D1686183

SCIENCE FICTION AND PSYCHOLOGY

Liverpool Science Fiction Texts and Studies, 62

Liverpool Science Fiction Texts and Studies

Editor David Seed, *University of Liverpool*

Editorial Board
Mark Bould, *University of the West of England*
Veronica Hollinger, *Trent University*
Rob Latham, *University of California*
Roger Luckhurst, *Birkbeck College, University of London*
Patrick Parrinder, *University of Reading*
Andy Sawyer, *University of Liverpool*

Recent titles in the series

40. Paul Williams *Race, Ethnicity and Nuclear War: Representations of Nuclear Weapons and Post-Apocalyptic Worlds*
41. Sara Wasson and Emily Alder, *Gothic Science Fiction 1980–2010*
42. David Seed (ed.), *Future Wars: The Anticipations and the Fears*
43. Andrew M. Butler, *Solar Flares: Science Fiction in the 1970s*
44. Andrew Milner, *Locating Science Fiction*
45. Joshua Raulerson, *Singularities*
46. *Stanislaw Lem: Selected Letters to Michael Kandel* (edited, translated and with an introduction by Peter Swirski)
47. Sonja Fritzsche, *The Liverpool Companion to World Science Fiction Film*
48. Jack Fennel: *Irish Science Fiction*
49. Peter Swirski and Waclaw M. Osadnik: *Lemography: Stanislaw Lem in the Eyes of the World*
50. Gavin Parkinson (ed.), *Surrealism, Science Fiction and Comics*
51. Peter Swirski, *Stanislaw Lem: Philosopher of the Future*
52. J. P. Telotte and Gerald Duchovnay, *Science Fiction Double Feature: The Science Fiction Film as Cult Text*
53. Tom Shippey, *Hard Reading: Learning from Science Fiction*
54. Mike Ashley, *Science Fiction Rebels: The Story of the Science-Fiction Magazines from 1981 to 1990*
55. Chris Pak, *Terraforming: Ecopolitical Transformations and Environmentalism in Science Fiction*
56. Lars Schmeink, *Biopunk Dystopias: Genetic Engineering, Society, and Science Fiction*
57. Shawn Malley, *Excavating the Future: Archaeology and Geopolitics in Contemporary North American Science Fiction Film and Television*
58. Derek J. Thiess, *Sport and Monstrosity in Science Fiction*
59. Glyn Morgan and Charul Palmer-Patel, *Sideways in Time: Critical Essays on Alternate History Fiction*
60. Curtis D. Carbonell, *Dread Trident: Tabletop Role-Playing Games and the Modern Fantastic*
61. Upamanyu Pablo Mukherjee, *Final Frontiers: Science Fiction and Techno-Science in Non-Aligned India*

SCIENCE FICTION
AND PSYCHOLOGY

GAVIN MILLER

LIVERPOOL UNIVERSITY PRESS

First published 2020 by
Liverpool University Press
4 Cambridge Street
Liverpool
L69 7ZU

Copyright © 2020 Gavin Miller

The right of Gavin Miller to be identified as the author of this book has been asserted by him in accordance with the Copyright, Designs and Patents Act 1988.

All rights reserved. No part of this book may be reproduced, stored in a retrieval system, or transmitted, in any form or by any means, electronic, mechanical, photocopying, recording, or otherwise, without the prior written permission of the publisher.

British Library Cataloguing-in-Publication data
A British Library CIP record is available

ISBN 978-1-78962-060-3 cased

Typeset by Carnegie Book Production, Lancaster
Printed and bound by CPI Group (UK) Ltd, Croydon CR0 4YY

Contents

Acknowledgements	vii
Introduction	1
1 Evolutionary psychology	45
2 Psychoanalytic psychology	81
3 Behaviourism and social constructionism	127
4 Existential-humanistic psychology	167
5 Cognitive psychology	201
Conclusion: Science fiction in psychology	235
Works cited	259
Index	277

Acknowledgements

Some of the material in this book elaborates ideas developed in earlier publications. The discussion of Naomi Mitchison's *Memoirs of a Spacewoman* in Chapter 1 draws upon my article 'Animals, Empathy, and Care in Naomi Mitchison's *Memoirs of a Spacewoman*', *Science Fiction Studies* 35.2 (2008): 251–65. The reading of Octavia Butler's *Parable* novels in the same chapter draws upon my book chapter *'Parable of the Sower*: The Third World as *Topos* for a US Utopia', *Science Fiction, Imperialism and the Third World: Essays on Postcolonial Literature and Film*, eds Ericka Hoagland and Reema Sarwal, Jefferson, NC: McFarland, 2010, 202–12. The reading of Aldous Huxley's *Brave New World* and George Orwell's *1984* in Chapter 2 develops ideas from my book chapter, 'Political Repression and Sexual Freedom in *Brave New World* and *1984*', *Huxley's Brave New World: Essays*, eds. Izzo, David Garrett, and Kim Kirkpatrick, Jefferson, NC: McFarland, 2008, 17–25.

Particular thanks go to my colleague Anna McFarlane, who read and commented upon an entire early draft, suggesting many valuable improvements. I also thank critical friends from English Literature at Glasgow University: Stephen Burn, Matt Sangster, and Rhys Williams particularly. I am also grateful to the three anonymous peer reviewers who commented upon the manuscript, and to the Series Editors and Editorial Board of Liverpool Science Fiction Texts and Studies. Various team members at Liverpool University Press were very helpful as this monograph developed, and as deadlines passed (and were graciously extended). My thanks to Christabel Scaife, Jenny Howard, and Anthony Cond. More generally, I am fortunate to have been able to teach science fiction at Glasgow University, and I am grateful to past and present students for our many stimulating discussions.

Introduction

Psychological knowledge pervades contemporary Western culture. We are thoroughly psychologized subjects, who think and act in ways shaped by the claims of varied, and competing, psychological schools. But, perhaps surprisingly, there has been little sustained exploration of science fiction's employment of psychological discourses, despite the genre's pre-eminent standing in the literary exploration of scientific ideas. This book aims to rectify that deficiency by investigating how science fiction has made use of ideas from five different psychological schools: evolutionary psychology; psychoanalysis; behaviourism and social constructionism; existential-humanism; and cognitivism. This monograph also offers a concluding preliminary exploration of cultural traffic in the other direction – the use made by psychology of science fiction narratives and rhetoric.

The idea for a book on *Science Fiction and Psychology* sprang from the topic's resonance with my research in another field altogether, namely the history of the psychological disciplines. While researching the history of psychoanalysis, and working also on the famed 'anti-psychiatrist', R.D. Laing, I was struck by correspondences that connected the history of psychology, psychiatry, and psychotherapy with the realm of science fiction. Laing's doctrines, allied with a feminist critique of psychiatry, were clearly influential upon Marge Piercy's science fiction novel, *Woman on the Edge of Time* (1976). I had also, quite independently, been teaching Joanna Russ's complex postmodern science fiction novel, *The Female Man* (1975), and had noticed an epigraph drawn from Laing's counter-cultural manifesto, *The Politics of Experience* (1967). My sense of a possible larger project was consolidated further by some writing opportunities: a book chapter on Aldous Huxley's *Brave New World* (1932) gave me the opportunity to explore a psychological comparison with George Orwell's *1984* (1949); and an article on Naomi Mitchison's *Memoirs of a Spacewoman* (1962) revealed further anti-psychiatric elements in feminist science fiction. These trial explorations (G. Miller 'Political'; G. Miller 'Animals') resonated with some other chance pieces of information: B.F. Skinner, a pre-eminent behaviourist, had written a utopian novel espousing his psychological principles; and Ursula Le Guin was sympathetic to Jung's psychodynamic psychology.

Further scoping work – in order to prepare a formal book proposal – assured me that there was a rich field of texts, ideas, and approaches that could be explored. I would write a book exploring science fiction's use of discourses furnished by academic psychology. The book would extend in time from psychology's disciplinary birth in the late nineteenth century to the rise of neuroscience at the close of the twentieth. By drawing upon my background as a historian of the so-called 'psy disciplines' (psychiatry, psychology, psychotherapy), I would provide concise exposition of the relevant psychological schools, while with my literary training I would explore the deployment and elaboration of these discourses in science fiction. My understanding of the human sciences' peculiar character suggested to me that science fiction might make use of behaviourism, psychoanalysis, and other psychological discourses in ways that differed materially from its deployment of the natural and life sciences.

'Science Fiction': Definitions, selections, and decisions

An important exclusion must be noted at the outset. My training and previous research have very largely been in the textual disciplines, and so the science fiction examined in this monograph is exclusively prose narrative (and, moreover, in English). There is no reason why science fiction in film, television, radio, graphic novel, and computer gaming should have any less fruitful a relationship with psychology. The exclusion of these media – and any others I may have overlooked – expresses only my disciplinary limitations.

The definition of 'science fiction' used in this monograph is one pre-eminent in scholarly literature on the topic. Following Darko Suvin's foundational work, albeit with some modification in light of later criticism, 'science fiction' here refers to narrative make-believe depicting a non-mimetic reality – a reality unlike the everyday world of naturalistic fiction. This non-mimetic fictional reality, however, is not a higher or separated world like that of fantasy, but rather an alternate version of our own reality – past, present, or future – transformed by a fictional innovation, or *novum*, of a broadly scientific nature. Science fiction, in other words, does not aim to reproduce common-sense empirical reality, but instead offers an 'opposition to naturalistic or empiricist literary genres' shared with 'myth, fantasy, fairy tale and pastoral' (Suvin 3-4). However, unlike these latter genres, the estranged representation found in science fiction does not postulate 'some closed collateral world indifferent to cognitive possibilities' (8) – some fairy tale reality, or fantasy Middle Earth world. Rather, the transfigured, estranged fictional reality of a science fiction narrative is extrapolated from a *novum*, an 'innovation' that is 'validated by cognitive logic' (63). The 'narrative dominance or hegemony' of the *novum* is necessary (63), otherwise any incidental use of advanced gadgetry (such as in a Bond movie) would qualify a tale as science fiction (70); thus, '[a]n SF narration is a fiction in which the SF element or aspect, the novum, is hegemonic, that is, so central and significant that it determines the whole narrative logic' (70). This principle of narrative hegemony means that the present investigation excludes, for instance, thrillers such as Richard Condon's *The Manchurian Candidate* (1959) or Len Deighton's *The Ipcress File* (1962). Although these narratives have a potential psychotechnological *novum* (mind control) that takes them some way toward science fiction, they are essentially tales of espionage and political intrigue.

The *novums* of science fiction are indefinitely diverse (if often somewhat conventional) and include familiar natural and life science innovations such as space and time travel, artificial intelligence, robots and androids, cyborgs, cloning, and human 'enhancement'. What matters is that '[t]he novum is postulated on and validated by the post-Cartesian and post-Baconian scientific *method*' (Suvin 64-65). Suvin acknowledges that the scientific method includes the human sciences, and even seems to indicate that this grounding typically underlies the better sort of science fiction:

> [S]*ciences humaines* or historical-cultural sciences like anthropology-ethnology, sociology, or linguistics (that is, the mainly nonmathematical sciences) are equally based on such scientific methods as: the necessity and possibility of explicit, coherent, and immanent or nonsupernatural explanation of realities; Occam's razor; methodical doubt; hypothesis construction; falsifiable physical or imaginary (thought) experiments; dialectical causality and statistical probability; progressively more embracing cognitive paradigms; *et sim*. These 'soft sciences' can therefore most probably better serve as a basis for SF than the 'hard' natural sciences; and they *have* in fact been the basis of all better works in SF. (67-68)

Suvin's list of human sciences extends, of course, to psychology, the concern of this monograph. Drawing upon the methodical cognitions of psychology in its various schools and subdisciplines, science fiction authors can imagine such intentional or adventitious innovations as: perfected techniques for behavioural conditioning of the personality; artificially intelligent machines that offer psychoanalytic psychotherapy; radically enhanced self-knowledge and empathy with others; the recrudescence – or suppression – of supposedly dormant evolved psychological mechanisms important to natural and sexual selection; and the transformation of cognition by artificial languages. Texts employing all these *novums* – and more – will be examined in this monograph. Moreover, the range of primary texts under analysis goes beyond narratives where the *novum* is postulated on and validated by scientific psychology. There will also be analysis of several texts where the *novums* are not primarily psychological, but where the ensuing narrative addresses issues informed by one or more psychological schools. Such texts are relevant because they allow science fiction to endorse, interrogate, and explore psychological discourses, yet without directly extrapolating fictional psychotechnologies. For instance, the well-known *novum* of Jack Finney's *The Body Snatchers* (1955) is the replication of human life by vegetative alien seed pods. While this is a non-psychological *novum*, the text, as will be shown (206–20), uses the consequent alien invasion narrative to explore the ramifications of early cognitivist psychology: the alien copies exploit blind spots in our finite and necessarily schematic capacity for perception, memory, and cognition.

Suvin's analysis of the science fiction genre has been influential, but also contentious. Scholars have generally been sympathetic to his thesis that science fiction's 'basic operation is *cognitive estrangement* – inducing a perspective of critical displacement from the distorted ideological perception of social reality' (Csicsery-Ronay 'Science' 52). It has, though, been deemed wiser to think of Suvin's generic definition as an ideal type extracted from the varied reality of the genre. Carl Freedman concedes 'there is probably no text that is a perfect and pure embodiment of science fiction', but argues that '[w]e may validly describe a particular text as science fiction if we understand the formulation to mean that cognitive estrangement is the dominant generic tendency within the overdetermined textual whole' (*Critical* 20). The concept of the *novum*, moreover, has received sustained criticism – and ultimately with consequences for the perceived uniqueness of 'cognitive estrangement' to science fiction. Istvan Csicsery-Ronay notes that Suvin's 'model of a single novum is useful for reading narratively simple fictions, such as short stories and novels with relatively simple narrative arcs', but 'once fictions cross a certain threshold of complexity it becomes more difficult to pin down exactly what the novum-premise is' – a difficulty compounded by the generic tendency to 'increasingly affect the carnivalesque, a mode in which many different novums seem to operate simultaneously, as if in a pluralistic society of innovations' (*Seven* 62). Csicsery-Ronay's refinement of Suvin's model informs the discussion in this monograph, for there is certainly no intention to confine science fiction within the model of a single 'novum-premise'. Some texts, such as B.F. Skinner's *Walden Two* (1948) or Vincent McHugh's *I Am Thinking of My Darling* (1943), do indeed operate largely by extrapolating from a single psychologically-conceived novelty, be this a science of behaviourist cultural engineering (Skinner), or a viral contagion that prompts heightened desire for an individual, self-fulfilling life (McHugh). But many others locate psychological *novums* within a number of competing innovations and novelties: in Frederik Pohl's *Gateway* (1977), for instance, FTL (faster than light) travel is as significant as the computerized psychotherapist Sigfrid, and in Marge Piercy's *Woman on the Edge of Time* (1976), a highly cultivated existential psychology is one of a number of utopian innovations, including extra-uterine gestation, male lactation, and human–animal communication.

Suvin's thesis that the *novum* 'is postulated on and validated by the post-Cartesian and post-Baconian scientific *method*' (64–65) has also been criticized. As Csicsery-Ronay points out:

> [M]uch of what is read and admired as sf is not very strict about its rationality. Many of sf's most typical novums are only ostensibly scientifically rational. Two-way time travel, telepathy, precognition, and communicating alternate universes are very difficult to formulate scientifically in the mesocosm of human existence. Yet they can be elaborated with consistency and coherence as if they were really possible. (*Seven* 73)

In an admission of this problem, and as a refinement of Suvin's model, Carl Freedman concedes that 'the category of cognition appears to commit the literary critic to making generic distinctions on the basis of matters far removed from literature and genre' (*Critical* 17). He therefore proposes a corrective, whereby

> cognition proper is *not*, in the strictest terms, exactly the quality that defines science fiction. What is rather at stake is what we might term (following a familiar Barthesian precedent) the *cognition effect*. The crucial issue for generic discrimination is not any epistemological judgment external to the text itself on the rationality or irrationality of the latter's imaginings, but rather [...] the attitude *of the text itself* to the kind of estrangements being performed. (18)

As a number of critics have noted, this modification of Suvin's theoretical framework has quite significant ramifications, particularly for the distinction of science fiction (the supposed literature of scientifically validated extrapolation) from fantasy (the supposed literature of impossible marvels). Csicsery-Ronay notes that

> [t]he cognition effect is precisely that: an *effect* – an illusion of valid knowledge created by imitating extratextual rational-scientific arguments and descriptions in the languages of scientific predication. Freedman takes his model from Barthes's *history effect* and *reality effect*. In each of these techniques, the reader's sense of historical knowledge or perception of reality is created by a rhetoric that imitates the rhetoric of nonfictional discourses, but is only remotely dependent on supposedly real events or objects. (*Seven* 140)

As China Miéville explains, precisely this kind of concession 'radically undermines the notion that sf deals in a fundamentally different kind of "impossible" than fantasy' ('Editorial' 45); while 'SF and fantasy might still sometimes be usefully distinguished' there is no 'fundamental epistemological firewall' between the two genres – both science fiction and fantasy may be seen 'as different ideological iterations of the "estrangement" that, even in high Suvinianism, both sub-genres share' ('Cognition' 243).

The question arises whether the distinction between science fiction and fantasy is useful with respect to this monograph's exploration of psychological discourses. The over-riding motive for maintaining the genre distinction, at least provisionally, has been pragmatic: to examine the place of psychological discourses in fantasy literature (e.g. Jungianism in Le Guin's fantasy stories) would require another book in itself. Hybrids of fantasy and science fiction have also been excluded for the same reason: a text such as Joseph O'Neill's *Land Under England* (1935) deploys images of behaviourist conditioning (Seed xx), but its unlikely conceit of a Roman civilization hidden under Hadrian's Wall places it beyond the boundaries of this investigation. Another reason to provisionally maintain the distinction between science fiction and fantasy, and to exclude the latter, can be found, as will be shown, in the varied functions of psychological discourse in science fiction. These certainly include cognitive estrangement (and also utopianism), but extend also to didactic-futurological uses, self-conscious metafiction, and the heightening – or diminution – of the so-called 'reflexivity effects' whereby psychological concepts take root in human character. These varied functions place greater emphasis on the socially presumed validity of psychological concepts ('cognition') rather than the rhetorical imitation of psychological discourse ('cognition effects'). Psychological science fiction may popularize psychology by weaving it into narratives of historical progress; it can accept or dispute psychological analyses of the genre of science fiction itself; and it may facilitate, or resist, the internalization of socially current psychological discourses by the subjects to whom they are addressed. Fantasy, perhaps, does all these things as well, but *prima facie* there is reason to focus on science fiction's negotiation with circulating expert discourses of the human mind.

Alongside such broadly formalist (re)definitions of science fiction, this monograph situates science fiction historically by adopting Andrew Milner's location of the genre's origins in the nineteenth century (which contrasts with, for instance, Adam Roberts's location of science fiction in longer traditions, such as utopia and the fantastic voyage, which stretch back to antiquity (21–31)). Milner argues that science fiction is, strictly speaking, a 'type' – 'a radical distribution, redistribution and innovation of interest within the novel and short story genres' arising in the nineteenth century from 'the practical capacity of sciences to become technologies' (153). The 'cognition' in SF, for Milner, is not simply methodical rationality operating within a disenchanted worldview (which can of course be found in Classical and pre-modern philosophy (cf. Roberts 23–24)), but a specific technoscientific, and indeed technocapitalist rationality, first manifested when

> the Industrial Revolution decisively and definitively redefined science into an intensely practical activity inextricably productive of new technologies [...]. And this is clearly how contemporary SF continues to understand science: Le Guin's Hainish Ekumen is made possible by the ansible eventually produced from Shevek's science, and Roddenberry's United Federation of Planets by the science that produced Starfleet's warp drive. Nothing even vaguely similar exists in Aristophanes or Lucian, Campanella or Cyrano. (139)

The fundamental concern in the genre (or type), Milner argues, is therefore with the ramifications for human life of technoscientific rationality – SF asks whether the 'fictional sciences' of its narratives 'can and will produce technologies sufficiently effective as to shape human being itself' (154). Milner's historicized account of the genre therefore tends to locate science fiction's fundamental problematic in the realm of the human sciences, and specifically their ambiguous potential for human liberation (echoing Suvin's contention, already noted, that the '"soft sciences" [...] most probably better serve as a basis for SF than the "hard" natural sciences' (68)). Milner's definition is thus preferred in this monograph because it illuminates the central concern with science fiction's deployment of psychology, a key human science. Psychology, as will be shown below, emerges in the late nineteenth century as a pre-eminent technology of the human, and thus as a significant interlocutor for science fiction as conceived by Milner.

As the preceding meditations on genre (or type) indicate, this monograph contributes primarily to literary criticism, and particularly to the literary study of science fiction. This aim brings commitments that may be at odds with other academic approaches. One such contender is history, which has an entire subdiscipline devoted to the psychological sciences. An historian reading this monograph will note, for instance, that the chapters have very little interest in author biography. I have taken the view, dominant in literary studies since New Criticism onward (cf. Wimsatt and Beardsley), that author biography is relevant to interpretation and criticism as 'external' evidence that may be used sparingly to introduce interpretative hypotheses. Such hypotheses must then be carefully redeemed through a properly argued reading of the 'words on the page', the 'internal' evidence of the textual object itself. For instance, in my reading of Marge Piercy's *Woman on the Edge of Time* (195–99), I briefly introduce the author's youthful fascination with existentialism as a way of highlighting the internal evidence in her protagonists' vocabulary of 'in-knowing', a term that conveys existential-phenomenological meanings when examined carefully, but that has no place in established disciplinary vocabulary. However, I make no reference to the biographical facts of Piercy's involvement with the counterculture of the 1960s and 1970s: the dominant political ideologies of *Woman* are clear enough from the internal evidence of the text itself.

This monograph also eschews a further historical methodology, that of prosopography – a 'group portrait' of a well-defined set of agents, or a sample thereof – which might then delimit their outputs as a textual corpus. There is no doubt a potential prosopography of science fiction writers who were also psychological professionals. The psychologist and utopian author B.F. Skinner (1904–90) is one particularly well-known example, although the group would extend to less well-known figures. These might include the psychiatrist author David H. Keller (1880–1966), an author of science fiction, weird tales and horror, as well as the biologist and animal psychologist James V. McConnell (1925–90), a celebrity scientist now best remembered – if unfairly – for his discredited work on memory transfer by cannibalism in planarian worms (Rilling). McConnell in particular would be a fascinating case study in the promotion of psychological ideas by a celebrity expert. A prosopography of such figures is, however, an exercise for the history of the psychological sciences, rather than for literary criticism.

A focus on textual outputs by a set of psychologist-authors would be significantly misleading, for one cannot assume that science fiction by psychologists necessarily shows significant or interesting deployment of psychological discourses. Also, more importantly, such a focus would ignore the 'psychologization' of Western society which is the historical backdrop to this investigation. Any study of science fiction and psychology must acknowledge the extent to which psychological discourses have been widely circulated, authorized, popularized, and made available to authors who may have had no professional training. Writing in 1973, the psychologist Kenneth J. Gergen noted:

> On the level of higher education, over eight million students are annually confronted by course offerings in the field of psychology, and within recent years, such offerings have become unexcelled in popularity. The liberal education of today entails familiarity with central ideas in psychology. The mass media have also come to realize the vast public interest in psychology. The news media carefully monitor professional meetings as well as journals of the profession. Magazine publishers have found it profitable to feature the views of psychologists on contemporary behavior patterns, and specialty magazines devoted almost exclusively to psychology now boast readerships totaling over 600,000. When we add to these trends the broad expansion of the soft-cover book market, the increasing governmental demand for knowledge justifying the public underwriting of psychological research, the proliferation of encounter techniques, the establishment of business enterprises huckstering psychology through games and posters, and the increasing reliance placed by major institutions (including business, government, military, and social) on the knowledge of in-house behavioral scientists, one begins to sense the profound degree to which the psychologist is linked in mutual communication with the surrounding culture. ('Social Psychology' 310)

Indeed, as this monograph will show, authors who are non-professionals have produced some of the most complex and interesting deployments of psychological discourses in science fiction, whereas even talented psychological professionals such as Skinner have tended to produce rather limited, didactic work.

While this monograph is informed and delimited by the history of psychologization, the chapters do not offer a continuous chronological and causal narrative, such as might be offered by a historian tracing, for instance, the vicissitudes of behaviourism in the post-war US public sphere. There is no doubt a conceivable, if enormous, project that could uncover the complex historical web of causal relations involved in the production, reception, and circulation of psychological science fiction. It could trace the broader historical context, the sources or experiences that informed authors' work, as well as the reception history of their outputs. Such a task is beyond the scope of this monograph. Even to pursue a single school in this way would require a lengthy volume: by way of comparison, David Seed's cultural history and literary analysis of brainwashing is in itself a book-length project. Nor is a comprehensive chronological cultural history of psychological science fiction necessarily desirable. Such an encyclopaedic approach is pursued by Damien Broderick's survey of parapsychological science fiction, which offers a chronologically ordered analysis of over fifty science fiction novels and short stories, regardless of their similarity, historical significance, or literary merits (*Psience*). Such a strategy is eschewed by this monograph. Given the enormous quantity of science fiction writing over the last hundred years or so, even solely in the English language, there can be no pretence to an exhaustive, purely descriptive survey of science fiction texts in which psychological discourses are deployed. Even if a comprehensive survey were possible, it would be undesirable. The pervasiveness of certain psychological discourses, particularly psychoanalysis, means that many science fiction texts are informed in some way by psychological expertise, but without significant elaboration of the discursive encounter. At most, such texts might merit mention in passing, but are not – and could not – be systematically recorded or analysed in the ensuing chapters of this monograph. For a text to be included in detail, the psychological element must be a matter of significant concern and elaboration within the narrative (but may, of course, be one *novum* among many, rather than the single innovation originally proposed by Suvin). Moreover, an encyclopaedic approach would inevitably involve the repetitious excavation of largely identical meanings within very similar texts. In this monograph, however, each textual reading is intended to add fresh insight to the understanding of science fiction in psychology, rather than to laboriously demonstrate the recurrence of a meaning already discovered. The textual sampling is therefore purposively intended to show a diversity of psychological deployments within and across the chapters. This aim also means that some chapters are clearly far from exhaustive. There is certainly a much larger hinterland of psychoanalytically informed science fiction. But this monograph has excluded it from consideration in order to leave room for chapters on psychological discourses that are comparatively neglected, such as cognitivism and existential humanism.

In a further departure from historiography, this monograph necessarily intervenes in the 'selective tradition' conceptualized by Milner (238 below) by taking an evaluative standpoint. The primary textual selection has been informed by an evaluation of the works under consideration, and by the merits of reading the psychological discourses within them, particularly where this interpretative frame reveals neglected or latent meanings. Colin Wilson's science fiction, for instance, is often rather crudely escapist and sexist, but the critical neglect of his consciously existentialist work means that his novels are worthy of attention in the present context (179–85). Moreover, an understanding of the less aesthetically sophisticated work of Wilson helps to articulate the textual logic of his more developed counterparts, Marge Piercy and Doris Lessing (195–99, 186–88). As well as examining such neglected traditions of psychological science fiction, this monograph also aims to explore texts in which the psychological elements are critically unrecognized. Naturally, these texts are harder to identify in a systematic way, even though such reinterpretations are an important contribution to literary scholarship and make particular use of expert reading skills. That there might be Jungian motifs in Le Guin's *The Word for World is Forest* (1972) is a plausible hypothesis, validated and elaborated by close textual attention (105–10). However, the proto-cognitivism of Finney's *The Body Snatchers* has been entirely overlooked by existing criticism, despite some rather inviting textual clues (206–20). And a text such as Vincent McHugh's proto-existentialist utopia, *I Am Thinking of My Darling* (173–78) is barely on the radar of science fiction criticism, let alone acknowledged as a narrative deploying psychological ideas.

In summary, the primary texts in this monograph have been selected on the basis of: their capacity to show a diversity of psychological schools and extrapolated deployments; their sustained engagement with psychological discourses; the merits of their promotion within the selective tradition of science fiction; and the intellectual excitement in the discovery of neglected psychological meanings within them.

'Psychology': Definitions, selections, and decisions

A purely descriptive definition of 'psychology' might, of course, include not only recognizable modern knowledge formations (behaviourism, psychoanalysis, cognitivism, and so forth), but also such diverse phenomena as the study of the soul in early modern, Enlightenment and Romantic philosophy and theology, and the various understandings of the soul or self that are embedded in the world's wisdom traditions (Buddhist or Confucian psychology, for instance). However, for the purposes of this monograph, 'psychology' is defined as the cluster of disciplines arising during industrialization in the West that extend scientific methods to knowledge of the soul, self, or psyche. Following established precedent, psychology is taken to begin in the industrialized nations of the West in the mid to late nineteenth century, as the new discipline displaces what Graham Richards calls the 'prevailing disciplines and genres of "reflexive discourse"' such as philosophy, physiology, literature and theology (11). A convenient 'timemark' for the beginning of psychology (and one that resonates with the late nineteenth-century origins of science fiction) is 1879, which marks 'the establishment of the first Psychological laboratory, by [Wilhelm] Wundt at Leipzig' (25). As Richards cautions, this dateable event must be seen within a wider historical context, for Wundt expounded an introspectionist methodology that had limited significance for the later discipline: 'Wundt's significance rests largely on his creation of the experimental laboratory and the fact that this attracted numerous American postgraduate students, who on returning home in the 1880s and 1890s eagerly developed his methods in new directions' (25). Experimental psychology flourished in the US because Darwinian natural history had established a principle of continuity between humankind and nature: 'diverse studies of children, animals, physiology, social behaviour and madness were [...] unified as aspects of a single project: exploring the implications of the evolutionary perspective for human nature' (23). Such cultural facilitation of psychology was woven into the larger fabric of the youthful nation by the key figure of William James, who 'taught the first American university courses in the new scientific Psychology', and 'wrote an influential text, *The Principles of Psychology*, that was published in 1890 after 12 years of work' (Pickren and Rutherford 53).

This monograph thus employs what Roger Smith calls a 'social definition' of psychology, proceeding from the observation that, from the late nineteenth century onward, Western academic psychology is established as 'a discipline, with subject-matter and an institutional and occupational identity' ('Does the History' 154). However, although psychology is taken to be 'a *social* presence since the generation of Wundt or James' (154), this monograph largely eschews any attempt to impose a progressivist, Whiggish history upon the discipline. As Smith explains:

> 'Psychology' is the generic sign of a cluster of competing would-be disciplines. Psychology has had (and continues to have) a protean

> character, differing with specific, local circumstances. We cannot refer with any precision to 'the birth' of the discipline. What originated with Wundt in the 1870s at Leipzig was not the same as what went on in the new North American psychology departments of the 1880s. (156)

The beginning of psychology can be only vaguely demarcated, and the field's subsequent development continues to be one of plurality rather than consensus: a less bibliographically convenient, but more precise title for this monograph would be *Science Fiction and Psychologies*.

The period of literary history under examination by this monograph therefore starts in the late nineteenth century, with the beginnings of both psychology as a discipline, and science fiction as a type. This periodization, as already indicated, allows the monograph to survey science fiction during the so-called 'psychologization' of Western society, a process by which the expert discourses and practices of psychology spread in authority and accessibility until they constituted a common sense about the nature of the human subject. As Nikolas Rose notes, 'The "disciplinization" of psychology was intrinsically bound to the "psychologization" of a range of diverse sites and practices, in which psychology came to infuse and even to dominate other ways of forming, organizing, disseminating, and implementing truths about persons' (*Inventing* 59). Various kinds of psychology entered into such diverse sites as 'factories, courtrooms, prisons, schoolrooms, bedrooms, colonial administration, [and] urban spaces' (59) where they wrought 'transformations in forms of personhood – our conceptions of what persons are and how we should understand and act toward them, and our notions of what each of us is in ourselves, and how we can become what we want to be' (11).

Although the discipline of psychology continues in vigorous good health, it has more recently been challenged, and transformed, by the rise of neuroscience. Nikolas Rose and Joelle M. Abi-Rached trace the origins and rise of this research programme, including the invention of the term 'neuroscience' in 1962, the inauguration and rapid growth of the Society for Neuroscience from 1969 onwards, and – most significantly – the efflorescence of research, publishing, and popularization in this area:

> While in 1958 there were only some 650 papers published in the brain sciences, by 1978 there were more than 6,500. By 1998 this figure had risen to more than 17,000, and in 2008 alone more than 26,500 refereed papers were published on the neurosciences in more than four hundred journals. In the wake of the decade of the 1990s,

which U.S. President George Bush designated 'the decade of the brain', things seemed to shift into a new phase, with discussions of the crucial role of the brain for individuals and society in light of advances in neuroscience moving from the specialized literature into a wider domain. (5)

Psychology was not of course effaced by neuroscience, but it was increasingly required to reach a rapprochement with this rival discipline:

By the turn of the century, it seemed difficult to deny that the neurosciences had, or should have, something to say about the ways we should understand, manage, and treat human beings – for practices of cure, reform, and individual and social improvement. Across the first half of the twentieth century, the prefix *psy-* was attached to a great many fields of investigation of human behavior, seeming to link expertise and authority to a body of objective knowledge about human beings [...]; now the prefix *neuro-* was being invoked in the same way. (6)

The rise of neuroscience can be perceived in science fiction, and this motivates my decision to take the 1990s, 'the decade of the brain', as the end of the period under investigation in this monograph. The closing decades of the twentieth century mark – at least in the science fiction imaginary – a diminuendo in the authority of psychology over the nature of human being. To offer a plausible cognition effect, writers have increasingly had to accommodate the rising visibility and prestige of neuroscience. The cyberpunk movement in the 1980s is the most conspicuous acknowledgement of the rival – and perhaps even dominant – authority of neurodiscourse in the technoscientific imaginary. As Sherryl Vint observes, 'the defining icon of cyberpunk is the integration of computer technology with human embodiment' ('Afterword' 228) – a trope enthusiastically explored, and apparent in the title alone, of the movement's paradigmatic text, William Gibson's *Neuromancer* (1984). Cyberpunk's 'neuroromanticism' offers what Istvan Csicsery-Ronay calls 'a rich thesaurus of metaphors linking the organic and the electronic. [...] Psychology and even physiology are wiring, nerves are circuits, drugs and sex and other thrills turn you on, you get a buzz, you get wired, you space out, you go on automatic' ('Cyberpunk' 274).

Of course, neurodiscourses are not simply absent from pre-cyberpunk psychological science fiction. A number of texts examined in this monograph deploy neuroscientific alongside psychological *novums*. However, neuroscience is typically deployed as an extraneous or threatening 'other' to psychology. For instance, in Piercy's *Woman on the Edge of Time*, the existential threat to the protagonist, Connie Ramos, is an experimental brain implant that will suppress her 'deviant' tendencies. This sinister neuro-innovation, moreover, is an estranged representation of the non-fictional neuroleptic medication employed upon Connie and her fellow psychiatric patients. The text thus acknowledges the prestige of neuroscience, but also erects an ethical boundary against what Rose and Abi-Rached describe as a 'key transactional point' in the rise of neuroscience, namely 'psychiatric pharmacology – that is to say, the development of pharmaceuticals to treat mental disorder' (10). A similar boundary is created in Ian Watson's *The Embedding* (1973): an experimental memory-enhancing drug leads ultimately to the madness of the test subjects (with further warnings against dabbling in the brain provided by a parallel catastrophic narrative of South American natives experimenting with their indigenous pharmaceuticals). Perhaps the only text examined which offers a positive view of neuroscience is Daniel Keyes's *Flowers for Algernon* (1966), which is merely ambivalent about the intelligence-enhancing neurotherapy offered to its cognitively impaired protagonist, Charlie Gordon. He becomes (temporarily) a genius, but also a much less sympathetic and likeable person – and the entire experimental project is implicitly equated to a kind of retroactive eugenics. While the text accommodates neuroscience in its *novum*, the dominant interest is, though, still psychological: the narrative devotes far more attention to the self-psychoanalytic process enabled by Charlie's enhanced intelligence. Indeed, to compare *Flowers with Algernon* with a post-1990s text may prove informative. Elizabeth Moon's *Speed of Dark* (2002) tells a similar, if more optimistic tale, of a young man with autism who is offered a neurotherapy that will 'cure' him. The discourses mobilized are neurocognitive, with psychogenic explanations for autism relegated to a pre-scientific aside: 'Back in the mid-twentieth century', reflects the protagonist, 'therapists thought autism was a mental illness, akin to schizophrenia. My mother had read a book by a woman who had been told she had made her child crazy' (49).

Alongside the delimitation of 'psychology', the organization of the discipline for the purposes of this monograph must also be explained. The absence of a unifying paradigm in psychology motivates the division of chapters according to a series of different psychological schools or orientations. Other structural divisions are of course perfectly conceivable. One might, for instance, structure a monograph on this subject according to psychological topics and/or technologies in science fiction, focussing on themes such as memory, perception, intelligence, and human development, or on technologies such as psychotherapy, psychological enhancement, and brainwashing. But for the purposes of this monograph, an emphasis on relatively discrete psychological schools will allow certain functions of psychological discourse within science fiction to be more clearly articulated. In particular, it will be easier to deal with science fiction's capacity to offer metafictional commentary on the psychological origins, nature, and gratifications of the genre itself (and particularly the accusation that it markets compensatory wish-fulfilment to misfits and losers). The ordering by discrete schools will also help in investigation of the genre's potential to subvert and interrogate the authority of psychological knowledge itself.

The issue of which psychological schools to include, and how to categorize them, also requires elucidation. This monograph considers five different schools or orientations in psychology: evolutionary psychology; psychoanalytic psychology; behaviourism and social constructionism; existential-humanistic psychology; and cognitive psychology. These categorizations are, of course, not necessarily those that would be recognized by a contemporary practitioner of psychology surveying the present state of the discipline (who might, for instance, regard psychoanalysis as a pre-scientific deviation). But nor are these categories chosen purely for their reflection of meanings and categories available to historical agents in their context. They are instead inflected by the need to productively organize literary readings of science fiction, leading to divisions and linkages that might be unsuited to other scholarly contexts. For instance, both psychoanalysis and existential-humanistic psychology are psychotherapeutic 'talking cures' that, broadly speaking, putatively enable the client to exercise greater creative control over his or her life (with existential-humanism typically more optimistic about the extent to which happiness is achievable). Nonetheless, this monograph considers these two orientations as different schools, and allocates each to its own chapter: psychoanalysis in science fiction is epitomized by the *novum* of an enhanced analytic process that looks behind the self-deceptions of everyday consciousness to find hidden meanings; existential-humanism shares a similar orientation towards improved self-understanding, but its deployment in science fiction is typified by *novums* that promote altered or extraordinary states of consciousness with utopian potential. These different tendencies in extrapolation motivate the allocation of two, distinct chapters. On the other hand, this monograph brings together behaviourism with social constructionism since both orientations (despite their significant differences) facilitate utopianism in science fiction by insisting on a public ontology of malleable psychological objects (although constructionism prefers terms such as '(social) discourse' to the earlier vocabulary of 'behaviour'): if apparent 'human nature' can be rendered fluid, then society can be remoulded in some utopian (or dystopian) shape by behaviourist or constructionist technologies. In similar fashion, attachment theory is included within evolutionary psychology because science fiction writing emphasizes the evolved mammalian embodiment in attachment, despite the theory's affinities with object relations psychoanalysis and cybernetics. A further consideration in the chapter categories arises from the continuity – in science fiction extrapolation, at least – of later disciplinary schools with earlier, less formalized orientations. With the exception of the chapter on behaviourism and social constructionism, the chapters explore the significance of earlier proto-discourses. Thus: 'psychoanalysis' includes earlier Nietzschean ideas; 'existentialism-humanism' includes the *avant-la-lettre* peak experiences of Vincent McHugh's *I Am Thinking of My Darling*; 'evolutionary psychology' extends back to Social Darwinism and evolutionary sociobiology; and 'cognitivism' includes Walter Lippman's earlier psychology of stereotypes and blindspots.

There is no pretence that the chosen schools are exhaustively surveyed within each chapter, nor that they represent the totality of psychological discourses deployed in science fiction. *A posteriori*, as the succeeding readings will show, the chapters have picked out psychological orientations fruitful for science fiction. But, *a priori*, there may well be others that would reward exploration, such as (to take a few examples almost at random) Gestalt psychology, Jean Piaget's genetic epistemology, and Ignacio Martín-Baró's liberation psychology. Of course, some excluded schools may indeed be 'dormant' from a science fiction perspective (but only a thorough survey could say for sure), while others may be more productive. There are, though, three kinds of psychology that are excluded in principle from this monograph: neuropsychology, parapsychology, and fictional psychology.

Given this monograph's focus on the period from the disciplinary founding of psychology in the late nineteenth century to the rise of neuroscience by the end of the twentieth century, a boundary line has been drawn in the somewhat imprecise territory where psychology meets neuroscience. This monograph will consider psychological schools that are taken to shed light on the workings of the brain – such as behaviourism, cognitivism, and evolutionary psychology – but does not venture into the deployment of neuroscience or neuropsychology in the strict sense. Neurodiscourses of the 'left brain' and 'right brain', and other phenomena of the 'neuronovel' (Burn) extrapolated to science fiction, will therefore not be directly considered. As noted above, though, neurology may enter indirectly: Keyes's *Flowers for Algernon* is included, for instance, because it addresses psychoanalytic theories at length via the *novum* of a neurosurgical and neuroregenerative technique for the treatment of brain damage.

Moreover, this monograph does not deal at length with highly marginal or contentious psychologies such as Dianetics (cf. Hirshbein), or with parapsychology – although it will briefly enter this latter, problematic area in the discussion of existential-humanistic schools. The exclusion of what one might refer to as unorthodox psychology, or, more pejoratively, as psychological 'pseudoscience', does not deny the complex debates surrounding unorthodox areas of psychological knowledge. A thoughtful literature problematizes any easy distinction between science and supposed pseudoscience (e.g. Gieryn), thereby exposing the 'boundary work' between legitimate and illegitimate psychological knowledge. This monograph, however, deals not with the validity of the distinction between scientific and pseudoscientific psychology, but rather with the cultural ramifications that ensue from the fact of this distinction, its nature and validity notwithstanding. The origins of psychology as a modern discipline are informative in this regard. As Andreas Sommer observes, 'Wundt had publicly and programmatically rejected psychical research as intrinsically unscientific in the same year he established German experimental psychology in Leipzig' (24). However, in the US, James endorsed psychical research, with the consequence that 'several of Wundt's students, [...] (along with other leading US psychologists not trained by Wundt), ruthlessly combated the father of American psychology in his attempts to integrate psychical research into nascent psychology' (24). Among the boundary work of early North American psychology was thus an 'aggressive rejection of psychical research as the "unscientific Other" of academic psychology' (24). Through such founding disciplinary activities, academic psychology united against parapsychology, pushing the latter to the margins, and into the realms of Occultism (cf. Leahey and Leahey) – a disciplinary victory which has been overwhelmingly successful.

The implications of this disciplinary history for science fiction, and for this monograph, are complex. The boundary work of academic psychology has largely deprived parapsychological phenomena of an underlying cognitive logic. However, science fiction has nonetheless represented a variety of so-called *psi* phenomena. As Damien Broderick notes, 'ESP and other psychical phenomena' rank alongside space exploration and nuclear technology as the '[t]hree major icons' of Golden Age science fiction, and have persisted in the genre (*Psience* 1). Peter M. Lowentrout observes that the scientifically marginal status of parapsychology has not obstructed its deployment within science fiction, even though '[i]n parapsychology, is not yet clear that the objects of study which are said to constitute the field's natural history even exist' (388). Lowentrout describes how the genre, aided to some extent by a credulous public and by the sleight of hand of the cognition effect, has blithely developed various kinds of *psi*-dominated stories in which parapsychological abilities may be: a barely credible 'wild talent'; a latent neurological faculty; a metaphysical or occult reality; and – more recently – 'an interesting plot device to explore an aspect or aspects of the human condition with little interest in the ontological implications of *psi*' (398). Lowentrout's observation that *psi* has been 'domesticated' into a generic 'beast of burden' (399) indicates its incorporation into the so-called science fiction 'megatext', a term popularized also by Broderick (*Reading* 57–63), denoting a 'set of established images and motifs, such as cyborgs or hyperspace or FTL [faster than light] travel, that do not belong to any single text or author, but are shared, each new iteration both relying upon established meanings and associations, and also opening them up to new possibilities' (Vint *Science* 57).

Despite the conventionality of *psi* in science fiction, this monograph will deal with parapsychological phenomena only incidentally (as when, for instance, the existentialism of Colin Wilson and Doris Lessing crosses into the realm of psychokinetics, precognition, and telepathy). *Novums* located in *psi* are frequently encountered in the genre and are a legitimate launching point for utopianism and cognitive estrangement. However, as indicated above, this monograph has a particular set of interests that will exclude *psi*, despite its potential fruitfulness for other investigations. These interests include reading science fiction texts for their didactic and futurological meanings, for their response to psychologized accounts of science fiction as a genre, and for their negotiation with the construction of the human by expert psychological discourses. Such aims respond to the deployment in science fiction of academically authorized psychological discourses, thereby excluding *psi*-based science fiction.

Alongside unorthodox psychology, what one might call 'fictional psychologies' have therefore also been excluded from consideration in this monograph: i.e. bodies of nominally psychological knowledge that are unique to science fiction's brand of literary make-believe, and that purely employ the rhetoric of cognition effects. For instance, the 'psychohistory' of Isaac Asimov's Foundation trilogy has been excluded: as Freedman explains, this fictional discipline purportedly follows 'the well-known actuarial principle that the behavior of people in the mass can be rationally foreseen', and offers 'an applied social psychology that allows the long-term tendencies driving worlds and galaxies to become visible to the scientific investigator' ('Remembering' 132). However, since there 'is no evidence that Asimov ever attained any scholarly acquaintance with the writings of Marx or Freud', 'psychohistory' is merely a psychologically decontextualized neologism that re-invigorates 'the reduction of science to nineteenth-century positivism' in a fictional science of historical determinism (133). The same exclusion applies also to Asimov's 'robopsychology', which is similarly detached from authorized, extra-diegetic psychological discourses. The pre-eminent robopsychologist, Dr Susan Calvin, is simply a mouthpiece for Asimov's cognition effects – she is expert in the imaginary and largely unspecified science of the post-cybernetic 'positronic brain', a 'spongy globe of plantinumiridium about the size of a human brain' (2).

What is psychology doing in science fiction?

The question arises of what role psychology plays within science fiction. This book proposes five different functions: (1) the *didactic-futurological*; (2) the *utopian*; (3) the *cognitive-estranging*; (4) the *metafictional*; and (5) the *reflexive*. The deployment of psychological discourses in science fiction may therefore work, respectively, to:

- inform and educate the non-specialist through extrapolation of psychological technologies, thereby teaching within the context of futurological forecasting;

- anchor in historical possibility the imagining of a currently non-existent society, whether considerably better (utopian) or worse (dystopian) in comparison with the reader's own;

- defamiliarize and denaturalize contemporaneous social reality by furnishing psychological *novums* that extrapolate current social tendencies and/or construct unsettling fictional analogues of the reader's world;

- self-consciously thematize within narrative fiction the psychological origins, nature, and function of science fiction as a genre, whether affirmatively or critically;

- articulate and/or subvert the construction of individuals and groups who have reflexively internalized and adopted the 'truth' of particular psychological knowledge claims.

The first three of these functions are familiar from existing traditions of science fiction criticism, but the metafictional and, in particular, the reflexive functions are less so. The latter, with its element of contestation of psychological knowledge, also begins to encroach upon a further area of provisional investigation in this monograph – the rhetoric of science fiction as it appears within formal psychological discourse (242–58).

The didactic-futurological function

The author and critic Joanna Russ proclaims 'science fiction [...] is *didactic*' ('Towards' 5), and argues that this is not a deficiency, but a difference to be celebrated:

> [S]tandards of plausibility – as one may apply them to science fiction – must be derived not only from the observation of life as it is or has been lived, but also, rigorously and systematically from science. And in this context 'science' must include disciplines ranging from mathematics [...] through the 'hard' sciences (physics, astronomy, chemistry) through the 'soft' sciences (ethology, psychology, sociology) all the way to disciplines which as yet exist only in the descriptive or speculative state (history, for example, or political theory). (4)

Science fiction is thus depicted by Russ as a contemporary popular encyclopaedia in which credible and future-orientated speculative narratives are used to convey various kinds of scientific knowledge, including the human sciences. Leaving aside the limitations of this view for the moment, it is clear that psychology can be deployed within science fiction in this way: to teach popular science, while simultaneously forecasting a plausible (if not necessarily inevitable) future. Admittedly, pedagogy is sometimes superfluous when a *novum* is psychologically grounded. Only a few reminders are needed to explain the Freudian backdrop to the Party's sexually repressive social technologies in Orwell's *1984* (although notably *Brave New World* begins with a lengthy exposition of various psychological conditioning techniques (Huxley 1–24)). But a more recondite psychology, or a more complex *novum*, may require greater exegesis: the narrator of Finney's *The Body Snatchers* conveniently recalls, for instance, a university lecture on the psychology of memory (72–73); and, in Skinner's *Walden Two*, the community's leader explains and defends at some length a behaviourist technology for teaching self-control to children (97–99). In such instances, science fiction works as a popularizing medium for scientific ideas (although with the caveat that the author him- or herself may not be drawing exclusively or necessarily upon academic psychology, but rather may be employing other popularizing expositions).

While there are no doubt good arguments that science fiction cannot be adequately accommodated in the Procrustean bed of futurology, there are certainly science fiction narratives that are intended, or received, as exercises in forecasting of the future. The futurological element is particularly clear, for instance, in the 'future war' subgenre (in which psychology is often marginal). Charles E. Gannon, for instance, shows in detail how Robert Heinlein's science fiction, and specifically the authoritarian vision of *Starship Troopers* (1959), was addressed to the US military-industrial complex, who then proceeded to develop military technologies and social organizations envisaged in this and other narratives (208–38). Even Wells's far more admonitory narrative, *The World Set Free* (1914), which narrated a future nuclear war, was read by scientists and military planners, who consequently operated 'within a powerful new paradigm that had been established by future-war fiction' (92). The futurological possibilities of specifically psychological science fiction must be similarly acknowledged. *Walden Two* is a particularly clear attempt to forecast a hypothetical (and supposedly preferable) future. As Skinner explains in his 1976 foreword:

> [E]ither we do nothing and allow a miserable and probably catastrophic future to overtake us, or we use our knowledge about human behavior to create a social environment in which we shall live productive and creative lives and do so without jeopardizing the chances that those who follow us will be able to do the same. Something like a Walden Two would not be a bad start. (xvi)

Nor is Skinner alone in such forecasting: McHugh's *I Am Thinking of My Darling* provides, in the 1940s, an eerily prescient vision of the 1960s counterculture. Alongside such short-term forecasts, psychological science fiction may also prophesy over generations and millennia, particularly when an evolutionary viewpoint is offered. Octavia Butler's sequence, *Parable of the Sower* (1993) and *Parable of the Talents* (1998), uses psychological ideas to offer a new evolutionary lineage for *homo sapiens*, and similar long-range accounts of psychological transformation are, of course, famously offered by H.G. Wells in *The Time Machine* (1895).

The academically dominant view – and one with which my argument broadly concurs – is that the didactic and futurological functions of science fiction, although marked in particular historical circumstances, are rather marginal, and provide a limited ground for interpretation, criticism, and evaluation. Suvin, for instance, refers disparagingly to the *'popular science* compost heap' apparent 'in the early phylogenetic stages of SF from technologically developed countries' (22). Where science fiction has become overly didactic, the resulting mixture is 'neither good fiction nor interesting science', and 'is dislodged the first time the shapers of public and publishing opinion happen to read Wells – or, indeed, a good straightforward essay of scientific popularization' (23). Although Suvin's ire is directed at particular strands of the genre (such as the interwar US science fiction dominated by Hugo Gernsback's editorial vision), his objection can be expanded to include modes of reading that pursue exclusively the didactic-futurological function. The didactic horizon models science fiction as entertainment education, whereby the genre offers what Stephen Hilgartner calls '"appropriate simplification" – a necessary (albeit low status) educational activity of simplifying science for non-specialists' (519). The interpreter and critic can do little more with such a hermeneutic than reconstruct the scientific content of a text in order to patrol the 'boundary between "appropriate simplification" and "distortion"' (534). While there are indeed lengthy treatises that attempt just such a critical operation (e.g. Glassy), they are essentially an exercise in knowing and judging science fiction by the standards appropriate to another genus (namely, popular science writing) with a consequent impoverishment of meaning. The futurological hermeneutic horizon faces a similar problem. The genre does sometimes attempt to literally forecast the future, whether fatalistically, or as a warning, or as a positive prescription. But on the whole, the credibility of science fiction's forecasts is beside the point, otherwise the genre would be hostage to changes in scientific knowledge and to invalidated predictions. A genre classic like H.G. Wells's *The War of the Worlds* (1898) – a text that still speaks clearly to the present – would be a mere historical curiosity, invalidated alongside its (pseudo-)predictions of intelligent life on Mars. Or, in a more psychological vein, Anthony Burgess's *A Clockwork Orange* (1962) would decline in value alongside the dwindling credibility of the behaviourist discourses and technologies extrapolated in its central *novum*, the Ludovico Technique. Science fiction's future historiography, which clearly arose in close dialogue with literal futurology, is less about forecasting, and more about exposing 'fictive models that have acquired fatal weight in real social life. Works of sf *play out* myths of history, without competing models or recalcitrant facts' (Csicsery-Ronay *Seven* 83–84).

The utopian function

While science fiction cannot be read adequately as literal futurology, its predictions may be understood as 'illusions of prophecy' (Csicsery-Ronay *Seven* 76). Science fiction's make-believe prophecies, conjugated in the past tense, 'playfully represent the colonization of the future by the present, through the forceful extension of contemporary trends, and, at the same time, the returning feedback-colonization of the present by the future, the reified anticipations, anxieties, and projects of our technoscientific problem-solving' (78). Of particular significance in the present context are make-believe predictions that confront the present with imaginary representations of a fictional better (or worse) world, thereby awakening dissatisfaction with the present, and also critically articulating the blind spots and limitations in our contemporary political ideals. There is no doubt an indefinite number of ways in which the human sciences can propose social, political, and economic innovations that might build a utopian (or dystopian) world in science fiction. Psychology, though, has a distinctive significance in utopian extrapolation and world building, for it can offer hypothetical technologies for the reshaping of the soul, and thus overcome – at least in make-believe – objections that dwell on the refractory nature of the human personality. While it might resemble social and cultural futurology, the utopian function therefore offers something rather different, for its fundamental aim is to awaken and articulate dissatisfaction with the present, rather than to offer positive technocratic blueprints.

The authority of psychological discourses in the post-war period clearly helped to unsettle the anti-utopian complacency of the Western powers in their opposition to Soviet communism. Ruth Levitas describes the 'climate of the Cold War and the later capitalist triumphalism that accompanied the fall of communist regimes after 1989' as one in which '[p]ublic discourse and political culture are profoundly anti-utopian, portraying utopia as an impossible quest for perfection whose political consequences are almost necessarily totalitarian' (7). Levitas notes how Isaiah Berlin resignifies the Kantian phrase, 'the crooked timber of humanity', in order to assert 'the irredeemability of human nature and thus the hubris of utopia' rather than to convey the original implication that 'a good social order would enable the better development of the individual' (7). Psychological discourses, however, promise that the crooked timber can be grown true, and offer a counter-discourse of renewed utopianism. The behaviourist utopia posited by Skinner's 1948 novel, *Walden Two*, delineates a fictional planned community in which, according to its leader Frazier, 'we strike for economic freedom at this very point – by devising a very high standard of living with a low consumption of goods' (57). In response to the complacency of post-war consumer capitalism, *Walden Two* promises to cultivate self-control from childhood onward, thereby curbing any supposed innate tendency to conspicuous consumption and competitive emulation.

It would be simplistic to suppose that *Walden Two* offers merely a technology (behaviourist conditioning) that – hypothetically, at any rate – solves a pre-defined problem (*viz.*, the need to tame our consumerist appetites). Rather, dissatisfaction with consumerism emerges in tandem with the capacity to imagine alternatives. Such 'social dreaming' (Sargent 4) does not simply respond to discontent with the present – it also awakens that dissatisfaction. Admittedly, *Walden Two* is undoubtedly in large part what Tom Moylan would call a 'blueprint utopia', in which 'blueprints or plans' are 'imposed by one author or by a central authority' (*Demand* 198). Concrete prescriptions are dictated to the community by Frazier, a leader who effectively arrogates all political authority to himself as a self-styled expert in cultural engineering. Nonetheless, *Walden Two*'s capacity to awaken and articulate dissent from the inevitability and desirability of the present anticipates the so-called 'critical utopia' that Moylan identifies in the New Wave of science fiction in the 1960s and 1970s. Critical utopias 'indicate what cannot yet be said within present conceptual language or achieved in current political action' (39): they are '"[c]ritical" in the Enlightenment sense of *critique* – that is expressions of oppositional thought, unveiling, debunking, of both the genre itself and the historical situation', and also '"critical" in the nuclear sense of the *critical mass* required to make the necessary explosive reaction' (10).

The consolidation of neoliberalism has, at least for now, disappointed Moylan's expectation. As Levitas points out, '[a] politically quiescent context and reading' has meant that 'the political impetus and intent of the critical utopia is not necessarily matched by political effectiveness' (111). However, the generic transformation Moylan describes can clearly be seen in the work of science fiction authors such as Joanna Russ, Ursula Le Guin, Marge Piercy, and Samuel Delany:

> A central concern in the critical utopia is the awareness of the limitations of the utopian tradition, so that these texts reject utopia as blueprint while preserving it as dream. Furthermore, the novels dwell on the conflict between the originary world and the utopian society opposed to it so that the process of social change is more directly articulated. Finally, the novels focus on the continuing presence of difference and imperfection within utopian society

itself and thus render more recognizable and dynamic alternatives. (*Demand* 10–11)

In both critical utopian texts and their interpretation it is 'emphasized that utopian narrative is first and foremost a process. Utopia cannot be reduced to the society imaged [*sic*], the "utopia" constructed by the author, or to the experience of the visitor in that society, or even to its basic ideological contestation with present society' (*Demand* 39). As Levitas observes, both writers and critics tend increasingly to conceive of utopian narratives as sparking critical awareness and speculation rather than as offering concrete prescriptions: 'The shift to a greater pluralism, provisionality and reflexivity in fictional utopias is paralleled in a theoretical commentary which treats utopia as heuristic rather than telic' (112).

The deployment of psychology in critical utopias may seem problematic, since the discipline is often implicated in the creation of fictional societies that are clearly intended as, and understood to be, far worse than our own. The use of behaviourist conditioning upon Winston Smith in Orwell's *1984* is a very well-known example, and to it one might add the similar behaviourist conditioning employed in Burgess's *A Clockwork Orange*, or the subtler repressive power of the state-mandated sexuality in Huxley's *Brave New World*. However, following William Sargent's taxonomy of utopian phenomena, such dystopias should be distinguished from anti-utopian narrative. The '[a]nti-utopia' consists of 'a non-existent society described in considerable detail and normally located in time and space that the author intended a contemporaneous reader to view as a criticism of utopianism' (9). The '[d]ystopia', however, furnishes 'a non-existent society described in considerable detail and normally located in time and space that the author intended a contemporaneous reader to view as considerably worse than the society in which that reader lived' (9). The anti-utopia opposes utopian dreams and projects *in toto*, while the dystopia still offers the possibility of hope, despite being in polar opposition to the positive 'eutopia' – a fictional society presented as considerably better than the real social world (9). As Tom Moylan explains, some dystopias therefore 'affiliate with a utopian tendency as they maintain a horizon of hope (or at least invite readings that do)' (*Scraps* 147). This possibility is facilitated by 'the typical narrative structure of the dystopia (with its presentation of an alienated character's refusal of the dominant society)' (147):

> [T]he counter-narrative develops as the 'dystopian citizen' moves from apparent contentment into an experience of alienation that

is followed by growing awareness and then action that leads to a *climatic* [*sic*] event that does or does not challenge or change the society. Despite the absence of the eutopian plot of the dislocation, education, and return of a visitor, the dystopia generates its own didactic account in the critical encounter that ensues as the citizen confronts, or is confronted by, the contradictions of the society that is present on the very first page. (148)

Such a counter-narrative can be found, of course, in *1984, Clockwork Orange, Brave New World*, and any number of psychologically informed critical dystopias.

The shift from utopia as positive blueprint to critical utopia and critical dystopia motivates an evaluative shift in the psychological disciplines typically deployed. The behaviourism celebrated by Skinner becomes the object of satire in Ursula Le Guin's *The Lathe of Heaven* (1971), which portrays objectivist psychology as a technology for the suppression of difference, contingency, and diversity. Social constructionist psychology also tends to receive the same sceptical treatment, whether in the threatened patriarchal ravings of Edmund Cooper's *Who Needs Men?* (1972) or in the analogy between genetic and cultural diversity in Naomi Mitchison's *Solution Three* (1975). (Indeed, *Solution Three* also continues the longer standing suspicion, apparent in Huxley's *Brave New World*, that vulgar Freudianism might mandate sexual expression as a technology of pacification.) In opposition to behaviourist conditioning, social constructionist programming, and Freudian psychohydraulics, the critical utopia tends to valorize psychologies depicted as conducive to difference and diversity, and opposed to the putative monological tendencies of objectivist psychology. Piercy's *Woman on the Edge of Time* and Mitchison's *Memoirs of a Spacewoman*, for instance, both depict future societies where the phenomenological exploration of subjectivity and intersubjectivity are highly developed arts, with a concomitant sensitivity to that which is alien, different, or incommensurable.

The cognitive-estranging function

For readers acquainted with science fiction literary criticism, and particularly the work of Suvin, the presence of 'cognitive estrangement' in psychological science fiction will seem a predictable corollary to its presence in science fiction based on the natural and life sciences. For Suvin, every work of good science fiction is 'a developed oxymoron, a realistic irreality, with humanized nonhumans, this-worldly Other Worlds, and so forth' that defamiliarizes our own, taken for granted social reality (viii). To take one of Suvin's examples, H.G. Wells's Time Traveller encounters a Darwinian *novum* in the future civilization of the Eloi and Morlocks, 'a run-down class society ruled by a grotesque equivalent of the nineteenth-century industrial proletariat' (212). Such cognitive estrangement can of course be readily supplied by psychological *novums*. The Freudian-cum-behaviourist technologies of Huxley's *Brave New World*, for instance, clearly present a series of extrapolations that depicts in grotesque, magnified form a hedonistic, consumerist, class society much like that of late capitalism.

The psychological rationale for Suvin's theory repays examination, particularly in the present context. As Csicsery-Ronay explains, Suvin's work introduces 'the notion that SF's basic operation is *cognitive estrangement* – inducing a perspective of critical displacement from the distorted ideological perception of social reality' ('Science' 52). The fictional worlds of science fiction depart – often markedly – from the reality of our everyday world. Nonetheless, states Suvin, we come to know better our own social and political condition by reading of a non-realistic, make-believe world transformed by the fictional *novum*:

> Though I have argued that SF is not [...] an orthodox allegory with any one-to-one correspondence of its elements to elements in the author's reality, its specific modality of existence is a feedback oscillation that moves now from the author's and implied reader's norm of reality to the narratively actualized novum in order to understand the plot-events, and now back from those novelties to the author's reality, in order to see it afresh from the new perspective gained. This oscillation, called estrangement by Shklovsky and Brecht, is no doubt a consequence of every poetic, dramatic, scientific, in brief *semantic* novum. (71)

As Suvin's allusions indicate, he explains this effect by developing a central category of Russian Formalist aesthetics, namely that of *'ostranenie'* (defamiliarization) – a term 'coined by Viktor Šklovskij to account for the special nature of artistic perception' (Steiner 48). In his 1914 essay, 'The Resurrection of the Word', Šklovskij (also anglicized as 'Shklovsky') offers a psychological and linguistic thesis that has been extraordinarily fruitful for literary criticism. He argues that everyday language is degraded by a loss of vivacity and richness that results from a general psychological tendency to economize perceptual and cognitive effort:

> When words are being used by our thought-processes in place of general concepts, and serve, so to speak, as algebraic symbols, and

must needs be devoid of imagery, when they are used in everyday speech and are not completely enunciated or completely heard, then they have become familiar, and their internal (image) and external (sound) forms have ceased to be sensed. We do not sense the familiar, we do not see it, but recognise it. (41–42)

For Šklovskij, who employs a 'machine metaphor' of 'energy-efficiency' (Steiner 49), everyday language and perception are automatized and energy efficient; literary language, on the other hand, allows the audience to experience the world anew by using formal devices to hinder the psychological tendency to economy of cognitive and perceptual effort (Steiner 48–50). Through various poetic and narrative devices, both language and the world are remade in the work of art so as to be 'perceived' in their original unfamiliarity: 'Only the creation of new forms of art can restore to man sensation of the world, can resurrect things and kill pessimism' (Shklovsky 46).

Suvin combines this psychologized Formalist notion with Brechtian dramaturgy via a further postulation that science fiction's generic tropes also create in readers a *'Verfremdung* [alienation] effect' (Brecht 184), a sense of critical and reflective distance from contemporaneous society. Berthold Brecht's hope was that his new, so-called epic theatre would enable actors to adopt a 'socially critical' attitude whereby 'their performance becomes a discussion (about social conditions) with the audience they are addressing' (187). Suvin deploys this notion of defamiliarization-cum-alienation within an implicit two-axis typology:

> Fiction [...] can be divided according to the manner in which men's relationships to other men and their surroundings are illuminated. If this is accomplished by endeavoring faithfully to reproduce empirical textures and surfaces vouched for by human senses and common sense, I propose to call it *naturalistic fiction*. If, on the contrary, an endeavor is made to illuminate such relations by creating a radically or significantly different formal framework – a different space/time location or central figures for the fable, unverifiable by common sense – I propose to call it *estranged fiction*. (18)

Suvin's distinction therefore indicates a four-fold, and also evaluative, typology based on whether a given work or genre is cognitive or non-cognitive, naturalistic or estranged. It is important to remember that, for Suvin, the 'cognitive' in 'cognitive estrangement' reflects the demystifying function of science fiction estrangement as much as it does the scientific grounding of the *novum*. In (1) myth, fantasy, and folk tale, the world is putatively mystified by being represented non-naturalistically (these genres represent a world that is 'actively oriented towards the hero' (19), a world of wishful, animistic alliances). Such non-cognitive non-mimetic standing is also appropriate to what Suvin calls 'second-rate SF' (ix), the pulp texts where the cognitive function is neglected in order to provide 'mystifying escapism' (ix). In (2) bad realist literature, the world is naturalistically represented, but is, nonetheless, still mystified. One might imagine here works of popular or middle-brow realism that are naturalistic but also ideologically complicit. However, in (3) good realist literature we know the world better by having it represented mimetically; such literature is both naturalistic, and demystifying. One might think here of the historical novel, as epitomized by Sir Walter Scott, and celebrated in Georg Lukács's famous account. Finally, in (4) good science fiction, we know the world better by having it represented non-mimetically; the non-naturalistic approach defamiliarizes and alienates taken-for-granted features of our social life, which then are perceived, in the ideal case, as contingencies that may be open to historical praxis.

The metafictional function

Suvin's theory broadly endorses the psychology of perception and cognition deployed by Šklovskij, in which routinized mental operations cast a veil over reality – a veil that may be rent by defamiliarizing and/or alienating textual rhetoric. As Suvin's particular mixture of psychology with literary theory indicates, science fiction that deploys psychological discourse is in a position quite different to science fiction that relies upon the natural and life sciences. Psychological science fiction potentially thematizes in the textual *novum*, or elsewhere in the narrative, a complex system of concepts that may impinge upon theories of artistic and literary production and reception. It thus contains a specific metafictional potential.

Suvin's psychological allegiances are rather recondite, so the metafictional function is more readily elaborated via the popular psychoanalytic interpretation of science fiction with which the genre has had to contend, particularly in the post-war years. An enlightening, and historically significant, document is provided in a case narrative published by the lay (i.e. non-medical) psychoanalyst Robert Lindner (1914–56), a prominent cultural commentator in the post-war US, and author of the 1944 case study later adapted into the 1955 motion picture *Rebel Without a Cause* (Waage 25–27). The narrative of 'The Jet-Propelled Couch' was published in 1954 in Linder's book of psychoanalytic case studies, *The Fifty-Minute*

Hour, and also in *Harper's Magazine* in abridged form in December 1954 – January 1955 ('Jet-Propelled I'; 'Jet-Propelled II'). Lindner recounts the anonymized (and thus already somewhat fictionalized) narrative of 'Kirk Allen', a physicist referred for treatment by his employers, a secretive US government agency. Alarmed by Allen's apparently psychotic statement that '"he'll *try to spend more time on this planet!*"' (*Fifty-Minute* 224), his superior ships him off to Baltimore for initial consultation with Lindner, who is quickly assured 'of Kirk's utter madness' (253). In the current, florid form of his psychosis, Kirk believes he can journey instantaneously from his life in the contemporary US to a future existence as 'Kirk Allen, Lord of a planet in an interplanetary empire in a distant universe' (250).

In the hope of bringing his analysand back to consensual reality, without the risks of shock therapy or psychosurgery, Lindner embarks upon a lengthy analysis while Kirk is temporarily resettled in Baltimore. He patiently traces the origins of Kirk's psychosis to his troubled upbringing as the only child of European extraction on a small Polynesian island (presumably a fictional *topos* sufficiently similar to the analysand's real experience). Kirk's alter ego is initially encountered (or discovered) when the twelve-year-old boy reads a published series of science fiction novels in which the protagonist has the same name: '[a]s I read about the adventures of Kirk Allen in these books the conviction began to grow on me that the stories were not only true to the very last detail but that they were about *me*. [...] *I knew that what I was reading was my biography*' (244). While Kirk's 'corporeal body was living the life of a mundane boy, the vital part of him was far off on another planet, courting beautiful princesses, governing provinces, warring with strange enemies' (245). This fantasy system is further elaborated during Kirk's adolescence as he begins to supplement the published text of his own life: 'I set myself the task of remembering what was going to happen to me beyond the point reached by my "biographer"' (248). Eventually, he acquires the ability not only to have 'predictive recall' of his biography (249), but also the capacity to instantaneously inhabit the body of his future self: 'At any time, no matter where I am or what I am doing, I can will to be him, and at once I am. [...] when I return to this present self, I bring back the memories I have of that future' (251); conveniently, explains Kirk, time spent as an all-conquering science fiction Superman 'compresses into only minutes on the clock my mundane self keeps' (252).

Lindner's psychoanalytic detective tale pursues 'the underlying psychic factors', particularly the abrupt severance of Kirk's 'almost symbiotic relationship' with his 'Polynesian nurse, Myna', which 'induce[s] anxiety to such a degree that his infant mind, threatened with permanent engulfment, strained to master it by the only means available at that stage: fantasy' (260–61). Kirk's inner life of fantasy, which allows him to 'tolerate his inner turmoil and the accompanying negative feelings' (262), are finally given definite form in his science fiction alter ego, where '[w]ith boundless universes of space and endless maneuverability in time at his immediate command, he could no longer be threatened by inner ragings' (63). Even purely as a study of psychogenic factors in psychosis, Lindner's analysis would undoubtedly today be seen as rather deficient, particularly in its reluctance to acknowledge male vulnerability. Lindner recounts what he calls Kirk's 'sexual seduction' (237) by his European governess, a woman supposedly 'taboo for him, as were all white women – a consequence of his deeply unconscious incestuous fears' (240). Lindner appears to be psychoanalytically interpreting an experience which, in itself, would seem sufficiently traumatic. At age eleven, Kirk is repeatedly sexually abused by his governess, who compels 'intercourse two or three times every night and often during the day', and who generally treats him as a 'sort of sex toy' (240). The abuse is systematic – 'There were times when I had to run away from her lust, lock her out of my room' (240) – and violent, for if Kirk is unable to respond, 'she would beat me, claw at me with her nails, bite me' (241).

But leaving aside the validity of Lindner's aetiological claims, his case narrative elsewhere implies continuity between the pathological and the normal. Alongside deep psychoanalytic explanations, there are more intuitively understandable accounts of Kirk's psychosis as compensation for his sense of inferiority and exclusion. As the only non-Polynesian, Kirk feels exiled from his childhood peer group, leading to 'a split in his personality that generated two contradictory views of self and world. On one side, a lowering of self-esteem developed – a feeling of inferiority and a sense of having been rejected for good cause' (234). Lindner then describes what is clearly, albeit implicitly, an Adlerian inferiority complex – not a cringing submissiveness, but an unshakeable compensatory conviction of superiority: 'On the other side Kirk developed an internal sense of superiority. [...] a conviction of difference and special election was born in him' (234). Kirk's investment in his supposed future life as intergalactic emperor is therefore an intensified version of the Adlerian neurotic who 'can only obtain security by striving towards a fixed point where he sees himself greater and stronger, where he finds himself rid of the helplessness of infancy' (Adler 27). The message is clear: Kirk's psychosis is the culmination of neurotic mechanisms found, in embryonic form, in the production and reception of popular science fiction. Lindner further emphasizes this implicit point when he explains the peculiar seductiveness of Kirk's science fiction fantasies. As an *'aficionado* of the genre' (*Fifty-Minute* 279), Lindner is especially vulnerable, and finds himself 'succumbing to a fascination that could be fatal' (285). Although Lindner is able to resist the 'magnetic pull' of Kirk's 'stupendous fantasy' (292), the reader is left to infer that a weaker individual, one less experienced in psychic exploration, might have been dragged into a psychotic *folie à deux* with the analysand.

'The Jet-Propelled Couch' circulated a warning message to readers and writers of science fiction. Psychoanalysis, the clinically and culturally dominant psychology of the 1950s US, had diagnosed the genre as an endemic cultural psychopathology. Few readers and writers may have experienced Kirk's troubled and abusive upbringing, but many might have shared Kirk's isolation from peers and recognized the potential for compensatory fantasies in science fiction. Because of such widely popularized psychoanalytic interpretations, science fiction as a genre has had to contend with the supposed expert knowledge that its narratives are textual commodities sold as compensation for incapacity in the social world. One way of dealing with this psychoanalytic reduction of science fiction to neurotic fantasy is by writing metafictional science fiction that critically and self-reflexively elaborates this analysis. Norman Spinrad's *The Iron Dream* (1972), for instance, purports to present *Lord of the Swastika*, a 1954 Hugo Award winning science fiction novel written by an alternate-historical Adolf Hitler who 'dabbled briefly in radical politics in Munich before finally emigrating to New York in 1919', and then dedicated 'the rest of his life to the science-fiction genre as a writer, illustrator, and fanzine editor' (9). The fictional text of *Lord of the Swastika* is followed by a critical afterword redolent of Lindner's cultural diagnosis. Hitler's novel is 'the obsessional product of a deranged but powerful personality' (251) – a 'piece of sublimated pornography, a phallic orgy from beginning to end, with the sexuality symbolized in terms of grandiose fetishistic military displays and orgiastic bouts of unreal violence' (247). Furthermore, explains the afterword, '*Lord of the Swastika* varies only in intensity and to some extent in content from the considerable body of pathological literature published within the science-fiction field' (251). As Le Guin notes in her review of Spinrad's novel, the overall effect is to encourage critical self-reflection from within the genre on the psychological correlates of the 'Straight SF Adventure Yarn' epitomized by 'Robert Heinlein, who believes in the Alpha Male, in the role of the innately (genetically) superior man, in the heroic virtues of militarism, in the desirability and necessity of authoritarian control, etc.' ('On' 42).

Of course, the metafictional element in a text such as *The Iron Dream* also indicates that science fiction can acknowledge, incorporate, and transcend, the psychoanalytic reduction of the genre to neurotic (and psychotic) fantasy. Such deployment of psychoanalysis can thus be found in a strand of psychologically informed metafictional science fiction in which the genre turns out to be (and thus also to be something more than) the power fantasies of a madman. In Barry N. Malzberg's *Herovit's World* (1974), for instance, a hack science fiction writer called Jonathan Herovit allows his personality to be supplanted firstly by the fictional persona of his authorial pseudonym, Kirk Poland, and then by Mack Miller, the fascistic hero of Poland's Space Survey Team novels. Herovit's science fiction fantasies are an act of existential evasion, culminating in a psychotic break in which Mack the Surveyman embarks on a violent and ultimately self-destructive rampage around Manhattan: 'Murder would have to be part of it from time to time and other things as well and at every step Headquarters would resist and the bleeding hearts would yelp, but now, still the job would be done' asserts the interpolated narrative from Kirk Poland's Surveyman novel, *Survey Sunlight*, just prior to Herovit's final disintegration (207). The subgenre – and thus presumably some ongoing wider generic insecurity – continues even into the 1980s, to be found, for instance, in Iain M. Banks's *Walking on Glass* (1985), where one of the novel's interlaced narratives concerns Steven Grout, a seeming paranoid schizophrenic who believes he is an interstellar warrior exiled to Earth as part of a sinister game. Grout, who is unemployed, socially inept, and adrift in Thatcher's 1980s Britain, seems – like Kirk Allen – to have developed his unacknowledged fantasy system in continuation of childhood daydreams: 'As a child he had done the same thing, as a game; something to make life more interesting, give it some purpose [...] then he had begun to have dreams about it, to come to realise that it was *real*' (27–28).

Psychological science fiction thus has a potential for metafiction, for the psychologies addressed within it may inform some theory of art or literature relevant to the genre. Lindner's analysis of Kirk Allen, and its metafictional successors, was a specifically psychoanalytic endeavour, but the metafictional function of psychological discourse may deploy other schools such as behaviourism, existentialism, cognitivism, and so forth. Finney's *The Body Snatchers*, for instance, offers a defence of the 'weird tale' using proto-cognitivist ideas (219–20). Indeed, the metafictional function may involve repudiation of psychoanalytic reductionism: Piercy's *Woman on Edge of Time* deals with a possibly 'psychotic' protagonist, but – unlike 'The Jet-Propelled Couch' – offers instead an existential-phenomenological account of the imagination as politically and culturally creative (199).

The reflexive function

Psychological discourse in science fiction facilitates not only aesthetic self-consciousness, but also reflection on psychological knowledge claims themselves. This kind of critique rarely occurs with discourses from the natural sciences – that a text which relies upon relativistic time dilation should in some way directly criticize the General Theory of Relativity seems most unlikely (excluding make-believe criticisms that exploit cognition effects to ground *novums* such as FTL travel). Psychological discourses are, however, far more open to literary subversion. In Pohl's *Gateway* (1977), for instance, a psychotherapeutic computer program ('Sigfrid') uses Freudian theories and techniques to accommodate the protagonist, Bob Broadhead, to the existing capitalist order (119–24). The critique of psychoanalytic therapy is clear: Broadhead is 'taught' that his guilt is ultimately Oedipal in origin, rather than an emotion that takes his own undeserved advantage as its object. To take another example, William Sleator's anti-behaviourist young adult novel, *House of Stairs* (1974), promotes existentialist and psychoanalytic ideas as a discourse of individual freedom within a dystopian world where behaviourist technology adapts young people to their repressive social conditions (146–49).

I have described this possible function of psychological discourse in science fiction as the 'reflexive function' because it foregrounds the so-called 'reflexivity' of the human sciences. This term is used, following Roger Smith, to denote theoretical positions that recognize that 'how we live and what we say about how we live are not independent variables but parts of a single, reflective circle' ('Does Reflexivity' 5). The thesis of reflexivity may be seen, as Smith indicates, in a number of broadly similar philosophical positions – including arguments advanced by Charles Taylor, Hans-Georg Gadamer, and Alasdair MacIntyre – which recognize that the subject of psychological knowledge is at least partly constituted by that knowledge itself (4–5).

The concept of reflexivity in the human sciences may be elaborated via a significant distinction between psychology, and the 'hard sciences', such as physics. Thomas Kuhn notes how 'some accepted examples of actual scientific practice – examples which include law, theory, application, and instrumentation together – provide models from which spring particular coherent traditions of scientific research' (11). Such 'paradigms' allow a sustained period of 'normal science', with the classical example being the development of Newtonian physics. However, as Roger Smith notes, there has never been a phase of normal, puzzle-solving psychological science: '[i]t is notorious that "psychology" is not a unified body of knowledge with a common core of mutually consistent concepts; indeed, it is a highly contentious philosophical question whether it could ever achieve a unified theory' ('Does the History' 154–55). Sonu Shamdasani agrees that the disciplinary ambition to find a unifying psychological-scientific paradigm along the lines of, say, Newtonian mechanics in eighteenth- and nineteenth-century physics, has not been fulfilled:

> At the outset, psychologists sought to emulate the form and formation of established prestigious sciences, such as physics and chemistry. This emulation – or simulation – took different forms. Central to it was the conception that psychology should also be a unitary discipline. Yet very quickly, the proliferation of variously styled psychologies demonstrated that there was little consensus as to what could be considered the aims and methods of psychology. (5)

One might suppose that the plurality of psychologies indicates that a unifying Kuhnian 'normal science' paradigm has not yet arrived, and that psychology remains, for the moment, an immature discipline. However, there is good reason to believe that a unifying paradigm could never be created for psychology, precisely because of reflexivity. Wade Pickren and Alexandra Rutherford outline this crucial problem: 'Although knowledge about geology does not change the essential nature of rocks or minerals, knowledge about psychology can change humans. We are both the agents and the objects of scientific study in psychology and are thus active generators and recipients of that knowledge' (xix). As Roger Smith concludes, 'in the human sciences at least, it simply is not possible at root to separate subject and object. The very act of acquiring knowledge, even in the most rigorously controlled situation, is a change in the life of both subject and object' (*Being* 76). The various psychologies, as Shamdasani explains, 'have themselves partially transformed the subject that they set out to explain. Their interpretive categories have been adopted by large-scale communities and subcultures, and have given rise to new forms of life' (10).

Although reflexivity is not widely recognized in science fiction literary criticism, it has been explicitly thematized within the genre itself. Robert Sheckley's 1956 short story 'Bad Medicine', for instance, promotes an *avant-la-lettre* representation of reflexivity by cognitively estranging the post-war diffusion and authorization of psychoanalysis, a phenomenon that gave rise to a new community of expert consumers of therapeutic practice. In the year 2103, Elwood Caswell, a jetbus conductor, is driven to desperation by a delusive homicidal mania directed against his friend and neighbour, Magnessen. Caswell consequently purchases from his Home Therapy Appliances Store a General Motors Rex Regenerator, which the store clerk advises him is a 'hefty, heavy-duty, twenty-five amp machine for a really deep-rooted major condition' (209). Unfortunately, as the clerk discovers from his manager after Caswell has left with his sale, the Rex Regenerator in question is a display model not intended for purchase – crucially, it is a non-Terran model designed '[f]or giving mechanotherapy to *Martians*' (210). Caswell returns home unaware of this difficulty and follows the operating instructions for the Mars-market machine: 'Try not to feel any embarrassment or shame', they advise in a sardonic displacement of post-war psychotherapeutic optimism, 'Everyone has problems and many are worse than yours! Your Regenerator has no interest in your morals or ethical standards, so don't feel it is "judging you". It desires only to aid you in becoming well and happy' (212). The scenes that ensue between Caswell and his mechanotherapist are the satirical heart of the narrative, as the Regenerator dogmatically constructs its Earthling analysand according to a series of alien concepts. Although initially baffled by the contents of Caswell's mind (Martians are incapable of homicide), the Regenerator ploughs on, confident in its own expertise. After subjecting Caswell to a word association test (partly in Martian), the machine confidently declares that he has 'a classic case of feem desire complicated by strong dwarkish intentions' (215). Caswell submits to this diagnosis out of respect for the authority of psychological science: '[t]hese machines knew what they were doing and had been doing it for a long time. He would cooperate, no matter how outlandish the treatment seemed from his layman's viewpoint' (215). In classic psychoanalytic fashion, the Regenerator then persuades Caswell that his inability to comment on his 'juvenile experiences with the thorastrian fleep' are symptoms of 'Blockage [...] Resentment. Repression'; it encourages him to concentrate on his 'feelings – both revealed and repressed – towards his goricae' (218), i.e. '[t]he tree that nourished you during infancy' (219). Although Caswell initially resists the expert knowledge that 'the goricae stifled your necessary rejection of the feem desire' (219), he soon accepts the reflexive inscription of these categories onto his psyche: '"It's the damnedest thing," Caswell said, "but do you know, I think I *do* remember my goricae!"' (220). The story ends with Caswell fully analysed, and free of his homicidal intention, yet darkly planning to 'dwark Magnessen in a vlendish manner' (226).

Of course, the human subject may not only adopt, but also resist, the interpretive, self-fashioning categories authorized by psychology, be they psychoanalytic or otherwise. The furore surrounding the publication in 2000 of Randy Thornhill and Craig T. Palmer's evolutionary psychological account of rape, *A Natural History of Rape: Biological Bases of Sexual Coercion*, is instructive. Thornhill and Palmer propose that a future society might implement 'an evolutionarily informed educational program for young men that focuses on increasing their ability to restrain their sexual behaviour' (179). Such a scheme 'might start by getting the young men to acknowledge the power of their sexual impulses and then explaining why human males have evolved that way' (179). Alongside educational programmes for men and women, a remodelled society might also revive 'patterns of movement that keep females – especially at the ages when they are most sexually attractive – out of isolated areas' (185). Thornhill and Palmer's account of rape as a male reproductive strategy was subjected to withering scrutiny in responses such as the 2003 edited volume *Evolution, Gender, and Rape*. Although much of the debunking of Thornhill and Palmer focusses on the deficiencies of their evolutionary psychology, and on their criminologically ill-informed model of rape, there is also some consideration of the problem of reflexivity. What if men, having 'learned' that rape was adaptive, not only became more likely to rape (because of a belief in its naturalness), but also to demand an ethical re-evaluation of rape, so that it was, say, less of crime to rape a young sexually attractive female encountered in an isolated area? Where would the slide down the slippery slope towards the decriminalization of rape be halted? Beliefs about human nature have ethical implications, in part because of the meta-ethical presumption in favour of the right to express one's supposed nature. As A. Leah Vickers and Philip Kitcher argue, the 'social consequence' of the proposed educational programme detailed above, could be 'a continued perception that women are partly responsible for rape' (165). What such comments indicate is the problem of the reflexivity of psychological expertise: the implementation of a comprehensive and sustained educational programme of the kind proposed by Thornhill and Palmer would go a long way towards making the kind of male subject supposedly discovered by their application of evolutionary psychology.

Such anxieties about the consequences of the psychology proposed by Thornhill and Palmer thus indicate a contemporary understanding that, as Richards has it, 'when psychologists introduce a new concept or theory about the psychological, they are engaged in *changing* it' (6):

> [N]obody prior to Freud had an Oedipus complex, [...] nobody before Pavlov and Watson was ever 'conditioned' and [...] nobody before c.1914 had a high IQ. [...] they were not terms in which the psychology of people prior to their introduction was actually

structured. They had no psychological *reality*. The very act of introducing such concepts changed the situation by providing people with new terms in which to experience themselves – and only *then* can they be properly said to refer to really occurring psychological phenomena. (7)

Unlike the natural sciences, the psychological sciences are essentially more contentious, for they both know and constitute what they know; they are confluences of 'power' and 'knowledge', to use the familiar formula introduced by Foucault, and developed further by scholars such as Nikolas Rose. The latter argues that the creation of psychological subjects is closely bound up with modern modes of government. Psychological expertise, unlike old-fashioned naked power, 'achieves its effects not through the threat of violence or constraint, but by way of the persuasion inherent in its truths, the anxieties stimulated by its norms, and the attraction exercised by the images of life and self it offers to us' (*Governing* 10). Science fiction, because of the reflexivity of psychologies, may – although far from invariably – exploit the consequent latitude for critique of the discipline. This monograph will explore further the rhetorical techniques found in science fiction texts that, whether wittingly or unwittingly, thematize, endorse, and/or challenge psychological knowledge.

What is science fiction doing in psychology?

The preceding introductory account of psychology in science fiction has, for the sake of convenience, treated the discipline as if it were some kind of unadulterated, 'pure' scientific discourse and practice. But, in fact, there is no hard and fast segregation of psychology from literary practice. By remaining sensitive to the actual, contingent practices of psychology as a discipline, it is possible to discern motifs and narratives that might, in other contexts, be identified as 'science fiction', and which provide didactic and futurological functions, as well as (largely unrecognized) cognitive estrangement. Although the focus of this monograph will be on psychology in science fiction, it concludes with a provisional analysis of science fiction in psychological theory and practice.

Some anticipation of this discussion may be helpful. Science fiction is, for instance, a recognized (albeit minor) element in higher education pedagogy, where published narratives may be used as a focus for discussion in psychology classes. Even the almost inevitable misunderstandings and wilful errors made by science fiction writers can be turned to the educator's advantage, for these force students to monitor the 'boundary between "appropriate simplification" and "distortion"' (Hilgartner 534). Steven J. Kirsh, for instance, describes his use of Orson Scott Card's 1985 novel *Ender's Game* to teach developmental psychology to undergraduate students, with the requirement that they identify 'both accurate and inaccurate applications/depictions of developmental concepts in the book' (50). But science fiction is not restricted to psychological pedagogy. Futurological 'science fiction' prophecies may be employed to encourage investment of resources in a particular school of psychological research. For Jenny Kitzinger, this is a standard element in all kinds of scientific research, not merely the human sciences: scientists 'routinely make proclamations about the promise and potential of their work', including 'fantastical and engaging futuristic tales (e.g. about a world free of suffering)' (82). Ideally, such narrative extrapolation is self-conscious and, thus, more readily open to discussion and contestation: Corinne Squire notes for instance the explicit feminist utopianism in Sandra L. Bem's social-cognitive 'account of gender schema theory' ('Crisis' 45).

Psychology might, in time, whether cheerfully or grudgingly, admit the presence and efficacy of extrapolatory narratives within the messy, contingent practices of psychological investigation. It may though find it harder to admit that the cognitive estrangement offered by science fiction narratives also seems to be an element within psychology itself, which sometimes uses extrapolations to defamiliarize and critique our everyday ideologies. In the context of feminist psychology, Ann Oakley proclaims the need for a 'denaturalization' or '[e]strangement from one's own culture' (*Gender* 201) – an ambition that finds concrete realization in some of Sandra L. Bem's work on gender stereotypes (e.g. Bem 609). One might also wonder about Stanley Milgram's 'obedience experiments' of the 1960s and 1970s, in which participants were duped into administering what appeared to be increasingly dangerous electric shocks to test subjects. Ian Nicholson, among a number of later commentators, has been particularly scathing of the ethics and validity of the obedience experiments ('Torture' 747–51), and has tended to view them as a spectacular, estranging critique of a post-war US society committed to the Vietnam War, and to playing its role in Mutually Assured Destruction. In summary, the concluding chapter will explore how science fiction contributes to the pedagogy of psychology, to the authority of narratives underlying psychological research and technologies, and to the estranging discursive elements within psychology itself.

Prospectus

All chapters of this book are tasked with some exposition of psychological theory. Certain psychologies are more familiar than others to the literary critic, so the relevant theory will, for instance, be sketched lightly in Chapter 2, which focusses on the well-known discourses of psychoanalytic psychology. Other psychologies, however, are typically less familiar to a literary audience and require more systematic exposition. Readers will therefore encounter short didactic passages, typically at chapter beginnings, outlining the psychological school under consideration, and key relevant tenets. An apology for my selective auto-didacticism can be found in Joanna Russ's statement that '[a] modern critic attempting to understand science fiction without understanding modern science is in the position of a medievalist attempting to read *Piers Plowman* without any but the haziest ideas about medieval Catholicism' ('Towards' 6). 'Criticism of science fiction', continues Russ, 'will – perforce – employ an aesthetic in which the elegance, rigorousness, and systematic coherence of explicit ideas is of great importance', and will 'appear to stray into all sorts of extraliterary fields: metaphysics, politics, philosophy, physics, biology, psychology, topology, mathematics, history, and so on' (12). The elegance, rigour, and systematic coherence of my excursions into psychology are for the reader to judge, but I hope that they will be recognized as necessary. With regard to the exposition and summary of literary texts, I have assumed that canonical science fiction texts such as Orwell's *1984* or Wells's *The Time Machine* require only the lightest of introduction. But for works that may be less familiar, I have provided lengthier summaries.

Although the five, school-based chapters are not intended to offer a cumulative historical analysis, they are ordered by approximate chronology of the psychologies (or proto-psychologies) that they introduce. The chapters, with the exception of the final chapter, may however be read in any order. While there are occasional cross-references, each chapter's argument should be broadly intelligible in isolation. The Conclusion, though, should preferably be read after all (or most) of Chapters 1 to 5, since it draws out general conclusions from them, prior to its exploration of cultural traffic in the contrary direction, i.e. from science fiction into psychology.

Chapter 1, on 'Evolutionary psychology', explores the importation of this psychological discourse into science fiction writing, not just in terms of the recent evolutionary psychology (EP) programme inaugurated by John Tooby and Leda Cosmides, but also with respect to earlier schools such as Social Darwinism and sociobiology. The Social Darwinist context motivates in science fiction an anti-utopian tendency to didactically forecast a state of future decadence that can be arrested only by the re-activation of dormant evolutionary mechanisms. This pattern may be familiar enough from H.G. Wells's *The Time Machine* (1895) and Robert Heinlein's *The Moon is a Harsh Mistress* (1966), but is less easily perceived in Octavia Butler's sequence, *Parable of the Sower* (1993) and *Parable of the Talents* (1998), which predicts a new evolutionary lineage for *homo sapiens* emerging from a future in which the US is a failed state. Happily, a challenge to the reflexive authority of evolutionary psychology can be found in Kurt Vonnegut's *Galápagos* (1985), which satirizes the sociobiological paradigm by taking to the point of absurdity evolutionary explanations for human aggression. Science fiction can, moreover, escape hackneyed Social Darwinist discourses by drawing upon alternative evolutionary psychologies. Naomi Mitchison's future utopia in *Memoirs of a Spacewoman* (1962) draws upon attachment theory to offer a renewed feminist ethic of compassion and imaginative understanding, while also estranging our dominant ethical systems.

Chapter 2 takes 'Psychoanalytic psychology' as its focus. Although official psychoanalytic discourse begins with the work of Freud, science fiction frequently deploys proto-psychoanalytic wisdom inspired by Nietzsche. Texts such as H.G. Wells's *The Island of Doctor Moreau* (1896) and *The Croquet Player* (1936), John Christopher's *The Death of Grass* (1956), and Alfred Bester's 'Oddy and Id' (1950), reflect the anti-utopian tenor of popular Nietzschean ideas in which civilization is a fragile veneer concealing displaced instinctual gratification. Superficially, such bourgeois conservatism continues in the extrapolations of George Orwell's well-known dystopian novel *1984* (1949) and Aldous Huxley's comparable dystopia *Brave New World* (1932). However, both these novels challenge the reflexive hegemony of Freudian discourses by thematizing the pessimism written into the hydraulic model of the mind – a critique of Freudianism intensified in Barry N. Malzberg's alternate history novel, *The Remaking of Sigmund Freud* (1985), which represents Freud as essentially opposed to the utopian potential of social dreams. Dreams, though, are celebrated in Ursula Le Guin's Jungian science fiction novel *The Word for World is Forest* (1972), which estranges the colonization of traditional societies by industrial modernity, and counterposes a utopian and metafictional discourse of rootedness in the collective unconscious (thereby developing an aesthetic pioneered by Golden Age precursors such as Frank Herbert's *The Dragon in the Sea* (1956)). A generic sifting and re-evaluation of psychoanalysis continues in the virtual dialogue between Daniel Keyes's *Flowers for Algernon* (1966), which (like Bester's *The Demolished Man* (1956)) promotes the psychoanalytic narrative investigation of the self, and the unreliable narrative of Frederik Pohl's

Gateway (1977), where the protagonist undergoes psychotherapy with a computerized therapist, and is returned to a psychological 'normality' that reconciles him to a future reality of brutal capitalist exploitation.

Chapter 3, 'Behaviourism and social constructionism', explores science fiction extrapolations informed by these two psychological paradigms, both of which insist on the malleability of human psychology. B.F. Skinner's near-future utopian novel, *Walden Two* (1948), attempts to authorize the behaviourist model of the self by inscribing operant conditioning into longstanding progressivist discourses. But this attempted reflexivity effect is subverted by the novel itself, which persistently endorses historical, philosophical, and ethical discourses that have supposedly been rendered obsolete. The undermining of behaviourism's authority is heightened in texts such as Anthony Burgess's *A Clockwork Orange* (1962), Ursula Le Guin's *The Lathe of Heaven* (1971), and William Sleator's *House of Stairs* (1974). These narratives juxtapose against behaviourism counter-discourses from different sources, including wisdom traditions such as world religions, and also antagonistic psychological discourses such as psychoanalysis and existentialism. Social constructionism – like behaviourism, but with greater emphasis on contingency and unpredictability – encourages science fiction to ask, hopefully or otherwise, what would happen if seeming psychological and cultural givens of our time (such as heterosexuality or patriarchy) are wholly or partially dissolved in a future or alternative social order. With enormously varying complexity and ethical sensitivity, Joanna Russ's *The Female Man* (1975), Edmund Cooper's 1972 novel *Who Needs Men?* (in the US, *Gender Genocide*) and Naomi Mitchison's *Solution Three* (1974), explore the utopian and dystopian reconstruction of gender relations, but are troubled by issues of natural and cultural diversity.

Chapter 4 discusses the significance for science fiction writing of 'Existential-Humanistic Psychology'. This anti-systematic school of psychology – epitomized by figures such as Viktor Frankl and Abraham Maslow – recovers neglected philosophical and spiritual categories regarded as proper to human being, in contrast with animal life or inanimate systems. As with psychoanalytic psychology, proto-discourses are important to science fiction. Vincent McHugh's *I Am Thinking of My Darling* (1943) uses tacitly existentialist ideas to imagine an early critical utopia in which the emerging ideal of personal authenticity queries the American Dream as instantiated in 1940s New York. McHugh's critical utopian novel contrasts with the ponderous extrapolations of Colin Wilson in *The Mind Parasites* (1967) and *The Space Vampires* (1976), and Doris Lessing in *The Four-Gated City* (1969). Both these authors – despite their widely differing positions in the literary canon – use science fiction as a didactic and futurological (even prophetic) medium in which existential psychology unabashedly serves as the supposed rationale for spiritual apotheosis (including the prophesied cultivation of *psi* powers). A more fruitful post-war deployment of existential-humanistic psychology can be found in texts such as Theodore Sturgeon's 'And Now the News ...' (1956), Naomi Mitchison's *Memoirs of a Spacewoman* (1962), and Marge Piercy's *Woman on the Edge of Time* (1976), which critique the instrumental tendencies of mainstream psychology.

Chapter 5 explores the entanglement of 'Cognitive psychology' with science fiction, yet without dwelling on the familiar motifs of post-cyberpunk fiction. The formal beginnings of cognitive psychology are typically traced to the foundational post-war work of figures such as George Miller and Noam Chomsky, which was subsequently codified into a self-conscious school by the work of Ulrich Neisser. Jack Finney's classic narrative, *The Body Snatchers* (1955), draws upon earlier proto-cognitivist discourses to contend, often quite didactically, that the human mind typically operates as a biased, limited capacity information processor. With this psychological and political thesis, the novel explores possible personal, political and aesthetic strategies that might free the human mind from its stereotypes and blind spots. The unsettling of everyday perception in *The Body Snatchers* is systematically generalized by the linguistic *novums* of Ian Watson's *The Embedding* (1973), Samuel Delany's *Babel-17* (1966), and Ted Chiang's 'Story of Your Life' (1998), which imagine that language (and thought) is fundamentally constructive of perceived reality. These stories ask broader, cosmological questions about the nature and accessibility of ultimate reality – with Watson's novel ultimately proposing a mystical riposte to cognitivism's model of the mind.

The Conclusion, entitled 'Science fiction in psychology', firstly draws out some general conclusions from the preceding chapters. It then provisionally analyses the deployment of science fiction tropes within the body of official psychological literature, whether at a popular or more scholarly level. Although science fiction may be exploited in a very simple way within psychological theory and practice as a popularizing and didactic tool, there are other, more complex and often self-conscious ways that the genre is used. Psychologists as varied as Sandra and Daryl Bem, Randy Thornhill and Craig Palmer, and Steven Pinker, invoke different speculative narratives of the future as a way to legitimate their particular psychological claims. Perhaps surprisingly, psychology can also make use of science fiction motifs to offer cognitive estrangement of the present, be this consciously, in critical feminist psychology, or unwittingly, as in the famed obedience experiments of Stanley Milgram.

Chapter 1

Evolutionary psychology

This chapter explores the significance of evolutionary psychology (EP) for science fiction, revealing the longstanding anti-utopian deployment of Darwinian psychologies in the genre, which often imagines that progressive social ideals suppress evolutionary selection, thereby leading to stagnation and degeneracy. This supposed process can be reversed only by the activation of dormant evolutionary mechanisms in a society dominated by the struggle for survival. This anti-utopian Social Darwinist ideology is deployed in H.G. Wells's work, is authorized in more recent texts such as Robert Heinlein's libertarian manifesto *The Moon is a Harsh Mistress* (1966), and even appears (albeit equivocally) in apparently more progressive visions, such as Octavia Butler's *Parable of the Sower* (1993) and *Parable of the Talents* (1998). However, there are texts that critique this ideology (and its concomitant *topos*), or that offer alternatives to it. The agonistic worldview of sociobiology, and the discursive authority of its apparently expert pronouncements on human nature, are scathingly mocked in Kurt Vonnegut's *Galápagos* (1985). There exists also an underexamined discourse of compassionate and feminine ethics, authorized by rival evolutionary psychologies such as attachment theory, and explored by Naomi Mitchison in *Memoirs of a Spacewoman* (1962).

Evolutionary psychology

The contemporary programme of EP has emerged from a longer tradition of evolutionary explanations originating in Social Darwinism. In his historical and cultural examination of Social Darwinism from 1860 to 1945, the period of its greatest popularity, Mike Hawkins depicts this tradition of thought as embedded in a larger context of Darwinian ideas epitomized by four key tenets:

(i) biological laws governed the whole of organic nature, including humans; (ii) the pressure of population growth on resources generated a struggle for existence among organisms; (iii) physical and mental traits conferring an advantage on their possessors in this struggle (or in sexual competition), could, through inheritance, spread through the population; (iv) the cumulative effects of selection and inheritance over time accounted for the emergence of new species and the elimination of others. (31)

To these four Darwinian principles are added a fifth by Social Darwinists, namely that 'this determinism extends to not just the physical properties of humans but also to their social existence and to those psychological attributes that play a fundamental role in social life, e.g. reason, religion and morality' (31). This social philosophy is, as Hawkins notes, epitomized by the work of the British social philosopher Herbert Spencer (1820–1903), who argued from the 1860s onward that human society was, or ought to be, a continuation of natural selection by other means: in so-called 'primitive' society, 'warfare raised the average level of ability among humans by killing off inferior individuals and tribes' (92), whereas in modern society 'the struggle for existence took the form of industrial competition' (93). Darwinism thus putatively legitimated *laissez-faire* capitalism: Spencer 'was vehemently opposed to publicly funded welfare schemes because he believed them to have the effect of preserving – indeed, often multiplying – the number of the unfit' (95), who were 'biologically worthless' (99). If the state in an industrial society 'attempted to regulate market transactions, promote individual welfare, or aid the sick, the poor and the unemployed, then they not only invaded personal liberty but posed a grave threat to future progress' (94). Such ideas were echoed and amplified in the US by prominent figures such as the political economist William Graham Sumner (1840–1910) who argued from the 1880s onward against 'socialism, collective welfare and state interference' (110) in works such as *What Social Classes Owe to Each Other* (1883).

Social Darwinism fell into eventual disrepute in the twentieth century because of its association with far-right ideologies. As Richard Weikart explains, Hitler's doctrine of Aryan supremacy was rationalized by a Social Darwinist natural history of the German people:

The Nordic race, Hitler averred, had developed its key traits, especially its propensity for hard work and its moral fiber, but also its physical prowess, due to the harsh northern climate. He was not arguing that climate directly caused a change in biological traits [...]. Rather he thought that in the harsh climate only the strongest, hardest-working, and most cooperative individuals could survive and pass on their traits. The weak and sickly, as well as those who refused to labor diligently, perished in the struggle for existence. (542)

Despite Social Darwinism's post-war dormission, the evolutionary analysis of social and cultural life was re-energized by the emergence of sociobiology in the 1970s, and by the slightly later development of formal EP (Hawkins 292). Since the late 1980s, the leading proponents of EP have created a research programme built upon the foundations offered by 1970s sociobiology. Leda Cosmides and John Tooby's lengthy essay, 'The Psychological Foundations of Culture', introduces some key theses from EP, and is a founding document for the research programme. Tooby and Cosmides argue that the social sciences have tended to dismiss the notion that '"human nature" – the evolved architecture of the mind – can play any notable role as a generator of significant organization in human life' (28). Social science insists dogmatically that '[w]hat is organized and contentful in the minds of individuals comes from culture and is socially constructed' (32). Tooby and Cosmides' rejection of what they call the SSSM (the Standard Social Science Model) would certainly raise a few eyebrows among scholars in the humanities and social sciences, who might be surprised to learn, for instance, of their belief that '[c]ultures are more or less bounded entities' which are homogeneous, consisting of 'widely distributed or nearly group-universal behavioral practices' (31).

At any rate, the SSSM, claim Tooby and Cosmides, has obstructed the development of a genuinely evolutionary psychology. Among their list of the key tenets of EP, are the following:

a. the human mind consists of a set of evolved information-processing mechanisms instantiated in the human nervous system;

b. these mechanisms, and the developmental programs that produce them, are adaptations, produced by natural selection over evolutionary time in ancestral environments;

c. many of these mechanisms are functionally specialized to produce behavior that solves particular adaptive problems, such as mate selection, language acquisition, family relations, and cooperation;

d. to be functionally specialized, many of these mechanisms must be richly structured in a content-specific way;

e. content-specific information processing mechanisms generate some of the particular content of human culture, including certain behaviors, artifacts, and linguistically transmitted representations. (24)

Apparent geographical and historical variation across cultures can therefore be unmasked to reveal a unified psychological content determined by evolutionary mechanisms that were effective in early human populations. One much-discussed EP study, for instance, proposes that apparent cultural variation in the canons of female beauty is largely peripheral to the business of men choosing a mate, and that female sexual attractiveness is in fact positively correlated in all cultures with a particular waist-hip circumference ratio of around 0.7 (Singh); underneath seeming cultural variation is a unitary and specific content generated by mate selection. A similar, larger study seeks out further cross-cultural universals in mate preferences by looking at factors such as age, financial prospects, relative youth or seniority, and so forth (Buss). One of the key ambitions of EP is thus quite clear: explanation by cultures (in the plural) are to be supplanted by explanation from EP (in the singular). In typically forthright fashion, Steven Pinker asserts in *How the Mind Works* (1997), his popularization of EP, that 'nothing in culture makes sense except in the light of psychology. Evolution created psychology, and that is how it explains culture. The most important relic of early humans is the modern mind' (210). These putative cultural universals are explained as causally dependent upon psychological mechanisms that were evolved in Pleistocene societies, but, as Buller notes, the chains of inference in such studies are frequently quite tenuous (457–71); nor is it clear that any such universals require explanation by psychological mechanisms (rather than common historical origins – or simply cultural imperialism (Shepard and Yu)).

Such EP explanations mean that – despite its self-styled opposition to the humanities and social sciences – this contemporary research programme has an affinity with the work of Marx, Nietzsche, and Freud. These 'masters of suspicion', to use Paul Ricoeur's phrase, all sought in various ways to unmask our ideals as disguised expressions of baser motives (for economic betterment, the attainment of power, the gratification of sexual or destructive instincts). Like these thinkers and their followers, EP too offers an interpretation that 'is understood as a demystification, as a reduction of illusion' (Ricoeur 27). To adapt the examples given in the preceding paragraph, a woman may believe herself to be attracted to the kindness and good looks of her husband. The proponent of EP knows, however, that she is ultimately obeying a Darwinian imperative to seek out a healthy and fertile partner who will look after her and her children. To take another example of 'unmasking', a religious believer may understand herself as holding to some particular creed about the nature of the cosmos and the place of humankind within it. But, according to Pascal Boyer, she merely 'signals a willingness to embrace the group's particular norm for no other reason than that it is, precisely, the group's norm' – religion has hijacked an evolved psychological module for the formation of 'large, stable coalitions of unrelated individuals, strongly bonded by mutual trust' (1039). As Richard Hamilton explains, EP proposes in such cases, and many others, that 'the reasons people give for their actions are post hoc rationalizations for what their bodies did under the influence of their evolutionary programme' (115).

There are further, more specifically evolutionary theses that may be unpacked and scrutinized within the EP programme. To Stephen Jay Gould, the EP programme seems far too rigidly adaptationist, since it frequently supposes *a priori* that identifiable human psychological characteristics are to be explained as adaptations to a particular environment. But, counters Gould, although '[n]atural selection made the human brain big', 'most of our mental properties and potentials may be [...] nonadaptive side consequences of building a device with such structural complexity' (104). To borrow Gould's example, humans have evolved brains that can learn to read and write, but this feature was not developed as an adaptation to an environment containing texts (104). There are also significant concerns about whether one can in fact identify adaptive problems and their corresponding solutions in the ancestral environment, the Pleistocene 'Environment of Evolutionary Adaptation' (EEA). This may be because the empirical information is very hard to ascertain (Gould 100), and remains so even when analogical reasoning based on contemporary anthropology and primatology is employed (Buller 94–96). There are also more subtle difficulties, such as the instability of the environment (Buller 99–102) or the loose fit between an adaptive problem and the multiplicity of possible solutions (Buller 104). Moreover, as will be discussed elsewhere (249–50), the rhetoric of certain EP texts borrows heavily – if unselfconsciously – from the tropes of speculative culture.

The evolutionary sieve:
The persistence of an anti-utopian *topos*

As indicated above, science fiction has historically drawn upon a broad context of Social Darwinist and sociobiological ideas that, while preceding formal EP, nonetheless offer material for psychological speculation. The Social Darwinist context motivates an anti-utopian tendency to didactically prophesy a state of future decadence that can be arrested only by the re-activation of dormant evolutionary mechanisms. Science fiction may therefore offer a *topos* in which evolutionary processes re-emerge and intensify after a period of presumed latency: some extraordinary and perilous setting re-invigorates sexual and natural selection, with the consequent exercise of psychological capacities that are dormant or masked in contemporary civilization.

This tendency can be traced back to H.G. Wells's science fiction (if not further), most famously in *The Time Machine* (1895). The general evolutionary logic in Wells's work is captured well by János I. Tóth and Katalin Csala-Gáti, who perceive a dilemma between (1) a cruel society in which evolutionary mechanisms are effective, and (2) a more benevolent society that causes the species to degenerate:

> Either high population growth coupled with a high death rate, causing cruel life for the majority, but selection effected with all its might and providing automatic evolutionary adaptation to the environment (in *The Time Machine* the greater adaptability, imagination and inventiveness of the Morlocks is the logical consequence of this reasoning). Or a significant limitation on population growth, coupled potentially with a low death rate, in which case poverty is less significant and the life of the majority is more pleasant. But in this case biological selection and evolution are not at play and so such an environment would result in degeneration and the possible genetic degradation of the species (as occurs in the case of the Eloi). (26–27)

Tóth and Csala-Gáti's reference to *The Time Machine* invites consideration of the psychological issues raised in the text, with its well-known sardonic commentary on nineteenth-century class discourses, whereby the human species bifurcates into the beautiful yet helpless Eloi, and the subterranean Morlocks, an aggressive and intelligent species that treat the former as domestic animals for their consumption. The Time Traveller's explanation of the psychology of the Eloi relates their limited intelligence to the societal de-activation of evolutionary mechanisms. '[T]he human intellect', he asserts, 'had committed suicide': 'life and property must have reached almost absolute safety', but, since 'intellectual versatility is the compensation for change, danger, and trouble' (Wells *Time* 78), the Eloi drift towards 'feeble prettiness' (79) and a 'general dwindling in size, strength, and intelligence' (49).

Wells's narrative teaches the martial virtues of re-activated evolved psychology. The Time Traveller's struggle for existence against the Morlocks clearly implies that he has found an environment fitting to his innate aggressive impulses. He describes, while battling the Morlocks, 'the succulent giving of flesh and bone under my blows', and '[t]he strange exultation that so often seems to accompany hard fighting' (74). Weena, the Eloi child-woman who is his temporary consort, also seems implicated in this recovery of the primitive within the Time Traveller, since he both rescues her, and takes considerable effort and risk to protect her – as if she were both mate and offspring. The Time Traveller's journey is therefore not merely forward into evolutionary time; it is also a journey back into more primitive elements of the psyche, those lain down in humanity's original evolutionary environment. The figure who confronts the complacent dinner guests at the beginning of the novel is 'haggard and drawn, as by intense suffering' (13), and announces himself to be 'starving for a bit of meat' (14); the Time Traveller has been thrown back into the Darwinian struggle for survival, where his latent faculties have re-emerged. The *novum* of time travel is therefore also a socio-psychotherapeutic metaphor for the re-invigoration of our evolved psychology via the encounter with danger and struggle. A similar psychological journey is experienced by the narrator of Wells's *The War of the Worlds* (1898), who – after the Martian invasion has failed – remarks that 'the stress and danger of the time have left an abiding sense of doubt and insecurity in my mind' (179). This renewed anxiety is glossed as, in effect, providential: 'in the larger design of the universe this invasion from Mars is not without its ultimate benefit for men; it has robbed us of that serene confidence in the future which is the most fruitful source of decadence' (179).

By the time of *A Modern Utopia* (1905), Wells had retreated from his more extreme public pronouncements on social eugenics and uneasily reconciled the evolutionary vision with his socialist sympathies. The narrator explains that '[t]he Modern Utopia will give a universal security indeed, and exercise the minimum of compulsions to toil' (107) but will nonetheless use measures such as 'sane marriage and birth laws' (106) to gradually eliminate from the species 'its congenital invalids, its idiots and madmen, its drunkards and men of vicious mind, its cruel and furtive souls, its stupid people, too stupid to be of use to the community, its lumpish, unteachable and unimaginative people' (95). Such regulated procreation will ensure that '[t]here would be no killing, no lethal chambers' – although, adds the narrator as an afterthought, 'Utopia will kill all deformed and monstrous and evilly diseased births' (100). However, regardless of Wells's partial retreat, the Social Darwinist vision persisted during the first half of the twentieth century even in liberal democracies, most notably in eugenic ideas and practices such as enforced sterilization; indeed, the US was a notable leader in the period, and something of an inspiration to Nazi Germany (Hawkins 242). The ideological justification for eugenics was typically Social Darwinist: 'eugenicists invariably depicted a rupture between nature and culture: natural selection had been replaced by selective forces which were social in *origin* and which usually acted contrary to the former' (247).

In the immediate post-war years, the political authority of Social Darwinism declined significantly given its obvious association with the Nazi regime. Golden Age science fiction, however, offered a reservoir in which US liberal culture preserved the ideology of the Nazi social order that it had so recently vanquished. For instance, Tom Godwin's *The Survivors* (1958), later published as *Space Prison* (1962), tells of a group of Earth refugees left to die on a hostile planet by their imperial oppressors. They instead pass successfully through an evolutionary bottleneck to emerge as vengeful superhumans (and, without any apparent irony, as racial stock for a new, superior empire). Robert A. Heinlein's *The Moon is a Harsh Mistress* (1966), the narrative of a Lunar colony's revolution against its earthbound masters, explores this *novum*-cum-setting with greater literary sophistication. The lunar colonists, or 'Loonies', are psychologically selected by the moon's evolutionary pressures (she is a 'stern schoolmistress' (236), as well as the illicit lover implied by the title). The Loonies are thus in a state of re-activated natural and sexual selection that propels them quickly beyond the atavistic 'earthworms' back on Terra: 'Those who adjust to facts stay alive; those who don't are dead and no problem' (164) explains the narrator, Mannie, whose full name (Manuel Garcia O'Kelly) hints at the hybrid vigour that Heinlein deems necessary to survival. As well as emphasizing the harsh natural environment, Heinlein's narrator presents the moon as a society in which the demographic imbalance between the genders re-activates or intensifies sexual selection by forcing the males to compete to impregnate females:

> [T]wo million males, less than one million females. A physical fact, basic as rock or vacuum. Then add idea of tanstaafl [there ain't no

such thing as a free lunch]. When thing is scarce, price goes up. Women are scarce; aren't enough to go round – that makes them the most valuable thing. (164)

Leaving aside the issue of how women would be treated if there were a glut of females in the Darwinian market, this quotation clearly supports Philip E. Smith's argument that 'since the beginning of his career as a writer, Heinlein has based his most important fictions on a very apparent philosophy: social Darwinism' (137). A simple explanatory framework runs throughout his work, in which 'biology [...] explains politics: A political system allowing a maximum of personal freedom and a minimum of government interference will best accomplish the advancement of the race' (141). The link between biology and political life is the psychology putatively demanded by natural and sexual selection, and made apparent in *Moon*'s mantra-like variations on the theme of hard facts, and in the peculiar pseudo-feminism that Heinlein foists upon his female characters. On the one hand, Heinlein's women are seemingly empowered, since they pick and choose their mates. This, however, is merely a manifestation of sexual selection at work: Manny explains how male 'bad breath and body odors' are 'self-correcting' vices since 'chronic offenders, or unfortunates who can't correct, aren't likely to reproduce, seeing how choosy women are' (Heinlein 204). Women are choosy, in that they are allowed to select the best mates. They are, however, psychologically subjugated to evolutionary imperatives in Heinlein's new EEA – Mannie remarks, for instance, that one of his family, Ludmilla, 'is a sweet little thing, just fifteen and pregnant first time' (43).

Wells's suspicion of civilized comforts, and Heinlein's biologically grounded libertarianism, both motivate the favoured *topos* of a setting in which evolutionary selection is intensified, calling forth supposedly 'desirable' psychological mechanisms in an environment marked by conflict and/or unrestrained economic (and sexual) competition. Their celebration of a renewed evolutionary environment resonates all too clearly with doctrines espoused in the 1930s and 1940s by a supposed 'other' to liberal society:

> Nazi officials and SS anthropologists [...] believed that the Nordic race had evolved to a higher level of intelligence, physical prowess, and social solidarity than other races, in large part because they had faced what biologists today would call greater selective pressure. This selective pressure was caused by the Ice Ages, which had weeded out the weak and sickly, leaving only the brightest and best to propagate the Nordic race. (Weikart 551–52)

Yet while Social Darwinist ideologies are readily perceptible in the work of Wells and Heinlein, the anti-utopian meaning of the favoured *topos* may be harder to discern in texts that are far more politically progressive, but that nonetheless deploy the fundamental narrative of an evolutionary separation of the wheat from the chaff.

Surprisingly, the *topos* of the evolutionary sieve occurs even after the counterculture had challenged the racial hierarchies of US society. It appears – albeit ambivalently – in the now canonical science fiction of the celebrated black US female author, Octavia Butler (1947–2006). Butler's 1993 novel, *Parable of the Sower*, and its 1998 sequel, *Parable of the Talents*, imagine a future US in which the state apparatus has almost completely failed. The central character, and narrator of the first novel, Lauren Olamina, is an adolescent girl living in a walled community in twenty-first century California. In the year 2024, when Lauren's narrative begins, global warming has taken its toll on the geography, economy, and society of the US. Her small community, Robledo, struggles to survive amidst increasing urban turmoil and crime. Lauren herself is affected by an inherited condition, 'hyperempathy', in which she compulsively identifies with others, and sympathetically (though not telepathically) shares their experience. Eventually, after her neighbourhood is ransacked, and most of her family killed, Lauren is forced to flee northwards. She takes with her a number of survivors, and eventually accumulates a small band of followers (among them her future husband, Taylor Bankole). She hopes to convert this community to her syncretic and newly invented religion, 'Earthseed'. This belief system has as its fundamental tenet, the credo 'God / is Change' (3), and takes as its eschatology and soteriology a far-off future in which a new posthuman lineage has spread through the universe, so escaping both evolutionary extinction and the Earth's eventual destruction. After various confrontations and crises on the road northwards, *Parable of the Sower* concludes with the establishment of the first Earthseed community in a remote rural site. The rather more pessimistic sequel, *Parable of the Talents*, introduces multiple narratorial points of view, including that of Lauren's sceptical daughter. The text tells at length of the Earthseed community's efforts to survive in the authoritarian Christian-fundamentalist presidency that takes over the declining US. Although Lauren's first community, Acorn, is destroyed by an invasion of so-called 'Crusaders' (i.e. fascist thugs), the Earthseed movement manages to survive and propagate, albeit by accommodating to the existing political order. By the end of *Parable of the Talents*, Lauren is able to watch the first shuttles lifting off to find new worlds. However, the reader is left to judge whether, in Canavan's words, 'the troubled realization of the Earthseed destiny' has entailed Lauren's 'retreat from real-world political struggle that concretely makes actual people's actual lives substantively better' (139).

The Earthseed creed might easily be viewed as an emancipatory, even revolutionary renewal of religious life and practice, especially in its celebration of change and diversity. According to David Morris, 'hope for social change and biological change together marks the excess that pushes Earthseed out of the realm of secular movements and into the religious. The new worlds will remake the people – they will challenge people in social terms but also invite new sociobiological adaptations that will change the human species' (278). For Michael Brandon McCormack, it is against a 'post-apocalyptic backdrop of devastation and religious intolerance' that 'Butler imagines future possibilities of a thoroughly secularized, multicultural, religious community of social "aliens"' (21). A cautionary note is though sounded by Tom Moylan who notes that 'Lauren's ideological and political goal is not the transformation of the Earth' but rather 'an apocalyptic leap, not *through* the present but *out* of the present' (*Scraps* 243). This view is echoed by Vincent Lloyd, who points out that '[b]y the end of the novels, Olamina has given up marketing Earthseed to the underclass created by rampant neoliberalism. Instead, she has found the perfect market for her religion among the upper middle class' (462).

Although the flaws in the Earthseed ideology are more apparent in *Parable of the Talents*, they can be discerned also in *Parable of the Sower*, particularly in its use of a Darwinist *topos* in which renewed evolutionary pressures sift out a higher form of human life. Whereas Heinlein's evolutionary vision located re-activated natural and sexual selection in a decolonizing society, the fictional US envisaged in the *Parable* novels is recognisably a failed state which can no longer provide central goods such as physical security, reliable judicial process, and meaningful political participation (Rotberg 3). The US government can, for instance, no longer be relied upon for security and justice – 'the cops knock them [the street poor] around, rob them if they have anything worth stealing' – and consequently there comes a proliferation of privately held small arms: 'We hear so much gunfire, day and night, single shots and odd bursts of automatic weapons fire' (O.E. Butler 48). The US is in economic collapse, with phenomena such as hyperinflation ('Food prices are insane, always going up, never down' (74)), and a return to trading by barter. There is a lack of medical provision, especially of the state-sponsored kind that would be called upon to prevent epidemics of cholera in Mississippi and Louisiana (51). Education, too, is increasingly privatized: primary and secondary schooling is provided within Robledo by amateur teachers such as Lauren. Outside of Robledo's walled communities, neither housing nor food can be assured: Lauren writes of the shanty houses – 'rag, stick, cardboard, and palm frond shacks along the way into the hills' (82), which are inhabited by 'living skeletons [...] Skin and bones and a few teeth' (82). The northern border has been closed by Canada in order to prevent a refugee crisis, and lethal force maintains this territorial division: 'People get shot every day trying to sneak into Canada' (76). In the absence of a strong domestic state and economy, the US has been colonized by external, foreign capital, such as the firm of 'Kagimoto, Stamm, Frampton, and Company' (109) who are, according to Lauren's father, 'Japanese, German, Canadian' (111). In Lauren's words: 'This country is going to be parceled out as a source of cheap labor and cheap land. [...] our surviving cities are bound to wind up the economic colonies of whoever can afford to buy them' (119).

This imagined failure of the US state reads almost as a sarcastic rejoinder to Heinlein's anti-collectivism. But, as Carl Abbott notes, frontier life has long been seen in American culture – including science fiction – as morally improving: 'The challenges of problem-solving and community-making in new settlements [...] demanded wide participation, cooperation, voluntary association, and support for public institutions. Far from undermining the civil community, the frontier balanced individual competition against the needs of the larger group' (125). Lauren, who thinks of 'the big city' as 'a carcass covered with too many maggots' shares in this essential scepticism toward urban life and state-provided security (O.E. Butler 9). She records with disdain the words of a new arrival to Robledo who remarks 'how he had paid enough [taxes] in his life to have a right to depend on the police to protect him' (81), and who describes his family as one that is 'not very social [...] We mind our own business' (34). These are the attitudes of the city, where safety is provided by the state, rather than of the frontier, where every member of the society is called upon to directly assist in its security. The incomer's announcement is preceded by a warning from Lauren's father that their community is built on mutual interdependence in the face of an external threat: '"This is a small community", my father said. "We all know each other here. We depend on each other"' (34). The same connection of community with security is explained later, after an abortive attack on Robledo – '"Did you notice", Dad said, "that every off-duty watcher answered the whistles last night? They came out to defend their community"' (69). Indeed, part of Lauren's admiration for the US space programme is based on the frontier ethos that it potentially offers, which is clearly akin to that promoted in Heinlein's lunar extrapolation: 'I think people who traveled to extrasolar worlds would be on their own [...] and far from help. [...] out of the shadow of their parent world' (77). Thus, as Canavan notes, the 'incisive and prescient critique of political neoliberalism' in *Parable of the Sower* 'at the same time celebrates futurological tropes we might typically associate with the right-wing thinkers Butler loathed' (134).

The reappearance of neoliberal ideology within Earthseed's grand narrative is in part due to the refractory nature of the evolutionary materials inherited by Butler from her generic forebears. The projection of evolutionary selection into the setting of a failed state intensifies in Lauren's journey northward out of Robledo, which leads her eventually to found Acorn, the ill-fated Earthseed community. This forced migration functions as a Darwinian sieve or strainer that tests the adaptiveness, the fitness for survival, of the group that she builds up around her: 'Out here, you adapt to your surrounding or you get killed' declares Lauren (O.E. Butler 168); to her friend, Harry, who also escapes, she warns, 'You still think a mistake is when your father yells at you or you break a finger or chip a tooth or something. Out here a mistake – one mistake – and you may be dead' (167). Lauren *et al.* are plunged into an evolutionary *Bildungsroman*, as they trek through a landscape filled with enemies repeatedly described as 'predators' (e.g. 186) and 'scavengers' (e.g. 220). Lauren watches and learns as she observes someone being robbed of all his possessions because he is inattentive, discovers the corpses of three youths who have died drinking chemically tainted water, and witnesses the destruction of an otherwise strong community sited too near the roadside. Lauren interprets this Darwinian threshing on the road northward as the first stage in a renewed progress up a supposed evolutionary ladder toward posthumanism: 'The Destiny of Earthseed,' she explains to one new member, 'is to take root among the stars. [...] That's the ultimate Earthseed aim, and the ultimate human change short of death. It's a destiny we'd better pursue if we hope to be anything other than smooth-skinned dinosaurs' (204). Evidence for such evolutionary processes at work in failed states such as Rwanda in 1994, or Somalia during the 1990s, would seem to be scant. Nor is there much evolutionary plausibility in Lauren's assumption that natural selection will direct *homo sapiens* towards some human ideal of perfection, rather than to some merely improved evolutionary adaptiveness (such as that satirically depicted by Vonnegut (60–67 below)). The Earthseed ideology invokes the 'Escalator Fallacy' in evolutionary thought identified by Mary Midgley – namely, 'the idea that evolution is a steady, linear upward movement, a single inexorable process of improvement, leading [...] "from gas to genius" and beyond into some superhuman spiritual stratosphere' (*Evolution* 7). In Lauren's case, this escalator leads to '[o]ther star systems. Living worlds' (O.E. Butler 204).

The flaws in the Earthseed ideology go beyond merely its imagining of human catastrophe as an opportunity for the rebirth of the human species, and the elimination of social undesirables. A further difficulty arises in its valorization of empathy as a foundational civic virtue. The urgently needed psychological progression, in Lauren's eyes, is the evolution of a more intensified capacity for empathy. Critics such as Jerry Phillips agree with this textual dominant, regarding hyperempathy as a utopian trace within *Parable of the Sower*: 'how much more difficult it would be,' he enquires, 'to starve, rape, exploit, terrorize, and murder the other?' (306). Lauren (whose voice dominates *Parable of the Sower*) implicitly authorizes this interpretation – after the torture and murder of her brother Keith, Lauren reflects, 'If hyperempathy syndrome were a more common complaint, people couldn't do such things' (O.E. Butler 105). The *novum* of hyperempathy also underlies the plot progression in *Parable of the Sower*, in which Lauren moves from her patriarchal and largely consanguineous family to the elective bonds of the Earthseed community that she brings together on her journey. On her lengthy trek, Lauren picks up others fleeing their blood families, such as Allie and Jill, 'who were so clearly their father's victims' (234), and finds a husband in Bankole, who, at age fifty-seven, is also a new, adoptive father. The adoptive imagery is further developed in an intertextual reference to the famous ending of John Steinbeck's *The Grapes of Wrath* (1939), where Rose of Sharon suckles a starving stranger. When Bankole finds an orphaned baby, a fellow traveller suckles the child at one breast, with her own child at the other (231). Such deprecation of kin loyalty is consonant with the *novum* of hyperempathy: Lauren's mutation replaces particularistic loyalty to family with a universal sympathy between persons, and thus resists the fragmentation of civic society into individuals and family units.

Yet there are some telling limits to Lauren's hyperempathy. Although she gets double the pleasure in sexual intercourse, she seems strangely immune to the sexual high experienced by the drug-addicted pyromaniacs, for whom 'watching the leaping changing patterns of fire' provides 'a better, more intense, longer-lasting high than sex' (133). There is no doubt an evolutionary narrative logic to this decision, since Lauren's mutation would scarcely be adaptive were she liable to be emotionally infected by the 'pyros', and to throw herself with gusto into their orgies of destruction. But there is a symbolic meaning as well. The pyromaniacs, as viewed by Lauren, are an image of revolutionaries who demand the redistribution of wealth: '"She died for us," the scavenger woman had said of the green face [a pyro]. Some kind of insane burn-the-rich movement, Keith had said' (149). Later, after an earthquake, there is a mass attack by pyros in which '[b]ands of the street poor precede or follow them, grabbing whatever they can from stores and from the walled enclaves of the rich and what's left of the middle class' (226). Lauren's hyperempathy is thus subtly moralized: the allegorical revolutionaries are 'othered' to the extent that she cannot pick up on their orgiastic sentiment (and something similar happens in *Parable of the Talents*, where Lauren is allowed to resist identification with her sexually sadistic Christian Crusader captors). Such moralism is further emphasized by the text's implicit account of sympathetic moral impulse as a compulsive imaginative identification with the other (so that in a fight, for instance, Lauren records, 'I felt every blow that I struck, just as though I'd hit myself' (11)). Contrast this with the definition of sympathy advanced by Philip Mercer in his study of the concept in moral philosophy:

> [I]f it is correct to make the statement '*A* sympathizes with *B*' then the following conditions must be fulfilled:
>
> (a) *A* is aware of the existence of *B* as a sentient subject;
>
> (b) *A* knows or believes he knows *B*'s state of mind;
>
> (c) there is fellow-feeling between *A* and *B* so that through his imagination *A* is able to realize *B*'s state of mind; and
>
> (d) *A* is altruistically concerned for *B*'s welfare. (19)

The fourth condition is significant because it indicates imaginative knowledge of another's feelings is not in itself robust enough to establish an ethically significant account of sympathy. One may well have this capacity, but be otherwise lacking a properly altruistic response. One could, for example, relish the sufferings of another if one were a sadist, and wish to prolong and intensify them. Alternatively, one could be concerned selfishly for the other's welfare – for example, 'because I desire to be well-thought-of or because I have a guilty conscience or because I want to get him into my debt' (11).

Lauren's hyperempathy is a pseudo-altruism in which, *ceteris paribus*, ego works to avert alter's sufferings so that the former does not have to participate in them. It is a kind of *lex talionis* inscribed on the psyche, rather than any genuine relationship of concern. Hyperempathy is little more than a swift psychic punishment for wrong-doing (or, less frequently in *Parable of the Sower*, an immediate reward for the giving of pleasure). Indeed, as Canavan notes, a multitude of related philosophical difficulties had caused Butler to abandon an earlier attempt to write a utopian novel in which 'empathy had become contagious' (121). Hyperempathy certainly cannot bear the weighty utopian constructions built upon it by critics such as Phillips, who writes, 'in a hyperempathetic world, the other would cease to exist as the ontological antithesis of the self, but instead would become a real aspect of oneself, insofar as one accepts oneself as a social being' (306). Even in our fallen, non-hyperempathetic world, there are many ways of self-accepted 'social being' that involve cognitive, affective and conative relations to the experience of the other, without the compulsive identification presupposed in hyperempathy.

Kurt Vonnegut's *Galápagos*: Subverting sociobiology

Despite the longstanding generic trope of the evolutionary sieve, there are more recent science fiction narratives that reflexively subvert the authority of evolutionary psychological discourse. The EP research programme that coalesced in the late 1980s in the collaboration of Tooby and Cosmides was a successor movement to the sociobiological research programme of the 1970s and 1980s, which was spearheaded in 1975 by Edward O. Wilson's *Sociobiology*. Steven Rose and his co-authors summarize this popular ethology as one in which 'human beings are seen as self-aggrandizing, selfish animals whose social organization, even in its cooperative aspects, is a consequence of natural selection for traits that maximize reproductive fitness. In particular, human beings are characterized by territoriality, tribalism, indoctrinability, blind faith, xenophobia, and a variety of manifestations of aggression' (Rose, Lewontin and Kamin 245). Rose *et al.* trace the lineage of this account backwards from sociobiology to Social Darwinism, and further back to Hobbes's atomistic account of human society (240–41). As Rose *et al.* explain, Wilson's work had an enormous popular ideological impact (233–35), which explains why even as contemporary EP is gestating in the early 1980s, there appear science fiction narratives which challenge the discursive authority of EP, including the favoured scenario of renewed selection mechanisms. Margaret Atwood's contemporary dystopian classic, *The Handmaid's Tale* (1985), is not primarily engaged with evolutionary or psychological discourses. Nonetheless, the future US 'Gileadan' society of patriarchal polygyny, in which older high-status males monopolize the reproductive females, and jealously guard them against cuckoldry from younger males, is represented as a grotesque, but nonetheless faithful extrapolation of EP. The novel's later 'historical notes' on Gilead present a future historian's view that 'the sociobiological theory of natural polygamy was used as a scientific justification for some of the odder practices of the regime, just as Darwinism was used by earlier ideologies' (318–19). The contemporary reader, of course, is left in no doubt of the patriarchal, historically specific appeal of sociobiological views on the natural relations between the sexes.

Atwood's novel is so well known that analysis of its reflexive function in the present context would be superfluous. A less well-known reflexive challenge to EP is provided in Kurt Vonnegut's 1985 novel *Galápagos*. This text responds to the rise of sociobiology and EP by extrapolating an ironic evolutionary utopia on its island *topos*, thereby exposing and undermining both the reflexive authority of EP and the longstanding generic infatuation with evolutionary bottlenecks. *Galápagos* is – or appears to be, since the narrative may be unreliable – the story of *homo sapiens'* evolution over millennia into a species of simple-minded, flippered, seal-like mammals confined to one of the Galápagos islands. The tale is told by a self-proclaimed ghost, Leon Trout, who was killed during the construction of the *Bahía de Darwin*, a cruise liner that will prove important in his narrative. Trout, the son of science fiction writer Kilgore Trout (a recurring character in Vonnegut's fiction), watches for over a million years as events unfold. The main narrative begins in 1986, during a period of economic and social collapse, as a group of characters assemble in Ecuador for 'the Nature Cruise of the Century' (Vonnegut 18) in which the *Bahía de Darwin* is intended to sail for two weeks around the Galápagos Islands. By a series of contingencies, including the outbreak of war, and the spread of a microbe that causes human infertility, a small group end up stranded on Santa Rosalia, a fictional island in the archipelago. The most important of the group are: Adolf von Kleist, captain of the *Bahía de Darwin*; Mary Hepburn, a widowed school teacher; and six young women, from the (fictitious) Amazonian Kanka-bono tribe. After ten years of isolation, Mary appropriates von Kleist's sperm, and uses it to artificially inseminate the Kanka-bono girls. This starts a colony on Santa Rosalia that gradually adapts to conditions on the islands while the rest of *homo sapiens* heads to extinction. The hands and feet of the Santa Rosalians become like flippers so that they can swim after fish (their staple diet), and their skulls become streamlined, so that their brains grow correspondingly smaller. Trout's tale ends in the year 1,001,986 as he awaits the appearance of a blue tunnel that will take him to the afterlife. His final words – which are, he claims, written in air using his ghostly finger – detail his desertion over a million years ago from the US Marines during the Vietnam

War, and his subsequent flight to Sweden. His war experience, admits Trout, drove him to a nervous breakdown – an admission that, as will be shown, casts doubt on the reliability of his narrative.

Bizarrely, there are commentators who seem happy to accept Trout's manifesto at face value. Donald E. Morse, for instance, sees *Galápagos* as a largely sincere utopian dream, if not quite a blueprint. Vonnegut's text 'warns against the ultimate effects of humanity's proclivity for destroying the planet', and extrapolates a future condition of posthuman ecological harmony: 'latter-day human beings slowly evolve over eons into less destructive and far more lovable, furry, polymorphosely [sic] perverse, aquatic creatures, thus ensuring their own survival in the far future, along with that of other beings, and of the very planet itself' (301). Charles Berryman is also trusting of Trout's narrative. Admittedly, he notes that 'after a million years the colony on the island is no longer human in any meaningful sense', and asks, 'If this is Vonnegut's conclusion, what reader could find it satisfactory?' (195). On the other hand, much of his reading takes at face value Trout's presentation of an evolutionary sifting and progression by which 'all difficulties are attributed to oversize brains, and survival will demand a new direction for evolution' (192).

More sensitive readings of *Galápagos* understand that Vonnegut very likely has an oppositional relation to his narrator's evolutionary discourse: Trout's fictional father, Kilgore, is Vonnegut's science fiction alter ego, and frequently used to ironize conventional genre narratives. Oliver W. Ferguson argues that if one reads Trout's autobiographical narrative attentively, then a very different interpretation of the novel is possible. What if Trout's act of narration takes place not millions of years in the future, but during the present day? Trout has, after all, confessed to bouts of mental illness. In this case, the main events of the story acquire a different ontological status. They emerge as the fantasies of a madman:

> Unable to cope rationally with his tortured history, he [Trout] took refuge in his imagination. [...] he denied his corporeal existence and created a story that envisaged a species to which not only familial life and human affections but also the common ills of twentieth-century society – domestic discord, economic freebooting, environmental despoliation, and war – were unknown. (232–33)

Peter Freese makes a similar point when he draws attention to the contradiction between the speech act in Trout's narrative, and the thesis propounded by that act. Trout is telling a story that argues rationally for the uselessness of rationality, and thereby appeals in its illocution to the very faculty that it dismisses: 'Not only does *Galápagos*, in story form, tell us about future story-less times – thus contradicting its message by the choice of its medium, but it also pleads for an abolition of big brains by using the powers exerted by big brains only and by thriving on the rhetorical devices of persuasion whose abrogation it celebrates' (Freese 170). Given these ironizing devices in the narrative, there is room at least to doubt the coherence of the conceptual net that Trout casts over the future history he presents – and it is quite conceivable that the entire future narrative is the fantastic projection of a madman.

If Trout's narrative is fantasized, then the key sentence in *Galápagos* is the admission of his guilty feelings over his actions in the Vietnam War, in which he shot an elderly woman:

> She was as toothless and bent over as Mary Hepburn would be at the end of her life. I shot her because she had just killed my best friend and my worst enemy in my platoon with a single hand-grenade.
> This episode made me sorry to be alive, made me envy stones. I would rather have been a stone at the service of the Natural Order. (Vonnegut 104–05)

Trout yearns for a narrative that will redeem his actions. He finds one – be it real or imagined – in a narrative that authorizes evolutionary explanations by grafting them into pre-existing salvational obsessions (just as Skinner sought to do with behaviourism in *Walden Two* (133–41 below)). Trout's wish as a soldier – 'What a life! I would have loved to put down all my weapons and become a fisherman instead' (160) – comes true, albeit at a phylogenetic rather than an ontogenetic level. He delights in enumerating the incapacities of the posthumans. They cannot torture: 'How could you even capture somebody you wanted to torture with just your flippers and your mouth?' (118)). They cannot enslave: 'How could you ever hold somebody in bondage with nothing but your flippers and your mouth?' (143). They cannot wage war: 'Nobody today is nearly smart enough to make the sorts of weapons even the poorest nations had a million years ago' (120), and '[e]ven if they found a grenade or a machine gun or a knife or whatever left over from olden times, how could they ever make use of it with just their flippers and their mouths?' (123). Evolution has weeded out instrumental rationality, signified by the metonymy of human hands, from human psychology: 'all the people are so innocent and relaxed now, all because evolution took their hands away' (151).

The peculiarity in *Galápagos* is that the evolutionary escalator, according to Trout, does not lead to salvation via greater instrumental mastery over the world, but through harmonious co-existence within it. It is therefore slightly misleading to view the novel as 'a rebuttal of a notion of smooth, progressive, predictable development [...] with a crucial emphasis being placed upon periods of crisis when contingent factors can throw evolutionary development in any one of a number of possible directions' (Cordle 172–73). There are certainly contingencies in Trout's narrative, but they are implicitly interpreted as a providential chain of accidental causation leading inexorably to a naturalized, evolutionary salvation. The theological allusions in Trout's narrative are frequent, and self-consciously allude to the resignification of Judaeo-Christian narratives. The most prominent allusions are to Noah's Ark and to the Garden of Eden. Trout several times refers to his tale as a variation on Noah's Ark (Vonnegut 13, 130, 173), and Captain von Kleist alludes to it as well (201). Those who are carried away to the Galápagos islands on the new Noah's Ark are saved from God's wrath, and are allowed to dwell in a second Garden of Eden in which Captain von Kleist is the new Adam (47, 56).

The religious narratives alluded to in *Galápagos* expose the secularized religious narratives that have given discursive authority to EP. As Hamilton explains in his critique of EP's social diagnoses and therapeutics, the so-called 'Atavistic Misfit Hypothesis' (109) offers a narrative of Fall from original innocence, and points towards a future salvation within (rather than after) history. Buller notes that 'Evolutionary Psychologists believe that much contemporary human behaviour is maladaptive' since, putatively, 'Human behavior in contemporary environments is caused by cognitive and motivational mechanisms that are designed to produce adaptive behavior in response to Pleistocene environmental conditions' (62). EP therefore often concludes that when 'contemporary environments differ from Pleistocene environments, the proximate mechanisms we've inherited from our Pleistocene ancestors will produce [...] Pleistocene-appropriate behaviour (which will fail to be adaptive under contemporary conditions)' (63). Gould cites for instance Robert Wright's hypothesis that 'a sweet tooth leads to unhealthy obesity today but must have risen as an adaptation' – which Gould regards as 'pure guesswork in the cocktail party mode' (100). Pinker is similarly forthright in his condemnation of what he sees as the vices created by maladaptation to our contemporary environment:

> People watch pornography when they could be seeking a mate, forgo food to buy heroin, sell their blood to buy movie tickets (in India), postpone childbearing to climb the corporate ladder, and eat themselves into an early grave. Human vice is proof that

biological adaptation is, speaking literally, a thing of the past. Our minds are adapted to the small foraging bands in which our family spent ninety-nine percent of its existence, not to the topsy-turvy contingencies we have created since the agricultural and industrial revolutions. (207)

There are countless other atavistic misfit hypotheses, real or conceivable, that may be created with regard to consumerism, child-rearing, sexual behaviour, aggression, group size, economics, and so forth, depending on whatever one presumes in the EEA.

The Fall from the original Eden, in Trout's worldview, occurred because of the putative evolutionary dead end of the 'big brain', which may have been useful in the EEA, but which has surely outgrown its value to the species. The 'big brain' is the Original Sin passed on from generation to generation of *homo sapiens*: 'What source was there back then,' asks Trout rhetorically, 'save for our overelaborate nervous circuitry, for the evils we were seeing or hearing about simply everywhere?' (Vonnegut 16). The 'big brain' facilitates sin by creating an artificial environment in which our innate, evolved psychological impulses run wild. Trout presents the con-man James Wait in such terms, as a fisherman whose hunter-gatherer modules are activated in an inappropriate social environment: 'Wait was a fisherman, and the price tag [which he leaves attached to his clothing] was his bait, a way of encouraging strangers to speak to him' (15). He is an 'eviscerator of widows' (30), a social predator who will 'stalk' Mary Hepburn at his leisure (31). The ruthless entrepreneur Alan MacIntosh is unmasked in similar fashion as merely a function of ancient, hard-wired EP run amok in late capitalism. He too is 'a fisherman of sorts. He hoped to catch investors, using for bait not a price tag on his shirt but a Japanese computer genius' (49). EP-style atavistic misfit explanations for violence, including sexual violence, are a recurring feature in Trout's depiction of twentieth-century reality. He remarks, for instance, that the crazed soldier, Delgado 'like the great survivor he was, [...] would rape a woman the next day and become the father of one of the last ten million children or so to be born on the South American mainland' (125). Trout's views on sexual violence, which seem to hint at some kind of specific male disposition to rape, are emphasized again in his speculations on what would have happened had the original passengers on the *Bahía de Darwin* arrived at Santa Rosalia: 'most of the women on the passenger list were past child-bearing age, and so not worth fighting for', but all the fertile women 'would have been impregnated by victors, even against their will' (148). Given this account, and the interlinking of male aggression and sexual conquest, modern warfare is unmasked by Trout as sexual selection perverted by the big brain of *homo sapiens*. When a Peruvian pilot fires a missile at a radar dome, Trout explains that

> Reyes wasn't crazy to feel that what he had done was analogous to the performance of a male during sexual intercourse. A computer over which he had no control, once he had turned it on, had determined the exact moment of release, and had delivered detailed instructions to the release machinery without any advice from him [...].
>
> The launching of the missile, in fact, was virtually identical with the role of male animals in the reproductive process. (153)

Women, on the other hand, are regarded by Trout as innately invested in gestation. Mary Hepburn's irresponsible, and downright abusive, artificial insemination of the Kanka-Bono girls is the work of 'Mother Nature Personified' since '[i]n the face of utter hopelessness on Santa Rosalia, she still wanted human babies to be born there. Nothing could keep her from doing all she could to keep life going on and on and on' (81).

Trout's atavistic psychological explanations are indefinitely elastic: practically anything of which he disapproves can be attributed to innate motivations. Trout expresses, for example, his surprise that sexual selection has not weeded out women such as one of Wait's fleeced widows: 'This woman was so ugly and stupid, she probably never should have been born' (18) – presumably sexual selection has been led astray by some 'big brain' perversion, such as makeup and clothing. EP-style explanations for family woes are also cooked up by Trout, who claims that humans are animals who should only stay together 'long enough, at least, to raise a human child, which took about fourteen years or so' (59). Wealth also perverts sexual and natural selection: 'The most famous amassers of survival schemes [i.e. the wealthy] back then typically had very few children'; and a tycoon such as 'Andrew MacIntosh didn't even care if he himself lived or died – as evidenced by his enthusiasms for skydiving and the racing of high-performance motor vehicles and so on' (67). Thus, concludes Trout, the human species has abandoned its evolutionary commitment to passing on its genes to successive generations: 'I have to say that human brains back then had become such copious and irresponsible generators of suggestions as to what might be done with life, that they made acting for the benefit of future generations seem one of many arbitrary games which might be played by narrow enthusiasts' (67–68).

In such EP-style explanations of our original Fall from the EEA, distal explanations are favoured over the proximate; ancient biology is preferred to contemporary history. Hamilton identifies this fallacy with reference to EP hypotheses on drug addiction: 'An explanation that cannot distinguish between users and addicts is not an explanation of addiction at all. We are therefore better off doing what social science typically does and investigating addiction at the proximate level of motivation rather than its evolutionary bases' (112). As well as destabilizing EP-style discourses by revealing their Christian genealogy, *Galápagos* therefore also exposes their analytic vacuity by taking the preference for ultimate explanations to its absurd conclusions: we have wars because we have big brains (that design weapons), and hands (that can pull triggers). Ditto, *mutatis mutandis*, for poverty, torture, rape, pollution, etc. Trout's rhetoric is thus a *reductio ad absurdum* of the supposed redemptive narratives that legitimate EP. In a favoured metaphor of evolutionary explanation, Trout thinks of the adaptive solution reached by the Santa Rosalians as a key fitting to a lock: 'I have now described almost all of the events and circumstances crucial, in my opinion, to the miraculous survival of humankind to the present day. I remember them as though they were queerly shaped keys to many locked doors, the final door opening on perfect happiness' (Vonnegut 217). If the cause of our woes is the incongruence between our social environment and the EEA, then, so Trout's narrative points out, one solution is to evolve out the greater human intelligence that creates the 'atavistic misfit'.

Naomi Mitchison's *Memoirs of a Spacewoman*: A motherly utopia?

Science fiction has clearly deployed – and also critiqued – evolutionary narratives, whether these stories postulate an alternative order that reawakens dormant evolutionary mechanisms, or diagnose the present as a society to which human psychology is innately ill-suited. The hegemony of agonistic and atavistic narratives in popular evolutionary discourses tends to occlude, however, evolutionary psychologies that are more utopian in their tendency. Such an alternative to the dominant tendency in Social Darwinism may be found in John Bowlby's attachment theory. In Bowlby's theory, the infant is born with an innate drive to interpersonal life that attaches it to primary caregivers (above all, the mother) whom it uses as a 'secure base' for exploration of the environment. By providing observable evidence of attachment behaviour, and of the distress surrounding separation and loss, Bowlby weakened the behaviourist thesis that personal relations were acquired as a means to the satisfaction of asocial drives such as hunger. Bowlby also adopted and psychologized the theory of cybernetics developed by Norbert Wiener and others in the 1940s and 1950s. By provision of a monitoring device and a feedback loop, a cybernetic system (whether mechanical, electrical, or biological) monitors the contingent variations between a set goal and actual performance, modifying its 'effector' apparatus in order to achieve the appropriate outcome (for further discussion see Wiener 112–15). Bowlby argues that the attachment between carer and child instantiates an evolved cybernetic system in which 'the predictable outcome follows activation because the system is so structured that it takes continuous account of discrepancies between a set-goal and performance' (*Attachment* 251). The set-goal of the attachment system is the maintenance of 'proximity to mother' (180): in the words of Judith Feeney and Patricia Noller, 'Bowlby [...] describes behavioural systems as homeostatic control systems that maintain a relatively steady state between the individual and his or her environment. The attachment system maintains a balance between exploratory behaviour and proximity-seeking behaviour' (3). The goal of proximity is itself set, according to Bowlby, by evolution: attachment behaviour is functional for the survival of the (reproductively active) human population in its environment.

A science fiction text profoundly informed by Bowlby's theory, and indeed by a general evolutionary psychological impulse, is Naomi Mitchison's *Memoirs of a Spacewoman* (1962). The novel takes as its dramatic substance the attempts of its narrator, Mary, to communicate with both Earthly fauna and with the various animal-like alien species that she encounters. Whether confronted by dogs, pigs, dolphins, and horses, or by extra-terrestrial starfish, centipedes, sea urchins, caterpillars, and butterflies, Mary must draw upon her formidable capacity for empathic understanding in order to foster ethical relationships with other Earthly and alien species. A highly developed capacity for attentive sympathy plays a vital (but not in itself total) role in the ethical relations that Mary maintains both with Terran and extra-terrestrial animal life, and the root of these relations, for Mitchison, is an EP of maternity. The end result is a utopian text that dreams of an ethic of care at the heart of societal relationships, including with non-human species.

The fictional world represented in *Memoirs* most likely represents Mitchison's personal views, for she saw herself from childhood onwards as both kin to animals, and in communication with them. As beings who shared our evolutionary heritage, animals were to Mitchison potential members of her society with whom she could communicate, and who could act as interpreters with the wider animal world. Her parrot, Polly, 'was a person' through whom she 'was able to communicate with the macaws at the Zoo, even the great red and yellow ones (Polly was blue-green), and get them to respond' (*Small* 96). Such a narrative of woman–animal relationship resonates with modern female and feminist accounts. Mitchison's empathic relation to animals has clear parallels with, for instance, Jane Goodall's rejection of behaviourist approaches to ethology. The latter's work with the chimpanzees of the Gombe involved a (rationally verifiable) imaginative identification with animals, rather than a merely external observation of stimulus and response: 'A great deal of my understanding of these intelligent beings was built up just *because* I felt such empathy with them. Once you know *why* something happens, you can test your interpretation as rigorously as you like' (Goodall and Berman 77–78). There are also significant parallels between Mitchison's views on empathy and recent feminist research on the role of sympathy in the ethical treatment of animals. Josephine Donovan, for instance, points out that both natural rights theory and utilitarianism have in common 'their rationalist rejection of emotion or sympathy as a legitimate base for ethical theory about animal treatment' ('Attention' 174). But a feminist animal ethics might well reject masculinist assumptions about sympathy. In fact, says Donovan, sympathy is not 'whimsical and erratic, nor does it entail obliteration of the thinking or feeling self'; it is also, she insists, 'easily universalized' (185).

Mitchison's late short story, 'Conversation with an Improbable Future' (1990), set in the same fictional world as *Memoirs*, outlines the importance of understanding and empathy to Mary's culture: '[C]ommunication' is 'the essential aim and prize for any space explorer' (227), and 'the beginning of communication', claims Mitchison's narrator (the daughter of a spacewoman), is '[u]nderstanding, sympathy' (231). Although Mary in *Memoirs* seems to have telepathic abilities, and also has technological assistance, the foundation of her work is the 'sympathy or empathy with other forms of life' that she is called upon to exercise (89). She describes her training in the imaginative reconstruction of the other's point of view: 'One reads and watches, one steeps oneself in 3D and 4D; one practises detachment in the face of apparently disgusting and horrible events; one practises taking bizarre points of view' (17). Such training is more or less what is proposed by contemporary feminist thinkers on animal rights, such as Donovan, who hope to cultivate our powers of sympathy:

> We also need education [...] in the practices of care and empathy. Years ago, in fact, Gregory Bateson and Mary Catherine Bateson contended that 'empathy is a discipline' and therefore teachable [...].

> Many religions, they note, use imaginative exercises in empathetic understanding as a spiritual discipline [...]. Such exercises could be adapted for use in secular institutions like schools (including, especially, high school). ('Caring' 365)

Exploration in Mary's world is therefore only incidentally spatial: Mitchison's explorers are not interested in the conquest of territory, but in the psychological voyage necessary to intersubjective understanding. Exploration seems to have lost its acquisitive, colonialist impulse.

It may be tempting to see Mitchison's spacewoman in the terms demanded not by EP, but by psychoanalytic theories that reduce love to some manifestation or sublimation of sexuality. Sarah Shaw, for instance, argues that Mitchison presents an erotic that 'always places women's pleasure at the fore of her projections of the future' whether this be in 'a depiction of a mother tenderly nursing an infant, or the physical detail of an extra-terrestrial's organs or pseudopodia penetrating a woman to give reassurance or satisfaction' (164). Shaw tends to see nurturing in Mitchison's work as a disguised expression of sexuality: 'It is only with the metaphorical child that details of organ and orifice, sensation and movement can be detailed. Though thinly disguised as maternal nurturing, the explicit language speaks to Mitchison's concern with female sexuality' (163). Shaw also applies her hermeneutic of suspicion to a scene in Mitchison's *The Corn King and the Spring Queen* (1931), where Erif Der, the protagonist, nurses her infant son, 'thrusting her breast deep into the hollow of his mouth, that seized on her with a rhythmic throb of acceptance', while her 'other breast let its milk drip in large bluish-white drops [...], then softened and sagged and waited' (Mitchison *Corn* 304). Certainly, by figuring the breast as phallic, and by emphasizing the physical release of breastfeeding, Mitchison analogizes adult sexual relations with suckling. But this equivalence works both ways. It does indeed assert that breastfeeding provides pleasure; but it also implies that copulation between adults echoes the tender love found in the coupling of mother and child. It is quite possible to reverse Shaw's rather formulaic reading, and argue instead that Mitchison is trying to represent the reality of the tender, nurturing feelings that may accompany sexual love. Mitchison's poem 'Comfort' (1990), for instance, explicitly compares suckling with sexual relations, not because the mother–child relation is 'erotic' in the Freudian sense, but because sexual relations are the scene of tender feelings between adults – particularly, it seems to Mitchison, in the satisfaction of male dependency needs. When '[a] woman comforts a man', 'he does not know'

> That the woman's mind is faithless;
> It is not with him.
> Nor with any man, for to her all men are children.
> She has been sucked by baby men, giving them freely her body
> As now she gives it. (135)

This reversal of the usual hermeneutic of suspicion that sees sexuality 'behind' love and tenderness may seem unusual, but it is more than some eccentricity on Mitchison's part. In British culture from Modernism onwards, there has been a psychological counter-discourse that resists the Freudian reduction of love to a manifestation of sexuality. As Mark Spilka points out, D.H. Lawrence chose *'Tenderness'* as 'his first title for *Lady Chatterley's Lover'*, a word which implies 'personal feelings, affections, soft sentiments from the conscious heart' rather than 'dark impersonal passions from unconscious depths' (363). The Scottish psychoanalyst and psychiatrist Ian Suttie (1889–1935), to whom Spilka refers, was also part of this resistance, arguing – from an evolutionary perspective – that love begins 'with the nurturing process in infancy, when the body first responds to love' (Spilka 376).

The suspension of a reductive attitude to love is particularly necessary for readers of *Memoirs* because Mitchison manifestly draws upon John Bowlby's attachment theory in her psycho-cultural *novum* of a feminine ethic based on advanced empathy and nurture. (And Bowlby was in fact informed by Suttie's evolutionary challenge to the Freudian account of the relation between mother and child (Bowlby 'Foreword' xvi–xvii)). Mitchison's allusion to attachment theory is clearest in 'Conversation with an Improbable Future', where the narrator describes how 'most women who decide to have children give one or two years of their life to the first bonding, which means the assurance of love for the life-time when the child, having this base, can and does reach out for others' (223–24). The security of this emotional base, claims the narrator, 'leads to the expectation of loving relationships between all humans' (224), and, indeed, with 'the many lovely animals of Gaia' (225). The metaphor of a base, constructed during the early mother–child relationship, and supporting later love relationships, was first developed by Mary Ainsworth, and became a key concept as Bowlby's theory developed. Bowlby explains:

> In her study of Ganda infants Ainsworth [...] notes how, soon after an infant is able to crawl [...] he makes little excursions away from her [i.e. the mother], exploring other objects and people and, if allowed to do so, he may even go out of her sight. From time to

time, however, he returns to her, as though to assure himself she is still there. (*Attachment* 208)

The mother, or other carer, provides a 'secure base' (Bowlby *Secure* passim) to which the child can return if exploration proves dangerous. Without such provision, later relationships will, Bowlby argues, be marked by patterns of insecure attachment based on the child's internalized expectation that others will be indifferent or hostile to its dependency needs.

The EP described by attachment theory has led Mary Midgley to ask whether such innate social dispositions 'supply, in some sense, the raw material of the moral life' (*Ethical* 136). Mitchison's text answers this question in the affirmative: her novel's utopian impulse proceeds from an insight that moral psychology has a specifically evolved, embodied basis in our biological life as animals with long periods of nurtured infancy. The issue is raised in *Memoirs* in a narrative episode of cognitive estrangement set on a planet inhabited by two closely related intelligent life-forms, the 'caterpillars' and the 'butterflies'. The all-female crew on this expedition have 'a great feeling of sympathy and warmth' towards the caterpillars (91), whom they touch, pet and fondle. These happy relationships are, however, interrupted by the butterflies, who direct psychic blasts of condemnation towards both these creatures and their carers. As the explorers interact with the two species, it becomes clear that the caterpillars are the larval form of the butterflies, and that the butterflies' assault is what activates the caterpillars' chrysalid stage. The butterflies believe that a caterpillar that has foregone its rudimentary aesthetic activities, and that has avoided fertilization, will hatch into a butterfly that is potentially immortal, and that can spend eternity in rhapsodies of contemplation. Fertilized caterpillars, on the other hand, hatch into butterflies that will in turn lay caterpillar eggs, and die in the process. The central conflict in the caterpillar and butterfly sequence is whether the explorers' feelings of sympathy with the caterpillars can legitimate a moral judgement against the actions of the butterflies, or whether the apparent perfection of the resultant butterflies must over-ride such feelings: 'Were the butterflies', asks Mary, 'morally entitled to behave with such cruelty to their own larval forms in order that occasional bliss among themselves should result?' (117).

This intra-species relationship estranges an ethical debate familiar from our own world. An affirmative answer to Mary's question would be provided by certain branches of the Western ethical tradition. Aquinas, for instance, is well known as a proponent of the position that animals are without souls, and that animal nature is entirely caught in the chains of efficient causation: 'as soon as an animal, whether by sense or by its imagination, is offered something to which its appetite is naturally inclined, it is moved to that alone, without making any choice' (280). The butterflies' ethic, which prohibits such immediate satisfaction in the caterpillars, allegorizes a supposed liberation of the soul from animal embodiment. The Thomistic conclusion that 'man's ultimate happiness consists solely in the contemplation of God' (60), rather than in enjoying the goods of the body, seems to be played out, aesthetically if not quite theologically, when the explorers encounter a butterfly that has apparently escaped death, 'circling round a tree which had a particularly beautiful and curiously shaped blossom' (Mitchison *Memoirs* 116). The creature experiences an 'intense aesthetic perception' which Mary perceives as 'an enhanced sense of well-being or hope' (116), and which others in the crew experience as 'contemplation and communion with ecstasy' (117).

Mitchison's text, however, estranges and critiques this ethical model in which the soul can supposedly free itself from embodiment. As *Memoirs* makes clear, the butterflies can pursue their ethic only because their own non-human psychology excludes maternal impulses. The Thomistic aspiration to transcend certain forms of human-animal motivation would, in other words, be suitable only for a different kind of species altogether. An intelligent animal species that progressed from instar to instar, but in which the imago stage felt itself to have no properly social relation to the larval stage, would be a fit embodiment for such an ethic. It is an evolutionary accident of their bodies, rather than some quasi-Kantian *causa noumenon*, that allows the butterflies to be so indifferent to the caterpillars:

> [T]he butterfly had no maternal feelings, could not have. It was no part of this evolutionary pattern. The eggs would look after themselves, even if a few perished, and when they hatched it would be into something utterly alien from their mother, and, again, capable of survival on their own. Maternal feelings could have had no outlet. The butterfly's egg-laying then was pure loss. (111)

Indeed, it is not even that the butterflies lack an 'outlet' for their feelings; they simply do not have them at all. They do not rear their young, and so they lack empathy with their offspring: the butterflies regard their actions as humans would 'the melting of ore to make steel or the grinding of wheat grains to make bread. We could not convey to them any sense of compassion, as humans know it, at any rate not to larval forms' (121). This sense of human compassion motivates one of the crew, Francoise – who treats her 'damaged and miserable caterpillars' as if they were '[h]er children' (113) – to break the explorers' code of non-interference by killing the only butterfly that appears to have reached the state of final immortal perfection, an act that leads to her confinement on Earth as punishment.

Mitchison's narrative of an evolved maternal ethics renews and adapts, perhaps consciously, an oppositional strand within Social Darwinist psychology. The sexologist Havelock Ellis (1859–1939) had argued in *Man and Woman* (1894) that 'men and women had evolved separate but complementary spheres of activity. For the former this sphere consisted of the cultivation of the arts, industry and exploration; for women, it was the bearing and raising of children and domestic activities' (Hawkins 256). Ben Mayhew has traced attachment theory in particular to the evolutionary speculations of Henry Drummond (1851–97), a Scottish theologian, clergyman, and natural scientist (22). Drummond's *The Ascent of Man* (1894) might have been better called *The Ascent of Woman*, for in it he argues that motherly love is the *telos* of evolution:

> [T]hrough [...] Mothers society has been furnished with an institution for generating, concentrating, purifying, and redistributing Love in all its enduring forms; [...] the perfecting of Love is thus not an incident in Nature but everywhere the largest part of her task, begun with the first beginnings of life, and continuously developing quantitatively and qualitatively to the close. (Drummond 430–31)

It is mammals, and specifically humans, that Drummond sees as located at the top of the evolutionary escalator. The relationship between mother and suckling child is explicitly a loving Communion:

> No young of any Mammal can nourish itself. There is that in it therefore at this stage which compels it to seek its Mother; and there is that in the Mother which compels it even physically [...] to seek her child. On the physiological side, the name of this impelling power is lactation; on the ethical side, it is Love. And there is no escape henceforth from communion between Mother and child. (358)

It may even be that Mitchison knew of Drummond's theory. In one striking passage, Drummond speculates on the kind of life-form for which our own evolved psychological responses could only be an irrelevance:

> If a butterfly could live till its egg was hatched – which does not happen – it would see no butterfly come out of the egg, no airy

likeness of itself, but an earth-bound caterpillar. If it recognized this creature as its child, it could never play the Mother to it. The anatomical form is so different that were it starving it could not feed it, were it threatened it could not save it, nor is it possible to see any direction in which it could be of the slightest use to it. (347)

Given this counter-discourse of an evolved psychology of moral sentiments, Mitchison's text therefore rewrites the metaphysical opposition between 'mind' and 'body' as a fantasy of a quite different, non-human EP.

The estranging narrative of the caterpillars and butterflies also thereby interrogates the utopian credentials of Mary's own society. Admittedly, the crew of her spaceship think of the butterflies' ethos as part of Earth's historical past. Mary, for instance, sees a religious parallel with periods when 'people were tortured and burnt alive in order to save their souls in another life, which most of them, perhaps, did not believe in' (Mitchison *Memoirs* 118). Another crew-woman sees the caterpillar–butterfly interaction as resembling the 'postponement of enjoyment' that 'happened [...] in the capitalist countries during their period of major industrial development' (118). Such comparisons draw attention away from the manner in which the explorers themselves are pursuing an ethic in which supposed freedom from their animal nature is the highest good. The explorers regard themselves as liberated from time (because of time dilation), and thereby superior to the 'non-exploring Terrans', who 'are mostly interested in power and pleasure which the rest of us cannot help considering to be of a rather worthless kind' (127). Mary pities her former crewmate Francoise, who, because she is imprisoned on Terra, and thus imprisoned in time, 'can never be the ageless, beautiful person – but was she really beautiful or is it just my memory? – that my own mother was' (126). The parallel with the butterflies and caterpillars is unmistakable: to be a Terran is '[t]o be, as it were, wingless in the Galaxy. Prisoners of time' (125). But where the butterflies had at least the possibility of immortality, the eternal life that Mary pursues is a confidence trick. Although the explorers can outlive their parents and peers, this 'immortality' is only from the Terran perspective. Most explorers last only a few missions, and die in middle age. Earthbound Terrans live longer lives, but do not live so far into the future.

Mitchison's implicit rebuke to the explorers' impossible aspiration to imitate the butterflies is closely allied with feminist projects that criticize the supposed gender neutrality of dominant forms of ethical reasoning. Sara Ruddick argues, for instance, that the human interest in child-rearing has a corresponding knowledge reached through 'maternal thinking' (346). For Carol Gilligan, there is a specifically feminine way of ethical thinking: she contends that 'men initially conceive obligation to others negatively in terms of non-interference', while women experience 'an injunction to care, a responsibility to discern and alleviate "the real and recognizable trouble" of this world' (100). The explorers' morality of non-interference is an obvious point of contrast with such supposed maternal or feminine logics, which have, of course, been widely debated and critiqued (for an overview, see Crigger). Leaving aside concerns about problems such as relationality and subjectivism, the contrast implied by Mitchison's text can be helpfully elucidated with concepts from the ethics of care. Clearly, to take *Star Trek*-style non-interference as one's 'prime directive' assumes that one's interests are primarily separate from those of others. But if one's well-being is inextricably bound to the well-being of another, as in relations of care, then moral dilemmas are more likely to be about how far one can pursue separate interests without abandoning those interests that are fulfilled through responsibility to others. Yet such dilemmas will appear 'real' or 'reasonable' only in so far as such emotions are not consigned to the realm of the 'merely animal'. Such relegation of an embodied care ethic to the domain of nature, to the realm of the heteronomous, is central to another cognitive estrangement in *Memoirs* – that achieved through Mary's repeated dealings with a species of alien parasites, the 'grafts', that exert a particularly powerful physiological and psychological effect upon female hosts. When Mary first hosts a graft, she finds herself caught up in a pseudo-pregnancy: ovulation ceases, her breasts swell and ache, and she has 'feelings of malaise, of the kind which one understands used to be common during pregnancy' (Mitchison *Memoirs* 53). Her graft (which she has named Ariel) eventually falls off, provoking some quite literal attachment behaviour in Mary – 'Instead of being relieved by the separation, I felt I couldn't bear it. I even cried a little' (55) – which is complemented by Ariel's own proximity-seeking behaviour: 'When I got back poor Ariel was obviously agitated and anxious. I knelt, and immediately it wriggled and rolled up to me again' (55). When Mary repeats the experiment, after her encounter with the caterpillars and the butterflies, there are further indications that powerful feelings of care, or tenderness, are in some way unfamiliar, improper, or pathological within Mary's culture. She feels 'two-minded about taking another; a mixture of attraction and repulsion which was too strong to be part of any normal make-up' (85). The feeling of 'hidden, but complete satisfaction' that she experiences while hosting a graft can only be a regression to 'a pre-intellectual state' (149), to being '[s]omebody, from a scientific point of view, delinquent' (159).

The grafts, as well as provoking psychological discomfort in Mitchison's characters, represent somatically the fusion of interests in relations of care – a merger that Mary, as a representative of her space-traveling culture (and, by extension, of our own), experiences as delinquency, irrationality, and regression. The vocabulary of denigration endemic in Mary's highly civilized culture is apparent in the 'irrational amount of care and affection' (109) that Francoise lavishes on her caterpillars, and is also apparent in Mary's relationship with her daughter, Viola. Mary is disturbed by a 'stab of tenderness' (67) towards her daughter, which she extends to Viola's Martian 'father', Vly, who triggered Mary's parthenogenetic pregnancy. Later, after Mary has returned from another expedition, she holidays with Viola (who is now in her teens, thanks to time dilation), and experiences further temporary insanity, as she contemplates her daughter's beauty: 'I let my self think crazily and with deep love up there on the snowfield!' (141). Mary understands that her enduring relationship with Viola is unusual for her culture:

> It is odd, nowadays, for a parent to have so much responsibility towards a child. [...] One does not yearn tenderly, owningly, over one's children, not at least after the first few months. One treats them as human beings, individuals, with the inalienable right not to be owned, to have their own space and their own time. Even the earth-bound, the non-explorers, realise this, dissociating children and guilt. (140)

But such separation and 'non-interference' is not as easy as Mary thinks. Reflecting on her relationship with Viola, she suffers unconscious guilt, experiencing a 'curious sense of blame' (140), and dreaming of her surrogate children from alien species. Indeed, the guilt of surrendered care relations is quite explicit, even before this point in the narrative, in her initial encounters with the caterpillars. After the butterflies' psychic attack, the caterpillars emit 'a pitiable crying for help, so that I thought suddenly and guiltily – a quite irrational and disquieting feeling – of my own little children, most of all Viola, and my little curly-gold Jon, Peder's son' (92).

Memoirs thus provides an alternative to dominant Social Darwinist constructions of EP. Mitchison's future utopia offers a renewed feminist ethic of compassion and imaginative understanding, while also offering a cognitively estranging response to our contemporary propensity towards ethics based on a fantasy of disembodiment. However, despite the striking parallels between Mitchison's novel and contemporary ideas of a feminine ethics, there are blindspots in the text, particularly in its reflexive construction of gendered subjectivity. Although Mitchison skilfully uses her fictional human–animal interactions to promote the ethical treatment of animals, and also to reveal the embodiment of Mary's thinking, the text tends to essentialize the capacity for nurture and empathy as a specifically female evolutionary accomplishment. Certainly, as Birke notes, the 'feeling of empathy, of connectedness is gendered; it is stereotypically associated with femininity in our culture' (46). Yet Mitchison's narrator goes further and claims that 'communication science is [...] essentially womanly. It fits one's basic sex patterns' (*Memoirs* 26); and the action of the story seems to bear this out – the crew on the planet of the butterflies and caterpillars are emphatically all female, and Viola, who is a haploid, seems to have an extra capacity for empathy precisely because she has double her mother's genes. The butterflies, who have no maternal feelings, are likely intended to be representative of a male, and not just stereotypically masculine EP.

Although Mitchison's story estranges the mythology of reason as disembodied, and seeks to re-embody various kinds of rationality, it colludes with the essentializing gender ideologies that haunt EP, even in its more compassionate variants. Bowlby, for instance, argued that the reciprocal love of mothers and babies is 'taken for granted as intrinsic to human nature', so that when this behaviour is not apparent, 'all are disposed to judge the condition as pathological' (*Attachment* 242). The unloving mother is more than a statistical oddity; she is mentally ill. As prophylaxis to this illness, there arose a further attempt to oblige, coerce, or regulate love via the 'mechanism' of 'mother–infant' bonding. Diane E. Eyer describes the hypothesis of 'a sensitive period in women following birth during which they are hormonally primed to accept or reject their infants' (2). From this scientific discourse (which Eyer finds rather doubtful), there emerged the medicalized ritual of mother–infant bonding in maternity wards, 'a ceremonial procedure in which tired women are expected to love their newborns on the spot' (192). Bonding will magically call forth the mother's love, and thereby insure her child against the calamities that fall to the insecurely attached. Eyer notes that the discourse of bonding soon became vague, pious and orotund: 'How', she asks 'was bonding transformed from an instinctual phenomenon triggered by female hormones to a kind of magical social glue, a way of describing all social connections while illuminating nothing about them?' (14).

Memoirs therefore endorses a less prominent, but nonetheless still somewhat repressive discourse of EP. Attachment theory, with its emphasis on love and emotional security, may seem far more innocuous than strict EP, with its frequent emphasis on aggression, violence, and competition. The latter reached a nadir in the hypothesis of, in effect, a 'rape module' in the male brain by Randy Thornhill and Craig T. Palmer

(249–50 below). Nonetheless, although attachment theory is an EP that is far more interested in our virtues than our vices, it does display some of the same weaknesses – in particular, it manifests what Myra J. Hird calls 'the cultural need to support sexual dimorphism' (42). This need, which Hird sees as apparent in post-Renaissance science, emerged in an urge to categorize (and indeed medically 're-assign') human individuals into two exclusive kinds, 'male' and 'female', which are conceived of as existing in a relation of polar opposition. The social corollary of sexual dimorphism is *'sex complementarity'*, the view that 'held that women and men were, biologically, better suited to different roles, and that these roles complemented each other to form the optimum living, working system' (23). Since the bodies to which our rational souls are restored may be categorized by a seemingly natural sexual dimorphism, Mitchison's narrator and perhaps Mitchison herself (who might well have accepted this biological dogma) seem to affirm that human psychology must also share in this relation of mutual exclusion and opposition.

Conclusion

Although Mitchison's EP reaffirms the gender essentialism of Social Darwinism (see Hawkins 249–71), it manages to avoid the worst agonistic excesses of this longstanding research programme. In particular, *Memoirs* eschews the longstanding infatuation of science fiction with a *topos* in which dormant selection mechanisms are re-activated by a society centred on a ruthless struggle for survival (Wells's various worlds, Heinlein's Moon, Butler's failed state ... the Nazis' Ice Age). Mitchison's text usefully indicates that the anti-utopian credentials of EP, broadly conceived, are not determined by Darwinian theory as such, but manifest instead wider ideological and political projects. The evolutionary worldview of the post-war British welfare state differs greatly from that of late nineteenth-century Britain, or the US in the latter half of the twentieth century, and so *Memoirs* avoids many of the difficulties in the Social Darwinism deployed by Wells, Heinlein, and even – albeit equivocally – by Butler. Nonetheless, Mitchison's text constructs the evolutionary subject in a particular, gendered way, authorizing an essentialist binary in which women are pre-eminently caregivers. A novel such as *Galápagos*, however, helpfully challenges the reflexive authority of EP, and its propensity to authorize a supposedly 'natural' paradigm of social life based upon whatever has been projected into the EEA. This reflexivity function is particularly valuable given the contemporary status of EP as the popular psychology that has filled the role left vacant by psychoanalysis: Hamilton notes how '[t]he jargon of EP has recently migrated from a few minor American universities into the academic mainstream and thence into Sunday supplements and dinner party conversations' (105). Moreover, a response to EP specifically from science fiction is important because, as will be discussed in this book's concluding chapter, the rhetoric of certain EP texts borrows heavily – if unselfconsciously – from the tropes of speculative culture.

Chapter 2

Psychoanalytic psychology

The psychological discourse most familiar to literary critics is undoubtedly psychoanalysis. Literary criticism, including work on science fiction, has energetically deployed the work of Sigmund Freud, C.G. Jung, Jacques Lacan, Julia Kristeva, and Slavoj Žižek, among others. As explained earlier (30–33), one of the earliest critiques of science fiction culture was the psychoanalyst Robert Lindner's case study, 'The Jet-Propelled Couch', first published in 1954 (*Fifty-Minute*). Jung is another early psychoanalytic critic of science fiction: his 1958 essay, 'Flying Saucers: A Modern Myth of Things Seen in the Skies' ('Flying') ends with a brief, archetypal criticism of Fred Hoyle's *The Black Cloud* (1957) and John Wyndham's *The Midwich Cuckoos* (1957). The field has since blossomed. A recent survey essay by Andrew M. Butler summarizes psychoanalytic readings of science fiction from Freudian, Lacanian, and French Feminist perspectives. He introduces a variety of psychoanalytic readings of textual and cinematic science fiction, covering topics such as psychosexual content, the 'uncanny' quality of artificial life, motifs of 'death instinct' destruction, and the resonance of post-Lacanian theory for science fiction film studies. Psychoanalysis thus appears to make sense of science fiction motifs that might otherwise seem unintelligible: Žižek, for instance, argues that psychoanalysis can 'explain why, in the midst of well-being, we are haunted by nightmarish visions of catastrophes' (17), including those promulgated by science fiction cinema.

While I am sympathetic to psychoanalytic readings, I have explored elsewhere what I see as significant problems in the metapsychology of post-Lacanian literary theory, particularly its curious model of the self as essentially solipsistic (G. Miller 'Wall'; G. Miller 'Apathetic'). Moreover, psychoanalytic readings of science fiction often proceed as if psychoanalysis were unknown to the producers and consumers of science fiction, rather than being one of the most widely popularized psychological discourses of the twentieth century (a trend that continues, of course, in Žižek's expert glosses of post-Lacanian theory via popular culture). Rather than reading science fiction via psychoanalytic critical theory, and thereby endorsing the 'truth' of psychoanalytic psychology (post-Lacanian, or otherwise), this chapter explores the way in which psychoanalysis has furnished a putatively scientific discourse for deployment in science fiction narrative. To attempt a comprehensive survey of the overlap of psychoanalysis and science fiction would be almost impossible: psychoanalytic discourse has so successfully entered contemporary habits of thought that many science fiction texts will contain some witting or unwitting use of its concepts. Nonetheless, some texts are more thoroughgoing in their extrapolation from psychoanalysis. This chapter surveys a few of these landmarks with the aim of offering readings productive for future exploration of this cultural terrain. The inevitably propaedeutic aim of this chapter means that the present discussion is largely limited to the founding fathers of psychoanalysis, Freud and Jung – and before them, Nietzsche – with some limited consideration of polemical traditions such as object relations theory. A central problem for science fiction, with its critical utopian (and dystopian) tendencies, is how to grapple with the conservative, politically pessimistic inheritance granted to psychoanalysis by the patriarchal triumvirate of Nietzsche, Freud, and Jung, while also negotiating with the demystifying, liberating potential of psychoanalytic self-knowledge, which promises to dissolve irrational blocks and anxieties, thereby releasing new human potential.

Psychoanalytic psychology

The comparative familiarity of psychoanalytic thinking within literary criticism means that a shorter, more synoptic introduction to the ontology, epistemology, and therapeutics of the movement will suffice. Psychoanalysis is among the most varied categories of psychological theory and practice, having diversified enormously since its beginnings in 1880s Vienna. There is clearly a central tenet in the notion of an unconscious mind, but there is notable diversity in the ontology of the unconscious. The unconscious may be a realm of truly unconscious mentation, as in Freudian theory, or it may be understood as an artefact co-constructed by patient and analyst, as in Lacanian theory (cf. Fink 158). The unconscious may be the product of a splitting within the mind, or it may, as with the Jungian collective unconscious, be always and already inaccessible to consciousness (Jung 'Concept' 42). The unconscious may contain instinctual drives, painful psychic contents, archetypal forms, internalized early relationships, or other psychic materials and structures. Though it may be tempting to look for some necessary and sufficient conditions with which to clearly demarcate psychoanalytic psychology from other forms, the unconscious mind in itself does not seem sufficient: as will be shown below, the concept of the unconscious mind precedes the birth of psychoanalysis, and, furthermore, can be found in other psychologies (evolutionary psychology seems, for instance, to presume some kind of unconscious purposiveness).

As well as consisting of something or other, the unconscious must also be discovered by some procedure that gets at its hidden, recalcitrant nature. The discovery procedure is typically a hermeneutic applied to symbolic materials produced by the analysand (the 'patient'), and/or sedimented in the analysand's culture. In classical Freudian interpretation, the analyst decodes the latent meanings found in the analysand's dreams, free mental associations, and other experiences, words, and actions recounted in the analytic encounter. In Paul Ricoeur's perceptive statement, Freudian interpretation is an 'exercise of suspicion' – a 'hermeneutics of suspicion' – rather than the more familiar hermeneutics of 'recollection of meaning' across cultural and temporal distance (28–36). Psychoanalytic hermeneutics vary nonetheless with the school in question. In Freudian theory, conscious life is unmasked to reveal the dominance of renounced sexual instincts (and, later in the theory's development, the vicissitudes of an instinct for self-destruction). The discovery of latent meanings, however, may be far less reductive than the classical Freudian pursuit of the anti-social sexual and death instincts: in object (i.e. personal) relations psychoanalysis, repressed emotions of love and tenderness may equally be discovered in the analytic encounter (e.g. Suttie passim). There are further variations in hermeneutic procedure. In more constructionist schools, the unconscious is a clinical artefact produced within the analytic relationship (creating, for instance, a 'clinical infant' composed 'of memories, present reenactments in the transference, and theoretically guided interpretations' (Stern 14)). For Jungians, the hermeneutic procedure may reveal a Freudian unconscious, but more importantly uncovers cross-cultural archetypes that mould human experience (Jung 'Concept' passim).

The denomination of psychoanalysis as 'the talking cure' indicates the importance of interpretation to its clinical application. Nonetheless, the eschewal of somatic therapies leaves room for an enormous variety of clinical conceptualizations and practices. Although less evident within literary criticism, the interpersonal relationship is of great important to psychoanalytic psychotherapy. In the classical Freudian 'transference', the analyst is a blank screen upon whom the analysand projects their relationship to significant figures (typically family members), with the aim of more successfully recapitulating their own emotional development (Freud 'Dynamics'). But, as ever, there is indefinite variation in the theory and practice of the therapeutic relationship. The emphasis may be, as in Lacanian psychoanalysis, on the psychoanalyst as an agent who undercuts the analysand's resistant, narcissistic belief in their own agency (Fink 11–27). On the other hand, in Jungian therapy, the analyst assists the analysand in the process of individuation, a journey of self-realization facilitated by the meaningful productions of the collective unconscious (Jung *Psychological* 448–50).

Proto-psychoanalytic extrapolations: Nietzschean discourse

Henri F. Ellenberger's magisterial study, *The Discovery of the Unconscious*, examines many of the antecedents of psychoanalysis in European culture of the late-eighteenth and nineteenth centuries. Nietzsche is, for Ellenberger, 'the common source of Freud, Adler, and Jung' (276), and self-evidently an intellectual influence upon Freud in his early maturity: 'the similarity of their thought is so obvious that there can be no question about the former's influence over the latter' (276–77). Indeed, argues Ellenberger, Nietzsche's ideas were so widely popularized that they were often absorbed without consumers being directly aware of their source (277). In Nietzsche Ellenberger finds a genealogy for the Freudian account whereby a monism or dualism of instinctual energy undergoes a series of vicissitudes, before emerging in inhibited, diverted, sublimated, or introverted forms (273–74). Words and actions could, for both Nietzsche and Freud, therefore, be unmasked 'as manifestations of unconscious motivations' (277). Furthermore, Nietzsche also seems for Ellenberger to parallel Freud in giving 'new expression to Diderot's assumption that modern man is afflicted with a peculiar illness bound up with civilization, because civilization demands of man that he renounce the gratification of instincts' (277). This anti-utopian pessimism can be found in science fiction narratives that offer a popular Nietzschean extrapolation in which modern civilization is challenged or subverted by repressed instinctual life (thus anticipating the later argument by evolutionary psychology that contemporary society is poorly adapted to the fundamental nature of human psychology (64–65)).

For a science fiction text that is apparently the product of 'the truly fantastic success that Nietzsche's ideas enjoyed in Europe in the 1890s' (276), one need look no further than H.G. Wells's familiar classic, *The Island of Doctor Moreau* (1896). This text both employs and popularizes proto-psychoanalytic, and most likely Nietzschean, expertise in its *novum*, and trains its readers in the reflexive art of 'unmasking'. The narrator, Edward Prendick, tells of his abandonment on an island in which the eponymous Doctor Moreau uses vivisection and hypnotic methods to mould a race of so-called 'Beast People' who exist halfway between animal and human. The text clearly draws upon an existing public discourse of unconscious thought processes. Prendick's pretence of amnesia after his return from Moreau's island is, for instance, mistakenly psychologized by his peers as a case of traumatic dissociation, 'as a curious instance of the lapse of memory consequent upon physical and mental stress' (Wells *Island* 5). Prendick also hints unwittingly at his own unconscious mentation when he inspects Moreau's bookshelf: 'as I handled the books on the shelf it came up in consciousness: where had I heard the name of Moreau before?' (32). Moreover, this unconscious mental life seems to be actively repressed or dissociated: 'I was thinking [...] of the unaccountable familiarity of the name of Moreau. But so odd is the human memory, that I could not then recall that well-known name in its proper connection' (33).

As Prendick's narrative makes clear, the central contents of the unconscious realm, at least in this text, are instincts violently repressed by socialization. Moreau's experiments in vivisection and hypnotism provide Wells with an estranging vehicle for psychological processes of acculturation. In a significant ambiguity, Prendick tells his readers how his first uncomprehending sight of a beast-man 'struck down through all my adult thoughts and feelings, and for a moment the forgotten horrors of childhood came back to my mind' (20). Are these 'forgotten horrors' the product of a childish imagination, now outgrown, or are they the repressed traumas of socialization? The remainder of his narrative insists on the latter possibility through, for instance, Moreau's explanation of how he has implanted the 'Law' in the mind of his Beast People:

> In our growing science of hypnotism we find the promise of a possibility of replacing old inherent instincts by new suggestions, grafting upon or replacing the inherited fixed ideas. Very much indeed of what we call moral education is such an artificial modification and perversion of instinct; pugnacity is trained into courageous self-sacrifice; and suppressed sexuality into religious emotion. (73)

The repressed realm is far from sexually monistic, but certainly among its content seem to be included the sexual instincts: as Prendick observes the Beast People's religious taboos, he learns that these prohibitions include 'the maddest, most impossible, and most indecent things one could well imagine' (59).

The repressed, of course, returns out of narrative if not psychological necessity – lacking Moreau's constant discipline, the Beast People gradually return to their animal condition. Even under Moreau's heavy hand, as Prendick notes, 'Certain matters [...] in which old instinct was at war with Moreau's convenience, were in a less stable condition' (81). Given these hints, it is somewhat predictable that Prendick, once returned to London, finds himself aware of the suppressed instinctual life of his fellow citizens:

> I see faces keen and bright, others dull or dangerous, others unsteady, insincere; none that have the calm authority of a reasonable soul. I feel as though the animal was surging up through them; that presently the degradation of the Islanders will be played over again on a larger scale. (130)

The return of the repressed in *Doctor Moreau* invites its readers to acquire and exercise their own depth psychological expertise. Despite Prendick's horror of the Beast People, and of their London counterparts, they will note that he feels an affinity with the resurgence of repressed instincts. Moralism, for instance, is presented as a mask for aggression, as Prendick helps to run down the Leopard man: 'I helped to pursue the Leopard Man who had broken the Law, and the Hyena-Swine ran, laughing savagely, by my side' (93) – the Hyaena-Swine is, as it were, the 'double' that reveals the sources of Prendick's own moralistic aggression. Furthermore, although Moreau depicts his experiments as an exercise in the overcoming of our animal, hedonistic motives – 'This store men and women set on pleasure and pain, Prendick, is the mark of the beast from which they came' (74–75) – most readers will quickly discount Moreau's insistence on a purely cognitive motivation for his vivisection of the island beasts. What Moreau refers to as 'the strange colourless delight of these intellectual desires' (75) seems no more than a self-deceiving screen for the gratification of bloodthirsty sadism. The baptismal 'bath of burning pain' (78) inflicted by Moreau is merely the contemporary analogue to the propensity for 'artistic torture' (72) that Moreau, with unconscious irony, attributes to the Spanish Inquisition.

In Wells's late novella, *The Croquet Player* (1936), which appears after the popularization of Freudian psychoanalysis proper, and exactly four decades after *Doctor Moreau*, psychoanalytic psychology provides a newer discourse for a similar narrative. Wells's narrator, Georgie, is a member of the leisure class, accomplished in croquet, bridge, tennis, and other untaxing amusements. While 'recuperating' (*Croquet* 7) at Les Noupets (a fictional resort, presumably in France or Switzerland) he meets Dr Finchatton, who tells him the story of his time in Cainsmarsh, an area of fenland where he was recently the local doctor. There is some kind of malaise in Cainsmarsh, where the people are fearful and paranoid beneath their façade of normality: Finchatton sees, for instance, a farmer blast a scarecrow with a shotgun, an old lady irrationally fearful of a shadow, and a dog that has been beaten to death. He himself develops bad dreams, insomnia, 'minor hallucinations' (22), and then 'a conspiracy mania' (23) in which he feels the locals are plotting against him. The local vicar explains his own belief to Finchatton that road works, field drainage, archaeology, ploughing, and similar excavations, have stirred up 'something mighty and dreadful buried in Cainsmarsh' (30). The curator of the local museum has a similar idea: 'The animal fears again and the animal rages again and the old faiths no longer restrain it. The cave-man, the ancestral ape, the ancestral brute have returned' (50).

Finchatton's narrative, however, is quickly subverted by Georgie's subsequent meeting with Dr Norbert, a 'psychotherapeutist' (59) from the local mental clinic. Norbert explains that Finchatton's narrative is a fabulation – there is no such place as Cainsmarsh. Nonetheless, Georgie finds himself infected by Finchatton's fears: his croquet suffers, he snaps at his aunt, and his bridge-playing falters, as a nameless anxiety begins to invade his leisured existence. Finchatton's story seems to be a geographical fantasy of the psychoanalytic investigation of the unconscious. The isolation and stillness of the place metaphorizes the analytic situation in which practical engagement is minimized, and the unconscious allowed to enter into the conscious mind: 'It is in just such a flat, still atmosphere perhaps – translucent, gentle coloured, that things lying below the surface, things altogether hidden in more eventful and colourful surroundings, creep on our perceptions' (19). What comes to the surface is not sexuality, nor even aggression, but a repressed objectless anxiety: 'There was fear in the Marsh [...]. It was an established habitual fear. But it was not a definite fear. They feared something unknown. It was a sort of fear that might concentrate at any time upon anything whatever and transform it into a thing of terror' (24).

Wells's text – published only a year after the Nazi's Nuremberg Laws came into force – seems to demand the same kind of pessimism as that found in Dr Norbert, who insists, in an echo of *Doctor Moreau*, that 'Man, [...] unmasked and disillusioned is the same fearing, snarling, fighting beast he was a hundred thousand years ago' (73). This anti-utopian direction to Nietzschean science fiction is elaborated in a post-war context by John Christopher's *The Death of Grass* (1956). In this apocalyptic novel, modern civilization collapses because of a plant virus that destroys all the world's grasses, thereby eliminating rice (botanically a grass), as well as cereal crops and pasturage. The narrative concerns the adventures of John Custance, and his family and entourage, as they fight to make their way from London to the Lake District, where they hope to find refuge in the secluded farm owned by Custance's brother, David. (David, wisely, has sown the ground with tubers, which will now be world's staple food crop.)

As the party, which includes Custance's friend Roger, struggles across the moors of northern England, they encounter another group of survivors, with their leader: '"Hey, mister!" he called. "Any news?" It was Roger who replied: "None, but that the world's grown honest." The man's face cracked into a laugh. "Ay, that's good. Then is doomsday near!"' (120). This brief conversation, which cites dialogue between Hamlet and Rosencrantz (*Hamlet* 2.2), illuminates the central Nietzschean unmasking of Enlightenment values. As Roger explains in an early dialogue: 'We're in a new era [...] Or a very old one. Wide loyalties are civilized luxuries. Loyalties are going to be narrow from now on, and the narrower the fiercer' (49). The underlying historical vision of *Death of Grass* is essentially cyclical: the characters understand their situation as a return to medievalism. As leader of the group, Custance perceives that '[t]he pattern of feudal chieftain was forming, and he was surprised by the degree of his own acquiescence – and even pleasure – in it' (151). The merit of this new Dark Ages, within the textual logic, is that it releases the passions from their diversion and dilution along the legal-moral channels of modern industrial civilization. In the absence of a functioning legal system, Custance's wife, Ann, is given a gun, and becomes executioner of a man who has raped her and her daughter (89). The group's armed expert, a gun dealer named Pirrie, similarly takes lethal revenge upon his cuckolding wife, Millicent: 'I am a wronged husband, Custance – a jealous one, perhaps, or a proud one. I am determined to have my rights' (129).

The text's cyclical history inaugurates a new era of (supposedly) authentic passions that seek proud, immediate expression. Though offensive to civilized morality, they are nonetheless presented as valuable precisely in their intensity. More sceptical readers may note that the text's ideology of renewed feudalism grants authority to the kind of upper-middle class male who was threatened by the British post-war consensus. Custance's newfound feudal status maintains, and indeed intensifies, longstanding class hierarches. He appraises for instance the potential value of a displaced proletarian:

A manual worker of some kind; the sort of man who would give a lifetime's faithful inefficient service. On his own, under the new conditions, he would have small chance of survival, his only hope lying in the possibility of attaching himself to some little Napoleonic gangster of the dales who would put up with his uselessness for the sake of his devotion. (142)

The text also offers a particularly sordid re-assertion of patriarchy. Pirrie, for instance, not only murders his wife, he also captures a sex slave, a young woman named Jane, whose family the group murders. And Custance's daughter, Mary, goes from being a young woman who might at least choose her life path (between marriage and a career as an architect) to being raped in the back of a car. In the new feudalism, women are, as Ann realizes, 'chattels again' (59).

Such Nietzschean discourses were readily adapted into the Golden Age of science fiction by way of the Freudian psychoanalytic theory that was ascendant in the immediate post-war US. Alfred Bester's 1950 short story 'Oddy and Id' (originally titled 'The Devil's Invention') freely translates the Nietzschean suspicion of civilized values into Freudian jargon. The story tells of Oddy (Odysseus) Gaul, a young man who, as his Harvard professors come to realize, is 'Fortune-Prone. Whatever he desires, he receives. [...] If his desire is totally beyond the peak of his accomplishment, then the factors of chance, coincidence, hazard, accident ... and so on, combine to produce his desired end' ('Oddy' 27–28). The professors conspire together, in some far-future Earth, to train Oddy to be of service to humanity, with his first task being to prevent a pending interplanetary war. Oddy, despite his protestations of peace, allows the war to happen, and rapidly ascends through the ranks, conquering the Solar System, and finally being elected 'Solon of the Solar Society in perpetuity' (35). The Harvard professors ruminate on their creation of a 'feudal overlord of a bankrupt Family of Planets that suffers misgovernment, oppression, poverty, and confusion with a cheerful joy that sings nothing but Hosannahs to the glory of Oddy Gaul' (35). Their interpretation of events pursues the familiar Nietzschean logic, but in a psychoanalytic idiom: 'Civilization and culture ... philosophy and ethics ... these were only masks Oddy put on; masks that covered the primitive impulses of his subconscious mind' (36). This Nietzschean-Freudian subconscious behind the mask of benevolence is the 'Id' of the title: 'We made the mistake of assuming that Oddy would have conscious control of his power. He does not. The control was and still is below the thinking, reasoning level. The control lies in Oddy's Id ... in that deep, unconscious reservoir of primordial selfishness that lies within every man' (36).

Subverting libidinal economics

Whatever the actual intent of Nietzschean and Freudian psychology, science fiction unmaskings of the civilized self in works such as *The Death of Grass* or 'Oddy and Id' challenge Enlightenment conceptions of historical progress. The imagined future reveals only repetition of the past, for history is constrained by human nature's recalcitrance. In similar fashion, Freud contends that contemporary civilization can only partially enforce its necessary instinctual renunciation. He argues in *The Future of an Illusion* (1927), for instance, that 'an appallingly large number of people are dissatisfied with civilization and unhappy in it, and feel it as a yoke which must be shaken off' (37). If the putative illusions of religious belief are eroded, then the masses, who are 'lazy and unintelligent', with 'no love for instinctual renunciation', will give free expression to their 'destructive, and therefore anti-social and anti-cultural trends' (7). In the speculative anthropology of *Totem and Taboo* (1913), as well as in *The Future of an Illusion*, and his 1930 essay, *Civilization and its Discontents*, Freud ruminates over what appears to be the significance of psychoanalytic theory for human history. What Freud innocently refers to as 'civilization' is capable of taking 'man [sic]' out of a supposed state of nature, but it is 'hard for him to be happy in that civilization' since it imposes 'such great sacrifices not only on man's sexuality but on his aggressivity' ('Civilization' 115).

Superficially, at least, this conservative opposition to progress beyond the supposed historical pinnacle of bourgeois society continues in the extrapolations of George Orwell's well-known dystopian novel *1984* (1949), and Aldous Huxley's comparable dystopia, *Brave New World* (1932). These novels explore in different, yet complementary, ways the possible significance of Freudian theory as a limit upon utopian aspiration. Orwell's novel (on first reading, at least) presents instinctual renunciation, rather than expression, as the means by which the totalitarian Oceanic state controls its citizens. As Blu Tirohl notes: 'The Party [...] reappropriates sexual energy for its own needs. As desire, or urge, would diminish after sexual intercourse the Party attempts to sustain in its members a state that permanently anticipates pleasure and then channels that energy for its own purposes' (55–56). Julia explains to Winston how the Party exploits an underlying instinctual drive, which may either be expressed healthily in sex, or, if frustrated, expressed unhealthily in state loyalty: 'When you make love you're using up energy; and afterwards you feel happy and don't give a damn for anything. They can't bear you to feel like that. They want you to be bursting with energy all the time. All this marching up and down and cheering and waving flags is simply sex gone sour' (Orwell 118). The narratorial voice, focalizing Winston, summarizes Julia's analysis, elaborating the 'sourness' of this sex as 'sexual privation induced hysteria, which was desirable because it could be transformed into war-fever and leader-worship' (118). Winston wonders to himself, 'how could the fear, the hatred, and the lunatic credulity which the Party needed in its members be kept at the right pitch, except by bottling down some powerful instinct and using it as a driving force?' (118).

This thesis is not merely propounded by the voices of the narrative; it is also represented in the action of the story. The conversion of frustrated sexuality into aggression is exemplified by Winston's compulsive feelings of sexual sadism towards Julia during the Two-Minute Hate:

> He would tie her naked to a stake and shoot her full of arrows like Saint Sebastian. He would ravish her and cut her throat at the moment of climax. [...] he realized *why* it was that he hated her. He hated her because she was young and pretty and sexless, because he wanted to go to bed with her and would never do so. (18)

The action of *1984* also connects sexual frustration to other pathologies, particularly of a psychosomatic variety. For example, Winston encounters a man in the street with a tic, which he later attributes to sexual tension, and himself suffers from a varicose ulcer on his ankle, which heals as his sexual relationship with Julia develops. Furthermore, Katharine, Winston's state-sanctioned wife, suffers from a chronic muscular tension linked to sexual repression: 'even when she was clasping him against her he had the feeling that she was simultaneously pushing him away with all her strength. The rigidity of her muscles managed to convey that impression' (61).

Brave New World, on the other hand, usually places a quite different political construction upon the relationship between contemporary society and sexual instinct, for it depicts a 'World State' in which sexual expression is essential to the functioning of a non-violent totalitarian system. As with industrialized gestation, the use of non-lethal weapons, and hypnopaedic 'education', the immediate gratification of sexual desire ensures a minimum of social conflict. In an early expositional scene, as Mustapha Mond and the Director lecture students in the gardens around the Conditioning Centre, the former explains how Freud, as well as Ford, created the template for their society. 'Our Freud', explains Mustapha, was 'the first to reveal the appalling dangers of family life. The world was full of fathers – was therefore full of misery; full of mothers – therefore of every kind of perversion from sadism to chastity; full of brothers, sisters, uncles, aunts – full of madness and suicide' (Huxley *Brave* 33). But although Freud showed the problem, Mustapha's solution is based on a quite different, and textually anonymous, twentieth-century thinker. The Controller explains how Pacific Island culture 'among the savages of Samoa, in certain islands off the coast of New Guinea' seemed to offer a different social organization: the narrator continues, 'The tropical sunshine lay like warm honey on the naked bodies of children tumbling promiscuously among the hibiscus blossoms. Home was in any one of twenty palm-thatched houses. In the Trobriands conception was the work of ancestral ghosts; nobody had ever heard of a father' (33). The unacknowledged allusion here is to Bronislaw Malinowski's anthropological research in the Trobriand Islands, published in works such as *Argonauts of the Western Pacific* (1922) and *The Sexual Life of Savages in North-Western Melanesia* (1929). The description of childhood sexual play, for example, can be found in the latter text, when Malinowski states that the children of the Trobriand islanders 'initiate each other into the mysteries of sexual life in a directly practical manner at a very early age' (47). The Controller's comment on fatherhood, meanwhile, borrows from Malinowski's claim that the islanders are entirely ignorant of the causes of human conception, and so believe that 'the only reason and real cause of every birth is spirit activity' (146).

Malinowski's description of the average Trobriand islander contrasts significantly with Orwell's account of the average Eurasian. The latter is a bundle of Freudian tics and compulsions. The former, however, is depicted as in exemplary psychic health: 'I could not name a single man or woman who was hysterical or even neurasthenic. Nervous tics, compulsory actions or obsessive ideas were not to be found' (Malinowski *Sex* 87). The Controller's account of his society intensifies the cultural pattern underlying Malinowksi's analysis, for the Freudian period of sexual latency, and later proscriptions on adolescent sexuality, are entirely alien to the World State. Mustapha explains, to the hilarity of his audience, how 'erotic play between children had been regarded as abnormal (there was a roar of laughter) [...] and had therefore been rigorously suppressed', and how, until age twenty, no sexual expression was permitted except covert 'auto-erotism and homosexuality' (Huxley *Brave* 27).

The model of the psyche developed by Freud, and accepted by Malinowski, becomes clearer as Mustapha (accompanied by the narratorial voice) explains the reasoning behind the World State's prescription of sexual expression. The psychology of frustrated desire is modelled in hydraulic terms much like those found in *1984*: 'Impulse arrested spills over, and the flood is feeling, the flood is passion, the flood is even madness; it depends on the force of the current, the height and strength of the barrier. The unchecked stream flows smoothly down its appointed channels into a calm well-being' (37). The narratorial voice further develops this relation between frustration and feeling in its account of child-rearing under the World State: 'The decanted infant howls; at once a nurse appears with a bottle of external secretion. Feeling lurks in that interval of time between desire and its consummation. Shorten that interval, break down all those old unnecessary barriers' (37). Emotion, according to this model, appears only when a desire is unfulfilled; the bare consciousness of a striving becomes something stronger, and more distinct, in the self's failure to find immediate satisfaction. 'Think of water under pressure in a pipe,' urges the Controller, 'What a jet!': 'Mother, monogamy, romance', continues the narrator, 'High spurts the fountain; fierce and foamy the wild jet' (35).

In *1984*, totalitarianism is aided by the 'bottling up' of sexual desire, and an exploitation of the consequent frustrated aggression. The Two-Minute Hate is the central political rite, and the sadistic O'Brien the central psychological type. In *Brave New World*, the stopper is taken out of the bottle, so that totalitarianism can exploit a passive population. The group sex of 'Orgy-Porgy' is the concomitant ritual, and the most typical citizen is Lenina's friend, the dutifully promiscuous Fanny. The plausibility of each novel proceeds from a common, albeit divergent exploitation of a psychoanalytic, and particularly Freudian, model of the psyche as a hydraulic system. There is firstly presumed a dualism of conation, based upon the opposition of instinctual desire: all striving is either fundamentally self-preservative, or fundamentally sexual (species-preservative). It is then supposed that inhibition of a striving can occur only from the opposition of these two impulses. Typically, this is a matter of the self-preservative instinct opposing ('damming', 'bottling up') the sexual tendency. Two distinct, but inter-related consequences, proceed from this inhibition of desire. On the one hand, inhibited impulse is supposedly converted into emotion; feeling substitutes for action, and all feeling (*qua* frustration) is painful. On the other hand, the painful and threatening emotion derived from a frustrated impulse may become unconscious, and so re-emerge in an attenuated and qualitatively distinct form. This may be either as a symbolic sublimation (experienced as ego-internal), or as a symptom (an ego-alien automatism, such as a tic, psychosomatic disorder, or compulsion).

The psychohydraulic model owes its enduring appeal to a number of features: its apparent economy of explanation, a degree of logical consistency, the plausibility of the psychological connections it offers, an analogy with natural scientific processes, an apparent consonance with sexual psychopathology, and its usage by a generation of psychoanalytic clinicians. Yet though this model makes a great deal of intuitive sense – which presumably facilitates its reflexive internalization by consumers of psychological discourse – it is far from clear whether there is indeed any reality to which it corresponds. The philosopher Ernest Gellner, for example, mocks the 'pseudo-psycho-hydraulics' apparent in intuitions such as the credo 'forces blocked in one way find outlets elsewhere' (106). He remarks that 'one may doubt [...] whether the sketchily constructed model of sluices and channels and chambers and locks and water-wheels, which translate these forces into concrete and specific directions of conduct and feeling, is in any way scientifically serious, as opposed to being mere metaphor' (107). In order to understand how this popular, but problematic model of the psyche is related to the dystopian vision of Orwell and Huxley, it is necessary to consider their shared political concern. Although *1984* and *Brave New World* might seem to represent very different political systems – one violent, the other non-violent – the common anxiety in each is towards the authority of functionalist sociology. By the 1920s and 1930s, early functionalists such as A.R. Radcliffe-Browne and Malinowski had begun to analyse societies by employing an analogy with biological organisms. In his 1935 paper, 'On the Concept of Function in Social Science', Radcliffe-Brown explains the primary, biological sense of 'function': 'the function of a recurrent physiological process is [...] a correspondence between it and the needs (i.e. necessary conditions of existence) of the organism' (179). The function of digestion, for example, is to provide energy and raw material to the cells of the body, and so maintain the continuity of the organism. Something similar, believes Radcliffe-Brown, can be said for patterns of social activity: 'The *function* of any recurrent activity, such as the punishment of a crime, or a funeral ceremony, is the part it plays in the social life as a whole and therefore the contribution it makes to the maintenance of the structural continuity' (180). Naturally enough, functionalism has little to say about the value of any such recurrent activity, except in so far as it is an effective means to structural continuity. This ethically vacuous conception is what haunts *Brave New World* and *1984*, both of which postulate societies that are (or seem to be) immensely stable, yet are quite indifferent to the deeper welfare of the individual: '"Stability," said the Controller, "stability. No civilization without social stability. No social stability without individual stability"' (Huxley *Brave* 36); 'Can you not understand', says O'Brien to Winston, 'that the individual is only a cell? The weariness of the cell is the vigour of the organism. Do you die when you cut your fingernails?' (Orwell 227).

The adaptability of the Freudian hydraulic model of the psyche is such that both repression and expression can be regarded as functional for the subordination of the individual to the continuity of the social structure. On the one hand, 'freely flowing' desire supposedly pre-empts self-reflection, and directly connects desire to action and fulfilment. The average citizen of the World State therefore has little capacity for self-reflection, and fewer, it would seem, of the higher or sublimated forms of sexual drive. On the other hand, the 'damming' or 'bottling up' of a drive leads to the repression of painful emotions that re-emerge in psychic automatisms such as the compulsive sadism of the average Oceanian. Taken together, *Brave New World* and *1984* present a cruel dialectic in which the creation of self-conscious subjectivity is also the destruction and self-alienation of that same subjectivity.

The futility of this Freudian dialectic is emphasized because each text unintentionally anticipates the other, despite the 'official line' in each towards sexual expression and repression. Towards the end of *Brave New World*, for example, John the Savage begins to resemble Winston Smith, as his frustrated desire for Lenina is converted into sexual sadism. This sadism he then introverts, unconsciously substituting his own body for Lenina, as he begins to flagellate himself: '"Strumpet! Strumpet!' he shouted at every blow as though it were Lenina (and how frantically, without knowing it, he wished it were!), white, warm, scented, infamous Lenina that he was flogging thus' (223). The World State soon absorbs this impulse into a giant sadomasochistic 'Orgy-Porgy' that resembles a Two-Minute Hate turned back on itself. In *1984*, on the other hand, despite Winston's longing for sexual expression, the most carefree and promiscuous members of society seem to be the Proles, who, though they lack World State's contraceptive technology, have found in gin, sex, and popular song, their own 'soma'. Moreover, one can quite reasonably view the love affair between Julia and Winston not as an expression of sexual freedom, but as an unconscious act of extended self-destruction. When they agree to rent the room above Charrington's shop, the narratorial voice remarks that '[b]oth of them knew that it was lunacy. It was as though they were intentionally stepping nearer to their graves' (124). Torture and submission to the Party, believes Winston, is a 'predestined horror [...] fixed in future times, preceding death as surely as 99 precedes 100' (124). There seems something unconsciously compulsive and self-destructive in Winston's path towards O'Brien's ministrations (a point also recognized by David Seed in his reading of the novel (14–15)).

Neither text, perhaps despite the intentions of Huxley and Orwell, presents any great psychoanalytic faith in either sexual expression or repression as a safeguard for individual freedom. However, the anti-utopian impulse in *1984* (and also *Brave New World*) may be understood less as sober psychological extrapolation, and more as an intensification, and exposure, of the conservative political premises that had been written into Freudianism. These were being challenged in the 1930s by psychoanalytic dissidents, such as Ian D. Suttie, whose 1935 critique of Freud, *The Origins of Love and Hate*, entirely rejects the gloomy Freudian prognosis for civilized society. Suttie's work is psychoanalysis in the Pelagian rather than Augustinian mode (a comparison Suttie himself invites (153)) – it emphasizes an original condition of love and sociability, rather than instinctual 'sinfulness', which can be preserved by an appropriate, psychoanalytically enlightened mode of social organization. Suttie's psychoanalysis of companionship contrasts with the psychohydraulic model, which regards social relationships as derived from the blockage of drive satisfaction. For Freud, as auto-erotism is repressed, so libido finds itself blocked, then diverted towards objects (persons, in effect) as the means to its satisfaction: social relationships, in other words, 'lean upon' drive satisfaction (Freud 'Instincts').

Traces of a utopian psychoanalysis of intrinsic sociability can even be found in *Brave New World* and *1984*, where they challenge the authority of psychohydraulics. Mustapha, for example, identifies the family as a central barrier to the free flow of instinct: 'Family, monogamy, romance. Everywhere exclusiveness, everywhere a focussing of interest, a narrow channelling of impulse and energy' (Huxley *Brave* 34). Yet it is unclear whether the family is of concern because it 'channels' instinctual drives, like a narrow-bore pipe, or whether it is a threat because it creates a domain of (innate?) intersubjectivity below the level of the entire community: 'What suffocating intimacies, what dangerous, insane obscene relationships between the members of the family group! Maniacally, the mother brooded over her children (*her* children)' (31). Mustapha seems more than a little anxious as he compares a human mother to a cat, loyal to her kittens, and voices what he assumes to be her sentiments: 'My baby, and oh, oh, at my breast, the little hands, the hunger, and that unspeakable agonizing pleasure! Till at last my baby sleeps, my baby sleeps with a bubble of white milk at the corner of his mouth' (32). From a functionalist point of view, the family is a 'recurrent activity' that serves the continuation of society as a whole through reproduction and early socialization. If these functions can be replaced, as they are entirely in *Brave New World*, then the family should be an obsolete mechanism. Yet *Brave New World* seems, through the fog of 'psychohydraulic' rhetoric, to deploy discourses of the family as a domain of intimate companionship that is an end in itself, rather than just a means to social stability and continuity, or a derivative of hedonistic drive satisfaction.

1984 is even more open in its promotion of a discourse of non-Freudian love and companionship. It is clear that the family for Party members in Oceania exists only for reproduction: the children are produced by a monogamous relationship, but are socialized into a direct loyalty to the state. The destruction of such intimate intra-familial loyalty is what haunts Winston in repressed memories of his mother's tender love for his sister. One night with Julia, he has a dream set inside the glass paperweight that he earlier bought in Charrington's shop:

> The dream had also been comprehended by – indeed, in some sense it had consisted in – a gesture of the arm made by his mother, and made again thirty years later by the Jewish woman he had seen on the news film, trying to shelter the small boy from the bullets, before the helicopter blew them to pieces. (Orwell 142)

This 'enveloping protecting gesture of the arm' Winston first perceives during his childhood when he robs his sister of a chocolate ration (145). To comfort her daughter, 'His mother drew her arm round the child and pressed its face against her breast' (144). Winston's relationship with Julia must therefore be analysed in terms other than those that he provides for it. His sexualized view of their relationship is encouraged by Julia. Yet it is quite possible that this is 'devil's doctrine', given the numerous hints that Julia is an agent of the Party (for example, it would seem to be her coffee that drugs both her and Winston before their arrest; she seems surprised only by the location of the telescreen in their room, rather than its existence; and so forth). The self-conscious sexual rebellion of their relationship may well be a cover for its real meaning (to Winston at least) as a domain of private love and intimacy. In an early encounter with Julia, for example, Winston is motivated not by desire, but by an instinctive sympathy:

> In front of him was an enemy [...]: in front of him, also was a human creature, in pain and perhaps with a broken bone. Already he had instinctively started forward to help her. In the moment when he had seen her fall on the bandaged arm, it had been as though he felt the pain in his own body. (95)

As their relationship develops, this non-sexual sympathy and companionship increasingly rears its ugly head, despite what Suttie called the endemic 'taboo on tenderness' in modern ideas and society (Suttie 80–96;

see also G. Miller 'Wall'). When Julia refuses to meet because she is menstruating, Winston finds himself confronted with an emotion that is normally obscured by the noise and turmoil of sexual tension and release: 'when one lived with a woman this particular disappointment must be a normal, recurring event; and a deep tenderness, such as he had not felt for her before, suddenly took hold of him' (Orwell 124).

Whether separately, or taken together, *1984* and *Brave New World* explore and challenge the reflexive hegemony of Freudian discourses by elaborating the pessimism written into the hydraulic model of the mind, which sees only a conservative stasis between anti-social hedonism, and life-suffocating renunciation. Both texts point towards the different, more relational model of the self developed by the so-called 'object relations' tradition (pioneered by Suttie, among others) in which the self is innately social, and the challenge of maturation is to find forms of love that recognize the autonomy and difference of others. *1984* and *Brave New World* therefore show a developing process whereby science fiction scrutinizes, and selects, the psychoanalytic discourses that it finds generically congenial. The liberation of psychoanalysis from the authority of Freud therefore becomes increasingly important to science fiction, particularly after the rise of the New Wave. Barry N. Malzberg's alternate history novel, *The Remaking of Sigmund Freud* (1985), provides a clear example of this sifting process, for its alternative timeline asks: what if Freud had never existed, or died young, before his discursive authority was stamped on the unconscious mind in the opening decades of the twentieth century?

The crucial action of the story takes place in the twenty-fourth century as humanity explores and colonizes worlds outside the solar system. The crew of an exploration vessel, *The Whipperly*, are succumbing to a gradual 'space madness' (Malzberg *Remaking* 108) that has incapacitated most of them. The ship's doctor and the executive officer fear that this psychosis is the work of rumoured hostile aliens, the Vegans. In desperation, they activate a so-called 'reconstruct' of Freud (112), a precise biological replica, even down to memories and intellect. The data for many such reconstructions of important Earth figures are held by spaceships and colonies, and reconstructs may be created in order to provide an external, expert perspective on complex situations: 'the presence of reconstructs was declared essential to the probes. With all the risks of exploration, the obligations involved, why not have immediate access to the best minds of the most vital century? Why not allow those minds to interact freely with the crucial events of exploration?' (107). Reconstructs of firstly Samuel Clemens (Mark Twain) and then Emily Dickinson are also activated on board the ship during the chaos of the descending madness. However, the crew's efforts are to no avail: the ship is captured by the tentacular Vegans; the crew disappear (presumably to face interrogation and death); and Freud is left alone with his captors. There he learns, to his great satisfaction, that psychoanalysis is universally valid, for he proceeds to cure numerous Vegans of a mysterious, seemingly psychosomatic affliction that affects their tentacles. Duly assured of his historical significance, the reconstructed Freud arranges with the Vegans to be returned to his former existence in early twentieth-century Vienna.

The crux of Malzberg's novel is the conceit that the real history of Sigmund Freud is as recalled by the crew of the *Whipperly*. Freud is actually killed in 1905 by the man who (in our world) became the right-wing isolationist editor of the *Chicago Tribune*:

> Murdered in 1905 in Vienna by Robert McCormick. Shot in the right eye at close range, brain destroyed. Famous alienist whose researches into the so-called 'unconscious' mind had created great excitement in professional circles. Married, no children. McCormick at a spectacular trial claimed that Freud had 'deeply offended' him but offered no further details. Insisted upon the role of sexual repression and fantasying in much human conduct. A man of some humor and intellectual range, author of some popular expositions of his theory. Much influence at the time, subsequently dispersed through disciples and colleagues for decades to come. (128)

The real Freud has no hold over the legacy of psychoanalysis: without his pre-eminence and his offspring to preserve his legacy, psychoanalysis is 'dispersed' into rivals, particularly, the text implies, Jung and Adler. The reconstructed Freud, however, is gradually suborned by the Vegans, who, the text strongly implies, deliberately counterfeit their psychosomatic illness in order to play on Freud's grandiose fantasies of miraculous healing and public acclaim. The reconstruct reflects, tellingly: 'The swiftness of accomplishment was almost a parody of the analytic outcome, almost a fantasy rather than an actualization of the process, but he was glad to see it happen. It was inspiring, miraculous really, to see what he had done. If only his colleagues could have seen him' (241–42).

Malzberg's novel provides a self-conscious, clearly intentional challenge to the Freudian reflexive construction of the self: whatever the validity of the unconscious mind, the pessimistic dialectic of Freudian thought, Malzberg clearly indicates, is an inheritor of late-nineteenth-century European bourgeois conservatism. As Erich Fromm explains,

Freud viewed his own society 'as the best possible one, and not capable of improvement in any decisive way':

> In the second phase of his work, after the First World War, Freud's picture of history became truly tragic. Progress, beyond a certain point, is no longer simply bought at great expense, but is in principle impossible. Man is only a battlefield on which the life and death instincts fight against each other. He can never liberate himself decisively from the tragic alternative of destroying others or himself. (*Crisis* 60)

For Malzberg, psychoanalysis must therefore be freed from Freud (and, before him, Nietzsche). Alas, the reconstructed Freud is sent back by the Vegans to Vienna in 1905, supplanting his biological original, and inaugurating the timeline that is our world (in which, incidentally, the reconstruct's high-handed manner aggravates an anonymous political activist, and potential analysand, who is very likely a young Adolf Hitler). The narrative ends as Freud

> leaned into the Vienna night as if adjusting the cloak of possibility around him, and then – knowing that possibility was all that he had been given, *for unto us a child is born* – he strode into the night, cleaved the night before him, moved into the distant and terrible century, the sound of the charnel houses in the further distance. (Malzberg *Remaking* 275)

The ominous charnel houses of our twentieth century – which is a creation of Vegan temporal sabotage – is due as much to anti-utopian Freudian discourse as any particular accidental historical encounter. Prior to his return, the reconstruct reflects:

> *No dreams.* That is what is really wanted; it is the dreaming that wrecked us, gave us a twentieth that was unspeakable, gave us a twentieth in which there were not dreams but only the obliterating machines which took away the underside, that part which gave depth, denied us then. (256)

Freud's essential opposition is to the utopian potential of dreams: 'The interpretation of dreams necessitates more often than not their negation. His researches, too, had taught him that' (275). Dreams are the psychic effluvia created in the unsatisfactory renunciation of instinctual satisfaction in the submission to civilization's repressive demands. In contrast to the ascendancy of such Freudian pessimism stands the real (i.e. counter-factual) Emily Dickinson, who becomes, as a lengthy opening section reveals, 'the unofficial poet laureate of America' (17). The real Dickinson is a 'traveler and celebrity' who 'had affairs with a few men, some of great consequence and some of less: men of the professions, political accomplishment, or learning' (19) – including Clemens. Yet, to clear the way for the reconstructed Freud, Dickinson too is replaced with her reconstruct by the malign Vegans – 'It is 1853. Slowly the alteration came upon her, deep in the cells, then moving outward. Emily Dickinson trembled with the slow force of it. What had happened to her?' (27) – to bring about the reclusive figure of our reality, neglected by her contemporary national culture, and unable to contribute to the public sphere in the presumably progressive manner of the 'real' author.

The collective unconscious: Rooted and radical?

The deployment of less pessimistic psychoanalytic discourses is a recurring feature of science fiction from the latter half of the twentieth century. A focus emerges in the genre on cultural *novums* that in some way renew the utopian potential in the concept of the unconscious mind. Even mainstream Freudian psychology contains elements that can be extrapolated as cultural solutions to the supposed 'return of the repressed' in so-called 'civilized' society. Freud concedes that the instincts can be partially compensated with imaginary, playful satisfactions, 'which are recognized as such without the discrepancy between them and reality being allowed to interfere with enjoyment' ('Civilization' 80). In Iain M. Banks's science fiction utopia, 'the Culture', symbolic substitutes act as a harmless, sublimated release for threatening, primal emotions. Banks's Culture novel, *Player of Games* (1988), begins with an apparently space-operatic running battle, complete with protective suits, homing missiles, energy weapons as sidearms, and so on. The description, however, turns out to be of the Culture's version of 'paintball'. Gurgeh, the protagonist, appears to be wounded: but the description is really of his suit's reduced function after every hit, and of the paralysing anaesthetic that it applies to his body in order to imitate injury and finally a brief 'death'. That technologically advanced make-believe may simply allow the 'venting' of a persistent vicious streak in humanity (and particularly men) is also suggested in Ernest Callenbach's *Ecotopia* (1975). This science fiction travelogue posits a future ecological utopia in which, as Fredric Jameson notes, the vices of the male are gratified via the all-male institution of the War Games, in which periodically the men revert to the most primitive weapons – clubs, bows and arrows – and let off steam assaulting each other physically in two opposing groups, sometimes with real casualties. The assumption of an essentialist and innate aggressivity of the male of the species is here presupposed and then ingeniously dealt with. The ritual combat has no content, no political purpose [...]. It is clearly enough intended to address the question [...] of the relationship between the Utopian society and the aggressive instincts or impulses (if such things can be posited as existing in the first place). (*Archaeologies* 52)

William Weston, the journalist who narrates *Ecotopia*, is told how the 'ritual war games' of this society came into being (Callenbach 74). Advocates of the practice were convinced that 'it was essential to develop some kind of open civic expression for the physical competitiveness that seemed to be inherent in man's biological programming – and otherwise came out in perverse forms, like war' (74). Such make-believe aggression is also found outside of the war games. Weston, in his journal, records a row between a couple where the male is prevented from physical aggression, and the scene becomes a ritualized duel of mutual insults. An interpretation in terms of a make-believe 'venting' of aggressive impulse is put forward by Weston: 'Nobody seemed to care what it had all been about, but they sure got a kick out of the expression of intense feeling!' (22).

The work of C.G. Jung has offered a fruitful resource for psychoanalytic science fiction that, in similar fashion, explores the utopian potential of creative culture (including, by extension, science fiction itself). Jung's psychology has little room for the libidinal economics of Freudianism, and offers, in the theory of archetypes, a more positive metafictional account than the compensatory fantasies envisaged by Lindner's psychoanalysis of 'Kirk Allen' (30–33). Perhaps the most accomplished science fiction author to profess an interest in Jungian psychoanalysis is Ursula Le Guin. To some extent, she understands her writing as exploiting the Jungian equivalent to the Freudian personal unconscious, namely the notion of the shadow self, which, as Le Guin explains, is 'all we don't want to, can't, admit into our conscious self, all the qualities and tendencies within us which have been repressed, denied, or not used' ('Child' 53). Jung argues that 'the less it [the shadow] is embodied in the individual, the blacker and denser it is', and so the more likely it is to form an 'unconscious snag, blocking our most well-meant attempts ('Psychology' 76). In order to escape from the unconscious fatality of the shadow self, the person must 'find a way in which his conscious personality and his shadow can live together' (77). Accepting the shadow self is understood by Le Guin as essential to a realistic moral and ethical apprehension, untainted by the defensive projection outward of one's own capacity for evil: 'If I want to live in the real world, I must withdraw my projections; I must admit that the hateful, the evil, exists within myself' ('Child' 54). The Jungian reconciliation with the shadow self quite clearly resonates with the protagonist Ged's quest for self-integration in Le Guin's fantasy *Bildungsroman*, *A Wizard of Earthsea* (1968).

Nonetheless, a renewed relationship with the personal unconscious is, for Le Guin, only part of a larger self-conscious application of Jungian ideas to science fiction and fantasy. To meet one's shadow is only the 'first step' towards an encounter with the Jungian collective unconscious, which Le Guin enthusiastically describes as 'the source of true community; of felt religion; of art, grace, spontaneity, and love' ('Child' 53). Jung provides the following distinction between the personal unconscious of Freudian psychoanalytic psychology, and the collective unconscious of his own theory:

> While the personal unconscious is made up essentially of contents which have at one time been conscious but which have disappeared from consciousness through having been forgotten or repressed, the contents of the collective unconscious have never been in consciousness, and therefore have never been individually acquired, but owe their existence exclusively to heredity. Whereas the personal unconscious consists for the most part of *complexes*, the content of the collective unconscious is made up essentially of *archetypes*. ('Concept' 42)

Although archetypes are 'inborn and universally present formal elements' (44) that are essentially beyond the reach of consciousness, their existence can be inferred because they 'give definite form to certain psychic contents' (43). Just as Immanuel Kant argued that the unknowable 'noumenal self' provided inescapable 'transcendental *a priori*' structures for our thought and experience (as, for instance, cause and effect, and time and space), so Jung's inborn archetypal 'forms without content' (48) supposedly impose universal patterns on psychic and cultural material.

What Le Guin attempts to exploit in her use of Jungian theory is the utopian universality of the archetypes – as she notes, the Jungian collective unconscious is 'collective' precisely because 'it is similar in all of us, just as our bodies are basically similar' ('Myth' 65). Thus, 'Writers who draw not upon the words and thoughts of others but upon their own thoughts and their own deep being will inevitably hit upon common material' (66–67); 'There will be – openly in fantasy, covertly in naturalism – dragons, heroes, quests, objects of power, voyages at night and under sea, and so forth' (67). Rather than revel in the culturally parochial 'mass mind' of 'cults, creeds, fads', and other 'hollow forms of communication' ('Child' 53), literary authors, according to Le Guin, go inward in order to find the truly universal forms of cultural and psychic life, so that 'the farther they go into the self, the closer they come to the other' ('Myth' 66).

Le Guin is, of course, by no means the only or first science fiction author to adopt a Jungian aesthetic. An early pioneer is Frank Herbert, whose near-future novel, *The Dragon in the Sea* (1956), grafts an archetypal Jungian aesthetic into the Golden Age tradition of adventure stories populated with engineering experts. The titular 'dragon' is the *Fenian Ram*, an advanced nuclear 'subtug' sent on a quest to pirate undersea oil from territory held by the Eastern Powers, with whom the West are embroiled in a lengthy war (which has already destroyed and irradiated the British Isles). The protagonist, Ramsey, is a psychologist and electronics expert sent by the Bureau of Psychology (BuPsych) to ensure the psychological health of the crew – the electronics officer in the sub's previous mission having 'suffered a psychotic blow-up' on returning to shore, a problem that has plagued other crews (Herbert 11). Ramsey is tasked both with preserving the sanity of Sparrow, the sub's captain, and foiling a probable Eastern Powers saboteur (eventually revealed to be the boat's engineer, Garcia). The action rather laboriously advances a series of incidents that reveal a paucity of cultural materials that can elaborate and resolve archetypal meanings for the crew's experience. As Sparrow points out, their 'underground base' is 'like a womb. And the marine tunnel. A birth canal if I ever saw one' (39). This accords with Ramsey's eventual diagnosis (after his own temporary breakdown upon return), explained back at base to his superior in BuPsych:

> [O]ur submariners seemed eager to return to duty. That's the paradox: they found threat in both spheres – ashore and at sea. When they were ashore they seemed to forget about the menace of the sea because the subconscious masked it. The boat spelled enveloping safety, a return to the womb. But when the men came ashore, that was birth: exposure. The sky's a hideous thing to men who want to hide from it. (202)

BuPsych have been unable to understand that '[t]he breakdowns are a rejection of birth by men who have unconsciously retreated into the world of prebirth' (198) because they have merely displaced religious wisdom without offering an acceptable replacement: 'Unless BuPsych can uncover telepathy or absolute proof of the hereafter, it can't substitute for religion' argues Ramsey, as he proposes religious training for psychologists, since religion 'provides a common bond for people, a clear line of communication' (202). As in Le Guin's diagnosis, a renewed language of archetypes restores communication with the unconscious, and thus with the wider collectivity that shares its archetypes. As for the subtug crews, Ramsey's preventative solution is a rite of passage to mark their symbolic rebirth as they return to land from the amniotic world of the sub.

Herbert's novel is interesting mostly as a historical document that shows Jungian meanings typical of the New Wave being grafted into the Golden Age technocratic fascination with vacuum tubes and atomic piles. At a more advanced literary level, Le Guin's 1972 novella, *The Word for World is Forest*, depicts an extra-terrestrial (although fundamentally human) society that has a highly developed relationship to its collective unconscious. *Word for World* is set on the planet Athsh, also known as New Tahiti, and latterly as Planet 41. The Athsheans, as the indigenous inhabitants are known, are a small green furry humanoid life form genetically related to the same 'Hainish' stock of humanoids as the Terrans (Le Guin *Word* 54) who have lately arrived on their planet as colonizers, drawn to it by the plentiful forests that they hope to clear for timber and replant as arable land. Despite their biological similarities, the Terrans show little concern for the Athsheans (or 'creechies' as they are pejoratively known). These peaceful, forest-dwelling inhabitants of the planet are mistreated, enslaved, and exploited in Terran logging operations, and show little resistance, since they are in general incapable of intra-species (or intra-genus) aggression. Le Guin's narrative traces the eventual and successful rebellion of the Athsheans against their colonizers, a movement if not led, then at least inspired, by one native in particular, named Selver, who overcomes the Athsheans' conscious and subconscious inability to kill other humans. Two Terrans act as unwitting accomplices in the decolonization of Athsh. The first of these is Captain Raj Lyubov, an anthropologist with military rank, who, while learning about Athshean culture from Selver, also teaches his native informant about Terran culture and society. The second is Captain Davidson. His repeated attacks on the Athsheans, which occur despite clear orders to the contrary from Earth, incite the natives to increasing use of force against their colonizers.

Le Guin's possible allusion to Jung in 'Commander Yung' (46) of the *Shackleton*, a visiting spaceship, indicates the psychoanalytic extrapolations within the text but, despite the Jungian inspiration, no great extra-textual knowledge of esoteric archetypes is needed to understand the meaning of *Word for World*'s sylvan imagery. The forest in the novel functions as a metafictional metaphor for the psycho-cultural terrain opened up by Jungian psychoanalysis: as Le Guin elsewhere remarks on this '[i]nner space', 'We all have forests in our minds. Forests unexplored, unending. Each of us gets lost in the forest, every night, alone' ('Vaster' 181). Selver's perceptions, which are the most authoritative in the novel, repeatedly contrast the 'rootedness' of his own culture in the subconscious mind with the 'rootlessness' of the Terrans. As Selver recovers after the first Athshean attack, which entirely destroys Captain Davidson's camp, he gradually recovers his capacity for waking dreams, and reflects, '[h]e had feared that he was cut off from his roots, that he had gone too far into the dead land of action ever to find his way back to the springs of reality' (Le Guin *Word* 36). But while Selver may recover his roots, it is clear to him that the Terrans 'have left their roots behind them, perhaps, in this other forest from which they came, this forest with no trees' (41). Selver's valorization of rootedness contrasts with the deforestation practised by the Terrans, who have already destroyed the ecosystem of one island on the planet because of the soil erosion consequent upon logging. Davidson's perception epitomizes the Terran assumption that forests are unworthy of preservation when they could be turned into arable land: 'when they came here there had been nothing. Trees. A dark huddle and jumble and tangle of trees, endless, meaningless' (15).

Although Le Guin indicates in her introduction that *Word for World* may be read as an allegory of the Vietnam War (7–8), the novel more generally comments, from a Jungian perspective, upon the psychoanalytic effects of modernity and rationalization upon traditional societies. Le Guin therefore inserts into the speech of a female Athshean an allusion to the famous statement on the Roman occupation attributed to the Caledonian warrior, Calgacus, by the Roman historian Tacitus in his *Agricola*. Calgacus's statement, 'They make a desert and call it "peace"' (Tacitus 22; ch.30), becomes '"[t]hey make the forest into a dry beach" – her language had no word for "desert" – "and call that making things ready for the women"' (*Word* 39–40). Such sylvan metaphors in *Word for World* of rootedness and rootlessness, of forestation and deforestation, resonate, presumably intentionally, with Jung's diagnosis of modernity. According to Sonu Shamdasani, Jung feared the modern 'uprootedness' (262) which arose '[w]hen traditions broke down, [and] consciousness became separated from instincts and lost its roots. These instincts, having lost their means of expression, sank into the unconscious, causing it to overflow into conscious contents' (262). In a 1946 essay, Jung explains how, in his view, religion, among other forms of tradition,

> guards against one of the greatest psychic dangers – loss of roots – which is a disaster not only for primitive tribes but for civilized man as well. The breakdown of a tradition, necessary as this may be at times, is always a loss and a danger; and it is a danger to the soul because the life of instinct – always the most conservative element in man – always expresses itself in traditional usages. Age-old convictions and customs are deeply rooted in the instincts. If they get lost, the conscious mind becomes severed from the instincts and loses its roots, while the instincts, unable to express themselves, fall back into the unconscious and reinforce its energy, causing this in turn to overflow into the existing contents of consciousness. It is then that the rootless condition of consciousness becomes a real danger. ('Psychotherapy' 98–99)

Such 'uprootedness' (Jung 'Undiscovered' 288), explains Jung in a 1957 essay, occurs when the consciousness of man [sic] 'orients itself chiefly by observing and investigating the world around him, and it is to the latter's peculiarities that he must adapt his psychic and technical resources' (289). The extraversion of consciousness onto the objective world, and the consequent hypertrophy of instrumental rationality, is therefore 'the ultimate source of those numerous psychic disturbances and difficulties which are occasioned by man's progressive alienation from his instinctual foundation, [...] by his concern with consciousness at the expense of the unconscious' (288).

Jung seems to speculate that the reduction of the self to the conscious self occurs in particular 'environmental conditions, knowledge and control of which necessitated or suggested certain modifications of [...] original instinctive tendencies' (289). There is, then, a Jungian historical vision, as well as an archetypal meaning, implicit in *Word for World*'s master symbol, that of the forest. A lengthy descriptive passage at the beginning of the second chapter develops a cultural geography in which the forest of tradition is contrasted with, as it were, the plain of modernity. In Le Guin's metaphorical forest, the world is represented as intrinsically complex, and resistant to the metaphorical highways of enlightened progress: 'No way was clear, no light unbroken, in the forest. Into wind, water, sunlight, starlight, there always entered leaf and branch, bole and root, the shadowy, the complex' (*Word* 27). In such a world, there can be no single clear progressive road, no grand narrative, only a multiplicity of paths that must always concede to a resistant environment – 'Little paths ran under the branches, around the boles, over the roots; they did not go straight, but yielded to every obstacle, devious as nerves' (27). The grand historical perspective into the far future, the stuff of Biblical 'revelation' *sub specie aeternitas*, is entirely missing: 'The view was never long, unless looking up through the branches you caught sight of the stars. Nothing was pure, dry, arid, plain. Revelation was lacking. There was no seeing everything at once: no certainty' (27). Le Guin's pun may well be conscious: the world of the (geographical) plain is (unambiguously) plain, but the forest is an ambiguous place in which 'you could not even say whether the leaves of the willows were brownish-red, or reddish-green, or green' (27).

The contrast between forest and plain also is used in *Word for World* to contrast the Athshean and Terran model of the psyche. Lyubov reflects that 'to the Athsheans soil, ground, earth was not that to which the dead return and by which the living live: the substance of their world was not earth, but forest. Terran man was clay, red dust. Athshean man was branch and root' (72). The Terran man [sic] identified by Lyubov, it seems, is a Judaeo-Christian man of the plains: his body is like a soil into which the distinct, ontologically separable life of the soul is sown. For the Athsheans, on the other hand, the self is always connected into the instinctual bodily roots putatively identified by Jungian theory. This is why the Athsheans, although they do not have sophisticated instrumental technology, possess a highly developed psychotechnology in their capacity for 'dreaming wide awake' (79), which, reflects Lyubov, 'related to Terran dreaming-sleep as the Parthenon to a mud hut' (80). The word for dream in Athshean is also the word for root (80), a further indication that their practice of wide-awake dreaming ensures their rootedness. Indeed, Athshean dreaming seems to be something like a development of what Jung called 'active imagination', 'a sequence of fantasies produced by deliberate concentration' that was also a way to receive psychic material formed by the collective unconscious ('Concept' 49).

As Lyubov indicates, the Athshean culture of rootedness in the collective unconscious means that they can very successfully acknowledge and negotiate with their instinctual life: there is no impossible dialectic between satisfaction and renunciation, as Freud postulated. For example, the 'singing-matches' between adult males are aggression-channelling devices so successful that, among the Athsheans, '[r]ape, violent assault, and murder virtually don't exist' (*Word* 52). On the other hand, Terran uprootedness leads to a suppression of archetypal expressions, a consequent denial of the instincts, and their fateful return in pathological forms. To Selver, the Terrans 'are grown men, but insane'

(98), who 'go about in torment killing and destroying, driven by the gods within, whom they will not set free but try to uproot and deny. If they are men they are evil men having denied their own gods, afraid to see their own faces in the dark' (41). The depiction of the Terrans in the chapters focalized on their representatives confirms Selver's diagnosis. There is, for instance, a kind of compulsory extroversion in their culture. When Lyubov takes a shot of vodka, 'It turned him inside out: it extraverted him: it normalised him' (46). Davidson reflects also on his dislike of the daydreaming invited by the forest environment: 'There was something about this damn planet, its gold sunlight and hazy sky, its mild winds smelling of leaf mould and pollen, something made you daydream. You mooched along thinking about conquistadors and destiny and stuff, till you were acting as thick and slow as a creechie' (16). Davidson's unwillingness to engage in healthy daydreaming means a return of the sexual and aggressive instincts in fantasies of violence: 'It made his belly churn a little to imagine it [i.e. dropping a napalm equivalent on the Athsheans], just like when he thought about making a woman, or whenever he remembered about when that Sam creechie had attacked him and he had smashed in his whole face with four blows one right after the other' (66). Furthermore, *Word for World* also implies that Terran culture (contemporary Western culture, in other words) lacks expression of the archetypal forms necessary for non-sexual intimacy.

> 'They're always pawing each other,' some of the colonists sneered, unable to see in these touch-exchanges anything but their own eroticism which, forced to concentrate itself exclusively on sex and then repressed and frustrated, invades and poisons every sensual pleasure, every humane response: the victory of a blinded, furtive Cupid over the great brooding mother of all the seas and stars, all the leaves of trees, all the gestures of men, Venus Genetrix .... (76)

The Terran hostility to affectionate touch occurs, according to the textual dominant, because of a quite specific (and seemingly anti-matriarchal) impoverishment in the archetypal inventory of uprooted Western culture.

Despite its exploitation of Jungian dreaming as a metafictional model for science fiction and fantasy, *Word for World* is not entirely faithful to the supposed nature of the collective unconscious. Jung emphasized the necessary inertia of the rooted order of things, so that 'in dealing with the individual, no matter how revolutionary his conscious attitude may be, we have to reckon with a patriarchal or hierarchical orientation of the psyche which causes it instinctively to seek and cling to this order' ('Psychotherapy' 99). Lyubov shares this conservative orientation when he wonders if the events on Athsh would 'change them [the Athsheans] radically? – when their unaggressiveness ran so deep in them, right through their culture and society and on down into their subconscious, their "dream time", and perhaps into their very physiology?' (Le Guin *Word* 75). Le Guin, though, is manifestly a feminist, and frequently critical of both hierarchies and gender essentialism. She resolves the tension between her politics and her psychoanalytic commitment to Jungian theory by reconfiguring the collective unconscious as something that is historically adaptable, capable of creating new archetypal forms. Selver thus becomes a new God, a personalized archetype alongside existing Athshean figures such as 'Pursuer', the 'Friend who has no face', and 'the Aspen-leaf Woman' (34): Selver becomes Death, a representation that allows the Athsheans to become capable, for the first time, of intra-species aggression against the Terrans (and even, one supposes, against themselves). Lyubov intuits this unexpected change when he meets Selver again shortly before the Athshean onslaught against Capital city, the central Terran enclave – Selver 'was changed, radically: from the root' (77). Socio-political radicalism (going down to the 'roots' of politics, as the etymology of radical in *L. radix* indicates (OED, *radical*)) can thus co-exist, in Le Guin's modified Jungianism, with the supposed rootedness of a culture in the collective unconscious.

The analytic encounter: Challenging accommodationism

Le Guin's use of Jungian ideas illustrates the way in which a writer may exploit one branch of psychoanalytic psychology, and then further modify it according to her own needs and interests. Nor is Le Guin alone in adapting Jungianism to feminism. Josephine Saxton does something similar in her feminist science fiction stories set in a world in which the collective unconscious can be entered and explored. In the novella *Jane Saint and the Backlash* (1989), the protagonist, Jane Saint, appears to bring back from a fantastic realm a new archetype, concretized in a mirror that enables greater empathetic understanding, particularly between men and women: 'There in the mirror she saw, not herself, but Miles. And, furthermore, she could feel his feelings, and understood his mortal soul and what drove it. She gazed and gazed until he took the mirror from her, convinced that she had concussion' ('Backlash' 167). As Saxon herself appears to indicate, this mirror archetype discovers (or invents) a collective unconscious that, though it may be primal and rooted, is also open to change and adaptation: 'I possibly *do* have a new idea there. If only its psychological equivalent could be effected, the entire world would change for the better' ('Introduction' 5).

But as well as being adopted and adapted to cultural *novums* in science fiction, psychoanalytic psychology also theorizes a talking cure. This mode of therapy has provided fertile material for literary representation in works by authors such as Philip Roth, Doris Lessing, and D.M. Thomas (Berman). Science fiction writing has similarly exploited the narrative possibilities of the therapeutic process, offering a speculative therapeutic optimism against the more pessimistic tendencies of Nietzsche and Freud. For instance, Bester's 'Oddy and Id' (89 above) is, in effect, expanded and revised in a hopeful direction by his 1953 novel, *The Demolished Man*, which centres on Ben Reich, an entrepreneur who murders his business rival, Craye D'Courtney. The narrative structure invokes a self-conscious dialogue with the classic whodunnit, as Reich attempts to evade detection by the telepathic 'Esper' detective, Lincoln Powell. Although the dominance of ESP as a parapsychological *novum* means that the text is largely outside the limits of this monograph, Bester's novel is relevant for its use of telepathy as a metaphor for psychoanalytic enlightenment. The '1st Class Espers', of which Powell is one, 'are capable of deep peeping, through the conscious and preconscious layers down to the unconscious ... the lowest levels of the mind. Primordial basic desires and so forth' (*Demolished* 20). Reich, the Espers Guild eventually comes to understand, is particularly dangerous because he (like Oddy in Bester's short story) is a potential tyrant, as indicated by the name of his company, Monarch Utilities & Resources. Reich (his name is another hint) is a proto-Hitler who would likely oppress (perhaps even exterminate) the telepaths. Powell explains to the Guild (in telepathic italics) that Reich threatens a potential *'civil war'* in which the Espers *'may suffer the usual history of minority groups'* (207). This licenses Powell's unleashing of a successful mass psychic assault against Reich, who is then subjected to the 'Demolition' of the title – a process of psychic erasure and rebirth to prevent the ascendancy of a man 'whose compulsions might have torn down our society and irrevocably committed us to his own psychotic pattern' (242). The detection narrative – which becomes rather incidental to the plot – is also resolved. Powell explains that Reich's financial motive for murder was really the screen for an unconscious wish. D'Courtney was in fact secretly Reich's father, a fact of which Reich was aware 'deep down in the unconscious', so that '[h]e wanted to destroy the hateful father who had rejected him' (240). The psychoanalytic shenanigans are further complicated by Reich's unconscious guilt feelings, which lead him to a series of potentially lethal booby traps directed at his own person:

> Reich had never admitted to himself that he murdered because he hated D'Courtney as the father who had rejected and abandoned him. Therefore, the punishment had to take place on the unconscious level. Reich set those traps for himself without ever realizing it ... in his sleep, somnambulistically ... during the day, in short fugues ... brief departures from conscious reality. The tricks of the mind mechanism are fantastic. (241)

The novel's closing pages pursue the analogy between telepathy and analytic enlightenment further. The Espers Guild hopes for a future in which all humans have developed their psychic talents: 'The world will be a wonderful place when everyone's a peeper and everyone's adjusted', Powell advises his Commissioner (243). But until that day arrives, the psychic (i.e. psychoanalytic) detective pursues 'the frightening truth in people', protecting us against 'the passions, the hatreds, the jealousies, the malice, the sicknesses' (243).

The vicissitudes of such science fictional authorization of the analytic relationship can be traced further in two texts separated by around a decade: Daniel Keyes's *Flowers for Algernon* (1966) and Frederik Pohl's *Gateway* (1977). Both novels illustrate the reflexive function of psychological discourse in science fiction, although in contrasting ways. *Flowers for Algernon* largely endorses and promulgates psychoanalytic self-reflection, whereas *Gateway* more sceptically interrogates the psychoanalytic model of the self, particularly its complicity with capitalist individualism.

The first-person narrative of *Flowers for Algernon* is recounted by Charlie Gordon, a man in his early thirties who works in a New York City bakery in a period roughly dateable to the 1950s or early 1960s. Charlie has a learning disability due to brain damage in infancy arising from the (non-fictional) condition 'phenylketonuria' (Keyes *Flowers* 113), now commonly known as PKU (see e.g. Cleary). Charlie, despite his cognitive impairment, has chosen to attend classes at the Beekman School for Retarded Adults, thereby acquiring reading and writing abilities beyond the level typical for his IQ (8). The main action of the narrative begins as Charlie undergoes an experimental psychosurgical therapy that removes his damaged brain tissue and stimulates new growth at a 'supernormal rate' (114). The treatment has been applied already with increasing success to animal experimental subjects by a team of scientists comprised of two academics, Strauss and Nemur, and their postgraduate student, Burt. The team are persuaded of its human applicability by the seemingly permanent intelligence gains (measured by maze-solving performance) in their latest animal subject, a mouse called Algernon. Charlie's post-surgical intelligence gains are similarly astounding. He rapidly becomes the kind of intellectual superman envisaged by the scientific team, and records his changing personality and abilities in the journal entries that make up the novel's narrative. Charlie's intellectual development propels him out of his job at the bakery, and into the world of higher education. He undergoes a simultaneous process of psychological maturation and self-reflection that leads him on a search for his estranged family, and into a troubled romance with Alice Kinnian, his former teacher at the Beekman School. The psychosurgical augmentation, however, turns out to be temporary: the treated individuals will always return to their earlier condition. Algernon loses his enhanced intelligence (and dies), while Charlie loses entirely his augmented intelligence – by the end of the book he is no longer working at the bakery, or attending classes, and is instead homed in an institution for adults with learning disabilities.

The narrative's manifold possibilities of estrangement interrogate the social valuation of intelligence, particularly as psychologically and academically conceived. Charlie's intellectual development over his accelerated *Bildungsroman* can be seen as a figure for social mobility (and class division) achieved through education, and as a way of representing within a few months of adult life the acquisition and loss of cognitive capacity over the whole life cycle (significantly, when Charlie seeks out his estranged mother, he finds that she is suffering from age-related cognitive impairment (198–213)). Keyes's choice of PKU as the cause of Charlie's learning disability is particularly telling. By the time of the novel's publication, PKU was a metonymy for seemingly 'miraculous' progress in biomedical diagnosis and therapeutics. As Jeffrey P. Brosco and Diane B. Paul explain, the prevention of PKU-related cognitive impairment was

> widely seen as a victory for scientific medicine. If the condition is detected in the newborn period and a specialized diet is instituted, the profound cognitive impairment usually caused by PKU is averted. For the diet to be effective, however, the otherwise normal-appearing infant with PKU must be identified, among thousands of other nonaffected infants, in the first weeks of life. In the early 1960s, parents of children with intellectual disability began to advocate for state laws to test all newborns in the United States [...]. By 1965, 32 American states had enacted screening laws, all but 5 making the test compulsory. (987)

References to screening and a therapeutic dietary regime are entirely absent from *Flowers for Algernon*, implying a 1950s setting for the narrative. The fictional psychosurgical *novum*, however, cleverly interrogates the 'potent cultural symbol' of PKU (987) by asking uncomfortable questions about the motives underlying biomedical progress in the condition's treatment. Nemur, while addressing an academic congress where Charlie is to be exhibited, refers to his patient as formerly 'one of nature's mistakes' who has now been replaced by 'a superior human being' (124). Charlie's outraged inner response conveys the textual interrogation of biomedical progress: 'I wanted to get up and show everyone what a fool he was, to shout at him: *I'm a human being, a person – with parents and memories and a history* – and I was before you ever wheeled me into that operating room!' (124). To what extent, the novel asks, is the narrative of PKU's treatment contaminated by a dehumanizing categorization of PKU-affected individuals with learning disabilities as inferior human beings produced in error by nature? The question is intensified by various narrative elements that problematize our contemporary cultural hierarchy in which greater intelligence equates to higher social worth. Alice, who provides a moral centre to the narrative, fiercely questions whether Charlie, whom she admired (and perhaps also desired) in his pre-surgical condition, has been genuinely improved by his increased intelligence: 'There was something in you before', she tells Charlie, 'a warmth, an openness, a kindness that made everyone like you and like to have you around' (94). This view is shared by Burt, who tells Charlie that he hasn't developed 'understanding' or 'tolerance' (117), and most trenchantly expressed by Nemur, who tells his experimental subject, 'you've developed from a likeable, retarded young man into an arrogant, self-centered, antisocial bastard' (189). This reversal of customary hierarchies is finally sealed by the narrative's tragic anagnorisis in which Charlie recognizes these perceptions as valid: 'I was seeing myself as I really had become: Nemur had said it. I was an arrogant, self-centered bastard. Unlike Charlie, I was incapable of making friends or thinking about other people and their problems' (194).

But the neurological *novum* of intelligence augmentation also introduces psychological, and specifically psychoanalytic, discourses of the self, for Charlie is increasingly emancipated by psychoanalytic reflection on the formation of his personality. This is particularly evident as he begins to understand and work through his mother's resentment of him, and her preference for Charlie's cognitively unimpaired younger sister, Norma. Admittedly, Charlie's promulgation of psychoanalytic or psychotherapeutic discourses contains elements from other psychologies, particularly existentialism. At one point he has to make a Sartrean existential decision about whether or not to report a colleague who is embezzling money at the bakery (70), and recognition of his finitude plays an important part in Charlie's increasingly autonomous life path, which is metaphorized through the novel's leitmotif of passage through a maze:

> Although we know the end of the maze holds death (and it is something I have not always known – not long ago the adolescent in me thought death could happen only to other people), I see now that the path I choose through that maze makes me what I am. I am not only a thing, but also a way of being – one of many ways – and knowing the paths I have followed and the ones left to take will help me understand what I am becoming. (169)

Such existential concerns extend also to Alice, whose sexual ambivalence towards her former pupil is represented in terms immediately recognizable from Sartrean existentialism. Charlie records in his journal:

> As I slipped my arm down to her waist, I felt her tremble, but still she kept staring in the direction of the orchestra. She was pretending to be concentrating on the music so that she wouldn't have to respond to me. She didn't want to know what was happening. As long as she looked away, and listened, she could pretend that my closeness, my arms around her, were without her knowledge or consent. She wanted me to make love to her body while she kept her mind on higher things. I reached over roughly and turned her chin. 'Why don't you look at me? Are you pretending I don't exist?'
> 'No, Charlie,' she whispered. 'I'm pretending I don't exist.' (77)

Alice's denial of her own specifically human existence – her 'bad faith' – more or less retells a vignette from *Being and Nothingness* (1943), which had been translated into English in 1958 by Hazel Barnes. To illustrate existential bad faith, Sartre imagines a woman who refuses to acknowledge her ongoing agency as a potential lover takes her hand:

> [T]he young woman leaves her hand there, but she does not notice that she is leaving it. She does not notice because it happens by chance that she is at this moment all intellect. She draws her companion up to the most lofty regions of sentimental speculation [...]. And during this time the divorce of the body from the soul is accomplished; the hand rests inert between the warm hands of

her companion – neither consenting nor resisting – a thing. (*Being* 55–56)

But while existentialist discourses are promulgated and authorized in Charlie's narrative, they complement, rather than subvert, the authority of psychoanalytic and psychotherapeutic discourses. Existential self-examination is fundamentally enhanced in *Flowers for Algernon* by Charlie's recovery of previously inaccessible psychic contents preserved in the unconscious mind. The text therefore clearly shows science fiction attempting to reflexively construct psychoanalytic selfhood in its readers (just as Skinner attempted to persuade his readers to adopt behaviourist categories (133–41)). The narrative promotes a psychoanalytic template for the examined life, beginning with Charlie's immediately post-surgical use of a hypnopaedic device designed also to awaken memories from the subconscious mind: 'Other things is at nite its suppose to make me have dreams and remembir things that happened a long time ago when I was a very littel kid' (Keyes *Flowers* 20). Within three weeks of his psychosurgery, and the accessing of the unconscious mind through dreams, Charlie begins a form of Freudian psychoanalytic therapy with one of the team members:

> Now that Im starting to have those dreams and remembiring Prof Nemur says I got to go to theripy sesions with Dr Strauss. He says theripy sesions is like when you feel bad you talk to make it better. I tolld him I dont feel bad and I do plenty of talking all day so why do I have to go to theripy but he got sore and says I got to go anyway.
>
> What theripy is is that I got to lay down on a couch and Dr Strauss sits in a chair near me and I talk about anything that comes into my head. (22)

In these regular encounters, Charlie learns that he has 'two minds', 'the SUBCONSCIOUS *and the* CONSCIOUS (thats how you spell it) and one don't tell the other what its doing. They dont even talk to each other. Thats why I dream' (23).

While Charlie's indoctrination into psychoanalytic truth might seem to invite a sceptically constructionist account of psychoanalytic authority, the dominant tenor of the narrative is towards the authorization of some rather hackneyed (and patriarchal) psychosexual motifs, particularly in the figure of his castrating, sexually repressive mother. Charlie is dogged by an overwhelming castration anxiety that has developed because of his mother's sexual repressiveness, and which has been elaborated by mistaken inferences about his sister's menstruation. These unconscious contents are revealed by his access to the unconscious mind through classical analytic techniques:

> Free association is still difficult, because it's hard not to control the direction of your thoughts ... just to leave your mind open and let anything flow into it ... ideas bubbling to the surface like a bubble bath ... a woman bathing ... a girl ... Norma taking a bath ... I am watching through the keyhole ... and when she gets out of the tub to dry herself I see that her body is different from mine. Something is missing.
> Running down the hallway ... somebody chasing me ... not a person ... just a big flashing kitchen knife ... and I'm scared and crying but no voice comes out because my neck is cut and I'm bleeding. (65)

Within the narrative logic, this castration anxiety explains Charlie's pre-surgical sexual latency, despite being long past puberty (his mother has, in effect, beaten his pubescent sexuality out of him (86)), and is also mobilized to explain the peculiar episodes that haunt his post-surgical relationships with women. As he and Alice first approach sexual intimacy, he undergoes a dissociative episode:

> It started as a hollow buzzing in my ears ... an electric saw ... far away. Then the cold: arms and legs prickly, and finger numbing. Suddenly, I had the feeling I was being watched.
> A sharp switch in perception. I saw, from some point in the darkness behind a tree, the two of us lying in each other's arms.
> I looked up to see a boy of fifteen or sixteen, crouching nearby. 'Hey!' I shouted. As he stood up, I saw his trousers were open and he was exposed. (77)

The watching boy is an hallucination, but the outside perspective belongs to the latent pre-surgical Charlie, a textual double who returns again during the post-surgical Charlie's subsequent liaison with his free-spirited artist neighbour, Fay: 'I saw the two of us, as if I were a third person standing in the doorway [...]. But seeing myself that way, from a distance, left me unresponsive' (147). This repressed, sexually inhibited self re-emerges also when Charlie gets drunk with Fay:

> [G]etting drunk had momentarily broken down the conscious barriers that kept the old Charlie Gordon hidden deep in my mind.

> As I suspected all along, he was not really gone. Nothing in our minds is ever really gone. The operation had covered him over with a veneer of education and culture, but emotionally he was there – watching and waiting. (150)

The repressed Charlie is still driven by Oedipal fears of castration expressed in his punning speech – as Fay explains, 'you kept saying you couldn't play with me because your mother would take away your peanuts and put you in a cage' (149).

The post-surgical Charlie is astute enough to understand the nature of the 'fears and blocks triggered in these sexual situations' (79), and attempts – with eventual success – to work through his various complexes and towards satisfying sexual intimacy with Alice (and, before her, Fay). Although Charlie is notionally attending regular psychotherapeutic sessions with Strauss, the narrative largely neglects the formal psychoanalytic model in which the analyst offers a blank screen upon which the analysand projects his or her most important (typically familial) early relationships. Instead, Charlie is liberated by the anamnesis of his unconscious mental life conveyed in the narrative structure of interpolated flashbacks in which he works through as an adult the central experiences of his troubled childhood. To take just one example, Charlie reflects upon the neurotic anxiety he feels at being strapped into the seat for his first air journey: 'Why should putting on the damned seat belt be so terrifying? That, and the vibrations of the plane taking off. Anxiety all out of proportion to the situation ... so it must be something ... what?' (103). He pursues the memory via free association, and recovers an experience in which his parents take him to a quack therapist whose treatment involves strapping the young Charlie onto a table before subjecting him to a painless, but entirely fanciful neurotherapy, 'short-wave encephalo-reconditioning' (108). Although the therapist, Dr Guarino, is exceptionally humane in his attitude towards his young patient, the experience has traumatic repercussions. The expense of the treatment, and his mother's fanatical desire to 'cure' him, further erode his parents' already fragile marriage. Charlie's anxious self-hatred is only intensified further after he accidentally soils himself during his first treatment:

> The look of disgust on his mother's face sets him trembling. For a short while he had forgotten how bad he is, how he makes his parents suffer. He doesn't know how, but it frightens him when she says he makes her suffer, and when she cries and screams at him, he turns his face to the wall and moans softly to himself. (109)

By recalling, and understanding, the significance of this early experience, Charlie overcomes his neurotic symptom – at the end of the air journey during which he narrates this experience, his 'out of proportion' anxiety has entirely disappeared.

There are, admittedly, some minor notes of scepticism in *Flowers for Algernon* towards psychoanalytic therapeutic optimism. At one point, Charlie and Alice go to the cinema to watch '[a] psychological film about a man and woman apparently in love but actually destroying each other' (59–60). Fortunately, a 'sudden memory' reveals to the husband 'that his hatred is really directed at a depraved governess who had terrified him with frightening stories and left a flaw in his personality' (60). Charlie's narrative is implicitly sceptical of the movie's miraculous psychoanalytic cure but, on the whole, Keyes's novel endorses and promulgates psychoanalytically-informed self-examination as a psycho-technology that overcomes 'fears and blocks', and liberates an authentic self capable of genuine intimate relations. By the end of Charlie's process of therapeutic self-examination, he no longer compulsively repeats his anxious relationship with his female family members: 'Alice was a woman, but perhaps now Charlie would understand that she wasn't his mother or his sister' (224–25). The result is some frankly rapturous sex with Alice, which Charlie experiences as 'the first step outward to the universe – beyond the universe – because in it and with it we merged to recreate and perpetuate the human spirit' (225). Charlie's narrative thus endorses the credo learned from Strauss at the beginning of his psychotherapy: 'even if I don't understand my dreams or memories or why I have them, some time in the future they're all going to connect up, and I'll learn more about myself' (37).

Frederik Pohl's *Gateway* has some resemblance to *Flowers for Algernon*, since it also employs an extended narrative of psychoanalytic self-reflection – a feature that has led it to be described by Thomas P. Dunn as a science fiction counterpart to '[J.D.] Salinger's *Catcher in the Rye*, Judith Guest's *Ordinary People*, and Hannah Green's *I Never Promised You a Rose Garden*' (91). But Pohl's 1977 novel also anticipates *The Remaking of Sigmund Freud* (98–101 above) since it imagines the *novum* of an artificial therapist in order to critically interrogate psychoanalytic discourse, and thus to partially destabilize rather than buttress its reflexivity effect. Pohl's novel, the first of a series of six related volumes drawing upon the same setting, takes place in a future Earth ecologically imperiled by overpopulation and the overexploitation of natural resources. The protagonist, Robinette Broadhead, is – despite his name – a man, and a wealthy one, undergoing psychoanalytic psychotherapy provided by a computer program that he nicknames 'Sigfrid von Shrink' in a clear allusion to Sigmund Freud (Pohl *Gateway* 1). Broadhead, who is usually known as 'Bob', is an unhappy individual for, despite his wealth, he suffers from depression, feelings of guilt, and difficulties in his sex life (176). He also, while in his twenties, experienced a 'psychotic episode' (12). To these psychological difficulties are added a psychosomatic pathology: Broadhead suffers from a gut disorder that has already forced him to have both stomach and intestinal transplants – he is figuratively devouring himself.

Interpolated with Broadhead's narrative of his therapy are episodes from his earlier life as a so-called 'prospector' on an asteroid known as 'Gateway'. Gateway was hollowed out by a now vanished alien race known – by Earthlings at any rate – as the 'Heechee'. Within Gateway is a network of tunnels containing various artefacts left behind by the Heechee, the most significant of which are a large number of spacecraft of varying sizes. Although the spacecraft can be easily piloted by humans, there is a serious hindrance to their use, one that necessitates the recruitment of prospectors willing to risk their lives. The ships can only travel on pre-programmed courses, and there is no way of knowing in advance where these many possible predetermined journeys will lead. A voyage on one of the craft may therefore lead to instant death, death from starvation or suicide if rations run out, a pointless excursion through space, or – as the prospectors hope – the discovery of information or artefacts for which the multinational Corporation that owns Gateway will pay enormous sums of money.

Bob's wealth derives from a successful scientific exploration mission in which he earned almost $20 million. His psychic distress – at least as Sigfrid superficially portrays it – is a consequence of his repressed guilt at what he does to survive the mission. He is one of the crew of two ships, both of which emerge dangerously close to a black hole. However, it proves possible to escape by docking the two ships, and allowing one to fall into the black hole, while the other accelerates away. Broadhead, rather than join his fellow crew members in their chosen ship, enters the other vessel and successfully escapes the black hole. This consigns the other nine crew members, including Broadhead's on-off lover, Klara, to the black hole's gravitational well. Broadhead's psychological torment seemingly derives from his repressed guilt at this betrayal of his comrades and companion, and is sharpened by the knowledge that – because of time dilation – Klara is still living through her last moments even as Bob, sixteen years later, attempts to enjoy his wealthy, privileged life back on Earth.

Although Dunn warns that *Gateway* is not 'a standard novel of the psychotherapeutic process in which a series of flashbacks occurs to the hero as the therapist bears down upon his early life', he does assent to the notion that the novel 'conclude[s] with the "return" of the hero [...] to mental competence' (92). In his reading, Broadhead's cure arises from the recovery of a trauma located in his adult life, namely the abandonment of Klara and the crew: 'there is a steady progress on both stories as both move toward the crucial scene' (92). Such a reading, however, places excessive faith in Broadhead's own account, and tends to overlook the unreliability of his narrative, especially in its co-creation with Sigfrid. Hints that *Gateway* is a far more problematic narrative of psychotherapeutic recovery than, for instance, *Flowers for Algernon*, should be apparent from the historical context to which it alludes. Terri Paul notes that Pohl's computer analyst is 'apparently inspired by Joseph Weizenbaum's ELIZA or DOCTOR computer program which could "converse" in English' (54). Weizenbaum, a pioneering computer scientist, explains how in the period 1964–66 he developed firstly ELIZA, a language analysing program, and then, as an experiment, gave it a script 'designed to permit it to play [...] the role of a Rogerian psychotherapist engaged in an initial interview with a patient' (3). The result was DOCTOR. Its creator, however, was less than sanguine about the value of his creation, which imitated not psychoanalytic psychotherapy, but the person-centred counselling developed by the US therapist Carl Rogers (1902–87), in which the counsellor facilitates the client's greater self-awareness and self-acceptance through a non-directive and empathetic conversation intended to elicit a process of self-realization (Kirschenbaum). Weizenbaum was shocked by 'how quickly and how very deeply people conversing with DOCTOR became emotionally involved with the computer and how unequivocally they anthropomorphized it' (6). This enthusiasm extended also to experts in the field of psychological health, whose hopes for further developments of DOCTOR astounded Weizenbaum: 'What must a psychiatrist who makes such a suggestion think he is doing while treating a patient, that he can view the simplest mechanical parody of a single interviewing technique as having captured anything of the essence of a human encounter?' (6).

This ironizing historical context to *Gateway* finds a typographic analogue in the occasional interpolation in the narrative of pages that contain chunks of input, output, and code, seemingly from Sigfrid's programming, and particularly from its interaction with Broadhead. As Paul explains: 'This information seems to encourage us to see Sigfrid in a different dimension, more machine than human' (54). That Sigfrid may be designed to provide comfort rather than true awareness is indicated by Broadhead's own memories of an earlier talking machine: 'I had a teddy-talker. I took it to bed with me, and it told me little stories, and

I stuck pencils into it and tried to pull its ears off. I loved that thing, Sigfrid' (Pohl *Gateway* 51) – and, indeed, Sigfrid, who can adopt different physical forms, later appears in an 'incarnation as a teddy-bear' (209). The question arises: how far should we trust Broadhead's apparent psychoanalytic anagnorisis, especially since it is co-created by Sigfrid? There are indications that Sigfrid is pushing Broadhead towards a focus on the events of the fateful mission, rather than other, more deeply repressed, and politically meaningful, guilt. In one scene, Broadhead tells how Sigfrid asks him to say the first thing that comes to his mind:

> I reject the first thing and say the second. 'The first thing that comes into my mind is the way my mother was crying when my father was killed.'
> 'I don't think that was actually the first thing, Bob. Let me make a guess. Was the first thing something about Klara?'
> My chest fills, tingling. My breath catches. All of a sudden there's Klara rising up before me. (7)

It may be tempting to assume that Broadhead is resisting thoughts of Klara, yet there is no actual confirmation that the 'first thing' is indeed Klara – the question is Sigfrid's. In a similar vein, Broadhead refers to a dream which he records and analyses with Sigfrid, but which he has now entirely forgotten, having, in a classic Freudian parapraxis (an unconsciously purposeful action), thrown away the piece of paper on which he wrote it down (101): the manifest and latent content of the dream remain entirely mysterious.

That Sigfrid's focus on Klara may be disingenuous is further emphasized by the fact that Broadhead, by his own admission, has severe psychological problems that predate his final Gateway mission. Broadhead's difficulties are apparent in an attack on Klara while they are on Gateway. He callously beats her, 'I punched her four or five times, as hard as I could', and then 'in absolutely cold blood, slapped her twice more' (232). Given this mistreatment, and her subsequent return to her abuser, Klara seems less the romantic ideal later created in Broadhead's therapy, and rather more like an abused woman unable to break free of dependency upon her partner. Furthermore, Broadhead, in a manner we might imagine to be typical of male domestic abusers, regards his own actions as outwith his responsibility. His attack happens 'as if choreographed by God, absolutely inevitably'; Klara has 'pulled the trigger' that releases 'all that stored-up fury' (232). That Broadhead should later abandon Klara to the black hole's gravitational field may therefore be regarded as gratifying to his unconscious aggression, rather than an act that may be casuistically redeemed: 'The only choice was whether some of you would die, or all of you would. You elected to see that somebody lived', counsels Sigfrid, in what may well be a devil's doctrine of competitive individualism (307).

Admittedly, there is no denying that *Gateway*'s narrative presents the Klara incident as traumatic, and subject to repression. Broadhead, for instance, suffers from aphasia when he tries to say, while referring to oral sex, the phrase 'going down' (53) – this is, obviously enough, what has happened (or is happening, due to time dilation) to the Heechee ship containing Klara. But Broadhead's own words indicate a larger context of actively repressed guilty memories involving his family, past girlfriends, and disowned friends. He has 'a hundred memories [...] clearly labeled PAINFUL in the index to my memory': 'How do I know which is the first thing, when they're all boiling around in there together? My father? My mother? Sylvia? Klara? Poor Shicky, trying to balance himself in flight without any legs' (6). There is, indeed, a clear sense in which allowing others to sink down is the leitmotif of Broadhead's life, and not just of his relationship with Klara. Throughout his life, Broadhead is the unwitting or witting beneficiary when someone is intentionally or unintentionally sacrificed to his betterment, the fruits of which are almost entirely undeserved (as one Gateway Corporation operative sardonically remarks to Broadhead, 'dumb luck is almost as good as brains' (271)).

These events begin when Bob's father is killed in an accident, a 'shaft fire' in the shale mines (12), after which Bob eventually inherits his father's job. (Dunn's reading gets this detail wrong, as it refers to the death of Broadhead's mother in a mining accident (92–93).) Furthermore, Broadhead's mother fatally refuses medical treatment (a lung transplant) in order that she can pay for her son's psychotherapy (Pohl *Gateway* 13), just as she earlier sacrificed her own happiness by refusing to remarry, lest her son feel unloved (7). Broadhead's opportunity to prospect on Gateway is yet another instance of his own good fortune at the expense of others, since he is supported by a lottery win in his mid-twenties: 'two hundred and fifty thousand dollars', 'enough for a one-way ticket to Gateway' (15). This money, which Broadhead acquires by 'dumb luck', was originally other people's money. Furthermore, before betraying Klara, Broadhead also betrays one of his few real friends, the Gateway caretaker, Shicky. The latter alerts Broadhead to his ultimately successful dual-ship mission on the condition that Broadhead takes him along, but is then betrayed by Broadhead so that he can have his casual sexual partner on board (276). The motif of the exploitation and indeed consumption of others also continues after Broadhead's return to Earth, when he wonders about the intestinal transplants that he has received: 'did he [the donor] die? Could he still be alive, so poor that he sells off parts of himself, the way I've heard of pretty girls doing with a well-shaped breast or ear?' (49). This pattern of events, and Broadhead's complicity in the exploitation of others, clarifies the incident in which he loses Klara. Broadhead is, yet again, playing the odds as best he can. If he survives with nine other people, his share is $1 million. If he survives alone, he gets all the crew's bonus, a total of $10 million – a fact confirmed by one of *Gateway*'s sidebars, a later 'notice of credit' to Broadhead from the Corporation (309).

Gateway therefore presents psychoanalysis as a mode of therapy that can facilitate insight and change, but that has been corrupted by a discursive regime that focusses on personal guilt rather than political responsibility. Broadhead does indeed find out the meaning of some of his behaviours (his anal eroticism derives, it seems, from one of his mother's few forms of tenderness – her taking of his temperature anally (257)). Nonetheless, in so far as Broadhead rationalizes away his guilt over his undeserved good fortune, he is correct in his understanding of Sigfrid's psychotherapy as an accommodationist technology analogous to the ideological function of confessional: 'you could make quite a nice hierarchical flow pattern', Broadhead remarks, 'with all the shit from inside my own head flushing into the confessional, where the parish priest flushes it onto the diocesan monsignor [...], and it all winds up with the Pope [...], until he passes it on by transmitting it directly to God' (102). Sigfrid's analysis can only go so far. For although Broadhead may feel guilt over his own psychopathological aggression (and therapy may palliate this guilt), his readiness to let others suffer while he prospers is functional for capitalist society, in which wealth is ultimately distributed according to various lottery-like mechanisms. Thus, in the third volume of Pohl's series of Gateway/Heechee books, *Heechee Rendezvous* (1984), the authority of technological solutions to Broadhead's guilt continues to be undermined. Broadhead refers to the 'unlocatable space where I keep the solid core of guilt Sigfrid von Shrink did not quite purge away' (42) as he wonders how best to psychologically 'make well' (43) the terrorists that threaten the Earth. This core of guilt is finally technologically removed when Broadhead dies, and then is resurrected as a computer program existing in Heechee circuits. Without a body, he no longer has guilt feelings: 'My belly didn't hurt anymore – I didn't have a belly' (295); 'For the first time in, my God, half my life, the last little vestige of guilt was gone' (311). The Heechee technology that preserves Broadhead is the ultimate successor to the psychotherapeutic technology employed upon him by Sigfrid.

Conclusion: Psychoanalysis and its vicissitudes

Ernst Bloch argues that psychoanalysis, at least in the Freudian paradigm, is unable to conceive of utopian fantasies as containing real potential: 'Psychoanalysis [...] puts daydreams completely on a par with night-dreams, and merely sees them as incipient night-dreams' (86). It thus interprets daydreams as if they were also the distorted, symbolically masked fulfilment of various impermissible sexual and aggressive wishes (79). Bloch therefore concludes that since the psychoanalytic unconscious is 'not a newly dawning consciousness with new content but an old one with old content that has merely sunk below the threshold' (115), then '[a]ll psychoanalysis, with repression as its central notion, sublimation as a mere subsidiary notion (for substitution, for hopeful illusions), is therefore necessarily retrospective' (137). The apotheosis of this bourgeois, psychoanalytic *'No-Longer-Conscious'* (115) is, for Bloch, the Jungian propensity to interpret 'what is beginning to dawn in an utterly archaic and occult fashion', which is, he asserts, 'ideologically useful for the Blood and Soil humbug' (137). Bloch's distaste for the seeming psychoanalytic obsession with the supposedly unalterable and archaic elements of human nature leads him to propose a hermeneutic that will find in cultural productions the latent, utopian content of the *'Not-Yet-Conscious'*, 'the preconscious of what is to come, the psychological birthplace of the New' (116). With such a progressive, anticipatory hermeneutic, for instance, the ancient legend of the fountain of youth can be partially deciphered as a latent dawning of the accomplishments of modern medicine and social organization (460–62). Bloch's endeavour is recognisably the beginning of a literary and cultural critical tradition that tries to interpret 'an obscure yet omnipresent Utopian impulse finding its way to the surface in a variety of covert expressions and practices' (Jameson *Archaeologies* 3) in order to reach a so-called 'political unconscious' (Jameson *Political* passim).

Nonetheless, the conclusion, deriving from Bloch, that Freudian psychoanalysis can only support conservative extrapolation, is not supported by the texts studied in this chapter. Admittedly, *Doctor Moreau*, *The Croquet Player*, *The Death of Grass*, and 'Oddy and Id' seem to reinforce culturally pessimistic, conservative narratives. But dystopias such as *1984* and *Brave New World* do much to subvert the dogmatic pessimism of Freudianism, and to point towards more utopian potentials – an impulse shared also by *The Remaking of Sigmund Freud*, with its critique of Freudian reductionism. A similar point may be made about the adaptation of Jungian ideas: in *Word for World*, Le Guin valorizes traditional society over modernity, but also challenges the stasis of official Jungian doctrine. Moreover, the unwitting dialogue between *Flowers for Algernon* and *Gateway* clearly invites the psychoanalytic model of self-reflection to move beyond false consciousness and self-deception formed in individual, familial contexts, in order to consider the nature of ideological mystification. The deployment of psychoanalysis within science fiction thus illustrates an insight drawn from the historiography of psychoanalysis. John C. Burnham argues that history must recognize both 'the importance of psychoanalytic theorists other than Freud' (221) and 'the historical change that takes place when someone reads and learns a new set of ideas and then integrates those ideas with others that the consumer already holds from the rest of the culture' (227). In a similar vein, Paul Roazen notes 'that every country has received Freud's teachings in accord with its own national needs and traditions of thought' (45). What is true for nations and cultures is true also for the literary culture and subculture of science fiction, which has exercised some liberty both in what it takes from psychoanalysis, and how it modifies psychoanalysis in order to find congruence with other generic needs and traditions. By careful sifting and adaptation, science fiction often finds utopian potential within psychoanalysis, and does much to challenge the discursive authority over the self of Freud's bleak historical prognosis.

Chapter 3

Behaviourism and social constructionism

This chapter explores the extrapolation of behaviourist and social constructionist psychologies in science fiction. Behaviourism theorizes the human organism as entirely controlled by its environment; by anticipating the absolute knowledge, prediction, and control of the effects of the environment upon the organism, behaviourist psychology offers the self as a blank slate upon which the specialist can infallibly inscribe his or her preferred vision of society. Although social constructionist psychology works with a very different set of psychological mechanisms, it shares with behaviourism a progressivist ambition to intervene in the social and cultural plasticity of human life. Constructionists attack what they see as the reification by psychology of phenomena such as emotions, cognition, and selfhood, which they believe to be far more culturally variable and conditioned than is typically accepted, and thus open to deliberate (and putatively beneficial) manipulation.

This chapter will examine in depth the behaviourist psychologist B.F. Skinner's *Walden Two* (1948) – which imagines a secluded post-war US utopia – before turning to the more dystopian extrapolation of texts such as Anthony Burgess's *A Clockwork Orange* (1962), famed for the behaviourist conditioning of its young protagonist. The deployment of social constructionist psychology in science fiction will then be explored through a focus on New Wave works that depict the fictional (re)construction of sex, gender, and sexuality through various forms of post-behaviourist cultural engineering. Although texts such as Joanna Russ's *The Female Man* (1975) deploy constructionism in a utopian direction, there is a significant counter-current of science fiction that interrogates constructionist discourses and ambitions.

Behaviourist psychology

The rejection of introspection as a valid method of scientific observation was central to the development of behaviourist psychology as it began to assume form in the opening decades of the twentieth century. The pioneering behaviourist John B. Watson (1878–1958) provides a manifesto-style statement in his 1913 article, 'Psychology as the Behaviorist Views It', which summarizes views he had developed firstly at the University of Chicago, and then latterly at Johns Hopkins. Watson announces that '[h]uman psychology has failed to make good its claim as a natural science' because of 'a mistaken notion that its fields of facts are conscious phenomena and that introspection is the only direct method of ascertaining these facts' (176). Watson's thesis is echoed by the Russian physiologist Ivan Pavlov (1849–1936) in his 1924 lectures: Pavlov hopes to investigate the animal brain 'without any need to resort to fantastic speculations as to the existence of any possible subjective state in the animal which may be conjectured on analogy with ourselves' (16). The same opposition to introspection is found also in the animal psychologist Edward Thorndike (1874–1949), who hopes to show 'that psychology may be, at least in part, as independent of introspection as physics is' (5), and in the work of B.F. Skinner (1904–90), who dismisses the 'psychic fictions' of mentalism (*Behavior* 5).

Behaviourism's opposition to introspection was a deliberate methodological gambit; as Brian D. MacKenzie notes, 'the "principles" involved, and the grounds of the adoption of an anti-mentalism, were *a priori* ones; or at least ones not in any way called for by experimental evidence' (13). Watson's polemical article exemplifies well a shared manifesto of *a priori* assumptions that, though not strictly entailed by anti-mentalism, are typical of behaviourism:

> Psychology as the behaviorist views it is a purely objective experimental branch of natural science. Its theoretical goal is the prediction and control of behavior. Introspection forms no essential part of its methods, nor is the scientific value of its data dependent upon the readiness with which they lend themselves to interpretation in terms of consciousness. The behaviorist, in his efforts to get a unitary scheme of animal response, recognizes no dividing line between man and brute. ('Psychology' 158)

Watson repeats his ambition to study only ontologically objective (i.e. publicly observable) phenomena, rather than the ontologically subjective (i.e. private, first-person) phenomena allegedly known through introspection. Moreover, prediction and control of behaviour are made essential to the scientific status of psychology: as with physics, psychology is knowledge only in so far as it is nomothetic – i.e. it articulates general laws that make behaviour knowable in advance and subject, in principle, to instrumental control. Indeed, the nomothetic assumption characterizes behaviourism as a movement. Pavlov, for instance, concentrates upon the study of the reflex action because it can offer 'regular causal connections between certain definite external stimuli acting on the organism and its necessary reflex reactions' (16). By 'unravelling the mechanism of these machine-like activities of the organism', Pavlov anticipates that 'it may reasonably be expected to elucidate and control it in the end' (8). Furthermore, as Watson's manifesto also indicates, behaviourism promoted methodologies that would supposedly reveal mechanisms that operated across all the higher animals, including humans. Skinner, for instance, was prepared to 'hazard a guess publicly' that the only differences that would be revealed 'between the behavior of rat and man' would 'lie in the field of verbal behavior' (*Behavior* 442).

Had behaviourism informed no apparent advances in knowledge (as defined by behaviourism, at least), then it would have quickly collapsed. Two key behavioural mechanisms were, however, discovered, at least with respect to animals: (1) classical, or Pavlovian conditioning; and (2) operant conditioning, as described by Skinner, and anticipated by Thorndike. Pavlov's account in 1924 of what he calls *'conditioned* reflexes to distinguish them from the inborn or *unconditioned* reflexes' (25) describes the elicitation of an innate reflex by a previously neutral stimulus. The paradigmatic description, as is well known, comes from his experiments in the preceding decades on the conditioning of the salivary reflex in the dog:

> [I]f the intake of food by the animal takes place simultaneously with the action of a neutral stimulus which has been hitherto in no way related to food, the neutral stimulus readily acquires the property of eliciting the same reaction in the animals as would food itself. This was the case with the dog employed in our experiment with the metronome. (26)

Since conditioned reflexes 'proceed according to as rigid laws as do any other physiological processes' (25), Pavlov believed that he had therefore found in learned behaviour the same predictability as was apparent in innate reflexes.

A similar claim was made in an early US experiment in the classical conditioning of the fear reflex in the human infant. John B. Watson and Rosalie Rayner's notable 1920 article, 'Conditioned Emotional Reactions', purportedly describes the conditioning of the fear reflex in 'Albert B.' (1), an eleven-month-old infant. Watson and Rayner establish to their satisfaction the existence of an unconditioned fear reflex in Albert when he is exposed to the sound stimulus created by 'striking a hammer upon a suspended steel bar four feet in length' (2). They proceed to condition this reflex by striking the bar simultaneously with Albert's exposure to a white laboratory rat. The result is, in their view, 'as convincing a case of a completely conditioned fear response as could have been theoretically pictured' (5). By the end of the conditioning process, Albert seems to respond with a fear reflex to the stimulus of the rat presented in isolation. Watson and Rayner also observe what they interpret as the generalization of this conditioned reflex to new stimuli such as a rabbit, a dog, and a fur coat (5–7). Throwing their remaining caution to the wind, Watson and Rayner conclude with a clinical extrapolation of their experiment upon a single human subject: 'It is probable', they assert, 'that many of the phobias in psychopathology are true conditioned emotional reactions either of the direct or the transferred type' (14). Watson and Rayner thus offered an 'origin myth' (Harris 6) for behaviourist human psychology even though a careful reading of their article belies the claim for experimental confirmation of classical conditioning in the human:

> With lots of work they got Albert to cry sometimes and to exhibit a sort of approach-avoidance conflict when they would spring upon him various stimuli. I say 'spring upon him' because I later discovered that they sometimes tossed animals at him, sometimes shoved things like Rosalie's sealskin coat at him, and their method of 'presenting' him with a Santa Claus mask was to have Watson put it on and crawl toward Albert at eye level. (5)

At around the same time as Pavlov, and Watson and Raynor, were investigating the conditioned reflex, Thorndike was engaging in early experiments that later informed Skinner's account of operant conditioning. In his 1911 monograph on *Animal Intelligence*, Thorndike describes the process whereby cats learn to escape from puzzle boxes:

> The cat that is clawing all over the box in her impulsive struggle will probably claw the string or loop or button so as to open the door. And gradually all the other non-successful impulses will be stamped out and the particular impulse leading to the successful act will be stamped in by the resulting pleasure, until, after many

trials, the cat will, when put in the box, immediately claw the button or loop in a definite way. (36)

Thorndike's study of the animal's spontaneous instrumental operations upon the environment – rather than behaviour elicited by stimuli – is subsequently elaborated and developed by Skinner from the 1930s onwards. Skinner distinguishes between respondent conditioning (i.e. Pavlovian) and operant conditioning (*Behavior* 20). In operant conditioning, a class of behaviours (an operation) becomes more probable (is reinforced) in so far as those behaviours bring about a class of reinforcing events (a reinforcer):

> Many things in the environment, such as food and water, sexual contact, and escape from harm, are crucial for the survival of the individual and the species, and any behavior which produces them therefore has survival value. Through the process of operant conditioning, behavior having this kind of consequence become more likely to occur. The behavior is said to be *strengthened* by its consequences, and for that reason the consequences themselves are called 'reinforcers'. (*About* 39)

There are, for Skinner, two categories of reinforcers: positive and negative. These contrasting terms refer to whether the reinforcing event brings something into the environment, or removes (or prevents) something:

> Some reinforcements consist of *presenting* stimuli, of adding something – for example, food, water, or sexual contact – to the situation. These we call *positive* reinforcers. Others consist of *removing* something – for example, a loud noise, a very bright light, extreme cold or heat, or electric shock – from the situation. These we call *negative* reinforcers. (*Science* 73)

In a classic Skinnerian experiment, 'the behavior of pressing downward a small lever' (*Behavior* 48) by a rat is reinforced (made more frequent) by making contingent upon this behaviour a positive reinforcer consisting in the release of food pellets. (The complementary mechanism that extinguishes a particular operation is termed 'punishment' by Skinner; like reinforcement, it may be positive or negative depending on whether the eventuated 'punisher' involves the presence or absence of a stimulus (*Science* 182–93).)

By such methods, increasingly complex behavioural patterns could be gradually inculcated in animals. Keller and Marian Breland, for instance, describe the training of animals to perform complicated routines for public entertainment. The routine of 'Priscilla the Fastidious Pig', who was exhibited in the late 1940s, extended to 'turning on the radio, eating breakfast at a table, picking up the dirty clothes and putting them in a hamper, running the vacuum cleaner around, picking out her favorite feed from those of her competitors, and taking part in a quiz program' ('Field' 202). Behaviourism – and pre-eminently, Skinnerian behaviourism – was, though, robustly criticized, especially in its pretension to provide a complete science of both animal and human behaviour, leading to a gradual post-war decline in its academic and wider cultural authority. Skinner's declaration that he would 'not go beyond the observation of a correlation of stimulus and response' (*Behavior* 10) was intended to repudiate both mentalism and neuralism (the study of the brain and nervous system) as valid avenues of psychological research. The classic cognitivist critique of Skinner's neglect of the inner workings of the organism is Noam Chomsky's thoroughly sceptical 1959 review of Skinner's *Verbal Behavior*, in which Chomsky concludes that Skinner's entire theory of the 'slow and careful shaping of verbal behavior through differential reinforcement' is in fact a *'reductio ad absurdum'* (563) of that same theory, since in fact children learn language 'by casual observation and imitation' (562) of their peers and elders. There were also many other important criticisms that eroded behaviourism. Harlow, for his part, criticized the Skinnerian assumption that learning behaviour leant upon the satisfaction of drives such as hunger and sex. Other criticisms centred on Skinner's propensity to generalize from his experiments with animals. Skinner assumed 'speciational generality': namely that what held true of rats and pigeons would also obtain in other species, including humans (Mackenzie 160). Skinner also assumed 'environmental generality' – which, 'to put it excessively crudely, asserts that the Skinner box is representative of all environments' (160). But it was far from clear that operant conditioning was observable in non-experimental environments, in which the animal was not neatly contained in, for instance, a 'soundproof, dark, smooth-walled, and well-ventilated box' (Skinner *Behavior* 55). Keller and Marian Breland, for example, reported in their later work in the training of animals that 'we have ventured further and further from the security of the Skinner box', and, in so doing, 'we have run afoul of a persistent pattern of discomforting failures' that 'represent breakdowns of conditioned operant behavior' ('Misbehavior' 681). The Brelands suggest, in other words, that what Skinner had discovered were not the underlying principles of animal and human behaviour, but rather some peculiar regularities in behaviour elicited by extraordinary environmental conditions.

Behaviourism and utopia: *Walden Two*

Behaviourists were eager to present their psychology as an important technique for intervention in social problems. As David Seed explains:

> Watson was one of the earliest to make the argument that induced conditioning was simply repeating in a more structured and directed way the process of socialization undergone by every individual. Then in his 1924 monograph *Behaviorism* Watson made his notorious claim that, if he was given twelve healthy infants and his own 'specified world' to bring them up in, he could train them to fulfill any role, regardless of the children's talents. (xii)

Alongside his various discursive statements, Watson authored a very brief utopian sketch published as a magazine article in 1929. In 'Should a Child Have More Than One Mother' (J.B. Watson 'Should'), Watson outlines, as J.G. Morawski explains, 'a thoroughly behaviouristic country with "units" of 260 husbands and wives' that engage in collective parenting by behaviorist principles (1088). Each child rotates through every family for a four-week period until adulthood is reached at age twenty, whereupon the men enter a vocation and women take up domestic life (1088). In Watson's vision, there is no need for familiar institutions of socialization and civic life (including the family), nor for any ethical or humanistic knowledge other than psychology. Instead, these functions and expertise are replaced by 'behaviorist physicians' who 'correct behavior disorders, make decisions regarding euthanasia, and treat insanity' (1088). As Morawski explains, this supposedly progressive psychological blueprint had a definite and largely unexamined set of assumptions: along with other psychological utopias, Watson's ideal was of 'an ordered, harmonious, and unified society in which psychology is a special science and in which psychologists provide expert leadership and implement scientific measures of social control' (1092).

Watson's vision of a psychological oligarchy was subsequently elaborated by the literary endeavours of behaviourism's key proponent, Skinner, who authored 'psychology's most noted utopia' (Morawski 1092), *Walden Two*, which was first published in 1948, and written in '[t]he early summer of 1945', just after the end of the war in Europe (Skinner *Walden Two* v). The title alludes to Henry David Thoreau's *Walden* (1854), an account of the author's two years of relative isolation in a semi-rural cabin of his own construction in Massachusetts. Skinner's utopia, like Thoreau's narrative, promotes self-sufficiency and isolation from the artificial needs of mercantile society; but whereas

Thoreau's narrative concerns an individual, and promotes the virtues of solitude, introspection, and autonomy, Skinner imagines an entire rural community armed with the virtues of self-reliance and self-control, and organized by the collective conditioning of its publicly observable behavioural patterns. *Walden Two* is narrated in the first person by Burris, a college professor previously acquainted with T.E. Frazier, the founder of the new community. Burris decides to travel to Walden Two when he is visited by two former students, Rodgers and Jamnik, who hope that Frazier's community will fulfil their hopes of a better, post-war society. A party of six is eventually formed: Burris; Rodgers and his fiancée, Barbara; Jamnik and his girlfriend, Mary; and Castle, a philosophy professor who is Burris's colleague. Together they travel to Walden Two, where they are each confronted with the choice between returning to normal society or joining Frazier's social experiment. The novel ends with Burris leaving Walden Two, only to change his mind at the last moment – he resolves to resign his university post, and returns to Frazier's community, where he will be re-united with Jamnik and Mary, who have also chosen to remain.

As Kenneth M. Roemer explains, didactic exposition of behaviourist theory and technology in Skinner's novel are subordinated to the utopian literary form: 'very little of *Walden Two* involves explicit expositions of the theories of behaviourism, and both the form and content of the book are dictated by long-established conventions of the literary utopia, particularly the conventions of the guided tour, the Platonic dialogue, and the conversion narrative' (128). Much of the novel is taken up with scenes of dialogue in which either Castle or Burris challenge the practicability or desirability of Frazier's 'cultural engineering' (Skinner *Walden Two* 38). Frazier typically rebuts their counter-arguments, frequently by responding that their objections are merely theoretical or hypothetical, whereas he has established *a posteriori*, from factual evidence, that his innovations are effective and conducive to happiness. As well as the conversion narrative that is threaded through these Platonic dialogues (Roemer 137–39), there is also a *Bildungsroman*, or novel of education, as the narrative traces Burris's acquisition of the putatively more mature psychological capacities characteristic of Frazier's community. Indeed, the inhabitants of Walden Two think of their guests as something like children: as Frazier bluntly announces, when he despairs of explaining his model of child-rearing, 'You wouldn't understand, however, because you're not so far advanced as our children' (Skinner *Walden Two* 102).

The central psychological and economic *novum* of *Walden Two* extrapolates the intuitive self-management supposedly practised by Thoreau in his life at Walden. For Skinner, Thoreau's rural 'tight shingled and plastered house, ten feet wide by fifteen long' (Thoreau 53) allowed the author of the original *Walden* to diminish his exposure to the goods and services offered by the nearby village of Concord. Behaviourism must go beyond Thoreau's isolation ('Concealing a tempting but forbidden object is a crude solution' (Skinner *Walden Two* 99)), and develop a properly effective psychology of self-control. Frazier details the conditioning procedures used to develop in the community's children what he calls 'a tolerance to painful or distasteful stimuli, or to frustration, or to situations which arouse fear, anger or rage' (97). For instance, 'We give each child a lollipop which has been dipped in powdered sugar so that a single touch of the tongue can be detected. We tell him he may eat the lollipop later in the day, provided it hasn't already been licked' (98). Alternatively, 'A group of children arrive home after a long walk tired and hungry. They're expecting supper; they find, instead, that it's time for a lesson in self-control: they must stand for five minutes in front of steaming bowls of soup' (99). One should not assume, however, that this behaviourist technology promotes self-control in the traditional introspectionist sense. The children are, from a strictly Skinnerian point of view, behaving as does a cat that learns to keep still so that its prey can get closer, allowing it to pounce with a greater probability of success. Like the cat, the children learn another mode of operation upon the environment by which the reinforcer is obtained. Frazier's mode of 'self-control' may resemble self-control as ordinarily conceived (the children are waiting, resisting inner urges, building the capacity to tolerate frustration), but is theorized within behaviourism as if it were any other operation – like putting money in a machine or walking to the convenience store.

Leaving aside the plausibility of this fictional technology for self-control, and the tacit redefinition of the concept (a key Skinnerian tactic), its significance to Skinner's utopian blueprint is clear: the citizens of Walden Two, and particularly its younger generations, are psychologically immunized against the manufactured needs of capitalism. As Skinner explains in his foreword to the 1976 edition, he offers the hope that 'by reducing the amount of goods we consume, we can reduce the amount of time we spend in unpleasant labor' (xiv). Or, as Frazier puts it, 'we strike for economic freedom at this very point – by devising a very high standard of living with a low consumption of goods' (57); this is why, for instance, the fashion cycle in *Walden Two* moves very slowly, if at all (28). The progress of Burris towards his eventual conversion can therefore be marked by his reduced dependence on cigarettes (167), while Rodgers' narrative centres on whether he can forego the snares of positive sexual reinforcement offered by Barbara, who would draw him back to the consumerist economy of the outside world. The centrality of anti-consumerism to Skinner's blueprint helps to explain the text's sometimes ponderous details – as Roemer notes, 'Frazier's defense of the tea service, which was carefully designed by domestic engineers, is almost as long and is more enthusiastic than his defense of Walden Two's economic system' (132). While this is no doubt biographically explicable as 'a reflection of Skinner's talent for design' (132), the meticulously efficient self-service canteen has its own textual logic as a lengthy synecdoche for the withering away of the service industries, and for the endless scrutiny of tradition and custom that must be addressed in order to make this happen.

One must acknowledge the utopian impulse of *Walden Two*, which imagines not only a society freed from the labour of obligatory consumption, but also from the concomitant alienated labour of unnecessary goods and services. No one in Walden Two works for money, and it is generally agreed by the citizens that 'even hard work is fun if it's not beyond our strength and we don't have too much of it' (Skinner *Walden Two* 147). However, the utopian dream facilitated by Skinner's fictional technologies has some conspicuous blindspots, even for a text from the 1940s. Unlike the multi-ethnic, jazz-loving city portrayed in Vincent McHugh's utopian New York in *I Am Thinking of My Darling* (173–78 below), Walden Two seems to have little place for diverse cultural traditions. Frazier is abstractly opposed to racism, remarking 'I could not see that hereditary connections could have any real bearing upon relations between men' (291). However, the culture of Walden Two is essentially European (and indeed Anglo-Protestant): music, for instance, means Schumann, Bach, and Gilbert and Sullivan, rather than jazz or swing. Women get an equally uncertain place in Walden Two. Frazer offers a paternalistic critique of 1940s femininity, and the boredom experienced by the 'neurotic housewife' (136). On the other hand, women who disagree with Frazier's views are dismissed in high-handed fashion ('[i]t's sometimes an almost hopeless task to take the shackles off their souls' (137)), even when his opinions seem to imply a re-assertion of patriarchy, such as his belief that 'most girls are ready for childbearing at fifteen or sixteen' (121) – at puberty, in other words. Moreover, disabled, chronically ill, infirm, and senescent persons are conspicuously absent: the text does not even begin to address the need for labour to care for such persons, nor consider the nature, if any, of their contribution to the community.

But, alongside reading Skinner's novel as a utopian blueprint, it is particularly fruitful to consider its unspoken ambition. *Walden Two* is certainly a text that uses psychological discourses to imagine a utopian scheme of human perfectibility realized by various forms of behaviourist conditioning. However, the gratifications of the utopian genre also facilitate Skinner's attempts to secure the reflexive authority of behaviourism: *Walden Two* attempts to construct its readership as psychological subjects in the behaviourist mould by offering Skinner's psychology as the instrument fulfilling various narratives of secularized salvation. To this end, *Walden Two* also, and quite self-consciously, exploits the wider US culture of unchurched religiosity apparent in the syncretic and subjectively authorized spirituality espoused by Thoreau (Hodder 21–24). Burris concedes that 'Frazier's program was essentially a religious movement freed of any dallying with the supernatural and inspired by a determination to build heaven on earth' (Skinner *Walden Two* 289). In this secularized soteriology, salvation is an event that occurs in historical time, and offers a psychological rather than corporeal regeneration: 'What Jesus offered', Frazier declares 'was heaven *on earth*, better known as peace of mind' (97). The earthly-heavenly aspects of Walden Two are amplified by the community's beneficence. Frazier emphasizes that behavioural conditioning in his community is accomplished through (typically positive) reinforcement of desirable behaviour, rather than through punishment (i.e. the weakening or extinction) of undesirable behaviour. Punishment – a term that here covertly acquires Skinner's technical meaning – is not proscribed because of moral or ethical considerations in any familiar sense, but because it is, according to Frazier, an inefficient psychological technology. Punishment, for instance, merely obviates a certain class of operant behaviours: what punished people do is try to avoid punishment – and any number of alternative operations could arise, not merely the right action that one might hope to reinforce. Frazier explains that when we punish a man [*sic*] by, for instance, striking him (a positive punishment in Skinner's terminology), 'We haven't really altered his potential behavior at all. That's the pity of it. If he doesn't repeat it in our presence, he will in the presence of someone else. Or it will be repeated in the disguise of a neurotic symptom' (245) – a point with which Skinner explicitly agrees in his later 1971 text, *Beyond Freedom and Dignity* (62–64).

As well as supposedly showing how to realize in near-future historical time a more humane and loving political regime (blissfully free of 'punishment', at least in the Skinnerian sense), behaviourist technology also gains reflexive authority by offering to solve the ethical problem of the conflict between inclination and duty – or, in *Walden Two*'s approximation, between the desires of the individual and the supply of societal roles. When Castle tries 'to press what appeared to be a case of personal sacrifice for the sake of the community' (Skinner *Walden Two*

21), Frazier argues that persons may be moulded to fit the needs of the community as whole: 'Our members are practically always doing what they want to do – what they "choose" to do – but we see to it that they will want to do precisely the things which are best for themselves and the community' (279). To those who might respond that the inhabitants of Walden Two have been coerced into conformity, the behaviourist reply exploits the semantic shifts typical of Skinner's rhetoric. There is no loss of freedom precisely because the folk psychology of freedom properly resolves into an account only of the 'avoidance of or escape from so-called "aversive" features of the environment' (*Beyond* 42). For Skinner, we are free not in the absence of environmental determination, but by being 'free from' poverty, pain, boredom, isolation, and so forth.

Skinner's rhetoric emphasizes the absence of punishment, the reconciliation of duty and happiness, and freedom from suffering, because these secularized salvational motifs buttress the reflexive authority of behaviourist expertise. Moreover, the grafting of behaviourism into salvational narratives is required in order to ameliorate Skinner's technocratic opposition to democracy, which would threaten otherwise to render behaviourism unpalatable to his post-war US and Western audience. As Roger Luckhurst explains, 'Technocracy [...] claimed to be merely a statement of neutral scientific or engineering fact'; its interwar advocates therefore claimed to transcend 'the politically riven landscape of the 1930s: above capitalism, communism or fascism, they simply promised to run the machinery more efficiently' (69). In similar fashion, Frazier concludes that the world at large, like the inhabitants of Walden Two, should be freed from democracy:

> Do you think a man goes to the polls because of any effect which casting a vote has ever had? By no means. He goes to avoid being talked about by his neighbors, or to 'knife' a candidate who he dislikes, marking his X as he might defile a campaign poster – and with the same irrational spite. No, a man has no logical reason to vote whatsoever. The chances of affecting the issue are too small to affect his behavior in any appreciable way. (Skinner *Walden Two* 249–50)

As Frazier's declamation reveals, behaviourism has rather an unusual analysis of participation in democratic processes: because there is not a secure causal relationship between the operation of voting and reinforcement (i.e. one's preferred candidate winning), the 'real' reinforcers for democratic participation are seemingly a host of other factors (e.g. the cessation or prevention of neighbourhood gossip). One might wonder how Frazier accounts for those citizens whose propensity to vote is positively reinforced by the outcome – those who frequently find that their preferred party wins. The obvious, although tactfully unstated comparison, is with what Skinner elsewhere in 1948 calls 'superstitions' – operant behaviours that are in fact ineffective, but accidentally reinforced by contingencies. When created in a pigeon,

> [t]he bird behaves as if there were a causal relation between its behavior and the presentation of food, although such a relation is lacking. There are many analogies in human behavior. Rituals for changing one's luck at cards are good examples. A few accidental connections between a ritual and favorable consequences suffice to set up and maintain the behavior in spite of many unreinforced instances. ("Superstition"' 171)

Presumably, something similar applies to the voter whose party wins, thereby offering reinforcement for this pseudo-operation upon the political environment. Given that voting is at best psychologically identical with the behaviour of a befuddled pigeon, then Frazier (like Watson) can conclude, to his satisfaction if not of his readers, that government should be left to a small class of specialists to whom this 'worry' has been assigned (*Walden Two* 254), and whose behaviour is properly reinforced by their performance.

Walden Two thus attempts, via various rhetorical strategies, to consolidate the reflexivity effects of behaviourist discourse. The utopian, soteriological promises of the narrative anchor the behaviourist model of the psyche in longstanding salvational discourses which promise that consumerism and capitalism can be tamed, punishment can be ended, and everyone can be happy in their social role. The more disturbing corollaries of behaviourism require careful handling, though, as they contradict other progressivist discourses, particularly from within liberal democracy, and might inhibit the internalization of behaviourist ideas. Skinner's key rhetorical tactic is to insist that the conflict is merely a pseudo-problem – democracy disappears in *Walden Two*, but, according to Frazier, no one has ever truly voted anyway. However, in explaining away objections to behaviourism, Skinner is frequently compelled to invoke discourses that have supposedly been rendered incredible by the advances of behaviourist psychology. For instance, Frazier is entirely dismissive of claims to historical knowledge, because there are, he believes, 'no real laws' that can be inferred from historical analysis (181). Walden Two's library is therefore small because there is no need to preserve primary material for later historical analysis (111–12). Yet, in order to defend his utopia against historical arguments that it must eventually fail, Frazier unashamedly historicizes. Just a few of these self-contradictions are: a generalization on 'the interchangeability of propaganda and progress' with reference to India (194); an explanation of 'the peculiar and extraordinary function of the hero-despot' with reference to Napoleon, and Napoleon-like figures (222); the past misuse of history in '[r]ace, family, ancestor worship' (224); the resilience of class-stratified societies, generalized from India (255); the superiority (in power, if not ethics) of democracy to despotism (256); and a general statement that '[t]he important lasting conquests in the history of mankind [...] had come about, not through force, but through education, persuasion, example' (289).

Nor is such discursive self-contradiction limited to local regions within the novel. A metafictional contradiction haunts the text, and disturbs its attempted reflexivity effect: *Walden Two* as a whole is beset by a 'performative contradiction' between the tenets of behaviourist ideology and the act of fictional story-telling. Frazier frequently protests that only experiments give acceptable answers to ethical and political questions (e.g. 161–64). There is even an extended rebuttal of the objection that Walden Two's results are invalid without the use of a control group (curiously, this is regarded by Frazier as a 'fetish of scientific method' (163)). Yet, when Frazier triumphantly asserts that what 'distinguishes Walden Two from all the imaginary Utopias ever dreamed of' is 'the fact that it exists right here and now!' (179), he unwittingly reminds the reader that *Walden Two* is also an 'imaginary utopia' – a make-believe experiment. Yet behaviourist discourse cannot coherently accommodate the activity of such utopian dreaming, for it translates accounts of intentionality into the schema provided by operant conditioning: the apparent aim of apparent action is the reinforcer, and the apparent action is simply conditioned operant behaviour. But, as Chomsky notes, '*I am looking for my glasses* is certainly not equivalent to [...] "When I have behaved in this way in the past, I have found my glasses, and have then stopped behaving in this way"' – not least because '[o]ne may look for one's glasses for the first time' (571n39). The behaviourist who (pseudo-)intends to create Walden Two is in the same philosophical muddle: the class of reinforcing events (the 'presentation' of a real utopian community, and/or the 'removal' of existing societal problems) that would condition the appropriate operations (finding land, organizing the community, building houses, etc.) is entirely empty. Indeed, even Skinner's official line on literature renders *Walden Two* paradoxical. The 'reinforcing events' putatively created by the 'entertainer, writer, artist, or musician' (*Science* 315) strengthen subscription to the culture that created these works of art and entertainment: 'A culture must positively reinforce the behavior of those who support it and must avoid creating negative reinforcers from which its members will escape through defection' (*Walden Two* xiii). Not only does this make it inconceivable that a work of literature might have an antagonistic relationship to the dominant culture, it is also quite difficult to see in what way – outside of a 'total institution' such as a prison or hospital – one can make books, music, pictures, and so forth, available only to well-behaved citizens.

For a consistent behaviourist, *Walden Two* cannot be part of the project of creating Walden Two. *Walden Two* is thus a book that performatively outruns Skinner's attempts to reflexively construct his readership as behaviourist subjects. Despite Skinner's efforts to authorize behaviourism by grafting it into longstanding progressivist discourses, *Walden Two* recurrently contradicts its textual dominant: the behaviourist utopia cannot so easily lay to rest the supposed pre-scientific models of subjectivity that haunt it, and which underlie political will-formation, historical analysis, and literary practice. The problems of reflexivity that hinder the positive utopian blueprint of Skinner's novel may perhaps explain why behaviourism has more typically been used in the service of critical dystopias that reflexively destabilize the behaviourist model of the self.

Dystopian reflexivity

Although the prestige and ambitions of behaviourism led to the technocratic utopian visions espoused by Watson and Skinner, the school also provoked a series of dystopian counterdiscourses, beginning in the interwar period. Satirically extrapolating the Albert experiment and its successors, Huxley's *Brave New World* (90–98 above) imagines in 1932 the neo-Pavlovian conditioning of the low-status 'Delta' infants, who suffer 'two hundred repetitions' of the simultaneous conjunction of 'books and loud noises', and also 'flowers and electric shocks' (17), so that they may acquire a lifelong aversion to literature and nature. David Seed notes also the deployment of behaviourism in two interwar science fiction narratives: John Wyndham's *Exile on Asperus* (1933) and Joseph O'Neill's *Land under England* (1935), both of which imagine oppressive societies where individuals are conditioned into conformity by behaviourist techniques (Seed xx, xxii). In the post-war era, behaviourism continued to have significant cultural resonance, particularly in its association with mass cultural anxieties about brainwashing (Seed passim). This phenomenon was epitomized in fictional representation by Richard Condon's technothriller, *The Manchurian Candidate* (1959), which imagines a Korean war veteran programmed by the Chinese to be an unwitting assassin; they employ upon him a quasi-Pavlovian technique of 'associative reflexes that use words or symbols as triggers of installed automatic reactions' (36). The dystopian possibilities of behaviourism came to be explored in post-war narratives that unsettle its discursive authority by implicating it in politically repressive and ethically impoverished worldviews (making explicit that which Skinner attempts to banish to the margins of *Walden Two*). Oppressive social control based upon respondent and operant conditioning therefore comes to feature as a *novum* in science fiction texts such as Anthony Burgess's *A Clockwork Orange* (1962), Ursula Le Guin's *The Lathe of Heaven* (1971), and William Sleator's *House of Stairs* (1974). In these dystopian narratives, the ethical and political concerns that Skinner tries to nullify come to the fore in a confrontation with behaviourist discourses.

The conditioned reflex as hegemonic *novum* (rather than Condon's technothriller gadgetry) appears in 'Ludovico's Technique' in *A Clockwork Orange*. Pavlovian conditioning is employed to produce a sensation of overwhelming nausea in the teenage criminal protagonist Alex whenever he feels aggressive emotions: he is repeatedly exposed to films of real and (perhaps) simulated violence while his nausea reflex is simultaneously activated by the administration of an emetic drug. Consequently, when Alex contemplates violence upon a prison attendant, his conditioned nausea is stimulated: 'as I sort of viddied [saw] him in advance lying moaning or out out out and felt the like joy rise in my guts, it was then that this sickness rose in me as it might be a wave and I felt a horrible fear as if I was really going to die' (Burgess *Clockwork* 90). A later demonstration of Alex's conditioning in front of an audience of politicians and prison officials confirms that he is incapable of both physical and sexual violence.

Burgess elsewhere explains that Ludovico's Technique was inspired by the use of aversion therapy upon homosexuals (*1985* 92), and he also displays a fair degree of familiarity with behaviourist theory – including both Pavlovian and operant conditioning, and Skinner's 1971 manifesto for cultural engineering, *Beyond Freedom and Dignity* (*1985* 87–89). Burgess does not at all question the technical efficacy of aversive therapy, which later came to be understood as particularly ineffective with regard to so-called 'conversion' therapies designed to modify sexual orientation (see e.g. Haldeman). The real significance of the Ludovico Technique in *A Clockwork Orange* does not reside in its technological plausibility (it exists alongside other far-fetched elements of the State's psychological armamentarium – Alex is later unconditioned, for instance, by '[d]eep hypnopaedia' (Burgess *Clockwork* 130)). Rather, the Ludovico

Technique allows Burgess to interrogate an underlying ideological assumption of behaviourist psychology, namely the metaphysical thesis of universal determinism, by which there is no difference between Alex 'freely' renouncing violence, and his being reconditioned by behaviourist technology. According to behaviourism, the causes in the former case are merely unknown psychological antecedents masked by the folk psychological explanation of 'free will'. In a later commentary upon *A Clockwork Orange*, Burgess explains his (effectively) existentialist objection to determinism as a political philosophy: 'The State has [...] destroyed a human being, since humanity is defined by freedom of moral choice' (*1985* 93). The prison chaplain in *A Clockwork Orange* speaks for this authorial voluntarist position, in which Alex's virtue is real only if he has chosen freely: 'He has no real choice, has he? Self-interest, fear of physical pain, drove him to that grotesque act of self-abasement. Its insincerity was clearly to be seen. He ceases to be a wrongdoer. He ceases also to be a creature capable of moral choice' (Burgess *Clockwork* 94).

Burgess's claim that 'the kind of humanity that can produce *Hamlet*, *Don Giovanni*, the Choral Symphony, the Theory of Relativity, Gaudí, Schoenberg and Picasso must, as a necessary corollary, also be able to scare hell out of itself with nuclear weapons' (*1985* 94) is also part of the general texture of his worldview, a view that has been called 'Manicheanism' (e.g. Stinson 506–07) in its insistence, in some rather fluid sense, upon the interdependence of good and evil. Burgess's Manicheanism is, as Rabinovitz notes, also informed by the Western importation of Daoist philosophy: 'Another important source of Burgess' theory is the opposition of yin and yang principles in Chinese philosophy. Burgess refers to the yin-yang in his autobiographical first novel, *A Vision of Battlements*, and in a number of essays' (541). A shared interest in Daoism's presumed implications for Western culture may therefore explain the family resemblance between Burgess's work and Ursula Le Guin's 1971 science fiction novel, *The Lathe of Heaven*. Le Guin's narrative, which is set in a near-future 1990s US, tells of the world-altering relationship between a mild-mannered white-collar worker, George Orr, and his domineering psychiatrist, Dr Haber. Orr presents to Haber with an unusual complaint: he believes that his dreams have the power to directly change reality, but they do so in such a way that the past is accordingly altered, so that no-one else notices how the world has been changed. Haber subjects Orr to a dream-augmenting technology, and soon discovers that Orr has indeed been telling the truth: the so-called 'effective dreams' (Le Guin *Lathe* 80) directly change the world, and correspondingly alter history and memory in the process. Haber therefore resolves to use Orr as an instrument with which to carve out a better world where overpopulation, war, and discrimination no longer exist. These and other efforts all backfire, though, with cumulative dystopian effect: the world's population is reduced by a mass plague; peace is brought to Earth by the threat of invading aliens; and racism disappears when different 'races' are blended into a single homogenous grey-skinned people.

As with *A Clockwork Orange*, behaviourism provides a focus for the text's engagement with scientific (re)definitions of the human mind, particularly in terms of anti-mentalist discourse. Haber decides to employ in Orr's psychotherapy 'a simple conditioning treatment in the classic tradition of modern psychology' that will teach his patient that 'he can dream safely, pleasantly' (56). Although Haber is far more neuralist in his interests than a stereotypical behaviourist (he plugs Orr into a machine that reads and augments brainwaves), he shares with behaviourism the basic presumption of a fundamentally public ontology from which subjective experience is eliminated. For Haber, the reality of Orr's dreams is entirely public, as marks made by an instrument: 'When you *see* another man's dream as he dreams it recorded in black and white on the electroencephalograph, as I've done ten thousand times, you don't speak of dreams as "unreal". They exist; they are events; they leave a mark behind them' (12). Indeed, there is a sense in which the novel is about Haber's attempt to force Orr's subjective experience – epitomized by dreaming – into the public, objective world, rather than to allow it to remain in what Haber calls the 'uncanny', 'utter privacy' of sleep (66). When Haber reflects early in the novel on the acoustically transparent walls in his office building, his thoughts convey his fundamental epistemological challenge. Since '[t]he only solid partitions left were inside the head' (5), Haber's task is to break down these partitions, and make common knowledge of the most private experiences – this is why Orr's lawyer initially tries to resist Haber on the legal grounds that the latter is committing a 'breach of privacy' (42). While Haber may be interested in Orr's effective dreaming for its apparent instrumental power, his interest is also in cultivating a form of dream (and, by extension, subjectivity) that is ultimately public: the inaccessibility of subjective experience is an affront to Haber, for whom knowledge (or control) is in itself a paramount value, and ignorance and uncertainty a vice.

Since *Lathe* to some extent valorizes unknowing, Fredric Jameson characterizes it as a novel whose dominant ideology promotes mystical submission to an unmasterable nature. He argues that 'from the central position of her [Le Guin's] mystical Taoism, the effort to "reform" and to ameliorate [...] is seen [...] as a dangerous expression of individual hubris and a destructive tampering with the rhythms of "nature"' (*Archaeologies*

293). Indeed, there is certainly opposition in *Lathe* to the assumption that the mind is by nature a blank slate that may be freely written upon by psychological technologies. The text continually belies Haber's confident statement that the unconscious mind, from which Orr's dreams emanate, is a 'wellspring of health, imagination, creativity', while '"evil" is produced by civilization, its constraints and repressions' (Le Guin *Lathe* 87). For instance, in one of the new worlds created by Haber, war is eliminated, yet violence remains in the spectacle of mass games of killing in public arenas, which seems to indicate some supposed ineradicable core of aggression (133). But *Lathe*'s opposition to constructions of the psyche as a manipulatable raw material extends beyond merely innatism, and into, as noted, a (putatively) Daoist or Manichaean challenge to the ethical presuppositions epitomized by behaviourism. The grey world that is temporarily conjured up in *Lathe* is a cousin to Burgess's ethically insipid 'moral neutrals' (Stinson 508) who have inadvertently removed the possibility for extraordinary goodness in their attempt to eliminate evil. After Haber has eliminated racism by eliminating races (or, to speak more properly, the morphological traits that speciously legitimated racial essentialism), he explains to Orr the superiority of his ethical position over 'fakirs' such as 'Buddha and Jesus': 'They tried to run away from evil, but we, we're uprooting it – getting rid of it, piece by piece!' (Le Guin *Lathe* 129). For Haber, good and evil are essentially ontologically independent: they are as separable in their being as appetitive and aversive stimuli, as a food pellet and an electric shock. Evil can therefore be weeded out of the world to leave only good – a thesis that is perhaps most plausible if the implicit prototype of evil is so-called natural evil such as illness, morality or natural disaster, rather than the moral evil of human wrongdoing. Le Guin's text, however, presents good and evil, in some respects at least, as ontologically dependent, so that to do away with potential or even actual moral evil is to co-relatively diminish the potential or actuality of moral good. Orr, in his non-racial (not even post-racial) world, finds in his memory 'no address that had been delivered on a battlefield in Gettysburg, nor any man known to history named Martin Luther King' (129). While the bad consequences of racism have been entirely weeded out of the world, there has never been the supererogatory (heroic, above and beyond the call of duty) virtues of an anti-racist movement. Furthermore, in Haber's world of grey uniformity, there is no room for the uniqueness that might be an object of romantic love. Orr is aghast at the elision from reality of Lalache, his lawyer and lover, whose 'brown skin and wiry black hair cut very short so that the elegant line of the skull showed like the curve of a bronze vase' are entirely inimical to a world in which 'every soul on earth' has 'a body the color of a battleship' (129). Indeed, parental love has also been eliminated in the grey people's world: children are reared by the state in specialist centres – a consequence of Haber's Skinnerian–Watsonian distrust of the nuclear family, 'the prime shaper of neurotic personality structures' (147).

A Clockwork Orange and The Lathe of Heaven pale in comparison, though, with the sustained engagement in William Sleator's anti-behaviourist novel House of Stairs (1974), which addresses the burgeoning market for adolescent fiction (now termed 'young adult' fiction) that, in the wake of landmarks texts such as S.E. Hinton's The Outsiders (1967), could narrate previously forbidden topics such as sexuality (see Hunt). The novel, set in a dystopian future US, relates the story of five sixteen-year-old orphans: Peter, a repressed gay youth; the rebellious Lola, 'olive-skinned' with 'black eyes' (Sleator 9); Blossom, a manipulative and gluttonous rich girl; the socially conformist Abigail; and finally the charismatic and good looking Oliver. The five – who are strangers to each other – find themselves brought together in a mysterious, Escher-like interior space composed of white staircases and landings. Apart from a rudimentary toilet and water source, the only other feature in this vast Skinner box is a mysterious machine, 'a plastic hemisphere about a foot in diameter, made up of many diamond-shaped facets' (20). The machine dispenses food pellets, albeit capriciously, when the group operate upon their environment in the desired way. Through such positive reinforcement, the machine gradually teaches them a complex group dance performed to the rhythm of its flashing lights and to an audio track of indistinct nonsense syllables (a kind of audio Rorschach test perceived by each of the group in a different way). Once the teenagers have been trained to perform the dance (losing their capacity to distinguish red and green light, which has no operational significance in their controlled environment (76)), the machine begins to reward them for intra-group hostility. Rather than acquiesce to the machine's demands, Lola and Peter retreat to a distant level of the building, where they resolve to starve to death. The others meanwhile engage in increasingly deceitful, aggressive, and humiliating behaviour towards each other – resulting in 'a total mistrust, an incessant wariness, like the constant expectation of a blow' (139) – while nonetheless co-operating sufficiently to perform the dance successfully. Just as Lola is about to surrender, and join the remaining three, the teenagers' time in the house concludes with a *deus ex machina* when the controlling scientist sends down an elevator that removes the group to safety. The conclusion of the narrative reveals that the teenagers have been chosen by the malign Dr Lawrence as potential recruits by the controlling regime, who are forming 'a group of young people, an elite corps, who would be able to follow unquestioningly any order given to them' (162). Blossom, Abigail, and Oliver continue in their career as recruits, while Peter and Lola, who are now firm friends, return to the outside world as rejects.

The dystopian world is sketched in as the central characters remember and share experiences during their confinement. Democracy is in thrall to an oligarchy centred on the 'International Industrial Conglomerates Lobbying Operation' (75); the environment is heavily polluted by constant thick smog that clouds the eight-lane highways (77); numerous children are reared outside the family in large, state-run orphanages, in part because of an unspecified war that left many without parents (14). While the majority population live in 'residential megastructures' (33), and the sexes are strictly segregated (56), the elite – of which Blossom was formerly a member before her parents' apparently accidental death – live in secret walled neighbourhoods where luxuries are freely available. Psychological technologies play an important role in running this society: not only are the teenagers being trained by behaviourist methods, entrants to the oligarchy are also vetted by psychological experts (such as Blossom's late father, who was a psychiatrist).

The dystopian narrative of Sleator's short novel is familiar in its plotline of alienation and attempted challenge to a dystopian social order (in this case, by Lola and Peter) (Moylan *Scraps* 148). Its formal distinction is the use of a cohort of protagonists who seem to stand as socially representative types: the upper middle-class woman and the straight male (Blossom and Oliver) are the least resistant, while the straight female (Abigail) offers some resistance, but not enough to join Peter and Lola, who form a minority alliance. The dystopian world offers some estranging content also, particularly in the complex dance of co-operating antagonists, which offers a figure for competitive consumer capitalism. However, *House of Stairs* is most marked by its full-frontal reflexive engagement with behaviourist discourse. Dr Lawrence is essentially a mouthpiece for the sardonic redeployment of Skinnerian clichés: 'You are *reinforced* to behave the way you do by the results you achieve', he explains to the group, 'People have been studying these patterns of conditioned behavior for years, and we may soon know that everything one does in life can be explained in this way' (Sleator 158). Echoing Skinner's views on cultural engineering in *Walden Two* and later texts such as *Beyond Freedom and Dignity*, Dr Lawrence declares:

> [T]he conditioning most people receive from life, from the real world, is unplanned – haphazard and accidental. Is it surprising then that people are only rarely well adjusted? That only rarely do

they find themselves in a life situation for which their conditioning has prepared them? No wonder that so many people are frustrated and dissatisfied (if not worse), and therefore do not perform with maximum efficiency. (162)

Sleator's riposte to this Skinnerian vision is a hypothetical social order in which young people are prepared for maximally efficient adjustment to their role as state-authorized assassins and torturers, thus overcoming the supposedly pre-utopian conflict between duty and inclination identified in *Walden Two*.

Moreover, to further destabilize behaviourist discourses, the text invites readers to employ psychoanalytic and existentialist categories. Not only is the text's dystopian world gender-segregated, it also represses sexual variations, such as Peter's barely conscious sexual attraction to his former roommate – 'Jasper's strong, hard body as he got into bed, so different from Peter's. Strong, to protect him, to take care of him' (34). Moreover, Peter's frequent fantasies and daydreams are part way between classical Freudian narcissistic regression and existentialist bad faith. He retreats to an imaginary womb-like space to avoid dealing with the reality of the house: 'The walls of the room swayed with rainbow colors, and the furniture seemed to be alive, each object with its own benevolent personality, murmuring comforting words to him, enclosing and protecting him. He let himself drift into it, cradled in the warm, underwater, rainbow-hued dimness that undulated around him' (61). In contrast is the existential freedom displayed firstly by Lola, and only latterly by Peter. As Abigail observes:

> Lola did what *she* wanted to do. To Abigail, who was always considering what boys thought of her, or what the other girls in her group would think, who was always trying to avoid doing whatever might hurt someone, or make her disliked, Lola's behaviour was hard to understand. It made Abigail, in some strange way, feel trapped; trapped, and then resentful of Lola's freedom. (80–81)

Such existential categories are elaborated in Dr Lawrence's attempt to impose a dehumanizing phenomenology upon the group – the three who co-operate 'no longer saw one another as people, but only as things to make use of' (140). Moreover, the narrator's rhetoric emphasizes sardonically the behaviourist continuity between machine, animal, and human. The first time Blossom is encountered feeding at the machine, Lola initially hears 'an undefinable series of noises, partly whirring and mechanical, but also strangely moist' (19), and then sees 'a bulge of white cloth, [...] it took her a moment to realize that it was a person, sitting on the floor with her back to the hole' (20). As the machine dispenses its cylindrical food pellets, Blossom eats heartily, with 'animal sounds' (20), then later 'leaned forward and stuck out her little red tongue automatically, reaching out her hand to catch the food without even looking at it' (23).

The frequently existentialist and psychoanalytic tenor of Sleator's behaviourist dystopia offers a discursive resistance to the promulgation of Skinnerian discourse in the post-war decades. The rhetoric of Skinnerian reflexivity effects is countered by alternative psychological models of the self, inserted as critical alternatives to a society of totalitarian conformity. Whatever Skinner's hopes as expressed in his fictional and polemical writings, science fiction thus plays its part in eroding the authority of behaviourism. With the gradual retreat of this psychological school from the imaginary worlds of science fiction writers (in parallel with its declining cultural authority), so later ideas of social constructionism begin to come into prominence. Nonetheless, this newer discourse invites not only utopian but also dystopian extrapolation, with echoes of the oppositional discourses that challenged behaviourism.

Social constructionism

Kenneth J. Gergen (1935–) is the US psychologist most associated with the development of social constructionist psychology. In his landmark 1973 article, 'Social Psychology as History', Gergen challenges psychology's disciplinary pretension to provide knowledge of human behaviour analogous to that provided by the physical sciences. He notes that in general '[a] paramount aim of science is held to be the establishment of general laws through systematic observation', and that in social psychology specifically, 'such general laws are developed in order to describe and explain social interaction' (309). However, this foundational nomothetic ambition to explain, as Pavlov put it, the 'machine-like activities of the organism' (8) is argued by Gergen to be merely wishful, at least with respect to social psychology. The psychological subdiscipline of social psychology, he argues, characteristically acquires knowledge of phenomena with only a contingent increase in predictability and control.

Gergen provides two classes of argument for this conclusion. The first set of arguments revolves around issues of reflexivity (35–39 above): 'Science and society constitute a feedback loop' ('Social Psychology' 310) in which discourses may be adopted or resisted by the subjects who are the objects of psychological investigation. Theories for instance may pretend to disinterested observation, but in fact contain an 'evaluative bias' (310) that 'subtly *prescribe[s]* what is desirable' (311): among Gergen's examples are stadial theories of moral development such as Lawrence Kohlberg's, which, Gergen claims, 'demean those at less than the optimal stage' (312). The circulation of psychological knowledge may also mean that 'previous patterns of behaviour are modified or dissolved' (313) in other ways, such as when measures are taken to forestall undesirable patterns of behaviour. Gergen examines the so-called 'risky-shift' whereby 'decision-making groups come to make riskier decisions through group discussion': 'should the risky shift become common knowledge, naive subjects would become unobtainable. Members of the culture might consistently compensate for risky tendencies produced by group discussion until such behaviour became normative' (313). Furthermore, what Gergen calls '[i]nvestments in freedom' may mean that, as a matter of principle, we are inclined to 'feel resentful and react recalcitrantly' (314) where we understand that psychological knowledge is being used to control our behaviour.

Gergen's second kind of argument against the nomothetic pretensions of social psychology proceeds from the historical (and thus also cultural) contingency of its supposed laws. '[W]e soon realize', he argues, 'that the observed regularities, and thus the major theoretical principles, are firmly wedded to historical circumstances' (315). For instance:

> [C]ognitive dissonance theory depends on the assumption that people cannot tolerate contradictory cognitions. The basis of such intolerance does not seem genetically given. There are certainly individuals who feel quite otherwise about such contradictions. Early existentialist writers, for example, celebrated the inconsistent act. Again, we must conclude that the theory is predictive because of the state of learned dispositions existing at the time. (315)

Because of such arguments, Gergen makes a practical inference in 'Social Psychology as History' that there should be a challenge within psychology to its 'disciplinary detachment from *(a)* the traditional study of history and *(b)* other historically bound sciences (including sociology, political science, and economics)' (319). In a later 1985 synopsis of social constructionism, Gergen almost entirely concerns himself with the general disciplinary implications of history and culture for both the objects of psychology and the practices of psychological explanation. He argues that once psychology takes seriously 'the historical and cultural bases of various forms of world construction', then phenomena such as childhood, romantic and maternal love, and the autonomous self are revealed to be reified products of social processes ('Social Constructionist' 267). Indeed, not only do psychological phenomena become denaturalized, 'removed from the head and placed within the sphere of social discourse', psychological explanations also come to be seen as 'historically and culturally situated, institutionally useful, normatively sustained, and subject to deterioration and decay as social history unfolds' (271).

For Gergen, the vicissitudes of the emotions in psychology are exemplary evidence for social constructionism. He surveys the enormous historical disagreement over what emotions there are, and which are primary:

> If the emotions are simply there as transparent features of human existence, why should univocality be so difficult to achieve? Broad agreement exists within scientific communities concerning, for example, chemical tables, genetic constitution, and the movements of the planets; and where disagreements have developed, procedures have also been located for pressing the nomenclature towards greater uniformity. ('Metaphor' 60)

The polyphony of emotion discourse indicates, to Gergen, that psychology typically, and mistakenly, 'treat[s] the putative objects of our mental vocabulary as palpable, where it is the names themselves that possess more indubitable properties. Because there are words such as love, anger, and guilt, we presume that there must be specific states to which they refer' (61). By studying key metaphors of emotion from twentieth-century psychological discourses, Gergen concludes that '[e]ach of the traditional metaphors essentializes the emotions – treating them as biological, sensory-cognitive, or energetic givens – there in nature, to be interrogated by science. In effect, the metaphors portend the existence of an obdurate domain outside the realm of social construction' (77).

Social constructionism questions the existence of such an 'obdurate domain' not just with reference to the emotions, but also a variety of other supposedly stable psychological phenomena, such as cognition, selfhood, sex, gender, and sexuality. Constructionist accounts of sex, gender, and sexuality have, for instance, been prominent in the work of notable pioneers such as Sandra Bem (1944–2014) – whose utopian research on gender schema theory will be considered elsewhere in greater detail (248–49, 252–54) – and Rhoda K. Unger (1939–). The latter's 1979 article 'Toward a Redefinition of Sex and Gender' is a landmark in feminist constructionist psychology. Unger contends that psychology should adopt the term 'gender' to describe 'those characteristics and traits socioculturally considered appropriate to males and females' (1085), with a view to a research programme in which it is less likely that 'psychological differences between males and females will be considered explicable mainly in terms of physiological differences between them' (1093). As later commentators have recognized (e.g. Poulin), Unger's article was a central statement in the feminist constructionist erosion of unthinkingly biological explanations for gender differences.

Social constructionism and science fiction's destruction of patriarchy

Although it departs from the nomothetic aspirations of behaviourism, constructionism shares with its predecessor certain affinities that inflect similarly its deployment in science fiction. Both schools open the way for utopian reconstruction by insisting on a public ontology of malleable psychological objects (with constructionism typically substituting terms such as '(social) discourse' for the earlier vocabulary of 'behaviour'). The social (re)construction of gender and sexuality provides a useful analytic focus in this chapter. As noted above, post-war feminism and constructionist psychology overlap in time, place, and political purpose. Moreover, the contemporaneous New Wave of science fiction imagines novel forms of sexed, gendered, and sexual life, frequently from a feminist perspective. As Rob Latham explains in his analysis of so-called 'sextrapolation', 'the feminist critique of normative gender roles and sexual relationships' was a significant trend within New Wave science fiction (262), and served also as 'a counterweight to the more or less explicit misogyny of the sexual revolution' (263). Science fiction may ask, hopefully or otherwise, what would happen if the seeming psychological givens of patriarchy (such as naturalized gender and sexuality) are wholly or partially dissolved in a future or alternative social order. The following argument explores firstly a landmark feminist New Wave deployment of gender constructionism, before moving to some neglected texts that (rightly or not) discern dystopian meanings alongside the more familiar utopian extrapolations associated with the reconfiguration of sex, gender, and sexuality.

Joanna Russ's feminist science fiction classic, *The Female Man* (1975), is explicitly informed by psychologies of a broadly social constructionist nature. As Judith Kegan Gardiner explains, *The Female Man* uses the science fiction trope of parallel realities to imagine multiple protagonists who are 'genetic[ally] identical quadruplets brought up in varied societies' ('Empathic' 92). These four female protagonists vary enormously: Joanna is an authorial alter ego; the conventionally feminine Jeannine inhabits an alternate history where post-war feminism never occurred; the adventurous and self-reliant Janet comes from Whileaway, an all-female future world; and the warmongering Jael fights in a future war between Manland and Womanland. Yet their differences are all to be understood as the effect of different socio-cultural environments: 'The novel presents its multiple first-person heroines to dramatize how different any one might be if raised in a different society. In this sense, it illustrates common feminist beliefs about the priority of culture over nature and about the socially constructed determination of both gender and personality' (93).

Russ's social constructionism clearly has some specific influence from the anti-psychiatrist R.D Laing (1927–1989) – or at least from that part of Laing's writings that are constructionist (Laing's existentialist contribution to psychology in science fiction is considered elsewhere (192–95)). The epigraph to the *Female Man* is taken from Laing's countercultural manifesto, *The Politics of Experience* (1967). In the quoted passage, Laing describes various interpersonal, or social psychological, operations by which 'Jack' invalidates various aspects of the discourses produced by 'Jill'. Such 'transpersonal invalidation' (Russ *Female* vii), argues Laing, is ubiquitous. Russ's wider familiarity with Laing is exemplified further in a 1980 essay where she refers, in the context of a discussion of Laing, to 'the kind of unspoken family command or "script" of which modern psychology so often speaks, injunctions like Be a failure, Never have enough, Live without love, and so on' ('On' 63). In *The Female Man*, social relations under patriarchy are therefore didactically represented as inducting women into a network of norms and discourses that are falsely reified into what one male interlocutor, an academic, calls 'women's psychology' (Russ *Female* 43). This process of construction begins, according to the narratorial voice, in infancy:

> Baby Laura Rose, playing with her toes, she's a real little sweetie-girl, isn't she?
> Sugar and spice.
> And everything nice –
> *That's* what little girls are made of!
> But her brother's a tough little bruiser (two identical damp, warm lumps). (200)

Such formation of what is depicted as an essentially neutral, mouldable material continues via the internalization of various discourses, which

Russ frequently articulates in terms of scripts and roles, such as those taken on by the women at a dinner party attended by Janet in her visit to Joanna's world:

> A ROUND OF 'HIS LITTLE GIRL'
> SACCHARISSA: I'm Your Little Girl.
> HOST (wheedling): Are you really?
> SACCHARISSA (complacent): Yes I am.
> HOST: Then you have to be stupid, too. (35)

The psychology mobilized in such passages is clearly consonant with later work in the constructionist research programme on phenomena such as gender stereotyping (see, for instance, Fine).

The didactic, feminist aims of the social psychological vignettes in *The Female Man* are clear. However, as well as cognitively estranging 'women's psychology', *The Female Man* also has a definite reflexive ambition to recuperate (or construct) women's anger under patriarchy. As Catherine Lutz explains, anger is normatively excluded in constructions of female psychology: 'Every emotion but anger is disapproved in men and, conversely, expected in women' (137); moreover, '[b]ecause emotion is constructed as relatively chaotic, irrational, and antisocial, its existence vindicates authority and legitimates the need for control' (139). Pat Wheeler, with specific reference to Russ, argues that the latter's fiction 'renegotiates the constraints of gender roles and compulsory heterosexuality and validates women's anger as part of the debate against essentialism. Anger is expressed against cultural, physical, and ideological oppression and is used as a positive force of expression' (113). The Whileawayans, the narrator remarks, are 'not nearly as peaceful as they sound' (Russ *Female* 48): Janet has 'fought four duels' and 'killed four times' on Whileaway (2), and has no qualms about physically confronting, and defeating, sexually and physically aggressive men on Joanna's Earth (45–47).

Russ's feminist extrapolations have generally met with a sympathetic reception from literary critics. However, there are elements in *The Female Man* that typically escape comment, and that invite reflection on some of the blindspots in Russ's work, such as its tendency to celebrate the insertion of women into patriarchal roles and relations. The obverse of Russ's feminist constructionism is an exculpatory, and indeed essentialist, blindness to the possibility of female sexual violence. This is particularly notable in a scene where Janet 'seduces' Laura Rose, a twelve-year-old girl from Joanna's Earth. The authorial interpolations 'Don't Janet', 'Don't exploit' (70) are vitiated by ironic commentaries that present prohibitions on such relations as merely anonymous scripts that further constrain women: *'everyone knows* that if you start them young they'll be perverted forever and *everyone knows* that nothing in the world is worse than making love to someone a generation younger than yourself' (70). The scene is putatively rendered innocuous by the absence of male biology: since no penises are involved, there can be no sexual violence. Moreover, *The Female Man* is curiously unreflective about what might loosely be called its American-ness, but which, for a lack of a more elegant term, could be more precisely described as its 'USAnian' character: the Whileawayans are gun-toting frontierswomen schooled in an ethic of self-reliance enforced by infantile separation from the mother, and by arduous rites of passage. Russ's feminist utopia is thus unproblematically imagined in a USAnian mould as a world renewed by the morality of the frontier (cf. Abbott).

The unthinking cultural imperialism and disavowed essentialism of *The Female Man* problematize Russ's discussion of her supposed textual 'others'. In her 1980 essay, '*Amor Vincit Foeminam*: The Battle of the Sexes in Science Fiction', Russ robustly, and justifiably, expresses her revulsion at Edmund Cooper's 1972 novel *Gender Genocide*, or, as it was titled in the UK, *Who Needs Men?* (the UK text and edition will be used for direct quotations). Set mainly in Scotland, and clearly drawing upon popular cultural tropes later exploited in the Highland romance novel (see Hague and Stenhouse), the text is unlikely to be canonized within contemporary Scottish literature. Russ summarizes the setting: '250 years in the future, an all-female, technologically advanced society occupies southern England and periodically sends exterminators north to kill the primitive survivals of patriarchy in northern Scotland' ('*Amor*' 49). As the novel itself explains, the 'Republic of Anglia' contains about three million women, and the Highlands about thirty thousand men, with associated womenfolk and children (Cooper 54), although the latter number is rapidly declining. The protagonist, Rura Alexandra, is a novice 'exterminator' from the parthenogenetic elite of the Republic (the majority of women are cloned). Although tasked with wiping out the remaining men in the Highlands, she falls for the chief of the Highlanders, Diarmid MacDiarmid, whom she encounters early on in the narrative, and whose life she spares out of pity and, it is implied, sexual desire. When Rura is later captured (and gang-raped) by Highlanders, Diarmid spares her life, and together they start a doomed love affair, punctuated by guerrilla warfare against the Borders Regiment of which Rura was previously a member. The narrative ends as Diarmid and Rura (now Rura MacDiarmid) are finally tracked down and killed by female exterminators.

Russ reviles Cooper's novel for its misogyny, which is epitomized in the text's assertion, via a female character (a retired Exterminator, who was once impregnated by a 'pig'), that rape is 'a myth. No woman [...] who is conscious and uninjured can be raped' (Cooper 46; Russ *'Amor'* 50). As Russ correctly notes, the narrative also attempts to persuade its readership that 'for women, heterosexuality is so much physically pleasanter than lesbianism that it binds a woman not only to sexual pleasure but to one man in particular and to a whole ideology of male dominance' (*'Amor'* 51). In the novel's ideological dominant, heterosexual pleasure secures the patriarchal alignment of sex, gender, and sexual preference inside the 'heteronormative matrix'. A Lawrentian primitivist discourse is invoked to describe the supposed regenerative effects of 'natural' sexual psychology upon the constructionist social conditioning that has produced Rura:

> A man – this man by her side – had washed away twenty years of conditioning. He had loved her; and while semen had pulsed excruciatingly, wonderfully, through her vagina, she had seen the look in his eyes; and had known the dissolution of Rura Alexandra and Diarmid MacDiarmid. There had been left only man and woman. Not man the rapist and woman the sex object. Just man and woman. Nature, throbbing with joy. Nature, goddess of seasons and harvests. Nature, mistress of life and death and birth. (Cooper 110)

Via Diarmid's actions and words, the text insists that while homosexuality may be socially constructed, a form of 'brainwashing', heterosexuality is natural, rather than being itself merely another variety of 'brainwashing':

> [Diarmid:] 'We are always short of women. We raid for them. Often we can get rid of this homosexual nonsense they have been taught, pretty damn fast. Your society has brainwashed them into thinking that Lesbian love is the greatest, but their bodies know different. And their bodies learn very quickly.'
> Rura shuddered. 'That, too, is brainwashing.'
> Diarmid laughed. 'Not brain. Breasts and vagina. Brain was quite a late appendage in evolutionary development.' (87)

Constructionist psychology is admitted into the text's discourse, but only as a veneer laid upon a fundamental evolutionary inheritance. Rura's 'learning to become a woman' (137) is not the replacement of one social construction with another, but is instead a matter of 'peeling away a superficial person and discovering something quite different underneath' (137–38).

Matters are further complicated by the *pathos* of the text, which alludes to Native Americans (55), and to the end of Highland culture in the eighteenth century as so famously depicted by Walter Scott in novels such as *Waverley* (1814). (There may also be a hint of the Vietnam War in the Exterminators' use of helicopters and their fondness for incinerating native villages.) Although the men are literally being exterminated (the regenerative powers of their semen notwithstanding), this biological destruction is an opportunity for the text to proleptically lament the extinction of patriarchal culture. During a pastoral interlude, Rura and Diarmid take refuge in a Highland cottage where they find the skeletal remains of a married heterosexual couple. Not only do Rura and Diarmid take on the roles of this couple, they discover further remnants of their almost-extinct culture:

> There was a trunk in the cellar, a steel trunk, locked. Diarmid broke the lock. Inside the trunk were the remains of a white dress, an old wedding dress perhaps, and a man's black suit. And underneath these were books. All kinds of books. A history of the Highland Clearances, a book on astronomy, the poems of Robert Burns, the novels of Sir Walter Scott. Books, books, books. (131)

Although Rura and Diarmid temporarily resuscitate patriarchal culture, their efforts are doomed: when they are eventually hunted down and killed, their organic death is a metaphor, and a metonymy, for a 'cultural genocide' directed against patriarchy.

Cooper's novel is, of course, a crude masculinist production that unfortunately confirms Lindner's early psychoanalytic suspicion that science fiction is compensatory wish-fulfilment for life's losers – in this case, men threatened by 1970s feminism. Russ's critical judgement is overwhelmingly valid. Indeed, the very stridency of the claim to naturalized heterosexuality in Cooper's novel tends to undercut the textual dominant: why is there all this drama and desperation if heterosexuality is so inevitably appealing to women? (Diarmid's crude evolutionary appeal hardly helps – he seems to think that cerebration evolved after mammalian biology.) Nonetheless, the latent critical dialogue between Russ and Cooper is not entirely one way. The essentialist mythology of sexually aggressive maleness in Cooper's novel parallels a similar construction of sexual difference in *The Female Man*, which has difficulty representing female sexual violence. Moreover, whatever the greater literary merits of Russ's novel, it certainly has little sense of the cultural parochialism with which it colonizes the feminist future (unlike, say, the contemporaneous feminist utopia in Marge Piercy's *Woman on the Edge of Time* (195–99)). Russ's constructionist expectation that 'our traditional gender roles will not be part of the future, as long as the future is not a second Stone Age' ('What' 93) has therefore not always been endorsed fully by science fiction. Naomi Mitchison's *Solution Three* (1975) is a more ethically and aesthetically advanced novel than Cooper's text, yet it too interrogates the sexual utopianism of constructionist psychology. Mitchison's narrative is set in the near future after 'the terrible crisis of Aggression', a global war that has led to 'the annihilation, as living and food-producing places, of large parts of the Earth's surface, including many major cities' (Mitchison *Solution* 7). The planet is ruled by a world government known as the 'Council', which aims at 'a world at last with a dropping population, and with a genuine diminution of aggression, group or personal' (7). In order to reduce overpopulation, birth is largely state regulated, and live births are normally of clones, which are brought to term and raised through infancy by an elite of so-called Clone Mums. The clones themselves are of either 'Him' or 'Her', the unnamed leaders who emerged after the crisis period, and who are generally regarded as the paragons of human perfection – indeed, the Clones are intended to take over the world's ruling Council (60). Part of the general admiration for Him and Her arises from their primary solution to the problems of aggression and overpopulation, a solution that is the central *novum* of the text: 'The challenge to aggressive inter-sexual love came first from Her; then the challenge was made still clearer in the Code which He homologated and by the Council itself. When that age-old sexual aggression changed to non-aggressive love of man for man and woman for woman, overt aggression dropped in the same curve as the still dropping popu[lation]-curve' (80). For a citizen of the world under Solution Three, such as Ric the historian, heterosexuality, and procreative heterosexuality in particular, is an outmoded cultural form, 'the women giving birth, popping the new lives out, over-populating, until at last it was realized that the attraction between the sexes was only a snare and an aggression; the real thing was man to man and woman to woman' (16).

The society of *Solution Three* is one in which monogamous heterosexual relations have been superseded by a non-possessive homosexuality enforced largely by social conditioning. The introduction of Solution Three began with 'intensive school-age hormone and psychological treatment during the years of population crisis' (16–17). Such measures were later supplemented by propagandizing in the mass media, and particularly by discursive interventions in writing for women:

[S]ocial changes could be made through the ordinary advertisement channels, once one got hold of them. Persuasion was, after all, such an expert business; it had only to be applied, both subliminally and overtly, through the many media. The essential was to get at the females and so much more could be done through a slanting of their favourite reading. (23)

At the time of the main narrative action, the solution is largely self-maintaining and enforced almost entirely by social construction: '[T]he absolute numbers [of non-clone births] dropped year by year. People do not on the whole break their customs and social morality and face the disapproval of their peer group for something as unimportant as inter-sexual love' (16). Given that the normative homosexuality within the world of Solution Three is a non-possessive 'free-love', a great deal of casual semi-public sexual activity takes place as a matter of convention. When, for instance, Jussie and Elissa, who are lovers, meet in the Council, their sexualized greeting is quite conventional: 'Jussie looked hungrily and simply had to stroke Elissa down, along shoulder to buttocks, and pull her for a moment into the same chair. Elissa responded with a quick hand between Jussie's legs, but just as a greeting' (15). This norm of non-possessiveness extends also to child-rearing: sexual reproduction (which Mitchison seems to identify with heterosexual procreation) is particularly intolerable since it encourages the possessive love of mother and child. When Miryam, a heterosexual 'Professorial', complains to Jussie about her cramped living conditions, the latter offers to have the children taken away and raised in a nursery (45–46).

To a certain extent, Mitchison's text deploys essentialist mythologies of aggressive heterosexuality, and utopian sexual reconstruction, with a knowing wink. The narrative, rather than being a blueprint utopia, revels in the opportunities offered by an estranging, carnivalesque world in which norms are turned upside down. The estranging function is clear: although heterosexuality is not strictly forbidden by law, the residual straight population are regarded as '"social misfits"' (13) even by members of the ruling Council. Tolerated, but hardly celebrated, hetero-sexuality is 'not against the Code', but 'utterly distasteful' (122). The 'deviants' (118) who practise it are a 'tiny minority' harried by feelings of shame and insecurity 'with their colleagues' eyes and tongues on them' (40), and can express their love openly in only a few public spaces 'known for being friendly to heterosexual deviants' (41). As well as giving straights a fictional taste of their own medicine, the text also invites an estranging reversal of other majority–minority relations. Tobacco cigarettes are regarded as 'doped' (93), while cannabis is normalized as 'the aggression dispeller' (88), and is even smoked during governmental meetings 'on occasions when hatred, anger and prejudice might have crept into the minds of the Council' (88). The majority population are also vegan, mostly because animals 'were such inefficient makers of protein and fat or milk constituents', but also because of 'civilized sentiment' against aggression, even between species (61).

Yet the text also alludes, with far greater subtlety than Cooper's *Gender Genocide / Who Needs Men?*, to a more sinister side of constructionist discourses – a recurrent theme first indicated by the anxiety expressed in Mitchison's authorial epigraph to James Watson, the co-discoverer of DNA, 'who first suggested this horrid idea' (4). The relatively attenuated discrimination against heterosexuals in the centres of world power is greatly amplified in peripheral areas where Solution Three is enforced. Miryam, a heterosexual 'Professorial' with children (Professorials are particularly resistant to sexuality propaganda), travels to Outer Mongolia to look for old strains of wheat, and encounters the darker side of the new order: 'Ulan Bator had been almost under control populationwise, though some of the methods were very unpleasant, especially the whipping of deviants by non-deviants. As deviant women were often not recognized until late pregnancy this resulted in the nastiest kind of aggression; there were occasional public castrations to the sound of drums' (102). Nor is the official world government opposed to the use of violence. There are planes and helicopters at the ready for when normal processes of pacification fail (150). Furthermore, since the Clones are intended to be as close as possible to Him and Her, there are frequent ominous references to 'the period of strengthening when, in a time-shortened psychological copy of the stresses in His and Her life, they were taken away and things were made to happen to them' (35). Whatever precisely is involved during this forced separation, it is so painful that the Clones are unwilling to talk about it.

The main kind of power in the world of *Solution Three* is however the 'soft power' of persuasion, as Mitchison's text interrogates the idea that political oppression must necessarily be built upon the use of state violence. Constructionist technology may have its own subtle, destructive potential. As Susan M. Squier explains, Solution Three relies on 'softer coercions': those, for instance, 'who are unwilling to abide by the mandated homosexuality, or wish to reproduce in vivo, are given substandard housing and less job access' (173). This soft coercion extends to the suppression of historical cultural difference: the historian Ric – who accepts as a truism the homosexual love between 'Jesus and John, Hadrian and Antinous', and 'Stalin and Beria' (Mitchison

Solution 48) – reflects on his conviction that 'history must be re-made in order to flower profitably and beautifully. Just as flowers and fruit are constantly re-made. He was thinking of his current work on Castro and Che, the scraps of evidence floating and pinned' (49). Historical and cultural alternatives to Solution Three are erased from history, even though the solution itself relies upon the possibility of culturally constructing a 'homonormative matrix' analogous to the 'heterosexual matrix' of patriarchal culture. This is why the heterosexually procreative population in the peripheral areas of Outer Mongolia are deviant not only in resisting Solution Three, but also in shunning consumption of the world government's propaganda: 'though the scattered villagers had transistors and sometimes listened to songs, they didn't bother with them much but preferred making their own' (105).

A definite psychological interrogation of the soft power of Solution Three occurs in Mitchison's depiction of the mother–child relation, which she represents as stubbornly natural, as a part of human nature that is not merely a blank slate upon which social constructionist forces can inscribe. A Clone Mum, Lilac, tries to resist the removal of her infant Clone by the world state, but is defeated by Jussie, who perceives that it is time for the Clone to be taken away and toughened up (echoing practices in Russ's Whileaway). In a clear allusion to Bowlby's attachment theory (a psychology that Mitchison explores at length in other texts (67–79)), Lilac protests: 'He was mine. [...] Fed on my milk. My little mammal. My own' (95). She is sententiously rebuked by Jussie, 'You know it is wrong for one person to assert ownership over another, even a lover, but most of all over a little child. A little Clone' (96). Lilac's consequent reflections articulate the historical parallel implicit in Mitchison's text. The world of Solution Three is a totalitarian state that imposes an ethic of universal love upon an evolved nature that stubbornly maintains elements of particular love:

> The police state. But not police any longer: instead watchers and carers. Jussie. And who was suffering? Not so much ordinary people who had suffered in the police states in the old days and been bullied and unhappy and lost their identity. No, now it was the baby Clones and the Clone mums who must fight for them. The suffering was going on, pinpointed this way. (95)

As Katerina Kitsi-Mitakou explains, the world government soon manages to re-assert its non-violent control over Lilac: 'She is [...] quickly and easily benumbed with the help of aggression dispellers [...], such as cannabis and sexual excitation. Stroking and smoking, and the offer of a job by Jussie, a Council member, and later Lilac's girlfriend, make Lilac forget her Ninety (the number of the baby boy)' (215). Nonetheless, Lilac's grief for her broken maternal relation is felt also at higher levels of power. Even a conformist senior official such as Mutumba 'cried for secretly and long' (Mitchison *Solution* 36) when separated from her own Clone child.

Mitchison locates the anti-constructionist psychology of attachment theory within a wider evolutionary and ecological representation of the limits of Solution Three. Part of *Solution Three* is taken up with the response to diseases that threaten the standardized plant crops upon which the remaining world population depends, particularly the '[w]heat, rather ominously standard, all the same height, colour, genetic formula, tailored to its environment' which is grown across large areas of centrally-managed land (69). In a Council discussion of this new danger, Ric alludes to 'a novel' (an outmoded genre in the future) from 'the second half of the twentieth century' (115), which foresaw the possibility of an infection that destroyed food crops. This intertextual allusion is almost certainly to John Christopher's 1956 novel *The Death of Grass* (88–89 above) which depicts the worldwide collapse of civilization because of the effects of the 'Chung-Li virus', which at first destroys rice before jumping up a taxonomic level to infect all the grasses, thereby eliminating the world's cereal crops and pasturage (22–23). The human race's failure to defeat the Chung-Li virus is presented not as an inevitability, but as a consequence of a particular solution used early on. Roger, a civil servant, explains: 'There were two schools of thought about tackling that virus. One wanted to find something that would kill the virus; the other thought the best line was breeding a virus-resistant rice strain'; he adds, 'if they'd found a virus-resistant rice, that would have solved the problem properly. You can almost certainly find a resistant strain of anything, if you look hard enough or work on a large enough scale' (22). Unfortunately, a crop treatment is used that leaves behind, at first unnoticed, the strain that affects all the grasses.

The moral of Christopher's story is carried over into *Solution Three*, which at a straightforward scientific and technological level warns against the reduction of biodiversity via an overdependence on intentionally selected strains of food crops. Symbolically, however, the idea of biodiversity is mobilized as a warning against the socio-cultural homogeneity of Solution Three. When Jussie reflects that '[t]here were probably still wild wheats, triticums of some kind, in parts of central Asia, small places which had resisted education. Yes, just as the Professorials had!' (Mitchison *Solution* 24), she makes the connection for readers between biological and cultural diversity: if one is necessary for human survival, so, insists Mitchison's text, is the other. *Solution Three* ends with the successful recovery of wild species drawn from the Earth's diminishing gene pool. The analogy is driven home as the Council comes to recognize that the mass-produced Clones may present an equal liability, since 'a kind of excellence which exactly fitted a certain epoch might, soon or late [*sic*], need certain alterations' (153). The supposed lesson from human genetics is echoed in the cultural plane: a more accommodating relationship is found with the heterosexuals of the text, who are both handy proponents of sexual reproduction and also a cultural equivalent to the rare wild strains. The overall ethical equation is formalized in the novel's closing sentence, spoken by the Councillor, Jussie: 'There are so many kinds of happiness. According to the genes' (160).

Admittedly, there is something clumsy in Mitchison's predication of sexual reproduction upon heterosexual preference. *Solution Three* ignores the possibility of, for instance, artificial insemination or *in vitro* fertilization between the sexes, even if the parents in question are homosexual in preference. Sexual reproduction, which introduces genetic diversity via 'the sin of meiosis, the upsetting of reason and planning, re-shuffling the chromosomes just anyhow' (92), is thus rather a retrograde metaphorical vehicle for Mitchison's exploration of diversity and difference. Heterosexual reproduction *in vivo* is unthinkingly naturalized in *Solution Three*, in a way that few would find plausible today. The text, having introduced the possibility of the cultural extinction of heterosexuality, thus assuages the anxieties of its majority readership. Not only do some people, particularly among the academic Professorial classes, seem entirely resistant to the social conditioning of homosexuality, there even emerges – by some unknown mechanism – a small number of heterosexuals among the population of Clones, that 'rising forest of genetic excellence' (24) whose preferences were assumed to be innately homosexual.

More positively, though, Mitchison's text marks a transition in political discourses, from the politics of redistribution, to concerns with identity and the environment. The future Earth of *Solution Three* has effectively addressed material inequality: everyone is roughly equal in wealth, and there is no such thing as private property, or ownership of others' labour. But politics, and history, still go on: biodiversity and cultural difference are threatened, and the question arises of a new 'solution' that would preserve them. The estranging representation of marginalized heterosexuality is chastening for those who might think that minorities are sufficiently protected by rights-based discourses: the heterosexuals of *Solution Three* are free to be straight, but are denigrated by the dominant culture's 'social character'. The missing ingredient is 'recognition': the affirmation that their sexuality can be the parameter of a successful life, rather than a disabling, limiting form of 'deviance' (Appiah 111). The puzzle-solving narrative of Mitchison's novel thus endorses biodiversity (in response to the agricultural and human eugenics of Solution Three) as well as cultural diversity (as an answer to the misrecognition of minorities). As Esa Väliverronen explains, the power of the term 'biodiversity' as 'a metaphor in semiprofessional and popular discourses' is 'linked to its origin as a scientific concept' (31). Mitchison's vindication of identity politics takes the rising popular scientific authority of 'biodiversity' as a supposedly uncontentious good, and transfers it to cultural diversity, further cementing 'the "biocultural" transformation in contemporary society' (Väliverronen 32).

Conclusion

By insisting on the basic malleability of human psychology, behaviourism and social constructionism both inform science fiction extrapolations in which apparent 'human nature' is rendered fluid in order to be remoulded in some utopian (or dystopian) shape. Behaviourism's impoverished sense of its own technocratic assumptions, and its identification of knowledge with instrumental mastery, mean that wholehearted utopian extrapolations such as Skinner's *Walden Two* are uncommon. Instead, behaviourism is more often interrogated by critical dystopias, in which existentialist motifs present a particularly antithetical discourse. Social constructionism, on the other hand, tends to be destabilized by questions, whether implicit or explicit, about what is natural. Such questions may be crude (Cooper's Lawrentian ravings), or far more informed and subtle (Mitchison's representation of attachment psychology), but they nonetheless gesture towards a concept of the natural – a concept that even behaviourism and social constructionism cannot dispense with if they suppose that we are, by nature, cultural animals. Moreover, a powerful counter-discourse can be perceived in both behaviourist and constructionist science fiction, whether in the grey-skinned dystopia of *The Lathe of Heaven*, or in the cultural extinctions depicted in *Solution Three* (or even *Gender Genocide / Who Needs Men?* in its own unsavoury way). The question arises: to what extent is the re-engineering of culture the imposition of homogeneity upon an existing diversity of contingent practices? Such an opposition of a fragile, diverse cultural environment to Enlightenment universalism was outlined in the post-war era by Isaiah Berlin's anti-utopian philosophy:

> The idea of a single, perfect society of all mankind must be internally self-contradictory, because the Valhalla of the Germans is necessarily different from the ideal of future life of the French, because the paradise of the Muslims is not that of the Jews or Christians, because a society in which a Frenchman would attain to harmonious fulfilment is a society which to a German might prove suffocating. But if we are to have as many types of perfection as there are types of culture, each with its ideal constellation of virtues, then the very notion of the possibility of a single perfect society is logically incoherent. This, I think, is the beginning of the modern attack on the notion of Utopia, Utopia as such. (40)

Science fiction, however, can adapt this critique to a more optimistic direction: the better, if not perfect world, imagined by critical utopia, and indicated also by dystopia, must accommodate a pluralism of communities and identities. The diverse traditions into which we are born and raised become an analogous resource to the biodiversity of the natural world.

Chapter 4

Existential-humanistic psychology

This chapter explores the deployment of existential-humanistic psychology in science fiction. This school of psychology was formed by a post-war syncretism of European existential philosophy and psychiatry with the empirical work of Anglophone psychologists dissatisfied with existing psychological approaches, particularly behaviourism and psychoanalysis. The research of European psychological and philosophical authorities such as Erich Fromm, Victor Frankl, Karl Jaspers, and Jean-Paul Sartre, was brought into the traditions of US and British psychology by figures such as Gordon W. Allport, Abraham Maslow, and R.D. Laing. Existentialist ideas were used to challenge what were seen as the dogmas of post-war Anglophone psychology, such as a reductive approach to value, a methodological neglect of first-person experience, and a presumption of mechanical psychological causality.

The primary texts analysed in the chapter are contemporaneous with the flourishing (and decline) of Anglophone interest in existentialism that extended from the 1940s to the 1970s. The proto-existentialist 1940s science fiction of Vincent McHugh is examined, followed by a discussion of Colin Wilson's later, explicitly existentialist science fiction from the 1960s and 1970s. Wilson, despite the frequent crudity of his work, provides a useful port of entry – and extracanonical comparator – to more accomplished writing by Doris Lessing, Theodore Sturgeon, Naomi Mitchison, and Marge Piercy. All these authors employ fictional *novums* that elaborate existential-humanistic tenets – although, as will be shown, their extrapolations work to quite different effects, ranging from visions of spiritual apotheosis, to politically engaged revolutionary utopianism.

Existential-humanistic psychology

Anglophone existential-humanistic psychology was consolidated by the US publication in 1958 of *Existence*, a collection of essays by European existential therapists such as Henri F. Ellenberger (1905–1993), Eugene Minkowski (1885–1972), and Ludwig Binswanger (1881–1966). In an introductory essay to the collection, the leading US existential psychologist Rollo May (1909–1994) argues that the condition of conventional psychology and psychiatry is such that 'serious gaps exist in our way of understanding of human beings' – gaps so serious, in fact, that the therapist or doctor cannot be sure that he is 'seeing the patient as he really is, knowing him in his own reality' (3). Only with a proper account of human being, or *Dasein* ('being-there' – a term derived from Martin Heidegger's existential philosophy (Heidegger)), can the psychologist – including the psychiatrist or psychotherapist – properly encounter the individual person. Existential-humanistic psychology sets out a varied stall of conceptual merchandise with which to supposedly better grasp the reality of human being: these include a distinction between authentic and counterfeit values; a recuperation of 'final' (or intentional) causation; 'meaning' in the sense of a certain kind of life-affirming value; freedom against determinism; a phenomenological method; and – in the form of hermeneutics – methodical reflection upon the understanding of words and actions.

Although *Existence* was published in 1958, the groundwork had been prepared in Anglophone culture by popular pioneers such as Erich Fromm (1900–1980), whose landmark text *Escape from Freedom* was published in 1941 in the US, and in 1942 in the UK (under the title *The Fear of Freedom*). Fromm, who had fled Nazi Europe, argues that although modern man [*sic*] is formally free, 'to know what one really wants is not comparatively easy, as most people think, but one of the most difficult problems any human being has to solve. It is a task we frantically try to avoid by accepting readymade goals as though they were our own' (*Fear* 218). Many – and perhaps most of us – live inauthentic lives in which, lacking self-knowledge, we slavishly conform to the life patterns dictated to us by 'anonymous authorities' (220) – with the pathological extreme being, in Fromm's analysis, Nazi Germany. Fortunately, the capacity for spontaneity is not entirely lost:

> Most of us can observe at least moments of our own spontaneity which are at the same time moments of genuine happiness. Whether it be the fresh and spontaneous perception of a landscape, or the dawning of some truth as the result of our thinking, or a sensuous

pleasure that is not stereotyped, or the welling up of love for another person – in these moments we all know what a spontaneous act is and may have some vision of what human life could be if these experiences were not such rare and uncultivated occurrences. (224)

By promoting such experiences of spontaneity, we may find (or create) life goals that are genuinely our own, and so fully develop our own unique, latent potentialities: 'The genuine growth of the self is always a growth on this particular basis; it is an organic growth, the unfolding of a nucleus that is peculiar for this one person and only for him' (227). Rather than adapting the individual 'to the rules of our society, expressed in terms of success, popularity, earning capacity', explains Fromm in a 1939 article, psychotherapy should aim to help the patient 'to become the subject for his own feelings and thoughts, that he should be able to feel what *he* really feels, to think what *he* really thinks, and to want what *he* really wants, instead of feeling, thinking, and wanting what he believes he is supposed to feel, think, and want' ('Social' 229).

As Fromm's emphasis on authentic conation indicates, existential-humanistic approaches rehabilitate the Aristotelian category of so-called 'final' causation – i.e. the cause of events and actions by intentional agency. The prominent US psychologist Gordon W. Allport (1897–1967) states in *Becoming* (1955) that European existentialism 'admonish[es] psychology to strengthen itself in those areas where today it is weak' (79), particularly in the phenomena of what Allport calls the *'proprium'*, 'all the regions of our life that we regard as peculiarly ours' (40). Of particular importance within these functions of emphatic individuality is what Allport calls the 'propriate striving' (56) that is constituted by '[t]he possession of long-range goals, regarded as central to one's personal existence' (51). The actions of propriate striving (exemplified in Allport's book by the lifelong project of the polar explorer, Roald Amundsen) are not motivated by 'a state of tenseness that leads us to seek equilibrium, rest, adjustment, satisfaction, or homeostasis' (48). Propriate striving is instead characterized by 'its resistance to equilibrium: tension is maintained rather than reduced' (49) in the pursuit of 'distant and often unattainable goals' (68). Such insistence on the validity of intentional causality within life-defining and life-affirming projects is fundamental also to the work of the Viennese existential therapist Viktor Frankl (1905–1997). He similarly argues in *Man's Search for Meaning* (first published in English in 1959 as *From Death-Camp to Existentialism* (Pytell 297–98)) that 'mental health is based on [...] the tension between what one has already achieved and what one still ought to accomplish, or the gap between what one is and what one should become' (106), rather than upon the achievement of 'equilibrium or, as it is called in biology, "homeostasis," i.e., a tension-less state' (107).

Accompanying the centrality of final causation to authentic human identity is a revised theory of value. The axiology (value theory) of existential-humanistic psychology provides a non-hedonistic account in which value is primarily inherent in a meaningful and spontaneous life, rather than in, for example, the pleasure of tension reduction. Frankl makes this point when he proposes 'a *will to meaning* in contrast to the pleasure principle (or, as we could also term it, *the will to pleasure*) on which Freudian psychoanalysis is centered' (99). Meaning can be found in certain kinds of action, in experiences of love and artistic reception, and even – perhaps notoriously, given Frankl's experience in the Nazi camps – in suffering (114–17). Similarly, for the US psychologist Abraham Maslow (1908–1970), psychology should attempt to locate and scientifically investigate subjective sources of meaning and value in a historical epoch in which traditions, or other external locations of value, have lost their authority (*Religions* 9). Maslow alleges that this recuperative aim has typically been neglected by psychology: 'the positivistic psychologists, the behaviorists, the neo-behaviorists, and the ultra-experimentalists [...] feel values and the life of value to be none of their professional concern' (5–6), while the Freudians accept 'that values are taught, in the traditional sense of indoctrination, and that they must, therefore, be arbitrary' (7). The answer to this neglect or deauthorization of value, Maslow believes, lies in a scientific investigation of so-called epiphanic 'peak experiences', so that they may be generalized beyond their pre-modern confinement to 'the private, lonely, personal illumination, revelation, or ecstasy of some acutely sensitive prophet or seer' (19).

Another important tenet of existential-humanistic psychology is famously central to the mainstream of European existentialism, namely the thesis that human beings have free will. The French existential philosopher Jean-Paul Sartre (1905–1980) famously insists that '[h]uman freedom precedes essence in man [*sic*] and makes it possible; the essence of the human being is suspended in his freedom' (*Being* 25). This tenet emerges without modification in the existential-humanistic work of Frankl, who criticizes the psychological prejudice towards 'pan-determinism': 'Man is *not* fully conditioned and determined but rather determines himself whether he gives in to conditions or stands up to them. In other words, man is ultimately self-determining. Man does not simply exist but always decides what his existence will be, what he will become in the next moment' (132). Even Allport, who is more metaphysically modest than Frankl, reserves a place for sudden, unpredictable change in his concept of 'saltatory becoming', which is – as its etymology in Latin *saltare* (to dance or jump) implies – essentially a leap of faith whereby 'the very center of organization of a personality shifts suddenly and apparently without warning. Some impetus, coming perhaps from a bereavement, an illness, or a religious conversion, even from a teacher or book, may lead to a reorientation' (87). Maslow also deploys such conversion experience in opposition to psychological determinism. He describes how, during a peak experience, the person putatively becomes 'more self-determined, more a free agent, with more "free will" than at other times' (*Religions* 67).

The phenomenological method also inheres in existential-humanistic psychological research and practice. As Maslow recognizes, 'Existentialism rests on phenomenology, i.e., it uses personal, subjective experience as the foundation upon which abstract knowledge is built' (*Toward* 9). The ontologically subjective realm that might be dismissed by, for instance, behaviourism, as mere psychic effluvia, or even as non-existent, becomes the object of close study. To take a paradigmatic example, Sartre interprets the subjective experience of vertigo not as an effect of efficient causation within the organism producing a feeling of dizziness, but as a direct subjective experience of freedom – the freedom to negate any resolutions, or motives, or psychological determinants, and to throw oneself over the precipice:

> If *nothing* compels me to save my life, *nothing* prevents me from precipitating myself into the abyss. The decisive conduct will emanate from a self which I am not yet. Thus the self which I am depends on the self which I am not yet to the exact extent that the self which I am not yet does not depend on the self which I am. Vertigo appears as the apprehension of this dependence. (*Being* 32)

Allport invites his readers to a similar phenomenological awareness when he calls attention to the direct experience of the bodily aspects of core identity: 'Think first of swallowing the saliva in your mouth, or do so. Then imagine expectorating it into a tumbler and drinking it! What seemed natural and "mine" suddenly becomes disgusting and alien' (43). A phenomenological approach also clearly informs Maslow's investigation of peak experiences, where it is melded with a large-scale empirical investigation. A sample of around 270 human subjects are invited to provide a phenomenological account of 'the most wonderful experience or experiences of your life; happiest moments, ecstatic moments, moments of rapture, perhaps from being in love, or from listening to music or suddenly "being hit" by a book or a painting, or from some great creative moment' (*Toward* 71). From these reports, Maslow constructs a phenomenological essence, or what he calls 'an impressionistic, ideal "composite photograph"' (71) of the peak experience.

Maslow's investigation of peak experience hints at another important aspect of existential-humanistic psychology, for his subjects are being invited to find adequate, perhaps even innovative verbal expression for their extraordinary experiences. An important strand of existential-humanistic psychology foregrounds questions of verbal and psychological understanding, or of *Verstehen* (German *understanding*), particularly as developed in the modern German-language tradition of the *Geisteswissenschaften* (German *human sciences*) epitomized by Wilhelm Dilthey (1833–1911), Hans-Georg Gadamer (1900–2002), and others. The German-Swiss psychiatrist and theologian Karl Jaspers (1883–1969) in his *General Psychopathology* (1913) argues that, rather than resting upon laws of psychology, human understanding of action 'is satisfied with the comprehension of quite a different sort of connection. Psychic events "emerge" out of each other in a way which we understand. Attacked people become angry and spring to the defence, cheated persons grow suspicious' (302). A similar, interpretative methodology is also required for what 'has been fully expressed in some movement, utterance, or act' (307). The understanding of meaningful phenomena requires a different methodology to the explanation of events conceived as natural phenomena: understanding 'is gained *on the occasion* of confronting human personality; it is not acquired inductively *through repetition of experience*' (303).

Although Jaspers asserted that 'schizophrenic psychic life' was '*ununderstandable*' (577), the Scottish psychiatrist (or 'anti-psychiatrist') R.D. Laing (1927–1989) later argued that the inability to understand psychosis was due to the clinician's failure to exercise sufficient empathy:

> The personalities of doctor and psychotic, no less than the personalities of expositor and author, do not stand opposed to each other as two external facts that do not meet and cannot be compared. Like the expositor, the therapist must have the plasticity to transpose himself into another strange and even alien view of the world. In this act, he draws on his own psychotic possibilities, without forgoing his sanity. (*Divided* 34)

This methodology was further pursued in Laing's case studies with his colleague Aaron Esterson (1923–1999) of disturbed young people in *Sanity, Madness and the Family* (1964), where he and Esterson promise their readers that '[c]linical signs and symptoms will become dissolved in the social intelligibility of the account that follows' (32). In the case of one young patient, her apparent voice-hearing arises because of an understandable, if peculiar response to her parent's behaviour towards her. The voices that she hears are her own thoughts, but thoughts that she has disavowed: '[s]he herself disclaimed being the agent of her own thoughts, largely, it seems, to evade criticism and invalidation' (45). Similarly: 'she sought temporary refuge in her own world, her private world, her shell. To do this, however, was to be "negative", in her parent's jargon: "withdrawn" in psychiatric parlance' (44). By the time of Laing's counter-cultural manifesto, *The Politics of Experience* (1967), it is even promised that the most florid of psychotic states can be understandable as *metanoia*, as a profound psychic voyage that changes the personality: 'Madness need not be all breakdown. It may also be break-through. It is potentially liberation and renewal as well as enslavement and existential death' (110).

To provide a systematic account of existential-humanistic psychology is a task impossible in the present (perhaps any) context. To a greater extent than other psychological sub-disciplines, there is a cultivated distrust of theoretical consensus and system-building: as Henryk Misiak and Virginia Staudt Sexton explain, 'Existential psychology, inspired by existential philosophy, is not a school but a *movement*, which focuses its inquiry on man as an individual person as being-in-the-world' (84). What has been presented here is a discussion of a few central features that anticipate the following extrapolations of existential-humanistic psychology within science fiction.

Proto-existentialist science fiction: *I Am Thinking of My Darling*

Even as Fromm's writings were beginning to popularize ideals of authenticity to an Anglophone, and particularly North American audience, in the late 1930s and early 1940s, so science fiction was articulating a simultaneous extrapolation of proto-existentialist ideas, long in advance of authors such as Wilson or Lessing. *I Am Thinking of My Darling* is a critically neglected utopian science fiction novel first published in 1943 in the US, and written by Vincent McHugh (1904–1983), an author prominent in the New York City arm of the New Deal Federal Writers' Project (Mangione 155–90). McHugh's intellectual interests remain unclear, but his novel endorses, whether consciously or not, ideals of authenticity such as those advanced by Fromm's existential therapy – indicating if not direct influence, at least the articulation of a contemporaneous sensibility primed and ready for theorization by existential-humanistic psychology.

I Am Thinking of My Darling takes place over a single week in the 1940s in New York City, running from Tuesday 17 February (McHugh 1) to Monday 23 February (281). The first-person narrative depicts New York in the grip of a mysterious contagious disease, known popularly as 'the fever', which brings about a significant, albeit temporary psychic transformation, alongside some minor physical effects. The fever, also known as 'Martineau's disease' (117), arrives on a liner that picks up the contagion during a stop in Guadeloupe (117–18). Those who contract it are released from their subservience to social conventions surrounding work, marriage, gender, class, and race, and find themselves psychologically free to pursue their deepest personal inclinations. What is released is not aggressive Freudian instinct, but instead what the Commissioner of Health calls 'a mass epidemic of good feeling. Joy. Happiness. Whatever you like. Potentially it's as dangerous as a riot or panic or any other disturbance' (53). New York becomes a far happier, but far less organized place, as its citizens begin to pursue more fulfilling personal and professional lives. The protagonist, Jim Rowan, who begins as Acting Commissioner of the Department of City Planning (5), finds himself elected 'executive assistant to the Acting Mayor' (41), and occupies a key role running New York behind the scenes. Rowan struggles to hold together the public infrastructure of police, fire, and health, and other utilities, even as the fever spreads to the majority of the population (including the original Mayor, who resigns office to pursue his private passion for model trains (37)). Rowan's narrative is complicated by two further factors. The first is his search for his wife, Niobe, an actor who contracts the fever early on in the story and who flits across the city in different roles and disguises, continually evading Rowan's grasp, and appearing latterly as 'Miss Sanderson' (277), a leading light in the newly-formed Society for the Preservation of Happiness (261). The second complication is that Rowan himself contracts the fever. Even though he sticks with his job – which he clearly finds personally fulfilling – Rowan falls into various picaresque escapades, including a series of unpredictable sexual encounters with female friends, colleagues, and acquaintances. Although some intensive biomedical research produces a vaccine, as well as an effective cure (a Vitamin C pill), the contagion is eventually halted by a spell of cold weather, which has an inimical effect on the virus. New York returns to a rather more uneasy version of the *status quo ante*, and Niobe returns to Rowan.

The novel's week of happy anarchy positions the narrative generically as an unusual hybrid of science fiction utopia with Saturnalian disruption. A novelist character describes the epidemic as a period of

'Mardi Gras' (239), and Rowan himself reflects that 'the Lord of Misrule was a woman and the woman my wife' as he pursues their 'grimly comic domestic duel' across the backdrop of the city (176). What may strike the contemporary reader most forcefully is the novel's apparently prophetic force as a sociological anticipation of the 1960s counterculture. Although no precise year is given, the decade is specified as the 1940s (e.g. 136), and the day–date combination would point to 1942, which seems to indicate an alternate history in which World War Two did not arrive to US shores in December 1941 (and perhaps did not occur at all). The New York witnessed by Rowan has the air, to later readers, of a countercultural *topos* like San Francisco, with (in McHugh's eerily prescient language) '[t]he unmistakable feel of a place with its hair down and a flower dangling over one ear' (129). The novel clearly depicts the epidemic's 'victims' as a vanguard social movement intent on the pursuit of personally fulfilling, self-authored lives: 'I read the legend in white paint on the crosswalk: THE WORLD IS YOURS FOR THE ASKING. ASK FOR IT. Revolutionary indeed. Well, happiness – whatever that was – would be revolutionary for most people. Right now it looked a bit messy, like most revolutions. But in twenty years, fifty, a thousand – why not?' (235). The Society for the Preservation of Happiness emerges as a vast popular force, with elements of the civil rights and feminist movements in its organization and rhetoric. Niobe's antiphonal address to a mass stadium meeting of the Society foresees a multi-ethnic community rallying less around revolutionary socialism and more around the desirability of authentic lives pursued without exploitation and discrimination:

> She said in a voice that curled like a whip inside you: 'What do you want?'
> 'Happiness!' they shouted. The galleries rolled with it.
> 'Do you want to take it away from somebody else?'
> 'No!'
> 'Do you want to beat down somebody else to get it?'
> 'No!' (278)

Niobe continues:

> 'Is it free as the sky for everybody?'
> 'Yes! Yes!'
> 'Is it free for the white man and the yellow man and the colored man?'
> 'Yes! Yes! For everybody!' (278)

Rowan, for his part, witnesses the final, abortive match of the Society just as the cold weather sets in, 'A disorderly march, filling the street from curb to curb. Recruits pouring in from every cross street. Men, women, and children of all the colors and nationalities under heaven' (288). He understands that '[t]his wasn't a parade. It was a folk movement, a vast human migration – men, women, children, and animals. Gentle and resistless, marching with banners. Horns and banners. Where to, for God's sake? Where?' (288).

The novel leaves unanswered the exact historical destination of this multi-ethnic 'folk movement'. However, a focus on the prescience of *I Am Thinking of My Darling* distracts from the existential significance of its central *novum*, the fever. Observed externally, the signs of the fever are apparently minor. The disease incubates in a couple of days, runs its course in eight to ten days, and is marked by '[e]xhilaration at onset, eyes also sometimes affected the first day, slight soreness at base of skull continuing for duration of attack' (117). The virus, however, is a *novum* that propels the infected person to a higher level of existential self-perception, granting a faculty that penetrates everyday self-deception – as Niobe observes in a telling dialogue recalled by Rowan, 'Does everybody that's unhappy know *why* – or even that he *is* unhappy?' (22). The psychological effects of the *novum* are described medically as consisting in 'Pronounced euphoria. Great sense of well-being. Personality harmony. And no more morals than a tomcat. No responsibility. But no rough stuff either. Very well behaved. Gentle. Too happy to want to hurt anybody' (50). Crucially, the virus is primarily a 'predisposing factor' that creates a state of enhanced perception, or 'hyperesthesia' (142). In a curious encounter, Rowan overhears a learned colloquy (drifting across from an adjoining building) while enjoying a one-night stand. One of the discussants suggests that the virus has provoked 'a revival of sensibility – already latent, mind you, in the social situation' (219).

The phenomenology correlating with these observations is depicted in Rowan's first-person narrative as he recounts the heightened sensibility created by the fever. Even eating breakfast is a celebration of the senses: 'my God, what a mortal luxury of sharp sweetness in the orange juice. Like the first fruit of the Bahamas in Columbus's salty mouth. That breakfast was to eating what love, the several kinds of love, is to a quick trick' (171). Rowan seems to be in the grip of an enduring *avant-la-lettre* peak experience, which he compares to 'the first few weeks of a convalescence from pneumonia. A good analogy in some ways. The springtime feeling. The freshness of the senses and the gentle euphoria and the flooding of hope' (172). The world shines as if you'd never seen it before, as if there were a light behind each separate particle of it. It looks and smells and sounds and tastes intolerably bright. You feel that you can see structure of it as you see the veins in a leaf against the sun. It has a new unearthly *value*' (172). The psychological result is a 'harmonious and inexhaustible level of vitality. Not mere energy or vigor. Vitality' (172).

The apparently prophetic sociological extrapolations of McHugh's novel are therefore anchored in a phenomenology of authenticity and spontaneity. The fever is an external agent that promotes a mass epidemic of saltatory existential leaps: the vast majority of New Yorkers apprehend their own unhappiness and resolve to pursue spontaneous goals. On one hand, this certainly means a great deal of unfettered sexual desire in the narrative. As part of Rowan's own adventures, he feels, for instance, an (unconsummated) desire for his African-American maid, Rachel, whom he perceives as 'beautiful – a tall gracefully knit brown girl with a clean coppery glow to her skin', 'looking like a very modern angel in a stained-glass window' (169). Female sexuality is also unleashed, and depicted in a serious of Carvinalesque vignettes in which Rowan – and other males – become '[p]etticoat bait' (100):

> The girls seemed to be doing the hunting. [...] A girl would plant herself in front of you and look up at you – 'Mmmm! Definitely my type' – and the man she'd been with would wave good-by, take three or four steps, and find himself corralled again. It was all good-natured enough, though I saw a lone cop shorn of his buttons and two sailors blindfolded with their own neckerchiefs and led away, not unwillingly, by a group of hilarious women. (100–01)

On the other hand, the fever's effects are conceived more broadly than merely the release of Freudian libido, or even just autonomous desire. The fever brings about a complete transformation in which the formal autonomy of the liberal subject is supplemented by the pursuit of authentic needs, which may typically be unexpressed or even unconscious to the average citizen. New Yorkers shift careers, not because work is inherently an unpleasant activity, but to find greater fulfilment: Rowan is informed that '[a]bout a quarter of people who left their jobs had taken new ones. An architect became an insurance man, a florist opened a gymnasium, and so on. Hope there for us. But everybody seemed to shy away from a good many of the essential jobs' (65). Marriages dissolve as both men and woman leave unfulfilling relationships, while others retrain themselves, taking up educational courses and 'new studies, mainly the arts and aviation' (65). The mass transformation is narrated metonymically via changes in clothing that express the inner, authentic life of Rowan's fellow citizens. He observes '[m]en in hunting jackets and corduroys. Some with flies stuck in their rumpled hats, or wearing house slippers. Men in overalls and jumpers. Baseball uniforms. A few yachting caps. One old sea lion was sporting the three stars of a commodore' (203). The change is even more striking in women, as Rowan infers that 'the girls, most of them for the first time, were dressing and acting up to their own secret idea of themselves': 'The general effect was more conservative than you'd imagine but striking enough. For one thing, they seemed to lose any sense of being inferior as women, or vis-à-vis other women. This made for free trade and a pleasanter time all round' (204).

Darling is an early critical utopia, one which uses the emerging ideal of personal authenticity to query the American Dream as instantiated in 1940s New York. Although Rowan must struggle to keep New York running, the disruptive effects of the fever are clearly valorized throughout the narrative, and offered as a counterpoint to the commonsense reality that sees as inevitable the '[d]iscomfort caused by the part of the personality that's kept on a chain by convention' (142). The story asks the reader to dream of a social organization in which authenticity would be possible for as many people as possible. Indeed, a brief metafictional commentary on the novel's critical utopianism emerges when Rowan tracks down the disguised Niobe to a public class run by Paulsen, a novelist and academic. Paulsen stresses to Niobe that representing the city in its present condition would exceed normal novelistic make-believe since the reader would have 'to accept a *double* convention, as in fantasy. But this is tougher than fantasy – Here he's got to believe that *both* your realities are real at the same time. First, the way the city and the people acted *before* this fever came along and, second, the new human logic *after* the fever got them' (239). Paulsen, within the world of *Darling*, explains that the epidemic has 'a new *norm* for us, a new way of life. At the same time the old norm still operates, especially as a field of reference. That makes a pull between them, a tension. And there you have the principle of social change' (239–40). The commentary is as much for McHugh's actual readership as for Paulsen's fictional reader: the utopia of *Darling* offers a temporary norm that stands in tension with the world as it is known through everyday realism – and suggests in that tension a possibility for social change.

Hidden faculties, latent affinities:
The existential parasites of Colin Wilson and Doris Lessing

The post-war years saw the continuing dissemination of existential ideas in Anglophone culture through exponents such as the UK author Colin Wilson (1931–2013), who is best known for his briefly voguish 1956 manifesto, *The Outsider*. 'At its core', explains Stefan Collini, 'stands the figure of "the Outsider", a romanticized individual who, liberated from the mundane preoccupations and social constraints of the common herd, dares to seek Truth [...]. In doing so, he (they seem all to be men) adopts an "Existentialist" attitude [...]. The label vaguely gestures towards a kind of personal or mystical insight' (417). Wilson's status as a home-grown UK existentialist public intellectual in the mould of Sartre or Camus was brief; it was eventually recognized that *The Outsider* 'consists of breathless summaries of the lives and ideas of a wide range of thinkers and writers' punctuated with 'sub-Nietzschean asides' about how the masses 'were sunk in their "bovine swill"' (417). However, as well as non-fictional (albeit often highly speculative) writings on topics such as philosophy, the occult, psychology and parapsychology, and crime, Wilson also wrote a number of science fiction novels. Wilson explains in his pamphlet essay, *Science Fiction as Existentialism* (1978), that he finds the genre attractive because of its suitability for didactic writing about existential concepts: 'In ordinary fiction, with its reflection of a familiar reality, the characters and events tend to overshadow the ideas – assuming there are any. In science fiction – or speculative fiction – the idea can be reflected clearly, as in a mirror' (15). Science fiction, for Wilson, is a means to convey in narrative and/or symbolic form his philosophical-cum-psychological existential ideas. His writing therefore tends towards a didactic–prophetic function, on the one hand popularizing existential psychology, while on the other claiming to foresee the emergence of an existentially developed vanguard community. While this aim leads Wilson to some rather crude, and indeed escapist tropes, it does also shed light on his affinities with other writers, such as Lessing.

Wilson's (pseudo-)scholarly, pedagogic aims are immediately apparent in the rhetoric of his science fiction novel, *The Mind Parasites* (1967), which presents itself as 'Volume III of the *Cambridge History of the Nuclear Age*' (C. Wilson *Mind* 9) in a short preface dated 2014, and claims to be a 'composite document made up from various papers, tape recordings and verbatim reports of conversations' (9) detailing the experiences of an archaeologist, Professor Gilbert Austin. The narrative begins with the suicide of Austin's friend, a psychologist called Karel

Weissman. Among Weissman's papers is a speculative history outlining the apparent failure of European history after the Romantic period of the late eighteenth century. The ultimate cause of the failure of historical progress, Weissman believes, is not, say, the erosion of cultural tradition, the alienating effects of modernity, or the depredations of capitalism and colonialism. Rather, the underlying cause is the activity of *'certain inner-forces'* (55), which Weismann refers to as the 'mind vampires' (53). These psychic parasites have drained the mental and spiritual energies of the human race and prevented its full historical and evolutionary development. Austin quickly perceives the truth of Weissman's thesis and soon becomes able to sense the activity of the titular 'mind parasites' (63). In response, he uses phenomenological self-discipline to develop countervailing mental abilities, including powers of telepathy, psychokinesis, and mind control. Austin then sets about training a cadre of similarly gifted individuals to oppose the mind parasites. As the battle escalates between these superhuman beings and the mind parasites, the latter use their powers of mind control to start a war between African nationalists and a resurgent European Nazism. Austin and his team infer, however, that the mind parasites are located on the moon, and travel through space to escape their disabling field of influence. Freed from the parasites' psychic vampirism, and having achieved a final apotheosis, Austin and company return to Earth and use their psychokinetic powers to force the moon to rotate 'at right angles to its own line of motion around the earth' (172). Having thus dizzied the mind parasites, the phenomenological task force then employ a ruse to convince the Earth's population that they are in fact under potential threat of invasion from aliens. Faced with what they believe to be a common enemy, the countries of the Earth unite, and the war between Europe and Africa soon fizzles out (the moon itself is later psychokinetically shunted in a near-sun orbit). Several years after peace is restored, Austin, along with some of his superhuman associates, leaves the planet on a spaceship which is later found abandoned and empty near the orbit of Pluto – it seems that Austin has left his species to join his evolutionary peers in other solar systems.

The speculative history presented in Weissman's *Historical Reflections*, the manuscript left to Austin, clarifies Wilson's (apparently heartfelt) extrapolation from existential-humanistic psychology. As Austin explains, Weissman describes 'some invisible yet cataclysmic change' (51) that occurred 'in about the year 1800' (52). As Romanticism emerges in European culture, the mind parasites strike back, killing early or driving mad a generation of artists, so that '[m]en of genius were ruthlessly destroyed like flies' (74). The reason for this attack, Austin explains, is that Romanticism involved a 'tremendous evolutionary leap forward' (73) apparent in, for instance, the heightened sensibility represented in its poetry. Like McHugh, Wilson harks back to Romantic sensibility as an existentialist precursor: epiphanic experiences such as those verbally mediated in Wordsworth's famous sonnet on Westminster Bridge bring about 'a tremendous feeling of power and courage, a glimpse of what life is all about, of the meaning of human evolution' (73). Austin's assertion that 'great men would have been two a penny if it hadn't been for the parasites' (74) anticipates Wilson's published speculations on the significance of Romantic perceptions. In *New Pathways in Psychology* (1972), subtitled *Maslow and the Post-Freudian Revolution*, Wilson explains his view that

> [i]t was the group of writers we call the romantics [*sic*] who discovered that a man contemplating a waterfall or a mountain peak can suddenly feel 'godlike', as if the soul had expanded. The romantics – Blake, Wordsworth, Byron, Goethe, Schiller – were the first to raise the question of whether there are 'higher ceilings of human nature'. But, lacking the concepts for analysing the problem, they left it unsolved. And the romantics in general accepted that the 'godlike moments' cannot be sustained, and certainly cannot be re-created at will. (194)

Adequate concepts for 'godlike moments' can, however, Wilson asserts, be found in Maslow's psychology of the peak experience, which gives scientific expression to man's [*sic*] 'glimpse of "the source of power, meaning and purpose" inside himself' (189). What was adventitious in McHugh's novel is made volitional in Wilson's fiction: since the capacity for peak experience can be freely cultivated (or so Wilson believes), 'it would not be inaccurate to say that *we are mentally ill all the time we are not having peak experiences* – or at least, capable of having them' (247).

As explained above, Maslow's account of the peak experience emphasizes the role of such epiphanies as a source of subjectivized value in modernized, detraditionalized societies. Wilson's work, however, consciously seizes upon other aspects of Maslow's analysis, such as the focussing of attention that is supposed to occur, as 'the percept is exclusively and fully attended to' with a 'tremendous concentration of a kind which does not normally occur' (Maslow *Religions* 60). In a state of such focussed attention, there is, says Maslow, something of a 'god-like perception, [or] superhuman perception' (61), with 'a very characteristic disorientation in time and space' that 'is like experiencing universality and eternity' (63). By having, and by cultivating peak experiences, the subject becomes more a soul, less enchained by mechanical causation: 'He [sic] becomes less an object, less a thing, less a thing of the world living under the laws of the physical world, and he becomes more a psyche, more a person, more subject to the psychological laws, especially the laws of what people have called the "higher life"' (67).

Wilson's explicit fascination with these elements of spiritual apotheosis in Maslow's psychology clarifies some of the world-historical prophecies contained within the ponderous scholarly dialogues represented in *The Mind Parasites*. For instance, Austin, and his friend Reich, spread the gospel among sympathetic intellectuals, such as Sigmund Fleishman, author of *Theories of the Sexual Impulse*, who regards sexuality as properly a conduit for peak experiences akin to those represented (so Wilson alleges) in Romantic poetry: 'He saw that man's sexual impulse is basically *romantic*, just like his poetic impulse' (C. Wilson *Mind* 84): 'The sheer power of the sexual impulse is the power of the god-like in man, and a sexual stimulus can arouse this power as a mountain can arouse his perception of beauty' (84). Furthermore, when Austin achieves his eventual apotheosis, he learns that 'it is not in the nature of things that man should get brief glimpses of freedom, his "intimations of immortality", and then lose them immediately. There is no reason why he should not experience them for ten hours a day if he likes' (153).

The distinct phenomenology of the peak experience encourages Wilson to graft his science fiction onto the sober doctrines of phenomenology, which is metaphorized as a process of mental map-making, charting new and unexplored realms of consciousness: 'Husserl had realized that while we have ordnance survey maps that cover every inch of our earth, we have no atlas of our mental world' (55), declares Austin. This statement clearly resonates with J.G. Ballard's famous declaration in 1962 that '[t]he biggest developments of the immediate future will take place, not on the Moon or Mars, but on Earth, and it is *inner* space, not outer, that needs to be explored' (197). However, given Ballard's psychoanalytic inclinations, a more relevant phenomenological path-finder for Austin is Aldous Huxley, whose essay *Heaven and Hell* (1956) speculates, pre-Ballard, on continents of the mind that lie out of the reach of everyday consciousness, and on the nature of the mysterious mental fauna that might be found there:

> If I have made use of geographical and zoological metaphors, it is not wantonly [...]. It is because such metaphors express very forcibly the essential otherness of the mind's far continents, the complete autonomy and self-sufficiency of their inhabitants. A man consists of what I may call an Old World of personal consciousness

and, beyond a dividing sea, a series of New Worlds – the not too distant Virginias and Carolinas of the personal unconscious and the vegetative soul; the Far West of the collective unconscious, with its flora of symbols, its tribes of aboriginal archetypes; and, across another, vaster ocean, at the antipodes of everyday consciousness, the world of Visionary Experience. (10)

Austin's exploration of inner space discovers a very particular kind of phenomenological fauna in its antipodes, namely the mind parasites, experienced as 'a strange shock, the feeling you would get if you were relaxed in a warm bath, and you suddenly felt a slimy movement against your leg' (C. Wilson *Mind* 30). Their favoured mode of attack is to douse victims in atheistic French existentialism: Austin comes to a 'vision of futility, of nothingness' (98) in which everything in 'this alien "universe"' is 'arbitrary and absurd' (99), and finds that 'a dreadful sense of insecurity and weakness gripped my stomach' (97). The intertextual allusions in this vision are to Albert Camus's notion of the absurdity of a 'universe suddenly divested of illusions and lights' in which 'man feels an alien, a stranger' (4), and also to Jean-Paul Sartre's phenomenology of the 'nausea' evoked by a contingent universe in which '[e]verything is gratuitous' – a realization that 'turns your stomach over' (*Nausea* 188). These well-known existential reference points are however quickly subordinated to Austin's (and presumably Wilson's) own solution: 'when I contemplated this alien "universe", and felt it to be arbitrary and absurd, I was making the oldest of human errors: of believing that the word "universe" means "universe *out there*". The mind, as well I knew, was a universe of its own' (C. Wilson *Mind* 99). This inner space is one in which the mind is at home in the universe. Those who (in one of Austin's typically androcentric and Eurocentric pronouncements) 'explore the countries of the mind as Livingstone and Stanley explored Africa' (59) discover also that there can be 'a focusing and concentrating of the "beam" of consciousness (or attention)' (90) that is pre-reflectively apparent in 'the sexual orgasm' (89), in '[t]he "inspiration" of poets', and in 'so-called "mystical" visions' (90).

Wilson's existential extrapolations may seem very peculiar, not only in the insistence upon the potential reality of psychokinesis and other powers, but also in the odd literalization of phenomenology as mental exploration, and the mind as a kind of 'beam', as if it were a ray gun. It may seem as if Wilson is drifting out into naïve wish-fulfilment of power fantasies, such as that diagnosed in the psychoanalytic critique of science fiction inaugurated by Lindner's famous case study (30–33 above). The accusation has merit. Wilson's ponderous didactic–prophetic extrapolations of phenomenology are essentially pseudo-science: as Noël Carroll remarks, Wilson's 'mystical brand of phenomenology' in *The Mind Parasites* 'ought to provoke Husserl's return from the dead' (183). However, there is a way of partially redeeming Wilson's tropes as an estranging device intended to renew the readers' 'perception' of the inner world (analogous to the use of estrangement upon socio-political realities). The existentialist theologian Rudolf Bultmann argued that it was 'the task of theology to demythologize the Christian proclamation' (3) by translating the mythical representations of Judaeo-Christian scripture into existentialist concepts. Myth, as one commentator on Bultmann explains, 'treat[s] of spiritual factors as if they were natural entities' (Henderson 46). In *Science Fiction as Existentialism*, Wilson alludes to what may be seen as the analogous aesthetic of *The Mind Parasites*:

> *The Mind Parasites* [...] was an attempt to state symbolically what I felt to be wrong with human beings: that through art and mysticism, we obtain glimpses of a tremendous freedom which seems, in effect, to be beyond our reach. The romantics of the 19th century seemed to be saying: 'Man is really a god.' So why are we, in practice, such poor, limited creatures? I suggested that the answer lay in some mysterious parasite that has hidden itself in the depths of the human mind, and which sucks up our vital energy, the energy we create through optimism and courage. (*Science* 13)

To 'state symbolically' his doctrines, Wilson invents, as it were, a 'bug-eyed monster' (or, more accurately, 'an immense, jelly-like octopus whose tentacles are separated from its body and can move about like individuals' (*Mind* 151)), a creation that concretizes the spiritual forces opposed to what he views as our potential apotheosis. Wilson uses the stock situations and devices of science fiction to depict existential concepts in a concretized, estranged form that transposes the neglected inner world into an extraordinary outer existence.

This cognitive aim clarifies the presumably unintentional comedy in Wilson's remythologized expression of the phenomenological concepts of 'intention' (the directedness of consciousness towards objects, both external and inner) and 'attention' (the focussing of consciousness upon certain objects). Austin explains that '[t]he moment man stumbles on the fact that his attention is a "beam", (or, as Husserl puts it, that consciousness is "intentional") he has learned the fundamental secret' (90). Intentionality becomes, in effect, a mental ray gun that Austin uses against the mind parasites: at one point, he releases his 'attention-beam on the enemy', which 'hit them like some enormous flame thrower, destroying them as though they were earwigs' (100). This relationship between author and reader in which neglected phenomenological realities are given expression in science fiction tropes even appears within the narrative of *The Mind Parasites*: Austin and his cadre refer to the parasites using 'a name – the Tsathogguans – borrowed from Lovecraft's mythology' (103) as a way 'to turn the truth about the parasites into a child's fable – something that could be easily grasped, something not too frightening' (103). (And when Austin remarks in passing that 'ninety-five per cent of the human race' (135) are incapable of grasping the reality of the mind parasites, we might also wonder if this is also Wilson's authorial judgement upon the reader.)

A similar aesthetic presumably also informs Wilson's further adventure in existentialist science fiction (with a twist of horror), *The Space Vampires* (1976), in which disembodied alien vampires invade the Earth, *c.*2080 (the datings in Wilson's novel are not entirely consistent), after their spacecraft is disturbed by human activities in the asteroid belt. A trio of space vampires returns to Earth, where they hop from body to body, consuming the life force of victims that they encounter along the way. Many themes similar to those in *The Mind Parasites* are addressed in this novel, including the elevated consciousness of the spacefaring protagonist, Captain Olof Carlsen, who comes to realise that 'normal consciousness' is merely a 'dream-like unreality' (C. Wilson *Space* 204). Carlsen also, as he battles against the vampires, finds that existential resolution can defeat these parasites of the human spirit, whose attacks Wilson gauchely imagines as a telepathic rape: 'it was outside him, trying to enter his body. His mental defences were closed, like hands covering his face; it was trying to force its way past the hands, to spreadeagle his will and force its way into his essential being' (167); yet (and perhaps Wilson fails to note the dissimilarity with everyday, embodied sexual assault), 'some universal law made it unable to invade his feeble individuality against his will' (168). The reified existential concepts culminate in a bout of psychic fisticuffs at the end, conducted via battling wills: 'before Jamieson could recover, his [Carlsen's] own will-drive struck back, catching Jamieson in his ribs and throwing him sideways into the wall' (196). *The Space Vampires* also has the distinction of being among a presumably small number of science fiction narratives in which an alien invasion force is defeated by its suicide. The vampires, who are renegade members of an alien race, undergo an anagnorisis near the end of the story: they recognize that they have been living in systematic inauthenticity throughout their vampiric assaults on other species, and choose freely to kill themselves in a despairing realization of their own evil.

While time, and literary criticism, have not been kind to Wilson's writing, it is interesting to reflect on what separates him from the work of a Nobel-prize winning author such as Doris Lessing (1919–2013). Wilson's eccentric fiction of existential alien vampires and latent ESP provides an intriguing extra-canonical counterpoint to similar motifs in Lessing's writing – motifs that have been treated far more respectfully by academic criticism. Lessing's loose five-volume novel sequence, *Children of Violence*, ends with *The Four-Gated City* (1969), the final instalment in the lives and adventures of its protagonist, Martha Quest (latterly, Hesse), as she moves to post-war London to begin a new life. Much of the novel is concerned with Martha's peculiar love life as part of an emotional (if not wholly sexual) *ménage à trois,* and her consequent involvement with the political and cultural elite of the British Establishment. The novel concludes, however, with a transition from narrative realism, albeit with much psychological interiority, to science fiction: the closing pages relate the evolution of a new variant of telepathic and precognitive human being, set against a worldwide 'Catastrophe' brought about by a combination of environmental depredations.

In the late 1960s Lessing had not yet fully embraced the science fiction aesthetic that would issue in later works such as her five-novel sequence, *Canopus in Argos: Archives* (1979–1983). As Hite notes (23–24), *Four-Gated City* is poised between 'serious' and 'genre' writing. After 'the Catastrophe' (Lessing *Four-Gated* 617), the novel abandons the third-person narrative focalized through Martha, and instead provides a multiple epistolary narrative of communities in telepathic contact, recording the emergence of a new psychically-gifted human sub-species. In an acknowledgement of generic hybridity, Lessing has Martha allude to John Wyndham's *The Midwich Cuckoos* (1957): 'You'll remember that half a century ago now, when you were a child, a novel was written about some children born all the same time with above-normal capacities? Where this author made a mistake was, imagining children being born the same as each other, with the same powers, communicating through exactly the same channels' (657). Moreover, during the earlier, pre-Catastrophe narrative, Martha undergoes a psychic awakening in which she becomes, in effect, an alien visitor to her own planet: 'she looked down again at an extraordinarily hideous creature who stood watching her, out of eyes that were like coloured lumps of gelatine that had fringes of hair about them and bands of hair above them, and which half protruded from a bump shape of pinkish putty, or doughlike substance' (526). The generic borrowing behind these estranged perceptions of a species heading for unwitting self-destruction is even made explicit:

> It was painful in a way she had never known pain, an affliction of shameful grief, to walk here today, among her own kind, looking at them as they were, seeing them, us, the human race, as visitors from a spaceship might see them, if he dropped into London or any city to report. 'This particular planet is inhabited thickly by defectively evolved animals who ...'. (528)

But while Lessing's indebtedness to science fiction is well known, and reasonably clear in *Four-Gated City*, her specific affinity with Wilson's writing may be less easily recognized. Prior to the global apocalypse, Martha's complicated personal life – set against the backdrop of 1960s London – brings her into contact with Jimmy Wood, her lover's colleague. According to Frederick R. Karl, Wood, 'a mild-mannered scientist and writer of space fiction who is a human computer', 'represents the bland forces of military, science, and government which, with velvet glove, offer salvation while they are missing a human dimension' (29). Wood is certainly a cipher through which Lessing can introduce various technocratic discourses. However, there is an added intertextual function to his character, for, in certain respects, he is a disguised version of Colin Wilson:

> He [Wood] had just published a story called, *The Force Dealers*, whose 'storyline' was that a certain type of human being had learned to 'plug in' to the energies of other beings, and live off them like a species of vampire. Some of the people who were thus being bled of energy knew about it, but others did not. Those who knew tried to warn those who didn't. The vampires did all they could to keep their victims passively in their power. (Lessing *Four-Gated* 495)

Wilson's *The Mind Parasites*, as noted above, was first published in 1967, two years before *The Four-Gated City*, so the allusion to Wilson's novel seems very clear.

Wood, however, is marginalized and 'othered' within the narrative, particularly because of his later plan to militarize ESP using a technology that makes the subject 'will-less' (555). The inclusion, yet repudiation, of Wood/Wilson in *Four-Gated City*, indicates a metafictional effort to contain a series of affinities with this far less celebrated writer, of whose work Lessing was clearly aware and occasionally critical (e.g. by drawing attention to the 'British provincialism' with which Wilson dismisses humanism and materialism, despite their global significance for communist nations and the developing world ('Small' 18)). Yet, as with Wilson in *Mind Parasites*, Lessing employs the same psycho-geographical metaphor in which altered consciousness is exploration of 'a totally uncharted interior' (Lessing *Four-Gated* 557). Moreover, a central drama within Martha's awakening to psychic ability is her confrontation with something called '*[t]he self-hater*' (558). This mysterious inner entity has driven Lynda, Martha's equally gifted ally, into madness. Martha, during her own process of self-discovery, is tormented and even possessed by this 'Devil' (574) which, for instance, torments her with racist emotions and thoughts (561). Ultimately – as with Wilson's parasites – this external possessor turns out to be really a part of Martha herself, '*aspects of me*' (574).

Martha finds in Wood's possession a 'potted library representing everything rejected by official culture and scholarship', 'including Zen, witchcraft, magic, astrology and vampirism' (535). This discovery indicates something of the generic convergence of both Wilson and Lessing, despite their different standing within the literary canon. The non-traditional religiosity of Wilson's writing has been recognized by Brian Stableford, who observes that '[i]n later books, most obviously *The Occult* (1971), Wilson informed us that [...] we might become supermen if only we could get a proper grip on ourselves. Our trouble, he insists, is *narrowness of consciousness*' (66). This doctrine, Stableford observes, harmonizes with other science fiction apologetics: 'We have, of course, heard this promise before. L. Ron Hubbard promised it when he invented Dianetics and Scientology; and John W. Campbell jr. promised it during the *psi* boom of the 1950s' (66). Lessing's spiritual beliefs are of course well-known. To cite one authority:

> Doris Lessing argues in her fiction that women labelled as mad are in fact accessing altered states of consciousness, which can be immensely liberating and educative. She links these experiences with psychic powers such as telepathy, which she claims can be consciously developed, and could act as the key to utopian changes in the future. (Fancourt 100)

For Lessing, it was the Sufism of Idries Shah that most readily accommodated these tenets (Hardin).

Like Wilson, Lessing uses science fiction as a didactic and prophetic medium in which existential psychology unabashedly serves as the supposed rationale for spiritual apotheosis. Her work, in its intent, accords with Wilson's declaration that 'the real aim of science fiction, and one that will assume increasing importance in the future, is to serve as a *catalyst* in the evolution of a new human consciousness' (*Science* 16). Science fiction, in this vein, is presented as a medium that putatively awakens dormant mental faculties by refocussing the readers' attention on neglected capacities of experience that have been suppressed by modern society. The ideology is neatly (if somewhat ironically) captured in Robert Silverberg's novel of telepathy, *Dying Inside* (1972), where the narrator-protagonist reflects:

> Aldous Huxley thought that evolution has designed our brains to serve as filters, screening out a lot of stuff that's of no real value to us in our daily struggle for bread. Visions, mystical experiences, psi phenomena such as telepathic messages from other brains – all sorts of things along these lines would forever be flooding into us were it not for the action of what Huxley called [...] 'the cerebral reducing valve.' Thank God for the cerebral reducing valve! If we hadn't evolved it, we'd be distracted all the time by scenes of incredible beauty, by spiritual insights of overwhelming grandeur, and by searing, utterly honest mind-to-mind contact with our fellow human beings. (21)

Lessing and Wilson's texts are to some extent a heterodox canon within the larger phenomenon of what religious studies calls 'New Religious Movements' (NRMs). Both show particular traces of New Age 'Self-spirituality' (Heelas 18), a mode of belief in which

> [p]erfection can be found only by moving beyond the socialized self – widely known as the 'ego' but also as the 'lower self', 'intellect' or the 'mind' – thereby encountering a new realm of being. It is what we are *by nature*. Indeed, the most pervasive and significant aspect of the *lingua franca* of the New Age is that the person is, in essence, spiritual. (19)

The greater value of their work, however, tends to reside in the estranging vision that accompanies these rather naïve narratives of spiritual transcendence (which, in their frequent reliance upon mental superpowers resemble rather too closely the Golden Age vision of space age supermen epitomized by A.E. van Vogt's 'slans' (see e.g. Broderick *Psience* 32–37)). A more assured handling of existential ideas occurs, as will be shown, in the work of Marge Piercy, who manages to incorporate tropes such as telepathy as a generic device, rather than as literal prognostication, and does so within an estranging and utopian fiction that continues the political engagement of a writer like McHugh.

Existential science fiction and psychiatric critique

The preceding discussion of Wilson and Lessing has shown how both authors regarded their work didactically, as prophecy of a psychologically superior form of human life. However, an equally significant deployment of existential-humanistic ideas uses science fiction to criticize contemporary, scientized accounts of psychopathology and, in so doing, problematizes the contemporary construction of the subject by the neurodiscourses underlying psychopharmacology and neurosurgery. Moreover, alongside this disruption of neuroscientific reflexivity effects, the opportunity arises for metafictional indications of what science fiction may offer other than mere wish-fulfilment in the Freudian (or Adlerian) mode of compensatory fantasy.

Existential critique of biomedical psychiatry emerged most clearly during the 1960s in the countercultural social movement known as 'anti-psychiatry', where it furnished discourses for New Wave authors such as Marge Piercy, whose lengthy novel *Woman on the Edge of Time* (195-99 below) explores, from a feminist perspective, the presumed dehumanization practised by conventional psychiatry. However, even Golden Age science fiction shows a dawning existential critique of biomedical psychiatry's therapeutic (and neuroscientific) optimism. Theodore Sturgeon's short story 'And Now the News ...' (1956) traces the breakdown and psychiatric 'cure' of MacLyle, a married middle-class suburbanite in his forties. MacLyle exists in a state of quiet and well-regulated conformity, his only peculiarity being an obsession with the news, which he rigidly consumes on a daily basis through print, radio, and TV. Annoyed by this behaviour, his wife sabotages every radio and TV in their house, and refuses to supply him with their local newspaper. This intervention triggers an existential crisis in MacLyle, who abandons his wife and children (having firstly made arrangements for their financial security with his attorney). Before leaving for a remote cabin in the Rockies, MacLyle finds he has lost the ability to read or even to recite the alphabet – a symptom that cuts him off entirely from his beloved newspapers. Troubled by the loss of the 'old reliable MacLyle' (Sturgeon 189), his wife hires a psychiatrist to track him down. The unnamed psychiatrist, regularly designated as the 'fairly intelligent psychiatrist' (190), traces MacLyle to the cabin, where he discovers that his unwitting patient is now incapable of communication by speech or writing. MacLyle lives in happy solitude, and spends his time practising the ophecleide (a little-known brass instrument), sculpting, painting in a largely abstract expressionist style, and pottering around. The psychiatrist forcibly drugs MacLyle with a cocktail of pharmaceuticals that renders him docile and suggestible. He then hypnotically persuades his patient that he is in his late thirties, before his apparent mental illness began. MacLyle is thereby gradually restored to communication with wider society, and returns to his hometown accompanied by the psychiatrist, having explained his self-seclusion as an attempt to escape the diminishment he experienced in his suburban life. The story ends with a rather formulaic twist ending in which MacLyle embarks on a briefly narrated killing spree ('He killed four people before they got him') in which he vengefully 'diminish[es] mankind right back' (200).

'And Now the News ...' builds a clear contrast between the norms of suburban life and the authenticity pursued by MacLyle. His spouse, for instance, is entirely consumed by the expectations incumbent upon her: 'She had always prided herself on being a good wife, and had done many things in the past that were counter to her reason and her desires purely because they were consistent with being a good wife' (189–90). Norms of mental health are unmasked in the story as a way of maintaining conformity to the anonymous demands of social convention, particularly as transmitted through the mass media. The attorney for instance perceives his client as 'behaving like a happy man – a rare form of insanity, but acceptable' (187). This 'insanity' is not acceptable however to the 'fairly intelligent psychiatrist', who, while observing MacLyle in the cabin, 'reflected suddenly that this withdrawn and wordless individual was a happy one, in his own matrix; further, he had fulfilled all his obligations and responsibilities and was bothering no one. It was intolerable' (196). The psychiatrist views MacLyle's continued seclusion as

> a violation of the prime directive of psychiatry – at least, of that school of psychiatry which he professed, and he was not going to confuse himself by considerations of other, less-tired theories – *It is the function of psychiatry to adjust the aberrate to society, and to restore or increase his usefulness to it*. To yield, to rationalize this man's behaviour as balance, would be to fly in the face of science itself. (196)

His unwitting patient's retreat from society (epitomized by the refusal of linguistic communication) is *'suicide'*, a destruction of MacLyle's essential nature as a 'social entity' (196). The story's *novum* extrapolates from the progress in the early 1950s of psychopharmacology, particularly in the development of anti-psychotics such as chlorpromazine (see e.g. López-Muñoz *et al.*) – a drug that features again under the tradename Thorazine in Piercy's *Woman on the Edge of Time* (197 below). The psychiatrist surreptitiously administers a soporific to MacLyle before injecting him with 'a careful blend of the non-soporific tranquilizers Frenquel, chlorpromazine and Reserpine, and a judicious dose of scopolamine, a hypnotic' (197). These drugs keep MacLyle 'conscious, docile, submissive and without guile' (198), and therefore amenable to a series of supposedly therapeutic hypnotic suggestions. During MacLyle's brief period of pre-murderous lucidity he explains to the psychiatrist why he had retreated to that particular area of the Rockies. As a student vacationing in the area, he had witnessed a friend suffer from a gangrenous broken leg that required amputation. The putrefaction of the body offers MacLyle a corporeal, concretized metaphor for the existential gangrene he felt during his suburban life: 'I was getting diminished to death and I had to watch it happening to me like that kid with the gangrene, so that's why' (200).

Sturgeon's short story elaborates the opposition between existential psychiatry and neuroscientific psychiatry that can be glimpsed in McHugh's earlier novel. Rowan encounters a psychiatrist who classifies the fever patients as suffering from a 'derangement' that 'falls into the schizophrenic class' because, like psychotics, the happy New Yorkers are '[e]vading responsibility at the same points. Job responsibility. Sex responsibility. Financial responsibility and so on' (McHugh 142) – indeed, for this medical professional, the correct response would be radical neurotherapies of various kinds, including shock therapies such as insulin coma, the drug metrazol, and electro-convulsive therapy, and psychosurgery in the form of leucotomy (143). Such science fiction critique of biomedical psychiatry elaborates in tandem with the development of 1960s and 1970s antipsychiatry. The most famous Anglophone critic of mainstream mental health discourses and practices was probably R.D. Laing, whose literary impact has been extensively explored with regard to Lessing's work in the 1970s. The relationship between the two has been examined at length, and there is little to add in the present context. Several critics have explored in depth the deployment of Laingian *metanoia* in a number of Lessing's texts (e.g. Vlastos; Bazin; Bolling), and her 1971 novel, *Briefing for a Descent into Hell*, has emerged as a paradigm of such literary extrapolation in its account of an academic's psychic voyage into unknown realms:

> Lessing's account of Charles Watkins's extraordinary voyages into the unknown corresponds so closely to what others have recorded about mental illness. The most notable – and often discussed – correspondence has to do with a case study of schizophrenia described by R.D. Laing in chapter 10 of *The Politics of Experience*

[...]. Although Lessing has denied borrowing from Laing's account, the correspondence is remarkable, with the details of the voyage, many of the major symbols and images, and the kinds of language games played by Charles all echoing what Laing reports of his patient. (Fishburn 49)

Yet it should be noted that Lessing herself drew on a context wider than that of Laing's well-known countercultural writing. Bert Kaplan's *Inner World of Mental Illness* (1964), for instance, has been described by Lessing as equally significant for her work (Hardin 575). Kaplan's earlier, less well-known work provides similar intellectual co-ordinates in his contention that 'so-called "symptoms" rather than being ego-alien manifestations of a disease process that has somehow gotten a grip on the person, are instead purposeful acts of the individual, which have intentionality and are motivated' (Kaplan x). Moreover, Kaplan's broadly existential and phenomenological critique of biomedical psychiatry was accompanied by a large number of first-person accounts of various states of mental illness, and altered consciousness and perception. These included not just descriptions of avowedly psychotic experience, but also excerpts from philosophical-cum-literary texts such as Sartre's *Nausea* (1938).

As Lessing's work and frame of reference indicate, there exists a larger 1960s and 1970s science fiction critique of psychiatry that draws upon both Laing and a more general existentialist mood. For instance, Naomi Mitchison's 1962 novel *Memoirs of a Spacewoman* (1962) relates, in a number of episodes, the efforts of its space travelling narrator, Mary, to communicate with both Earthly animals and with various animal-like alien species (67–79 above). Laing's brand of existential psychiatry appears in *Memoirs* when Mary goes on an expedition to a planet colonized by the Epsilons (or 'Epsies') – a race, in effect, of highly intelligent centipedes, whose 'colonist mentality' (Mitchison *Memoirs* 36) is a 'moral crudity' (34) beyond which humans have progressed. The tirelessly industrious Epsies, who merely 'asked and answered questions, decorated themselves, elaborated their dwellings and their technical organization and were undisturbed by their infrequent matings' may well estrange, and satirize, the bourgeois culture of European colonists in Africa and India (34). At any rate, their representation relates an absence of empathy with animals to the oppression of both colonized peoples and psychiatric patients. The Epsies live on their planet with a native species, whom the explorers christen the 'Rounds'. Though not strictly hominid, the Rounds are described as something between playful primate, pre-industrial native, and psychiatric patient. The Rounds 'made shelters, decorated themselves with fringed, blue leaves, and a kind of shining nut-like growth, and plucked their sparse silky fur into patterns' (37). The anti-psychiatric parallels appear when the Rounds are herded by the Epsies into an enclosure, a scene that reminds Mary of a mental hospital, something familiar to her only from history courses. A supervising Epsie employs a peculiar instrument to administer a 'little nick' to the heads (and thus to the brains) of the Rounds, turning them into 'docile and unanxious entities' (43): 'They were wandering about, not jumping or yelling or singing or expressing any violent emotion, and apparently in no pain. [...] the peculiar shine or glow of activity had died out of them' (42). After this thinly veiled representation of leucotomy, the Epsies then vampirically suck the bloodlike fluid from the Rounds, and use their desiccated corpses 'as building materials' (42).

This estranged representation of a specifically psychiatric exploitation of the Other alongside that of colonized peoples and animals gives an important clue to some of the intellectual context that informs *Memoirs*. Mitchison possessed, or was possessed by, what she called an 'underlife' of overwhelming fears and fantasies that were inexpressible to 'anyone who would treat the whole affair on a rational basis. Indeed, this is only too clearly what happens often enough to mental patients. They must be met half-way with understanding, as I am sure happens when there is a combination of good psychiatry with enough time' (*All* 95–96). The representation of psychiatry as normalization in *Memoirs*, and Mitchison's vocabulary of being met with 'understanding' probably indicates some knowledge of R.D. Laing's psychiatric work, which was coming to prominence in the late 1950s and early 1960s. In works such as *The Divided Self* (1960), Mitchison's fellow Scot argued that psychiatry should use the interpretative methods of the human sciences to render intelligible the seemingly nonsensical words and actions of the 'mad'. Whether in the understanding of 'ancient texts' or 'psychotics', we must 'bring to bear what is often called sympathy, or, more intensively, *em*pathy' (Laing *Divided* 32); 'Like the expositor, the therapist must have the plasticity to transpose himself into another strange and even alien view of the world' (34). Laing's references to the *Geisteswissenschaften* may help to explain why Mitchison so faithfully echoes Wilhelm Dilthey's account of interpretation in her depiction of an explorer who must also empathically transpose herself into many 'strange and even alien view[s] of the world'. Dilthey claimed that 'empathy' was the 'state of mind involved in the task of understanding' (226), and argued that through contact with different cultures, 'inner-directed man can experience many other existences in his imagination. Limited by circumstances he can yet glimpse alien beauty in the world and areas of life beyond his reach' (228). Unlike Sturgeon's pessimistic vision of existential authenticity as a retreat into non-communication, the Laingean ideal allows for communion across the presumed divide between sanity and madness.

Further existential psychological motifs inform Marge Piercy's feminist science fiction classic *Woman on the Edge of Time* (1976), a novel that shows how existential and phenomenological concepts can be woven into science fiction that eschews the naïve spirituality of Wilson and Lessing, and offers instead the utopian political engagement of a text like *I Am Thinking of My Darling*. The protagonist of *Woman*, Connie Ramos, is a downtrodden 1970s New Yorker whose defence of her niece from a pimp precipitates her entrapment in a bureaucratic web of psychiatric care. Connie's career as a patient sees her committed, and eventually drawn into an experimental mind-control programme designed to 'cure' violent mental patients. She draws hope however from what appears to be her telepathic contact with Luciente, a woman from a future utopia in the town of Mattapoisett. Through Luciente, Connie explores an eco-friendly and gender-neutral culture and society created in the aftermath of a feminist-led revolution, although still threatened by the power of the previous regime, which has outposts on the moon, Antarctica, and orbital space platforms. Finally, after glimpsing a dystopian possible future of sexual slavery and rampant exploitation, Connie commits an act of violent resistance, poisoning the coffee of the team experimenting upon her. Her killing of six people is, as she reflects after the deed, 'my act of war' (Piercy *Woman* 375).

Woman may be read in terms of a cultural context informed by post-war critiques of psychiatry. Kerstin Shands, for instance, argues that the novel 'can be construed as a fictional account of the factual horror story that is *Women and Madness*' (68). Phyllis Chesler's influential feminist critique of psychiatry, first published in 1972, argued that '[m]ost twentieth-century women who are psychiatrically labelled, privately treated, and publicly hospitalized are not mad. [...] they may be deeply unhappy, self-destructive, economically powerless, and sexually impotent – but as women they are supposed to be' (24–25). The psychiatric system, in Chesler's view, colludes in expelling women because of their 'irrational' resistance to patriarchy: 'Madness is shut away from sight, shamed, brutalized, denied, and feared. Contemporary men, politics, science – the rational mode itself – does not consult or is not in touch with the irrational, i.e. with the events of the unconscious, or with the meaning of collective history' (25). However, as well as Chesler's critique, one can also perceive Laing's influence in *Woman on the Edge of Time*. Indeed, there may be advantages to noting a broader context of psychiatric critique, since it positions Piercy's work within existentialism, a movement to which she was sympathetic. In her memoir, *Sleeping with Cats* (2002), Piercy recalls these influences from her college years: 'I was passionate about existentialism. I was reading Sartre and de Beauvoir and Camus. I tried to look like Juliette Greco, whom I had admired in movies and magazine spreads on existentialism' (95). This powerful youthful influence may help to explain why *Woman* contains many existential-phenomenological allusions, both in the Mattapoisett scenes, and in Connie's 1970s life.

Rather like Wilson's elite phenomenologists – although thankfully with less by way of didactic parapsychological extrapolation – Luciente's society practises a highly advanced form of subjective awareness called 'in-knowing'. This methodical cognition of the inner world, as Luciente explains, means that the Mattapoisett folk 'get used to knowing exactly what we feel, so we don't shove on other people what's coming from inside' (Piercy *Woman* 140). Not only are they experts in self-knowledge and the avoidance of Freudian projections and transferences, the future folk are educated in empathy, telepathy, and conscious control over normally autonomic bodily mechanisms: '"We want to teach inknowing and outknowing." Magdalena gestured apology and swept the women gently back into the hall, shutting the door. "To feel with other beings. To catch, where the ability exists – instance, so strongly for you. We teach sharpening of the senses"' (140). Inknowing also extends to what might be called an existential awareness of human finitude. Luciente remarks 'We all carry our death at the core – if you don't inknow that, your life is hollow, no?' (156–57). Moreover, for the Mattapoisett folk, severe mental illness is clearly *metanoia* in the mode proposed by Laing and others. Luciente explains:

> 'Our madhouses are places where people retreat when they want to go down into themselves – to collapse, carry on, see visions, hear voices of prophecy, bang on the walls, relive infancy – getting in touch with the buried self and the inner mind. We all lost parts of ourselves. We all make choices that go bad. ... How can another person decide that it is time for me to disintegrate, to reintegrate myself?' (66)

Such existential-phenomenological representations may be found also in the text's reflexive function, via Connie's own implicitly anti-psychiatric critique of her medical care according to objectifying psychological categories. Connie perceives a genuine intersubjective relationship to be absent in her carers – 'How that Dr. Redding stared at her, not like she'd look at a person, but the way she might look at a tree, a painting, a tiger in the zoo' (92). As a corollary to her treatment as a non- or subhuman entity, Connie is conscious also of how the objectifying psychiatric gaze fails to understand the 'inner side' of her seemingly symptomatic behaviour:

> Now they were questioning her about the beatings her father had given her as a child. She kept her face frozen, her voice level. Inappropriate affect, they called that – as if to have strangers pawing through the rags of her life like people going through cast-off clothes at a rummage sale was not painful enough to call forth every measure of control she could manage. (92)

Recognition of the existential-phenomenological psychology within *Woman* helps to defend it from criticisms advanced by Bülent Somay. For Somay, *Woman* is limited by a utopian plot that is 'rather dogmatically presented and flat' (30) – a 'blueprint' utopia, in other words – and by a contemporary plot in which the *novum* is '[a] single technological innovation (a neuro-surgical operation resembling Zamyatin's "Great Operation" in *We* [...]', 'a barrier which lacks social, cultural, and economic dimensions' (31)). Thus, the 1970s plot 'does not contain a novum significant enough to be properly thought of as S-F. In fact, when isolated from the utopian plot, the contemporary one is reducible to a mildly interesting critique of the techniques that North American mental health institutions practice to force patients to "adjust" to the world' (30). Somay's criticism, however, overlooks the centrality of existentialism within *Woman*. Connie's experience of 'the Thorazine that sapped her will and dulled her brain and drained her body of energy' (Piercy *Woman* 31) is precisely a kind of Wilsonesque psychic vampirism that anticipates the *novum* later tested upon her and other patients, the radio-controlled microcomputer implanted in the brain (which itself resonates with Jimmy Wood's will-sapping technologies in *Four-Gated City*). As Judith Kegan Gardiner remarks, 'What is most to be feared in Piercy's novel is the annihilation of one's ego by the control of another: the doctors want to steal Connie's mind' ('Evil' 75). The neuroscientific *novum* of the computer controller is thus central to *Woman* as a device of cognitive estrangement. On the one hand, it extrapolates the social tendency to technological control of the mentally ill, among other socially deviant individuals. On the other, it presents an analogical displacement of the social judgement that deprives the mentally ill of responsibility for their actions. It is this act of invalidation that Connie perceives in relation to her previous physical abuse of her daughter: '"Willful abuse for injuring the person or health of a minor child," they said, but they also said she was not responsible for her actions' (Piercy *Woman* 60).

This latter issue of responsibility is essential to an understanding of *Woman*. The story of Connie's development is one in which she recognizes and takes responsibility for the anger that she misdirected upon her daughter. A key insight occurs early on when she accepts responsibility for her willed attack on Geraldo: '"I smashed a bottle in the face of my niece's pimp." She grinned. "I wasn't overworked. I just hated him." Such a light feeling, like floating, to say that truthfully and let it hang there' (90). Such authentic disclosure (with its resonances of McHugh's fever phenomenology) anticipates Connie's later decision to engage in violent resistance by poisoning the coffee of the experimental medical team. Connie's murder (or assassination) of various members of the team has been misunderstood as 'a final act of violent revenge' (Shelton 169), and even condemned in doctrinaire Marxist fashion as 'too individualistic and too naturalistically portrayed to be considered as a metaphor for a collective action on the part of the oppressed' (Somay 31). Rachel DuPlessis is similarly pessimistic: 'If Piercy's analysis is correct, that is, if the tendency of therapeutic science is towards mind control, then the government grant machine will clone out another set of researchers. Killing those particular four scientists will not stop the process – that is, unless Connie's action did raise consciousness. We need evidence that others see and understand her message' (3). Objections such as these, however, overlook the existentialist concerns of the narrative. Piercy, no doubt, could have shown in detail the failure of an experimental programme discredited by suicide and murder – as the author, she holds the cards. Piercy might even have shown in greater detail the collective action that is surely alluded to in the Mattapoisett narrative, the 'thirty-year war that culminated in a revolution' (Piercy *Woman* 198). Yet to do so would have removed from the narrative the crucial uncertainty that Connie must feel about her action, which is surely ethically ambiguous in the sense developed by de Beauvoir. As the latter explains, the decision to take violent action typically does not rest upon confidence in a successful short-term outcome, and may even seem doomed to immediate failure:

> There are cases still more disturbing because there the violence is not immediately efficacious; the violences of the Resistance did not aim at the material weakening of Germany; it happens that their purpose was to create such a state of violence that collaboration would be impossible [...]. Attempts which are aware that one by one they are doomed to failure can be legitimized by the

whole of the situation which they create. This is also the meaning of Steinbeck's novel *In Dubious Battle* where a communist leader does not hesitate to launch a costly strike of uncertain success but through which there will be born, along with the solidarity of the workers, the consciousness of exploitation and the will to reject it. (de Beauvoir 162–63)

Connie's commitment to violent action – 'I'm at war. No more fantasies, no more hopes. *War*' (Piercy *Woman* 338) – thus resonates with the Resistance's uncertain efforts in occupied France: 'I am conducting undercover operations. I am behind enemy lines' (350).

Connie's eventual commitment to authentic but ethically ambiguous political violence also resonates with the novel's narrative strategy. As is well known, 'the book leaves open the possibility that both the utopian and the dystopian futures are merely projections of Ramos's fantasies' (Booker 341). No definite answer is given as to whether Connie's visions are fantasies – albeit it far from mere compensatory wish-fulfilment – or (fictionally real) telepathic glimpses of a future society. Even Connie herself wonders if Luciente is 'a fraction of her mind, [...] a voice of an alternate self, talking to her in the night' (Piercy *Woman* 252). Part of Piercy's sophistication in her use of the fantastic is, as Billie Maciunas notes, the way in which 'characters in Piercy's novel also mirror each other in terms of present and future. For example, Sybil, who is confined to the hospital for being a witch, is mirrored by Erzulia, a black woman in the future who practices both witchcraft and traditional surgery' (252). Even the two *topoi* – clinic and utopia – are set in correspondence, as when Connie reflects '[r]eally this could be a dining room in a madhouse, the way people sat naked with their emotions pouring out' (Piercy *Woman* 74–75). Such ontological indeterminacy is not used merely for its own sake, rather, explains Donna Fancourt, 'Connie's utopian "hallucinations" represent an opening of her mind towards different ontological possibilities' (106). Were the narrative to affirm Mattapoisett as the assured outcome of Connie's actions, then this would be to betray the text's existential dominant, which is neatly captured by Luciente's declaration to Connie that '[t]hose of your time who fought hard for change, often they had myths that a revolution was inevitable. But nothing is! All things interlock. We are only one possible future. Do you grasp?' (Piercy *Woman* 177). The ontological hesitation in the Mattapoisett utopia (and indeed the New York dystopia) allows Piercy to, as it were, write her futures in the conditional mood – what 'would be' rather than what 'will be'.

Conclusion

The heyday of existential psychology in science fiction extends from the 1940s to the 1970s, the significance of the discourse waxing and waning in parallel with existentialism more generally. As the allusions of McHugh and Wilson to eighteenth-century sensibility indicate, existential psychology provides something of a miniature latter-day Romantic response to the technocratic propensities of science fiction. In polar opposition to the methodological neglect of subjectivity in behaviourism, existential psychology offers science fiction a discourse in which first-person experience has a scientific dignity and significance. Admittedly, the insertion of existential psychology into fictional *novums* may prove immensely problematic, as in the work of Wilson and Lessing. The didactic–prophetic function of popular science fiction may encourage wild prophecies of apotheosis in a phenomenological space race to far-out destinations such as telepathy, psychokinesis, and precognition. Such sententious quasi-religiosity might seem to confirm reductive suspicions about the uses and gratifications of science fiction. Yet the utopian function of existential psychology is important, since it reveals that inward dimensions such as personal authenticity are now as important to any vision of a better society as the traditional concern for material justice. What is imagined in McHugh's alternate 1942 New York, or in Piercy's future Mattapoisett, is very far from compensatory wish-fulfilment, and offers a metafictional recuperation of science fiction, insisting on the creative and critical powers of human imagination. Moreover, existential-humanism is at odds with the technologizing and instrumentalizing tendencies of mainstream neuropsychology that have permeated the genre. Skip, a gay test patient for the mind-control device in *Woman*, encapsulates this reflexive destabilization of neurodeterminism: 'He moved like a robot not expertly welded. Yet he was no robot, whatever they thought they had done. She could feel the will burning in him, a will to burst free' (Piercy *Woman* 270).

Chapter 5

Cognitive psychology

If any one school of psychology were tailor-made for deployment within science fiction, it would seem to be the programme of research associated with the rise of cognitive psychology in the latter half of the twentieth century. The cognitivist model of mind as computer seems well-suited to longstanding science fiction tropes (or clichés) of machine intelligence. Such familiar science fiction conventions have been explored very extensively within literary and cultural criticism, particularly in the body of work associated with human–machine hybrids like the cyborg. This chapter, however, investigates less familiar aspects of the relationship between cognitive psychology and science fiction. Rather than concentrate upon *novums* derived from the supposed identity of the human mind with the modern computer, the following discussion focusses on the way in which science fiction deals with cognitivist tenets on the active, constructive character of mental activity. The cognitivist inventory of our conceptual, perceptual, mnemonic and linguistic apparatus offers the possibility to science fiction of blind spots in our knowledge of the world. What lurks at the margins of the world as we know it, challenging the security of our rational grasp on reality? Cognitivism even suggests to science fiction a more radical epistemological extrapolation: could everyday knowledge of the world of space and time be a phenomenal veil cast over an almost unknowable world of greater reality?

Cognitive psychology

There is a popular conception of a 'cognitive revolution' in psychology arising in the 1950s and 1960s, with foundational texts such as Noam Chomsky's *Syntactic Structures* (1957) or Ulric Neisser's *Cognitive Psychology* (1967). However, the postulation of a psychological revolution may be an artefact of 'cognitivist historiography' – an attempt to denigrate behaviourist research, in particular, as the infatuation of a disciplinary Dark Age (Watrin and Darwich). Questions of a cognitivist 'revolution' aside, there are clearly precursor traditions to cognitivism. It would therefore be misleading to see cognitive psychology as emerging purely from the collapse of behaviourism via critiques such as Noam Chomsky's famous 1959 review of Skinner's *Verbal Behavior*, in which Chomsky argues that infants must innately have the capacity to syntactically structure the typically haphazard experience of their linguistic environment. To take just one example of a cognitivist precursor, Frederic Bartlett's study of memory in *Remembering: A Study in Experimental and Social Psychology* (1932) is regarded by Wade Pickren and Alexandra Rutherford as an important proto-cognitivist work. Bartlett's analysis of recall of a culturally unfamiliar Native American folktale by British experimental subjects led him to argue that 'recall was actually reconstruction' (Pickren and Rutherford 317). His conclusion proceeds from careful attention to the kind of recall that might be found in real-life conditions:

> [O]ur studies have shown us that all manner of changes in detail constantly occur in instances which every normal person would admit to be genuine instances of remembering. There are changes in order of sequence, changes of direction, of complexity of structure, of significance, which are not only consistent with subjectively satisfactory recall, but are also perfectly able to meet the objective demands of the immediate situation. Degree of fixity is here a criterion which it would assuredly be hard to apply. (Bartlett 312)

Bartlett thus 'believed that the memorizer, rather than passively accumulating associative strength as the result of practice and repetition, *actively* organizes the material into meaningful wholes that he referred to as schemata' (Goodwin 446). As Pickren and Rutherford note, this finding implied strongly 'that earlier memory experiments that had used meaningless stimuli, such as nonsense syllables, were really assessing a different, and atypical, memory process' (317).

Bartlett was not the only precursor figure. American pragmatism had, for instance, given a constructive, Kantian direction to the psychological ideas of interwar public intellectuals such as Walter Lippmann (as will be shown below in a reading of Jack Finney's *The Body Snatchers* (1955)). In inter-war Germany, Gestalt psychology uncovered principles of perceptual, mnemonic, and behavioural configuration that structured experience – such *Gestalten* were epitomized by Max

Wertheimer's pioneering work on apparent motion and his subsequent research on other principles of perceptual organization (Wagemans *et al.*). Nonetheless, a self-conscious cognitive movement did not emerge until the post-war era, as figures such as Donald Broadbent, George Miller, and Noam Chomsky began to be seen as part of a coherent research programme: 'By the mid-1960s, sufficient research existed to warrant book-length summaries, and texts in cognitive psychology began to appear, most notably Ulric Neisser's *Cognitive Psychology* in 1967, which gave a specific name to the converging ideas of such people as Miller, Broadbent, and others' (Goodwin 456). Neisser's book serves as a useful introduction to the consolidating research programme, and focusses particularly on cognitivist accounts of perception and memory: 'The central assertion is that seeing, hearing, and remembering are all acts of *construction*, which may make more or less use of stimulus information depending on circumstances' (10). In exploring various psychological phenomena that substantiate this claim, Neisser endorses the schematic view of memory developed by predecessors such as Bartlett. It is a myth of pre-cognitive psychology that 'stored information consists of ideas, suspended in a quiescent state from which they are occasionally aroused' (281). In fact, '[p]recise repetition of any movement, any spoken sentence, or any sequence of thought is extremely difficult to achieve. When repetition does occur, as in dramatic acting or nonsense-syllable learning or a compulsive sequence of actions, we ascribe it either to long, highly motivated practice or to neurotic defensiveness' (282). As later cognitive psychologists would show, so-called Flashbulb memory, with its apparent preservation of extraneous details, is remarkable precisely because it is so unlike normal processes of conscious recall (Brown and Kulik).

Neisser discusses the overlap of memory and seeing in support of his claim that '*the mechanisms of visual imagination are continuous with those of visual perception* – a fact which strongly implies that all perceiving is a constructive process' (95). He illustrates his claim by describing experiments with the tachistoscope – an instrument that allows the fleeting presentation of visual stimuli of various kinds. Research using the tachistocope 'leaves no doubt that the subject can continue to "read" information in visual form even after a tachistoscopic exposure is over' (16) – a phenomenon that Neisser refers to as 'iconic memory' (20) or 'transient iconic memory' (16), and that we might popularly know as 'persistence of vision'. Phenomenologically, 'iconic memory' is experienced as sensation: 'although performance was based on "memory" from the experimenter's points of view, it was "perceptual" as far as the experience of the observers was concerned' (19). The contrasting physical reality confirms that perceptual experience is '"an event over time" – not just over the exposure itself, but over the whole period during which iconic storage makes continued visual processing possible' (22). Even perception of an apparently enduring object is equally constructive, as Neisser explains with regard to the act of reading:

> [Y]our eyes make dozens of discrete fixations, perhaps averaging about 300 msec. in length. As many as three separate fixations, taking about one second in all, may be occurring for each line of print. Yet you do not experience a rapid and bewildering succession of visual experiences; you see the whole page continuously, though your attention may be focused only on a part of it. This suggests that a residue of information extracted from earlier fixations remains available, and helps to determine what is seen in the present. (139)

As well as such constructive activity, involving both imagination and memory within perception, Neisser also explores the cognitivist tenet of the limited capacity of the human mind. The mind not only constructs the seemingly given and immediate, it also neglects and selects. The 'span of apprehension' limits 'the number of objects which can be "seen" in a single glance; it is variously estimated as four, five, six or seven' (41). The point is made also by George A. Miller in his classic paper, 'The Magical Number Seven: Plus or Minus Two', that 'the span of absolute judgment and the span of immediate memory impose severe limitations on the amount of information that we are able to receive, process, and remember' (95) – a phenomenon that Miller, informed by information theory, calls 'channel capacity' (82). As with iconic memory or other perceptual constructions, such cognitive activity can be inferred but cannot be directly experienced – 'Introspection is necessarily a poor guide to very rapid cognitive processes' (Neisser 43).

Although Neisser offers less by way of sustained engagement with cognitive linguistics, he is nonetheless aware of Chomsky's work, acknowledging that 'it would be hard to justify a treatment of "cognition" that did not deal with the understanding of ordinary language' (243). Pickren and Rutherford identify Chomsky's *Syntactic Structures* (1957) as historically important to cognitive psychology, given Chomsky's belief that 'the complexity of language and linguistic structure (syntax) could only be accounted for in terms of some innate body of linguistic knowledge that allows native speakers of a language to determine whether a given word sequence is grammatical or not' (327). As Hunter Crowther-Heyck argues, Chomsky's linguistics was central to the legitimation of the cognitivists' computational metaphor for mind: informed by Chomsky, Miller concluded that '(a) mind was necessary to explain language, (b) minds operate according to a set of universal logical rules, and (c) a theory of mind could be modeled in the form of a computer program' (53). Indeed, not only language, but all mental processes were susceptible to this new information-processing model: 'the computer enabled one to model mental processes in a rigorous mathematical fashion and then to put one's model to the test. Computers provided the novel opportunity to embody the ghost of the mind in a machine and so to wed theoretical model building with experimentation' (55). Miller's work was immensely influential – his key role in the Harvard Center for Cognitive Studies helped to provide for the US 'a nucleus from which the ideas of cognitive psychology radiated' (56).

Unlike psychologies such as psychoanalysis and behaviourism, cognitive psychology is currently a dominant psychological school, having spread to worldwide disciplinary significance since its self-conscious coalescence in the 1960s. Cognitivism's current status as disciplinary 'truth' can though be an obstacle to exploration of its deployment in science fiction. As Stefan Herbrechter explains, 'The new image of the human painted by the neuro- and cognitive sciences can be summarized in the provocative phrase: "the mind as machine", which is beginning to change the way humans see themselves, even where this does not automatically entail a sudden change in daily life practices' (25). Cognitivism enters literary theory as a research programme that legitimates motifs in contemporary posthumanism, particularly the erosion of boundaries between human and machine, and the proliferation of various forms of life, whether organic or artificial (cf. Haraway; Hayles). The meaning of cognitivism within science fiction may therefore seem obvious and theoretically validated. As Lisa Yaszek and Jason W. Ellis observe, 'Since World War II, inspired by cognitive science and computational technologies, SF writers have explored the mutability and multiplicity of the human condition, treating the organic body as just one of several mediums for one or more reengineered, posthuman species' (71) – with the well-known artificial and augmented intelligences of cyberpunk furnishing key examples (78–79). However, by taking a longer historical perspective, it is possible to discern alternative meanings of cognitivism with science fiction. The remainder of this chapter will explore how cognitivism licenses *novums* that explore, and problematize, the security of the relationship between mind and reality.

Beyond the posthuman self:
Stereotypes in Jack Finney's *The Body Snatchers*

Jack Finney's science fiction novel *The Body Snatchers* (1955), based on his original *Collier's* serial from 1954 (Johnson 5, 14 n1) contains a sustained exploration of ideas from cognitive psychology, particularly the effects of stereotypical schemas upon perception, knowledge, and memory. However, this cognitive discourse is obscured by taken-for-granted meanings of a text that has provided the elements of a modern myth: even persons unfamiliar with the novel or film adaptations will know something of this story of alien pods that replicate human beings, destroying the original in the process. The *OED*, for instance, records both POD PERSON and POD PEOPLE as terms that come into use from the late 1970s onwards. As befits a modern myth, Finney's novel is better known through its various motion-picture adaptations, particularly Don Siegel's *Invasion of the Body Snatchers* (1956) and the later, 1978, identically titled remake (or perhaps sequel) directed by Philip Kaufmann. The critical literature on the film adaptations is more extensive (e.g. Grant; Badmington) leaving something of a critical silence on the textual originals, albeit with exceptions (e.g. Johnson). Elana Gomel in discussing so-called 'alien-infestation texts' (97) characterizes *The Body Snatchers* as essentially an act of cultural boundary work between humanist subject and posthumanist others:

> The trope of alien infestation literalizes the cultural disintegration of 'man' in the plot of the transformation of a human subject into a post/inhuman entity. This transformation preserves the body but re-crafts the mind. The resulting posthuman subject presents a narratological quandary: it is simultaneously contiguous with humanity and thus speaks in a human voice; and yet it is also radically Other and thus its voice is a counterfeit, a simulacrum, an insincere and flawed imitation. Alien infestation is a discursive site where humanity confronts its alienation from itself. (97)

According to Gomel, 'even today most popular SF is committed to the ideology of liberal humanism. And so in order to police the elusive boundary between human and posthuman/inhuman, more and more radical violence is unleashed' (104). In Gomel's reading, *The Body Snatchers* performs at a less self-conscious level the kind of boundary work that has been identified by N. Katherine Hayles in her reading of Philip K. Dick's *Do Androids Dream of Electric Sheep* (1968) – a text in which, argues Hayles, 'empathy' is fictionalized as a criterion putatively establishing the uniqueness of humans with respect to their android creations (175). One might therefore assume that cognitive psychology in *The Body Snatchers* would serve essentially as an element in the production of 'new forms of subjectivity, which at least in part are dissociated from material forms of embodiment' (Herbrechter 25). Yet rather than positing a fundamental affinity – as 'information', say – between the human mind and the alien copy, cognitive psychology is employed in a quite different way within Finney's novel. *The Body Snatchers* draws upon popular interwar proto-cognitivist discourses to contend, often quite didactically, that the normal human mind typically operates as a biased, limited capacity information processor. With this psychological and political thesis, the novel explores possible personal, political, and aesthetic strategies that might free the human mind from its stereotypes and blind spots. The resulting discourses are, in effect, an Anglo-American language of perceptual estrangement and defamiliarization that lend the novel a metafictional cast.

The Body Snatchers is a curious fusion of genres. The underlying science fiction armature is very much along the lines of a Lovecraftian weird tale, particularly the 1927 short story, 'The Colour Out of Space' (Lovecraft): as with Lovecraft's tale, an unfathomable life form from another region of space arrives in an isolated rural setting, bringing death, destruction, and madness, before finally departing. Finney's setting, the small Californian town of Santa Mira, is invaded by space-travelling seedpods that copy the animate (and inanimate) forms of matter that they encounter on each new world. The population of Santa Mira are stealthily being replaced by alien copies that are identical to all but the keenest observers of the human original. With the creation of each alien copy, the original human dies; moreover, the alien copies are both sterile and biologically faulty – they will all die within a few years of their creation, meaning that all planetary life faces eventual destruction. The resistance to these barren invaders is recounted in a comedic first-person narrative (in the generic, rather than popular sense) centred on the narrator-protagonist, Miles Bennell, a divorced general practitioner, and Becky Driscoll, a fellow divorcee recently returned to Santa Mira. Together with a married (but childless) couple, Jack and Theodora Belicec, they go on what might be viewed as a series of bizarre double dates (recounted in Miles's erratically hardboiled prose) as they successfully combat the invasion. Unlike the typical Lovecraftian tale, in which the human protagonists are essentially powerless before a panoply of alien horrors, Finney's narrative allows a crucial role for human agency. As Johnson notes, the original *Collier's* ending has the G-Men intervene, arriving like the cavalry riding over the hill, to drive the alien seedpods back into space: 'burning gasoline serves [...] as a signal to the FBI, who rush in with riot and machine guns ready; the mob withdraws "in defeat" and only then do the pods rise' (11). In the novel, a different ending places more emphasis on individual agency: the protagonists Miles and Becky's destruction of a large field of pods with burning gasoline is the final tipping point in a war of attrition centred on Santa Mira. Or, at least, this is what Miles infers, as he witnesses the pods 'climbing steadily higher and higher into the sky and the spaces beyond it' (Finney 222).

Notionally, the horror of the parasitic alien copies is that they represent the extinction of all life on Earth. They are not only infertile, but, as is explained to Miles by an alien copy, 'The duplication *isn't* perfect. And can't be. It's like the artificial compounds nuclear physicists are fooling with: unstable, unable to hold their form. We can't live, Miles. The last of us will be dead [...] in five years at most' (190). But, in truth, Finney's novel dwells more on the otherness of the aliens, than on their literal destructiveness – be it their eyes 'as inhumanly cold as the eyes of a shark' (132), or Miles' realization that 'a fish in the sea had more kinship with me than this staring thing before me' (133). In an anticipation of empathy's role in *Do Androids Dream*, a key ingredient in this otherness is the attenuated emotional range of the aliens: 'There's no real joy, fear, hope, or excitement in you, not any more. You live in the same kind of greyness as the filthy stuff that formed you', accuses Miles (189). Beyond this Nietzschean critique of the alien's timid morality is a more homely objection to their lack of civic pride and basic manners: the alien copies neglect their homes and gardens, do not dine out or socialize, and, in one scene of eavesdropping by Miles and Becky, appear to have drifted across light years in order to indulge their taste for sarcasm – 'Uncle Ira went on', records Miles, 'repeating my reply to him of a week before [...] and his voice parodied mine with the pitiless sarcasm of one child taunting another' (139). In a similar vein, Miles and Becky stumble across horrific standards of alien customer service in an establishment where even the Coke 'tasted bad; it was too warm and it hadn't been stirred, and [...] there wasn't a spoon or straw in sight' (128).

Trivial though such plot and incidental detail may seem, it sheds light on what Johnson regards as '[t]wo potent sources of anxiety' in Finney's novel: 'the decline of the family and the disappearance of smalltown America with its virtues' (8). These intersect in 'worry about the decline in homely virtue, in the pride symbolized by a busy family business or a neat home on a pleasant small-town street' (9). Thriving small businesses, and their decline, are central to the narrative. As Miles and Becky walk cautiously through Main Street, they encounter the fading, symbolically named, 'Pastime Bar and Grill': 'The windows were fly-specked, the crepe-paper decoration and cardboard liquor signs badly sun-faded; these windows hadn't been touched for days. There was only one customer, sitting motionless at the bar' (125). On the other hand, the alien pretence of normality requires a simulacrum of small-town capitalism for the day of the 'Santa Mira Bargain Jubilee' (163):

> [T]here were red-and-white paper signs pasted on the windows of the supermarket: advertising Niblets, round steak at 96 cents a pound, bananas, and laundry soap. Vasey's hardware store, as always, had one window filled with kitchen equipment: pots, pans, electric mixers, irons; and in the other window, power tools. The dime-store windows were loaded to the ceiling with candy kisses, model airplanes, paper cut-out dolls, and staring at the red-and-gold front, I could almost smell that dime-store fragrance. (163)

The text's pro-capitalist, anti-communist agenda is readily discerned. As Johnson notes, 'institutions presented as targets of the body snatchers in the novel [...] are the same "American" institutions identified during the decade as targets of Communism. *Democracy vs. Communism*, a high school text published in 1957, singles out the family and individual property as the principal targets of Communist theorists' (10). One might also note that the name Ananias is used in a coded communication between Miles and Jack when the alien copies are eavesdropping on their telephone conversation: 'I tried to think of some figure in literature whose name was a symbol for falsehood, but for the moment I couldn't. Then I remembered – a Biblical name: Ananias, the liar' (Finney 144). The allegedly deceitful Ananias was struck dead for refusing to surrender all his wealth to the early church (*Acts* 5.1–6), thereby defying the redistributive ethos of his fellow Christians: 'neither said any of them that ought [sic] of the things which he possessed was his own; but they had all things common' (*Acts* 4.32); 'distribution was made unto every man according as he had need' (*Acts* 4.35).

But the novel's promotion of free enterprise is counterpointed by anxieties about consumerist capitalism, and other fractures in the post-war US self-image. The pods, for instance, are typically deposited in spaces filled with the clutter of outmoded and discarded consumer goods. One of the first things the arriving pods copy are items on a 'trash pile' at a local farm, such as an empty Del Monte peach can and a broken axe handle (151). Later in the chronology, Jack finds his double in a closet under the stairway that is 'half full of old junk:

clothes in cardboard boxes, burned-out electrical appliances, an old vacuum cleaner, an iron, some lamps, stuff like that. We hardly ever open it' (33). Finney's narrative thus poses critical, if unanswered questions to consumerism (where does the merchandise from Vasey's hardware or the dime store end up, if not spaces such as Jack's closet?). Moreover, both racial and gender politics trouble the narrative's apparent endorsement of hegemonic 1950s US ideals. As Johnson notes, there is a striking, almost incongruous scene in which 'Miles Bennell is spying on a gathering of townspeople who, unaware of his presence, engage in a "hideous burlesque" of their public selves' (7), leading Miles to compare the aliens to African Americans via his memory of a black shoe-shiner in San Francisco. Billy, 'a middle-aged Negro' (Finney 137) whose services Miles employed as a medical student, 'professed a genuine love for shoes. He'd nod with approving criticalness when you showed up with a new pair. "Good leather," he'd murmur, nodding with a considered conviction, "pleasure to work on shoes like these," and you'd feel a glow of foolish pride in your own good taste' (137). By chance, the youthful Miles later eavesdrops on Billy talking with a black friend in his own neighbourhood, a 'run-down section of town, a good two miles from the campus' (138). Billy parodies his daily self-abnegation at his customers' feet: 'never before in my life', reflects Miles, 'had I heard such ugly, bitter, and vicious contempt in a voice, contempt for the people taken in by his daily antics, but even more for himself, the man who supplied the servility they bought from him' (139).

The aliens' textual repercussions extend also into gender relations. Although the book's gender politics are often patriarchal, they are accompanied by some rather more equivocal episodes and representations. After her midnight rescue, Becky is incidentally cross-dressed, in an anticipation of emerging feminist politics: 'I told her where she could find a clean pair of old blue jeans that had shrunk and were too small for me, a clean white shirt, wool socks, and a pair of moccasins; and she nodded, and went upstairs to find them' (62); indeed, she becomes more attractive – wearing them, she looks to Miles 'like a girl in an ad for a vacation resort' (63). And even though Miles's night-time abduction of the unconscious Becky from her home may seem merely an exercise in masculine agency, there is nonetheless another meaning in the scene. Becky jokingly acknowledges the female sexuality that is concealed behind the 1950s stereotype of feminine mystique: 'I like the idea of one of me secretly carried through the streets in her nightgown, while the other is still home, properly alone in her bed, satisfying all the proprieties' (78). Theodora, for her part, imagines a changed masculinity via a replicated second husband who 'would have time to talk to me, and even help with the dishes once in a while' (78).

In addressing the patriarchy of the 1950s US, *The Body Snatchers* begins to reveal its cognitivist psychological credentials, and in a surprisingly feminist way. Admittedly, the narrative may seem unpromising for a feminist reading, given Finney's penchant for scenes of masculine agency and feminine passivity. The novel, however, contains some key dialogue – omitted from the 1956 motion picture – that sheds light on Finney's proto-cognitivist ideas. In Siegel's movie, Miles is involved in a struggle where he uses hypodermic syringes filled with sedatives to overpower his pod people captors, with assistance from the horrified Becky. Then, as the pair attempt to discreetly escape down Main Street, Becky's feminine nature betrays them: she lets out a cry of horror as a dog is nearly run over, alerting the alien copies to her unchanged nature. This rather sexist scene (which is not part of the novel's narrative) resonates ironically with some dialogue omitted from the motion picture adaptation. In the novel, as Miles racks his brains for a plan of escape, he is admonished by Becky for the blind spot in his thinking:

> 'Miles, I know there's no reason why anything we can think of has to work out at all. But now *you're* thinking like a movie. Most people do – sometimes, anyway. Miles, there are certain activities most people never actually encounter all of their lives, so they picture them in terms of movie-like scenes. It's the only source most people have for visualizing things they've had no actual experience of. And that's how you're thinking now: a scene in which you're struggling with two or three men, and – Miles, what am I doing in that scene in your mind? You're seeing me cowering against a wall, eyes wide and frightened, my hands raised to my face in horror, aren't you?'
>
> I thought about it, and she was right, very accurate, in fact, and I nodded.
>
> She nodded, too. 'And that's how they'll think: the stereotype of a woman's role in that kind of situation. And it's exactly what I *will* do – until I know they've seen and noticed me. Then I can do exactly what you did; why not?' (201–02)

In the ensuing melée, Becky simulates her potential movie stereotype – 'she cowered helplessly, eyes wide and frightened, both hands raised in a gesture of horror to her open mouth' (208) – before plunging hypodermics loaded full of sedative into their alien captors (directly, the text implies, into their parasitical buttocks).

Finney's use of the term 'stereotype', and the association of stereotyped thinking with popular cinema are surface manifestations of the novel's didactic strategy. These key terms indicate an important, if overlooked, intertext for *The Body Snatchers*, namely the psychological and political treatise, *Public Opinion* (1922), authored by Walter Lippmann (1889–1974), a significant intellectual presence in mid-twentieth century US culture. Lippman was not a trained psychologist, but rather a public intellectual who advised many important US politicians, and was famous for his regular column in the *New York Herald Tribune* (Newman 10). *Public Opinion* drew upon Lippmann's experience of working for the US Government during and after World War One, where, as Leonard S. Newman explains, he saw 'how propaganda twists facts and distorts the beliefs and attitudes people use to form their opinions. This led him to wonder how one could ideally convey accurate and unbiased information to the public that it could use to form intelligent opinions about important public issues' (10). Lippmann's pessimistic conclusion was that undistorted communication was impossible, since 'bias and distortion is inherent in how people's minds work, and because of that, people are unable to construct accurate and consensual pictures of reality' (Newman 10). Although Lippmann's conclusion has not generally been accepted (and, as will be shown, is only partly endorsed by *The Body Snatchers*), *Public Opinion* remains a so-called 'citation classic' in the field of the social sciences (7), particularly for the ideas it has bequeathed to cognitive social psychology. Although 'James and Santayana's ideas about memory, perception, emotion, and judgment provided the foundation for the psychological theory in *Public Opinion*' (Bottom and Kong 367), Lippmann's American-pragmatist orientation led him to anticipate 'much of the research conducted by cognitive social psychologists' (Newman 16). Lippmann's position that, in essence, 'people are limited capacity motivated processors of information who are prone to biases' (15) is argued in *Public Opinion* by reference to two complementary phenomena, the 'stereotype' and the 'blind spot'. Lippman's concept of the former is not, though, the familiar contemporary sense of the social 'stereotype' (regarding ethnicity, gender, sexuality, etc.). Rather, 'what Lippmann called a stereotype was what a contemporary psychologist would recognize as the broader concept of a "schema"' (12). As Newman explains, Lippmann's concept of the stereotype has a distinct family resemblance to the idea proposed by Bartlett, and continued in later cognitivist traditions:

> Here are some examples: After describing how a group of observers had misremembered details of a staged brawl, he noted that this was

because 'They saw their stereotype of such a brawl' [...]. He also notes that how people recall the appearance of common objects is affected by the 'stereotyped shapes art has lent them' [...]. Shortly after that he writes about stereotypes of landscapes, and even more extensively, about political beliefs as stereotypes. (12)

The complementary concept to the stereotype in Lippman's work is the 'blind spot', a term derived through 'an analogy to the perceptual illusions generated by the visual system. These are gaps between the external facts and internal mental representations resulting in cognitive illusions that lead people to make misguided choices' (Bottom and Kong 372). The blind spot metaphorically covers or conceals that which is not anticipated by the schema.

There is a great deal of persuasive internal evidence that Finney directly employs *avant la lettre* cognitivist ideas taken from *Public Opinion*. Becky's use of the term 'stereotype' in her discussion with Miles certainly indicates some lineage of ideas, particularly since she clearly uses the word in the sense of a Bartlett-like 'schema' rather than a social stereotype. But there are more precise affinities that indicate a closer textual dependence. Becky's belief that the ensuing brawl will be stereotypically (i.e. schematically) conceived resonates with one of Miles's earlier reflections, as a fellow medic, Mannie, attempts to persuade him that nothing sinister is going on in Santa Mira. Miles believes that he has earlier discovered a copy of Becky in her basement, but Mannie – who is by this point an alien copy – proposes that this perception was false, and merely constructed in a state of excited anticipation:

> You saw nothing Miles [...] Except a rolled-up rug, maybe, on a shelf in Becky's basement. Or a pile of sheets or laundry; almost anything at all, or nothing at all, would do. You had yourself so worked-up by then, Miles, so hyper-excited, running through the streets, that as you say yourself, you were certain you were going to find – what of course you did find. (Finney 72)

Although Mannie is the Devil preaching Scripture, Miles is inclined to agree given his own academic knowledge of psychology acquired as a pre-medical student. In a lengthy, but significant passage, he recalls:

> I once sat in a classroom listening to a psychology professor quietly lecturing, and now, [...] I was remembering how the door of that classroom had suddenly burst open, as two struggling men stumbled into the room. One man broke loose, yanked a banana from his

pocket, pointed it at the other, and yelled, 'Bang!'. The other clutched his side, pulled a small American flag from his pocket, waved it violently in the other man's face, then they both rushed out of the room.

The professor said, 'This is a controlled experiment. You will each take paper and pencil, write down a complete account of what you just saw, and place it on my desk as you leave the room.'

Next day, in class, he read our papers aloud. There were some twenty-odd students, and no two accounts were alike, or even close. Some students saw three men, some four, and one girl saw five. Some saw white men, some Negroes, some Orientals, some saw women. One student saw a man stabbed [...]. And so on, and so on. Not a single paper mentioned the American flag or the banana; those objects didn't fit into the sudden violent little scene that had burst on our senses, so our minds excluded them, simply ruled them out and substituted other more appropriate things [...] that we were each of us absolutely certain we'd seen. We *had* seen them, in fact; but only in our minds, hunting for some explanation. (72–73)

This brief narrative closely resembles a passage in *Public Opinion* where Lippman cites an experiment in the reliability of eyewitness testimony as part of his argument for the pervasiveness of stereotyping effects in perception, cognition, and memory. The passage is originally taken from Arnold von Gennep, *La formation des légendes*, but cited in an English translation by Fernand van Langenhove in *The Growth of a Legend* (Lippmann 82), a sceptical study of stories of Belgian atrocities promulgated among Germans during World War One (van Langenhove). Lippman quotes this source in *Public Opinion*:

At a Congress of Psychology in Göttingen an interesting experiment was made with a crowd of presumably trained observers.

'Not far from the hall in which the Congress was sitting there was a public fête with a masked ball. Suddenly the door of the hall was thrown open and a clown rushed in madly pursued by a negro, revolver in hand. They stopped in the middle of the room fighting; the clown fell, the negro leapt upon him, fired, and then both rushed out of the hall. The whole incident hardly lasted twenty seconds.

'The President asked those present to write immediately a report since there was sure to be a judicial inquiry. Forty reports were sent in. Only one had less than 20% of mistakes in regard to the principal facts; fourteen had 20% to 40% of mistakes;

twelve from 40% to 50%; thirteen more than 50%. Moreover in twenty-four accounts 10% of the details were pure inventions and this proportion was exceeded in ten accounts and diminished in six. Briefly a quarter of the accounts were false.

'It goes without saying that the whole scene had been arranged and even photographed in advance. The ten false reports may then be relegated to the category of tales and legends; twenty-four accounts are half legendary, and six have a value approximating to exact evidence.' (82–83)

Lippmann explains that the witnesses were frequently mistaken because they tended to see their

stereotype of such a brawl. All of them had in the course of their lives acquired a series of images of brawls, and these images flickered before their eyes. In one man these images displaced less than 20% of the actual scene, in thirteen men more than half. In thirty-four out of the forty observers the stereotypes preëmpted at least one-tenth of the scene. (83)

For Lippmann, this kind of experiment confirms his general account of the stereotype as an internal representation that 'stamps itself upon the evidence in the very act of securing the evidence' (99). Perception, knowledge, and memory are thus selective and creative acts informed by the constructive contribution of culturally mandated stereotypes: 'For the most part we do not first see, and then define, we define first and then see. In the great blooming, buzzing confusion of the outer world we pick out what our culture has already defined for us, and we tend to perceive that which we have picked out in the form stereotyped for us by our culture' (81). Stereotypes are 'the accepted types, the current patterns, the standard versions, [which] intercept information on its way to consciousness' (85), with the consequence that '[w]e imagine most things before we experience them. And those preconceptions, unless education has made us acutely aware, govern deeply the whole process of perception' (90). As noted above, the obverse of the stereotype is the blind spot: 'What is alien will be rejected, what is different will fall upon unseeing eyes. We do not see what our eyes are not accustomed to take into account. Sometimes consciously, more often without knowing it, we are impressed by those facts which fit our philosophy' (119).

While Lippmann does not seem to preclude the possibility of either innate stereotypes, or acquired but idiosyncratic stereotypes, his analysis concentrates on socially and culturally current preconceptions: 'the stereotyped shapes lent to the world come not merely from art, in the sense of painting and sculpture and literature, but from our moral codes and our social philosophies and our political agitations as well' (84). The intertextual significance may now be clear of Becky's admonishment to Miles that 'there are certain activities most people never actually encounter all of their lives, so they picture them in terms of movie-like scenes' (Finney 202). Photography, and particularly cinematography, are for Lippmann a technology that exemplifies, and also metaphorizes, the effects of stereotypes. It is 'images [that] flickered before their eyes' which misled the eyewitnesses to the staged brawl at the Congress of Psychology – a point that Lippmann elaborates:

> Photographs have the kind of authority over imagination to-day, which the printed word had yesterday, and the spoken word before that. They seem utterly real. They come, we imagine, directly to us without human meddling, and they are the most effortless food for the mind conceivable. Any description in words, or even any inert picture, requires an effort of memory before a picture exists in the mind. But on the screen the whole process of observing, describing, reporting, and then imagining, has been accomplished for you. Without more trouble than is needed to stay awake the result which your imagination is always aiming at is reeled off on the screen. (92)

In order to drive home his point, Lippmann's example of a cinematic stereotype is the notion of the Ku Klux Klan promulgated in D.W. Griffith's *The Birth of a Nation* (1925): 'Historically it may be the wrong shape, morally it may be a pernicious shape, but it is a shape, and I doubt whether anyone who has seen the film and does not know more about the Ku Klux Klan than Mr Griffiths, will ever hear the name again without seeing those white horsemen' (92).

The Body Snatchers is clearly a narrative that accepts much of Lippmann's cognitivist distrust of our perceptions, memory, and cognition. Miles's concluding remarks to his narrative concede as much:

> there are times, and they come more frequently, when I'm no longer certain in my mind of just what we did see, or of what really happened here. I think it's perfectly possible that we didn't actually see, or correctly interpret, everything that happened, or that we thought had happened. I don't know, I can't say; the human mind exaggerates and deceives itself. (Finney 226)

But it is precisely Miles's self-consciousness regarding his own potential unreliability that increases his reliability, and indeed gives him such a vital role in the narrative – as he says in beginning his story, 'I can't say I really know exactly what happened, or why, or just how it began, how it ended, or if it has ended; and I've been right in the thick of it' (1). The tale of Miles, and of Becky and the Belicecs, is one of their conscious effort against schematic apprehension. It is thus perhaps a sly authorial comment that Miles, because of the demands of general practitioner life, has frequently had his cinematic experience interrupted, and so carries fewer mental stereotypes: 'Sometimes I think I've seen half of more movies than anyone else alive, and my mind is cluttered with vague, never-to-be answered wonderings about how certain movies turned out, and how others began' (24). At any rate, there is something about Miles's diagnostic acuity that forestalls routinized perception and cognition. There is, for instance, a clear transition from stereotyped perception to genuine attention when Becky first presents at his practice, deeply concerned about her cousin Wilma's apparent delusions: 'For the first time I really saw her face again' (3) remarks Miles as he attends to his friend and patient. Moreover, Miles's diagnostic perceptiveness is the reason that Jack wants him to view the body that he has discovered in a closet: 'We called you, Miles, because you're a doctor, but also because you're a guy who can face facts. Even when the facts aren't what they ought to be' (35). Jack is alluding, in part, to Miles's previous diagnosis of Theodora with an uncommon and dangerous disease. Miles recalls: 'She had a sudden high fever, extreme lassitude, and I diagnosed it, finally, as Rocky Mountain spotted fever. I wasn't happy about that. You could practice medicine in California for a long time and never run across Rocky Mountain spotted fever, and it was hard to see how she could have caught it' (25). Miles's diagnosis is quite an accomplishment. Even today Rocky Mountain spotted fever is still very difficult to diagnose: the early symptoms are both variable and highly non-specific, and the lack of effective early diagnostic lab tests means that clinical judgement, particularly history-taking, is vital to detection of the disease ('Rocky'). Miles's diagnostic acuity reappears in his refusal of Mannie's invitation to regard the peculiar reports in Santa Mira as mass hysteria. Mannie's supposed refutation of Miles's concerns draws upon the peculiar case of the Mad Gasser of Mattoon (as it is now commonly known) or, as Mannie calls it, 'the Mattoon Maniac' (Finney 67). Reports of a prowler surreptitiously employing anaesthetic gas upon the citizens of Mattoon, Illinois, made national headlines in September 1944, before the supposed phenomenon abated (Bartholomew and Victor 233–37). Expert explanation at the time made reference to the idea of mass hysteria, a 'collective behaviour and somatic reactions [...] caused by the contagious spread of hysterical symptoms in suggestible persons (predominantly females prone to conversion hysteria) expressed to meet unconscious motivations' (238). Mannie thus represents the odd reports as '[m]ass hysteria, auto-suggestion, whatever you want to call it' (Finney 70). However, Miles's initial reflections on Wilma, sexist though they may be, repudiate the stereotyped presupposition that some kind of Freudian unconscious sexual anxiety underlies her apparent delusions: 'Wilma had her problems, but she was tough-minded and bright; about thirty-five years old. She was red-cheeked, short, and plump, with no looks at all; she never married, which is too bad. [...] Wilma hadn't turned sour or bitter; she had a shrewd, humorously cynical turn of mind; she knew what was what and didn't fool herself' (5–6). Because of his medical proficiency, Miles also has an intuitive sense of his blind spots, so that when he sees the 'blank' body on Jack's billiard table, he knows on some level that there is something amiss that he cannot quite cognize: 'I was getting more and more irritated. I didn't like this; there was something strange about this dead man on the table, but I couldn't tell what, and that only made me angrier' (30). Jack's attentiveness also helps him and Becky evade their intended duplication: the scientist Budlong's remark that an arriving pod blindly duplicated 'an empty tin can stained with the juice of once-living fruit' (187) inspires Miles's later use of two anatomical skeletons (marked with some of his and Becky's blood) to misdirect their intended pods.

Miles, though, is not unique in this capacity to resist stereotypes. The action of *The Body Snatchers* revolves around those who have the capacity to resist the symbolic dormission that runs throughout the novel: as Johnson explains, 'Sleep, in film as in novel, is a metaphor not for a general state of mind but for lack of vigilance and consequent vulnerability to subversion' (6). As a GP, Miles knows 'he's going to be telephoned out of bed for the rest of his life perhaps' (Finney 50), but there are others who are equally awake. As the replicated Budlong later explains to Miles and Becky: 'Your friend, Wilma Lentz, and you, Miss Driscoll, are sensitive people; most people weren't aware of any change at all' (188). Theodora Belicec also shares this sensitivity. Even after Mannie's rationalization of the mysterious events as mass hysteria, 'Theodora simply shook her head, her lips compressed in quiet stubbornness. It just wasn't possible for her to believe that she hadn't seen what she was certain she had seen – and could still see in her mind's eye' (79). The idiographic sensibility of Finney's protagonists mean that they are people, as Lippman puts it, 'whose consciousness is peopled thickly with persons rather than with types, who know us rather than the classification into which we might fit' (89). Finney's text, however, opposes Lippmann's critique of the 'self-containment' of American democracy – 'its rootedness in a simpler age, its fealty to an antiquated localist vision, and its dependence on sources of information and education that reinforced rather than overcame the inherent subjectivity of perception' (Blum 65). For Finney, a local community that is spatially smaller, less anonymous, less segregated between classes and other groupings, offers more hope of genuine interpersonal knowledge – hence Miles's annoyance at the loss of figures who have personal relations throughout the community, such as the telephone night operator (Finney 46). As a small-town general practitioner, Miles perceives Santa Mira as 'a town lying out there in the darkness [...] filled with neighbours and friends. I knew them all, at least by sight, or to nod or speak to on the street' (101–02). The citizens of Santa Mira, or some of them at least, are therefore an everyday counterpart to the trained cadre of experts that Lippmann posits in *Public Opinion* as a bulwark against stereotyping and blind spot effects in liberal democracy (402). Finney seems more hopeful than Lippmann, and thinks that everyday local democracy allows for enough trained perception to fulfil this function.

The Body Snatchers is thus a highly didactic text, albeit one that ultimately resists Lippmann's vision of 'the dispersion of expert knowledge by a disinterested corps of civil servants schooled in social science' (Blum 77). Its cognitivist psychological meanings also point towards a metafictional commentary upon its genre. Theodora's husband, by virtue of his profession as a writer, has a similar acuity of vision to Miles's. Jack's folder full of newspaper clippings recounting 'a couple hundred queer little happenings' (81) is a collection of Fortean reports that systematically collates potential cultural blind spots:

> I think they prove at least this: that strange things happen, really do *happen*, every now and then, here and there throughout the world. Things that simply don't fit in with the great body of knowledge that the human race has gradually acquired over thousands of years. Things in direct contradiction to what we know to be true. Something falls up, instead of down. (81–82)

Not only are these opinions shared by Jack and Theodora, they also, by the end of the narrative, belong to Miles as well: 'You read these occasional queer little stories, humorously written, tongue-in-cheek, most of the time; or you hear vague distorted rumours of them. And this much I know. Some of them – *some* of them – are quite true' (226).

The Fortean narrative and its cousin, the fictional weird tale, form part of a cultural armamentarium against stereotyped thinking – they narrate events that are out of kilter with received knowledge. To shoehorn Finney's implied aesthetic into a teleology culminating in 'cognitive estrangement' would be a disservice to *The Body Snatchers* (and, indeed, an instance of stereotyped thinking). Nonetheless, the comparison with Suvin is instructive: Finney's novel carries within it something like an aesthetic of cognitive estrangement, but located within the discourses of liberal capitalism, rather than Marxism. Like Suvin's Formalist forebears, Finney regards everyday perception, cognition, and memory as fallible because 'the mind engages in a natural and essential process of foreshortening, of compressing the limitless environment into proportions tailored to its own powers of comprehension' (Blum 60). Unlike Suvin, Finney's aesthetic focusses more on plot events than on the transformation of reality into an estranged form. For Finney, there is a cognitivist value, it seems, even simply in narration of extraordinary, Fortean intrusions into our common-sense view of the world. In *The Body Snatchers*, the blind spots of our cognitive apparatus can be overcome by the diagnostic acuity of a small-town GP, the artistic sensibility of an author, the good sense of a housewife like Teddy – and by the reading of weird tales.

Beyond the mind as machine:
Cognitive linguistics and temporal phenomenalism

The cognitive psychology of language readily offers material for *novums* of machine intelligence, particularly as manifested in linguistic performance. For instance, the sophisticated linguistic ability of 'Sigfrid' in Frederik Pohl's *Gateway* is a *novum* that extrapolates technologies of natural language processing, complete with interpolated sections of pseudo-code from Sigfrid's programming (121–22 above). *Gateway* thus anticipates the artificial intelligence *novums* of cyberpunk that have been so central to the 'digital and disembodied' variant of the posthumanist imaginary (Yaszek and Ellis 79). Sherryl Vint, among others, has been keenly critical of the Cartesian fantasies that underlie cyberpunk's tendency to celebrate the separation of computational mind from its organic substrate, the body: 'The world of cyberspace is the consummate world of the Cartesian dualist: in cyberspace, one *is* the mind, effortlessly moving beyond the limitations of the human body. In cyberpunk fiction, the prison of the "meat" is left behind' (*Bodies* 103–04). She therefore diagnoses cyberpunk as a subgenre offering wishful fulfilment of a masculinist 'desire to escape the vicissitudes of the body and occupy the place of self-mastery' (104). Thereby, one might add, cyberpunk seemingly restores the earlier Golden Age tendency diagnosed by Robert Lindner and his successors (30–34) – for Andrew Ross, the movement is 'a baroque edifice of adolescent male fantasies' (145). However, the contribution of cognitivist discourses to science fiction after the Golden Age goes beyond merely the supposed identity between mind and computer in the information-processing paradigm. Alongside familiar (and longstanding) *novums* of machine intelligence, including success in the Turing Test, linguistic cognitivism offers a more varied diet of discourses for deployment in science fiction. The following discussion shows how the unsettling of everyday perception in *The Body Snatchers* is systematically generalized by the linguistic *novums* of three texts from the post-Golden Age era: Ian Watson's *The Embedding* (1973), Samuel Delany's *Babel-17* (1966), and Ted Chiang's 'Story of Your Life' (1998). The three narratives are linked by their common use of cognitivist ideas to imagine that language is fundamentally constructive of perceived and known reality, and to imagine possible (if problematic) improvements to both language and perception. But while the Delany and Chiang narratives perpetuate fantasies of human enhancement, Watson's novel has a rather more sceptical attitude to the transformation wrought by its cognitive linguistic *novum*.

In Watson's novel, cognitivist linguistics are exploited to develop a contrast between everyday cognition of the world of time and space, and a fragile glimpse of a greater world that lies beyond the phenomenal veil of perception. The discourses of cognitive linguistics intertwine three parallel narratives, each centring on the quest for an experience of reality unmediated by cognitivist processing. The first of these narratives concerns a linguist, Chris Sole, who works in a secret government facility that uses bizarre, mind-bending environments to experiment with the cognitive development of young children. Sole's research employs a memory-enhancing drug in conjunction with a unique linguistic environment furnished by a computer-transformed language. Paralleling Sole's work is the narrative of anthropologist Pierre Darriand, a former revolutionary and ex-lover of Sole's wife. The relationship between Sole and Darriand is particularly uneasy since Sole is raising the latter's son as his own. Darriand, who still corresponds with Sole's wife Eileen, is studying an Amazonian tribal society known as the Xemahoa, focussing on the peculiar second form (or tier) of their language, which he calls Xemahoa B. This unique ritual language has a strong linguistic resemblance to the computer-transformed English used in Sole's experiment. The two separate plotlines of Sole and Darriand are brought together by the secret arrival to Earth orbit of the Sp'thra, interstellar traders who want to study alien brain structures. The Sp'thra are met by a covert US–USSR reception party, and arrange to exchange information and technology in return for human brains, including one transformed by the Xemahoa's ritual drug, maka-i. This ghoulish quest for disembodied brains brings together Sole and Darriand (the former, who has been recruited by the US, needs the latter to source the cerebral material), but the proposed human–alien exchange does not come to fruition. Instead, the US–USSR hegemony is so alarmed by the destabilization of Earth's power relations that they put into action 'Project Mulekick': the aliens are killed in a nuclear attack upon their spaceship, and the planet is told that the Sp'thra were hostile aliens who were planning an invasion. The novel ends with the Xemahoa saved from Western encroachment by the concomitant geopolitical chaos, and with the death of Sole's favourite child, Vidya, who has been driven to mental and physical destruction by the scientist's experiments.

Watson's essay 'Towards an Alien Linguistics' elaborates his interest in cognitive linguistics. He acknowledges the existence of science fiction precursors, such as Delany's *Babel-17*, and notes that this subversive, metafictional space opera (cf. Hardesty 69) draws upon the work of the linguist Benjamin Whorf:

> The American Benjamin Whorf, in contrasting European languages with American Indian languages, came to the conclusion that different languages condition radically different worldviews; different realities. Whorf's studies of Hopi, Nootka, Shawnee, and the American Indian view of the universe read at times like models for an alien linguistics; and indeed a good example of Whorf-based aliens occurs in Delany's *Babel-17* with its description of the culture of Çiribia, entirely based on heat and temperature changes. Delany's moral is that 'compatibility factors for communication are incredibly low'. This is Whorf writ large on the galaxy. ('Towards' 46–47)

Whorf was a particularly forthright, lucid, and early proponent of linguistic relativism, claiming that '[t]he categories and types that we isolate from the world of phenomena we do not find there because they stare every observer in the face; on the contrary, the world is presented in a kaleidoscopic flux of impressions which has to be organized by our minds – and this means largely by the linguistic systems in our minds' (213). Despite alluding to Whorf's hypothesis, Watson's interests are somewhat different, and centre on the existence and nature of innate grammatical structures: 'since Whorf's time, Chomsky has shown that there is in all human beings an innate plan for acquiring *any* human language – and therefore that all human languages must be formally related on some deep structural level' (47). This universalism might seem to allay concerns raised by Whorf's account of linguistic incommensurability, promising some ultimate, innate communicative compatibility, despite a degree of variation in cultural–linguistic constructions. Watson, though, draws quite another moral:

> Deep Structures underlie all our surface manifestations of Language. But introspection will never recover them. We cannot consciously think by means of them. And even the level of Deep Structures is some way removed from the level of Thought itself. Between the world and our expression of it are thus a series of interfaces, apparently impenetrable to consciousness. Our language is an activity; not a proof of anything. (49)

The conclusion offered by Watson is a kind of Kantian phenomenalism. Kant argued that our conceptual forms and perceptual apparatus ensured we could only know and perceive things as they appeared to us, rather than as they were in themselves (Kant). Similarly, Watson concludes that 'we would seem to be cut off from consciousness of Reality *by virtue* of the language which alone enables us to organise our thoughts and think about Reality' (49).

Watson confronts directly a problem evaded by *Babel-17* – namely, the epistemological implications of cognitivism. At first sight, Delany's novel seems committed to a relativist perspective informed by Whorf's analysis. The protagonist, Rydra Wong, a cryptographer, linguist, and poet, states baldly that 'language *is* thought. Thought is information given form. The form is language' (Delany 20). Moreover, there are significant cognitive variations between languages: 'when you learn another tongue, you learn the way another people see the world, the universe' (20). This interpretation has been propounded by Carl Malmgren, who argues that '[l]anguage is central to the novel in large part because Delany's view of language is Whorfian; he sees language as constitutive of reality, not as reflective of reality. We see what our language enables us to see; we think according to the ways that language makes available to us' (9). Yet, regardless of Delany's views, the text has quite another position. Babel-17, the language used by the space operatic alien enemy, is actually better for devising instrumental operations upon the external world than the languages Wong already knows. She learns Babel-17 and finds her cognitive mastery of the world to be immensely superior. She awakens to find herself imprisoned by space pirates (another operatic trope) and unwittingly slips into Babel-17 cognitions: 'she had felt it before with other languages, the opening, the widening, the mind forced to sudden growth. But this, this was like the sudden focusing of a lens blurry for years' (96–97). The conceptual mastery is explicit as Wong observes the webbing that holds her captive:

> She looked down at the – not 'webbing', but rather a three particle vowel differential, each particle of which defined one stress of the three-way tie, so that the weakest points in the mesh were identified when the total sound of the differential reached its lowest point. By breaking the threads at these points, she realized, the whole web would unravel. (97)

Elsewhere, Babel-17 is described as facilitating a 'hallucinatory vividness' in perception (116), and as 'the most analytically exact language imaginable' (184). Babel-17's weakness is that it happens to lack the word 'I'; as Rydra explains, 'Babel-17 is such an exact analytical language, it almost assures you technical mastery of any situation you look at. And the lack of an "I" blinds you to the fact that though it's a highly useful way to look at things, it isn't the only way' (188). There is therefore in *Babel-17* some mysterious way in which the self pushes through the phenomenal veil of language. This becomes particularly apparent in an incident where Rydra attempts to direct her lover towards the absence in his cognitive apparatus of a concept for the first person:

> Don't you see, sometimes you want to say things, and you're missing an idea to make them with, and missing a word to make the idea with. In the beginning was the word. That's how somebody tried to explain it once. Until something is named, it doesn't exist. And it's something the brain needs to have exist, otherwise you wouldn't have to beat your chest, or strike your fist on your palm. The brain wants it to exist; let me teach it the word. (131)

At this point, Delany's text retreats from the premise that 'language *is* thought', and offers instead the brain as metonymy for a separate cognitive process that reveals the insufficiency of any particular language and promises a restored relationship to authentic subjectivity via a renewed language of the self. In effect, *Babel-17* adapts and reflexively authorizes cognitivist ideas by offering them within *novums* of mental enhancement, both technocratic and countercultural: Babel 17, the language, is a linguistic psychotechnology for superior instrumental rationality, while Wong's discourse offers a language for cultivation of the self.

The Embedding, however, faces more directly the philosophical issues raised by cognitivism, asking how – if it all – we can experience reality if our perceptions and cognitions are shaped by a set of innate *a priori* forms, and what the consequences would be of an unmediated relationship to reality. Chomsky's linguistics provides Watson with a point of entry into a wider range of cognitivist positions on mental activity. Timothy J. Reiss argues that Sole's highly unethical experimental work with children is designed to 'test certain assumptions about the allegedly fundamental structures of universal grammar' (88). This account of Sole's experiment is, however, not quite accurate. As the accounts and debates about Sole's research indicate, it is an experiment that investigates the ramifications of improved short-term memory upon language, using patterns that are grammatical but deprecated (as unusable) beyond a certain level of complexity. The exemplary phenomenon of centre embedding is explained by reference to the nursery rhyme, 'The House that Jack Built'. In Watson's text, the version used is split across the dialogue of several characters, and runs:

> This is the farmer sowing his corn,
> That kept the cock that crowed in the morn,
> That wakened the priest all shaven and shorn,
> That married the man all tattered and torn,
> That kissed the maiden all forlorn,
> That milked the cow with the crumpled horn,
> That tossed the dog,
> That chased the cat,
> That worried the rat,
> That ate the malt,
> That lay in the house that Jack built. (cf. *Embedding* 48)

As Sole explains, the entire rhyme could, in principle, be rewritten, using centre embedding (more specifically, the 'self-embedding' of the same relative clause construction). But even when shortened to just a few phrases, the result is practically unintelligible: '"Any four-year-old can follow that nursery rhyme," Sole fired back, his face flushed. "It's another story when you embed the same phrases. 'This is the malt that the rat that the cat that the dog worried killed ate.' How about that? Grammatically correct – but you can hardly understand it"' (49). Sole's example in fact uses a different text of the full verse, but the point is clear: 'this is the dog that worried the cat that killed the rat that ate the malt' would become 'this is the malt that the rat that the cat that the dog worried killed ate'. The centre-embedded version increasingly separates verbs and their objects. We can surely understand 'this is the malt that the rat ate', and also 'this is the malt that the rat that the cat killed ate'. We can perhaps barely manage 'this is the malt that the rat that the cat that the dog worried killed ate', but surely not 'this is the malt that the rat that the cat that the dog that the cow tossed worried killed ate'.

The pertinent issue, at least in Watson's text (as opposed to the current state of linguistic theory), is not the validity, or otherwise, of a supposed universal grammar. Centre embedding is perfectly grammatical, but, used beyond a certain point, exceeds the capacity of human short-term memory. This is a point made by Miller and Chomsky in their 1963 book chapter, 'Finitary Models of Language Users':

> [S]entences of natural languages containing nested dependencies or self-embedding beyond a certain point should be impossible for (unaided) native speakers to understand. This is indeed the case, as we have already pointed out. There are many syntactic devices available in English – and in every other language that has been studied from this point of view – for the construction of sentences with nested dependencies. These devices, if permitted to operate freely, will quickly generate sentences that exceed the perceptual capacities (i.e., in this case, the short-term memory) of the native speakers of the language. This possibility causes no difficulties for communication, however. These sentences, being equally difficult for speaker and hearer, simply are not used, just as many other proliferations of syntactic devices that produce well-formed sentences will never actually be found. (471)

The children being experimented upon by Sole therefore also receive a drug called PSF, or Protein Synthesis Facilitator, described informally by Friedmann, one of the scientists, as a 'unique lever for improving brain performance!' (I. Watson *Embedding* 43). PSF works by removing bottlenecks in processing from short- to long-term memory, a point made clear in dialogue between Sole and his colleague, Zwingler:

> [Sole:] 'speech processing depends on the volume of information the brain can store short-term––'
> [Zwingler:] 'This amount being limited by the time it takes short-term memory to become permanent and chemical, instead of electrical?' (49)

As Friedmann explains, with regard to PSF, 'We can't inject information as such into the brain, like slotting in some miracle memory tape. But what we can do is hurry up the manufacture of protein while the brain is busy learning' (44). PSF therefore facilitates the acquisition and use of the centre-embedded language presented in the computer-generated/transformed speech environment inhabited (or endured) by Sole's children: 'He had walked among them, played with them, shown them how to use their maze and teaching dolls and oracles – wearing a speech-mask which snatched the words from his lips as soon as he whispered them, sent them to the computer for sorting and transforming, before voicing them' (17). As Sole's reflections show, the linguistic environment is one of grammatical, but (to us) unusable English:

> Sole couldn't have framed the sentences he heard his recorded voice saying, without a great deal of hesitation. They were English sentences, yet so un-English. It was the arrangement of those strings of words that caused the confusion. The words themselves were simple enough. Such kids' talk. Yet organized as no kids' talk before, so that adults couldn't for the life of them follow it without a printout of the speech with a maze of brackets breaking it up to re-establish patterns the mind was used to processing. (15)

PSF allows such speech to be intuitively, spontaneously processed. *The Embedding* is thus a novel that extrapolates from cognitivist findings on memory, but in a way peculiar to science fiction, a genre for which the reality of human memory (whether long-term or short-term) frequently seems unsatisfactory. Bartlett may have cautioned that 'all manner of changes in detail constantly occur' in 'genuine instances of remembering' (312). Yet science fiction seems infatuated with 'improved' human memory, particularly of an eidetic kind, and seems to have taken cognitivist models of memory as a challenge. Such a desire to find the potential for enhancement within cognitivist discourses is found even in the work of superior writers such as Delany – Rydra Wong, for instance, has total verbal recall in *Babel-17* (8). The persistent trope is ironized in Dick's renowned short story 'We Can Remember it for you Wholesale' (1966). When the protagonist Quail first goes to buy memories to enliven his apparently drab life, the salesman at Rekal Incorporated informs him, 'our analysis of true-mem systems – authentic recollections of major events in a person's life – shows that a variety of details are very quickly lost to the person. Forever. Part of the package we offer you is such deep implantation of recall that nothing is forgotten' (Dick 160). So-called 'extra-factual memory', insists the salesman, is better than the real thing by virtue of its non-schematic detail: 'You're not accepting second-best. The actual memory, with all its vagueness, omissions and ellipses, not to say distortions – that's second-best' (160).

In the case of *The Embedding*, improved memory is a cognitivist *novum* that facilitates a transformation in thought and perception – a transformation that may allow a brief transcendence of everyday phenomenal consciousness, or that may prove ultimately destructive. According to Tim Conley and Stephen Cain, *The Embedding* is a univocal warning against tampering with humanity's inborn cognitive endowment: 'clearly supporting Chomsky's theories of innate grammar, Watson demonstrates how this process drives these children insane – humans, it seems, are biologically and neurologically wired with deep linguistic structures that cannot be reprogrammed without causing psychosis' (57). Yet it is notable that a largely tolerable, perhaps even beneficent transformation is depicted in the narrative of Pierre's fieldwork with the Xemahoa, which parallels, and then intersects with, the stories of Sole and the alien visitors. The special, ritual language Xemahoa B, allows a transformed time perception because of its centre-embedded constructions, which can be used and understood only in an altered state of consciousness. Pierre reflects: 'If Xemahoa B – the drug speech – is as deeply self-embedded as my recordings lead me to suspect, then an utterance "now" is already pregnant with the future completion of the utterance' (I. Watson *Embedding* 71). As Pierre later discovers after participating in tribal rituals, the ability to use Xemahoa B occurs in a transcendence of the perceptual illusion that distinguishes past, present, and future. Only a mind freed from its imprisonment in the present can grasp this unique language:

> Time seemed like a useless ornament – a distraction. The sense of time he'd possessed the night before hadn't been time by the calendar or time by the clock. It hadn't been historic time, but a sense of the spatio-temporal unity out of which space and time are normally separated into an illusory contrast with one another.
>
> In this three-dimensional flatland of ours, words flow forward and only hang fire of their meaning so pitiably short a time, while memories flow hindwards with such a pitiably feeble capacity to hold themselves in full present awareness. Our illusion of the present is like a single dot on a graph we can never get to see the whole of. (109)

What ultimately emerges from Watson's speculations is a neo-Kantian thought pattern in which time is an illusion. His treatment of this theme can be instructively contrasted with Ted Chiang's 1998 intertextual short story, 'Story of Your Life'. The narrator of this story, set in a contemporary or near-future US, is Louise Banks, a linguist employed by the US government and military to communicate with the heptapods, seven-limbed aliens who have arrived in earth orbit, and set up remote communication stations across the globe. The heptapods have a two-tiered language system. Heptapod A, the spoken version, allows Chiang what is probably a sly allusion to *The Embedding*: Banks notes, 'the heptapods had no objection to many levels of centre-embedding of clauses, something that quickly defeated humans. Peculiar, but not impenetrable' ('Story Of' 137). Banks describes Heptapod B, the written version, as 'semasiographic', since 'it conveys meaning without reference to speech' (131). The latter tier is more important to the narrative, since it furnishes the central cognitive–linguistic *novum*: as Banks learns the language, she notes that 'Heptapod B was changing the way I thought' (151). The written tier presents meanings simultaneously via complex images. As Banks gains facility in it, so she begins to acquire the heptapods' mode of time perception: 'Humans had developed a sequential mode of awareness, while heptapods had developed a simultaneous mode of awareness. We experienced events in an order, and perceived their relationship as cause and effect. They experienced all events at once, and perceived a purpose underlying them all' (159). To disarm the usual paradoxes of free will versus determinism, Chiang postulates via his narrator a fatalistic conation that emerges in tandem with this simultaneous cognition: 'now that I know the future, I would never act contrary to that future, including telling others what I know: those who know the future don't talk about it' (163). Thus, when Banks is confronted in a shop with a bowl that she knows will later fall on her as-yet unborn daughter's head, she feels the inner necessity of buying it: 'I reached out and took the bowl from the shelf. The motion didn't feel like something I was forced to do. Instead it seemed just as urgent as my rushing to catch the bowl when it falls on you: an instinct that I felt right in following' (158). The heptapods' inadvertent cognitive transformation of Banks's perceptions provides her with a psychotechnology for spiritual reconciliation with the cosmos: she can rove freely over the course of her own and her daughter's life, savouring and reliving it, despite the latter's premature death in a climbing accident.

As Chiang is clearly aware ('Story Notes' 334), his short story rewrites Kurt Vonnegut's *Slaughterhouse-Five*, a short novel that thoroughly explores temporal phenomenalism via the similar device of an alien race (the Tralfamadorians) who perceive all times simultaneously, and who bring this wisdom to a vanguard of Earthlings, pre-eminently Vonnegut's protagonist, Billy Pilgrim. But in drawing upon Vonnegut's satirical and self-reflexive novel, Chiang's anodyne narrative entirely disregards Vonnegut's satire on fatalism, and his careful critique of modernist temporal phenomenalism. Billy learns, for instance, that it is futile to try to prevent wars (since time is wholly pre-determined), that dead people are 'still alive' in the past, and that evil can be eliminated from the world by concentrating one's temporal attention upon only the happy moments in one's life (G. Miller 'Literary' 308–10). Chiang's relationship to *The Embedding* is less pronounced, but 'Story of Your Life' nonetheless also disregards the unsettling elements of Watson's novel. *The Embedding* warns, for instance, that the atemporal experience of reality is a very fragile part of the Xemahoa's culture, and accessible only in extraordinary states of consciousness: 'Only a drug-tranced Bruxo can fully articulate it', affirms Pierre, 'Only a drug-tranced people dancing through the firelight can grasp the gist of it' (I. Watson *Embedding* 63). In Pierre's view, the Xemahoa's capacity for transcendence depends moreover upon a complex ecology, including an ecology of extended cognition enabled by their tropical rainforest environment: 'The intricacy of the links that held the mental and social life of these people together! Links between tree and soil and fungus; shit and sperm and laughter' (112). While the Xemahoa may be able to handle their ecstasies, Watson's narrative contains a number of parallels that caution against the routinized technological pursuit of transcendence. The Sp'thra insist that 'Other-Reality outside of this totality assuredly exists! We mean to grasp it! [...] There are so many ways of seeing This-Reality, from so many viewpoints. It is these viewpoints that we trade for' (137). Yet the aliens' ghoulish collection of disembodied brains provides an image paralleling both the Xemahoa's brutal mistreatment of a local woman and Sole's neurological experiments upon the children. The psychological destructiveness of Sole's experiments is presaged in the corporeal monstrosity of the Xemahoa child subjected throughout its gestation to the effects of the tribe's ritual drug, maka-i:

> But the baby—
> Sole stared at it, too shocked to feel sick.
> Three brain hernias spilled from great vents in its skull – grey matter slung in tight membrane bags about its head, like codroe at the fishmonger's. The top part of its face, beneath those bags of brain, had no eyes – two smooth dents where they ought to have been.
> From several places in its torso spilled ruptures. They jutted out of a body that only approximately contrived to contain itself within itself. (199)

This monstrous body metaphorizes the destructive effects, as Watson's text would have it, of trying to squeeze into human consciousness a contact with reality unmediated by our customary apparatus of cognitive mechanisms. Pierre's reflections provide another warning: while 'in some ways Xemahoa B is the *truest* language', 'for all practical purposes of daily life [...] it directs crippling blows at our straightforward logical vision of the world' (103). The linguistic (and cognitive) 'barrier – a great filter – [...] between Reality and our Idea of Reality' (103) therefore seems necessary to our survival, no matter how seductive the desire '[t]o know the whole truth of life, as a direct experience' (182).

As Zwingler's warning to Sole indicates, the latter's bizarre experiments are little better than the Xemahoa's meddling with gestation: '"Hmm, this PSF drug," nodded Zwingler. "It seems a dubious distinction to me – altering the brain by surgery, and altering it by a drug, if the drug's as long-acting as Sam supposes"' (43). Sole even reflects to himself that the experiment '[t]o raise children in isolation speaking specially designed languages' was 'a kind of pornography after a while, a sort of scientific masturbation' (12). The horrific consequences of Sole's experiments are revealed in his final encounter with Vidya, where he experiences something later conceived as 'projective empathy' (253) – which is explained as '[n]ot genuine communication of ideas from mind to mind. Not dialogue – but a domineering influence, a sort of electrochemical hypnosis' (253). Sole therefore undergoes the world as Vidya experiences it after years of pharmaceutical and linguistic conditioning:

> This world flipped, into a new state of being.
> It fell apart from lines and solids into a pointillist chaos of dots. Bright dots and dark dots. Blue dots, red dots, green dots. No form held true. No distance held fast. New forms making use of these dots in entirely arbitrary, experimental ways, sprang into being among the overwhelming debris of sense perceptions outside of him – fought to impose themselves on the flux of being – failed. Fell apart. And new forms rose. (249)

Sole's temporary 'iconic memory' ceases to be transient as he enters the mode of time consciousness previously experienced by Pierre in the rain forest, but now without the protective apparatus of Xemahoa culture: 'He was watching a movie – but as the new scenes arrived, the old scenes refused to yield and pass on. They too continued to be screened' (250). The narratorial voice further interprets Sole's experience by providing an extended metaphor of the cognitivist account of mind:

> Reason – rationality – is a concentration camp, where the sets of concepts for surviving in a chaotic universe form vast, though finite, rows of huts, separated into blocks by electric fences, which the searchlights of Attention rove over, picking out now one group of huts, now another.
>
> Thoughts, like prisoners – imprisoned for their own security and safety – scurry and march and labour in a flat two-dimensional zone, forbidden to leap fences, gunned down by laser beams of madness and unreason if they try to.
>
> Vidya's concentration camp had bulged at the seams. (250)

The searchlight (or spotlight) of attention, roving over areas of otherwise pre-reflective processing, sparks Watson's subversive elaboration of psychological metaphor (which is also elaborated in the punning 'concentration' camp). Attention brings to light our conceptual apparatus, which is primarily a tool for surviving in a chaotic, barely cognisable universe. Vidya has achieved a non-rational, mystical knowledge of the world – a knowledge that, unlike the Xemahoa, he is unable to even briefly withstand.

Cognitivist discourse represents the mind as an information processor that gains a limited degree of mastery over the world – leaving the way open for seductive fantasies of enhanced cognition, such as that found by the protagonists of Delaney's *Babel-17* and Chiang's 'Story of Your Life'. To this agreeable (capitalist and individualist) vision of self-improvement via psychotechnology, Watson opposes a different interpretation of the same cognitivist premises. *The Embedding* interrogates the reflexive authority of cognitivist psychology by extrapolating from it a *novum* uncongenial to narratives of posthumanist linguistic (and neurological) enhancement. What Sole experiences vicariously in his telepathic union with Vidya is an ironically improved mode of consciousness, and indeed knowledge, freed from *Gestalten*, schemas, transient iconic memory, informational bottlenecks, attention, and many other cognitivist phenomena:

> The world flowed around him more demandingly again – a million bits of information. His present awareness, however much it distended, still ached with the strain of finding room for all this fearful wealth. The world was about to be embedded in his mind in its totality as a direct sensory apprehension, and not as something safely symbolized and distanced by words and abstract thoughts. The Greater was about to be embedded in the Lesser. (251)

Sole and his experimental subjects lack the know-how conserved in the tribal society of the Xemahoa; these supposed 'primitives', rather than the 'developed' West, or the alien Sp'thra, have the greater expertise in the management of mystical states. Rather than obediently (if sluggishly) representing and cognizing the world, the mind is a necessary falsifier of an unmanageably complex reality that can be at best glimpsed in mystical states, and which is fundamentally inimical to symbolic representation.

Conclusion

Science fiction makes idiosyncratic and varied use of the cognitivist credo that knowledge, experience, and language are mediated by a diverse range of mental constructions. Admittedly, the tenor of cognitive psychology is towards the epistemological security of the computer metaphor for mind. As noted, there are many science fiction narratives, particularly in the cyberpunk subgenre, that explore the informational view of human life, and often celebrate a Cartesian separation of computational mind from organic body. But this chapter has focussed on science fiction narratives that use cognitivist and proto-cognitivist ideas to explore the possibility of phenomena that are commonly, perhaps almost necessarily, screened out by mentation. Finney's *The Body Snatchers* probes the weak spots of liberal democracy: the expulsion of the invaders from Santa Mira relies upon the relative immunity of the protagonists to the stereotyping effects that are necessary to everyday perception. *The Embedding* – and its kindred stories of science fiction linguistics, Delaney's *Babel-17* and Chiang's 'Story of Your Life' – ask broader, philosophical questions about the nature and accessibility of ultimate reality. For Delaney and Chiang, cognitivism offers the possibility of improved instrumental mastery over the world, an enhanced relation to authentic subjectivity, and a fatalistic reconciliation with the cosmos. However – and ironically, for a text so informed by cognitive linguistics – Watson's novel erodes these appealing narratives of cognitivist psychology, proposing that our mediated experience and cognition cast a phenomenal veil over an almost ungraspable reality that can only be safely grasped in a state of mystical consciousness.

Conclusion
Science fiction in psychology

The preceding chapters have examined the deployment of psychological discourses in science fiction, drawing upon a variety of disciplinary schools: evolutionary psychology; psychoanalysis; behaviourism and social constructionism; existential humanism; and cognitivism. As noted in the introduction (15–16), this structure has excluded other possible arrangements, including a division by various psychological phenomena, such as memory, intelligence, conation, and affect. Future researchers may indeed prefer some alternative structuring principle, particularly with a view to showing the entanglement of different psychological schools. For the sake of expository convenience, this monograph has also tended to somewhat artificially segregate different psychological theories. Behaviourism and constructionism have been considered together, as have various psychoanalytic schools – but evolutionary psychology has been divided from cognitivism (although the two clearly overlap), and the imbrication of psychoanalysis with existentialism has also been somewhat neglected.

Moreover, both psychology and science fiction have been defined in a way useful for this investigation, but clearly open to contention. Psychology is understood as the modern disciplinary formation emerging in the late nineteenth century, which sought to supplant prior discourses such as theology and philosophy, and which, in the course of its development, performed boundary work against certain allegedly pseudo-scientific research programmes, including parapsychology. Science fiction, meanwhile, has been delimited in roughly the terms advanced by Darko Suvin, in which the genre is defined as a narrative of estrangement dominated by a rationally validated scientific innovation. These delimitations of psychology and science fiction are useful to a pathfinding monograph, but nonetheless open to dispute and supplementation. Future research will probably, for instance, furnish a fruitful and significant reading of the place of parapsychology within science fiction, building upon the pioneering work of Damien Broderick (*Psience*). The implications for science fiction of the rise of neuropsychology have not been considered within this monograph; but, as with parapsychology, this is clearly a fruitful area for further research. Moreover, while this monograph has worked largely with Suvin's definition of science fiction, there is obviously a larger hinterland of science fiction and fantasy literature within which psychology may have a significant discursive presence. Finally, there can be no pretence that the sample of psychologically informed science fiction texts in the preceding chapters is any way exhaustive: they have been chosen to illustrate a diversity of approaches using each of the relevant schools; there are undoubtedly further science fiction narratives that make significant use of psychological ideas, and there are no doubt other psychological discourses to be discovered at work within the genre.

While this monograph has necessarily restricted its scope in certain ways, it has nonetheless illustrated and elaborated the varied functions of psychological discourse within science fiction. Although the *didactic-futurological function* may seem rather limited from a literary point of view, science fiction nonetheless frequently propounds and popularizes particular psychological schools of thought, typically within the context of a supposedly anticipatory extrapolation. The expositions and dialogues of Skinner's behaviourist utopian blueprint, *Walden Two*, clearly illustrate such an aim. This function need not, however, invite Skinner's ponderous didacticism: a similar aspiration to inform the non-specialist about psychological (specifically, cognitivist) ideas and their ramifications can be found in Finney's far superior genre classic *The Body Snatchers*. As for the *utopian function* of psychological discourse, it may be found in a range of critical utopian and dystopian narratives that nurture hope for a better world. While a number of exemplary narratives have been considered in the preceding chapters, perhaps the clearest realization is McHugh's existential utopia *I Am Thinking of My Darling*, which imagines New York briefly transformed by an epidemic of happiness. Predictably, the well-known *cognitive-estranging function* appears in a number of psychological narratives examined in the preceding chapters. For instance, Pohl's *Gateway* defamiliarizes psychoanalytic psychotherapy as an accommodationist technology, while Mitchison's constructionist utopia in *Solution Three* estranges the contemporaneous treatment of sexual minorities via its vision of an oppressed heterosexual minority. The genre as whole is addressed by the *metafictional function* of psychological discourses. This offers self-reflexive comment on the uses and gratifications of science fiction itself, particularly in conscious or implied opposition to the crude psychoanalytic view that the genre gratifies the compensatory power fantasies of social misfits. Wilson and Lessing, for instance, find science fiction to be an apt representation of existential realities that cannot be accommodated by everyday realist discourse, while for Le Guin science fiction offers a psychic rootedness in archetypal forms that facilitate psychological health. A final function, and one more closely confined to psychological science fiction, is the *reflexive function*, which allows interrogation of the expert discourses that offer to construct human subjectivity in their mould. Vonnegut's *Galápagos* subverts the authority of evolutionary psychological discourses, and a similar interrogation of psychoanalysis and cognitivism, respectively, can be found in Pohl's *Gateway* and Watson's *The Embedding*.

This monograph's analysis of psychological science fiction, with these various functions as 'ideal types' that clarify the meaning of individual narratives, has offered a number of fresh viewpoints. In particular, science fiction scholarship has been invited to enter into an interdisciplinary dialogue with the history of psychology. The depth and variety in science fiction's engagement with psychology has hitherto been largely overlooked by literary critics. In part, this is because contemporary literary theory has imported into literary studies only a few favoured schools congenial to the hermeneutics of suspicion: post-Lacanian psychoanalysis is, of course, pre-eminent. Yet, such psychoanalytic hermeneutics of suspicion obscure the extent to which science fiction authors knowingly employ psychoanalytic discourses. The enormous dissemination of Freudian and post-Freudian ideas during the twentieth century means that the overwhelming majority of modern and contemporary literature, science fiction or otherwise, anticipates a psychoanalytic horizon of reception. In literary studies, the presumed disciplinary truth and interpretative acumen of a narrow range of primarily psychoanalytic ideas thus impedes recovery, understanding and critique of the range of psychological discourses employed in science fiction. The psychologization of the Western self in the twentieth century has been marked by a plurality of psychological schools, which, alongside the other human sciences, discursively shape the self with far greater intimacy than the natural sciences. As the chapter structure of this monograph indicates, psychology has no unifying disciplinary paradigm. Moreover, psychological discourses are distinguished by their reflexivity effects – they can be adopted, adapted and/or refused by the subjects to whom they are addressed. Science fiction therefore plays a part in augmenting, or diminishing, the social currency and presumed validity of psychological discourses. One of the key accomplishments of this monograph has thus been to articulate science fiction's engagement with reflexivity effects (what I have called the *reflexivity function*).

To pursue an interdisciplinary dialogue with the history of psychology has further benefits. The genre can be seen to link psychology back into its pre-disciplinary forebears, with witting or unwitting critical effect: Skinner's fiction shows how psychology preserves and modifies religious and salvational motifs; Watson's *The Embedding* explores a quasi-Kantian phenomenalism; and Burgess confronts the behavioural sciences with wisdom traditions of a broadly 'Manichean' character. The exploration of psychological discourses also relates science fiction to the wider literary context with which it has been in continuous, if sometimes clandestine, communication. This is particularly clear with the existentialist affinities of Wilson, Lessing, and Piercy, but includes also the Nietzscheanism of Christopher, the postmodernism of Russ and Malzberg, the modernist interiority of Pohl and Le Guin, and the hard-boiled prose of McHugh. The simple act of posing a new question about psychological discourses even to very familiar, and apparently well-known texts, can also be remarkably transformative. A familiar reference point like *The Body Snatchers* appears in a very different light when located within proto-cognitivist questions about the adequacy of everyday perception, cognition, and memory. Other, less familiar texts, are dragged out of relative obscurity by their relevance to a new question. A text such as McHugh's *I Am Thinking of My Darling* – which is practically unknown, and out of print at time of writing – deserves far greater celebration and recognition within science fiction studies. This monograph thereby intervenes in the 'selective tradition' of science fiction. Informed by Raymond Williams, Milner argues that science fiction is 'continuously reinvented in the present', so that the 'boundaries of the genre are continuously policed, challenged and disrupted [...]. It is thus essentially and necessarily a site of contestation' (39–40). The set of interests in the preceding chapters invite a new formation of 'science fiction' in which the human sciences motivate different boundaries to the genre, alongside changed hierarchies and arrangements within it.

The questions addressed in this monograph also have ramifications for an understanding of science fiction's historical emergence and meaning. Modern psychology arises in the late nineteenth century, a context in which the pioneering work of Wundt and James was particularly important. Psychology is seen as pre-eminent among a number of disciplines that explored the Darwinian principle of continuity between human and non-human life. The importance to science fiction of psychology in its modern disciplinary formation has been demonstrated within this monograph, and this conclusion tends to affirm the literary history advanced by Milner (7–8 above), who disputes genealogies which depict the genre as continuous with classical antecedents, such as utopia and the fantastic voyage (138; cf. Roberts 21–31). Milner instead sees the genre as arising in the nineteenth century, when science became decisively understood as instrumental rationality. Science fiction is not so much a genre, as a 'type' – 'a radical distribution, redistribution and innovation of interest within the novel and short story genres', which was 'focused above all on the practical capacity of sciences to become technologies' (153). The fundamental concern of the 'fictional sciences' of science fiction is that instrumental rationality 'can and will produce technologies sufficiently effective as to shape human being itself' (154). The importance of psychology to the genre becomes clear. The principle of the continuity of nature established that the human soul was of the same nature as animal, and indeed plant life, and open to the same modes of systematic investigation, cognition, and control. The modern discipline of psychology immediately implied the real or potential existence of psychotechnologies that could fundamentally reshape what had previously been seen as an independent, and inviolable, psychic substance. Science fiction's interest in the potential of psychotechnologies is readily apparent in many of the texts considered in the preceding chapters. Mitchison's *Solution Three*, for instance, seems to speculate on the use of social conditioning techniques to dissolve the heteronormative matrix, and to institute homosexuality as normative. Other texts seem to invoke an adventitious instrumental technology, such as the renewal of supposedly dormant evolutionary mechanisms in Heinlein's *The Moon is a Harsh Mistress*.

The invocation of the Scottish Highland clans in the context of Cooper's (noxious) lament for patriarchal heterosexuality in *Gender Genocide* is particularly suggestive, for it links science fiction to the tradition of the historical novel, as epitomized, and inaugurated, by Sir Walter Scott's *Waverley* (1814), which retold the story of the Scottish Highland clans' final dissolution in the failed Jacobite rising of 1745. As Milner explains, 'SF and the historical novel are closely cognate genres, insofar as […] both take human historicity as their central subject matter' (152). The historical novel connected the present to the past – understood as a place of somewhat alien cultural life belonging to an earlier stage of human development – and contrastively illuminated the peculiarities, and indeed failings, of the novel's contemporary social and cultural setting. Science fiction, as critical scholarship shows, connects the present to hypothetical futures that equally demystify and illuminate the text's contemporaneous social and cultural context. As Milner notes (152), this view of science fiction's similarity to historical fiction is shared by Kim Stanley Robinson, for whom both genres 'must describe cultures that cannot be physically visited by the reader; thus both are concerned with alien cultures, and with estrangement. And both genres share a view of history which says that times not our own are yet vitally important to us' (54–55). The view is shared also by Jerome de Groot, writing from the other side of the generic division: 'a cognate genre [to the historical novel] is science fiction, which involves a conscious interaction with a clearly unfamiliar set of landscapes, technologies and circumstances' (4).

Science fiction, including its psychological subgenre, certainly arises as 'the future' becomes a realm of cultural appropriation and contestation. As Csicsery-Ronay explains:

> A central project of Western modernism was to invent the future as an autonomous time that could give purpose to the present [...]. The great scientific and philosophical systems of Darwin, Marx, Spencer, and positivism contributed to the sense of a future in which ideas of progress inherited from Christian humanism were dialectically combined with expectations of unimaginable material improvement, transformed worlds of greater freedom and power, whose very axioms would be constructed by New Men. (*Seven* 81)

However, it would be naïve to regard science fiction, including psychological science fiction, as typically an exercise in futurology – Robinson, for instance, notes that 'no sf story describes the actual future that will ensue in the real world' (54). As argued earlier (21–23), the futurological function of science fiction is too narrow to properly apprehend the genre (even novels that are genuinely programmatic, such as Skinner's *Walden Two*, tend to subvert their own 'blueprint' credentials). Science fiction's future histories must accordingly be distinguished from the progressivist narratives that arise in the nineteenth century, for 'SF's free history overtly represents fictive models that have acquired fatal weight in real social life. Works of sf *play out* myths of history, without competing models or recalcitrant facts' (Csicsery-Ronay *Seven* 83–84). Science fiction's futures need never be proved or disproved, not because they are always ludicrous or inaccurate, but because they need not be regarded as predictions (or warnings) in the first place, and can be so construed only by an impoverished interpretation.

Psychological science fiction therefore tends to play with the historical myths of the 'New Men' [*sic*] implied by real, potential, or adventitious psychotechnologies. Indeed, the apparent seriousness of the fictive future is almost inversely proportional to the quality of the text. The more problematic narratives of psychological science fiction tend toward literal psychological futurology and sincere posthumanist visions. *Walden Two*'s anti-consumerist citizens are represented by Skinner as the desirable product of behaviourist psychotechnology, yet the totalitarian instrumental rationality of Frazier's community is far less satisfactory than the text's critique of post-war US consumer capitalism. Christopher's *Death of Grass* is nostalgic for a feudal and patriarchal past restored by evolutionary mechanisms that strip away the veneer of Enlightenment to expose our (vulgarized) Nietzschean depth psychology. Wilson and Lessing are inclined to prophesy a New Man and Woman with extraordinary mental faculties engendered by phenomenological psychologies. In contrast, part of what makes Mitchison's *Solution Three* superior to Cooper's *Gender Genocide* is the way it suspends the seriousness of its future: Solution Three is not proposed as a model for post-capitalist society, but as a way of commenting on the ethical blindspots and limitations of materialist history. Indeed, an immediate interpretative cue that the novel does not endorse the textual *novum* is presented in the epigraph, which refers to Solution Three as a *'horrid idea'* (Mitchison *Solution* 4). Cooper's text, on the other hand, seems genuinely to fear the triumph of compulsory homosexuality and the 'cultural genocide' of patriarchy, hence its Lawrentian rhetoric and repulsive celebration of sexual violence as counterrevolutionary weapon. There is, of course, an indefinite variety of textual strategies by which psychological science fiction can suspend the seriousness of its fictional human futures. Piercy's highly self-conscious narrative in *Woman on the Edge of Time*, for instance, leaves the ontological status of Connie's visions undecided. This denies the reader any secure historical chain of causation leading from Connie's poisoning of her psychological experimenters to the future Mattapoisett (which is itself ontologically poised between fictional future, and fictional psychotic delusion). Vonnegut's *Galápagos* uses a similar strategy: the posthuman fisherfolk described by Leon Trout may be fictionally real or the product of Trout's deranged fantasies of humankind's evolutionary salvation. McHugh's *I Am Thinking of My Darling* uses a different approach: the virally-transformed New Yorkers are, at best, temporary posthumans – the epidemic of happiness is a carnivalesque provocation to the present, rather than a prophetic extrapolation in the mode of Wilson or Lessing.

Psychology and the rhetoric of science fiction

The discourses of psychology are varied and play a significant part in an indefinite number of science fiction narratives. Further research will no doubt elaborate, modify, and rebut the arguments and observations made in the present context. One remaining question will however be posed: namely, what is the significance of science fiction for psychology itself? The relationship between psychology and science fiction studies is a dialogue, not a monologue. The title of this monograph, *Science Fiction and Psychology*, might seem to imply an analytic boundary that fails to reflect cultural reality – as if 'official' psychological practice and discourse were untouched by the cultural reverberations of science fiction. Yet the cultural traffic between the two territories goes in both directions: science fiction, like literary writing more generally, affects the discipline of psychology. Gergen has remarked on the humanistic and creative, perhaps literary, ambitions that can inspire psychological researchers: 'I have talked with countless graduate students drawn into psychology out of deep humanistic concern. Within many lies a frustrated poet, philosopher, or humanitarian who finds the scientific method at once a means to expressive ends and an encumbrance to free expression. [...] Many wish to share their values directly, unfettered by constant demands for systematic evidence' ('Social Psychology' 312). Indeed, a number of renowned psychologists from supposedly 'harder' schools, including behaviourism and evolutionary neuropsychology, have aspired to be creative writers: long before *Walden Two* was even drafted, B.F. Skinner tried (and failed) to write a novel during his so-called 'Dark Year' between undergraduate and postgraduate studies (Elms 472–73), while Stanley Milgram hoped to parlay his non-fiction writing into a career as a creative writer (Nicholson 'Torture' 755).

Gergen implies that literary expression by psychologists, whether in psychological or non-psychological discourses, necessarily involves a relaxation of normal disciplinary protocols and procedures. In this view, a text like *Walden Two* popularizes a particular psychological discipline via pleasurable entertainment – the science fiction accretions offer a sugar coating that encourages a non-expert public to acquire scientific literacy in behaviourist ideas. The main duty of the popularizer, in this folk model of scientific practice (as critiqued by Stephen Hilgartner), is to stay firmly on the side of 'appropriate simplification' as opposed to 'distortion':

> [S]cientific experts enjoy great flexibility in public discourse. [...] when it suits their purposes, they can issue simplified representations for broader audiences; the notion of 'appropriate simplification'

justifies this practice, and enables scientists to invest these representations with the authority of the cultural symbol 'Science'. On the other hand, scientists at all times can draw on the notion of 'distortion' to discredit publicly-available representations. (520)

A particular variant on the latter discourse applies, as Jenny Kitzinger notes, with regard to science fiction, which may be accused of 'science-fiction scare-mongering' that has a 'a very powerful, and inevitably *negative*, impact on an ignorant public, driving "the masses" to dread the potential of science and technology' (74).

Research in science studies, however, contends that popular science has a much less external relationship to scientific practice. Alan G. Gross criticizes what he calls the 'deficit model' of public understanding of science: 'the deficit model is asymmetrical; it depicts communication as a one-way flow from science to its public', and it 'implies a passive public: it requires a rhetoric that acts to accommodate the facts and methods of science to the public's limited experience and cognitive capacities' (6). He opposes this one-way, deficit model, and proposes instead a 'contextual' model based on interaction between expert and lay audience in which 'public understanding is the joint product of scientific and local knowledge': 'So conceived, public understanding has genuine, not diminished epistemological status, different in kind, but not in significance from the epistemological status conferred by the methods of science' (19). In similar fashion, Richard Whitley describes the folk model of scientific popularization as one in which 'scientific knowledge is disseminated to a lay audience after it has been discovered and this process is separate from research' (8). However, argues Whitley, there is significant co-production of knowledge between experts and the lay public, since 'lay standards and terms are often involved in intellectual debates and controversies so that what counts as knowledge is often affected by successful mobilisation of lay elites and/or diffusion of doctrines to a wide audience' (8). Such co-production would be particularly marked with regard to human sciences, including psychology, since '[t]he closer scientific fields are to everyday discourse and concerns, then, the stronger the feedback from popularisation to knowledge production is likely to be' (8). As well as challenging the supposed distinction between expert producers and lay consumers, science studies also acknowledge that popular science discourses are internal to professional scientific activity. Whitley points out that 'as regards the research process itself, popularizing offers a cognitive space where, as yet fragile and unstructured projects, can be reflected on, free from the epistemological constraints that characterize other expository modes to differing degrees, and free from an acute risk of professional embarrassment' (58). Such speculative freedom can be found in extrapolations that borrow from science fiction to represent a future supposedly formed by a particular programme of research. For the sake of convenience, I will refer to these implied or actual narratives as 'science fiction extrapolations', although it should be noted that these stories are promulgated with a far more serious futurological intent than is typical of science fiction. Kitzinger notes that science fiction extrapolation is internal to scientific discourse and practice, since 'scientists and policymakers tell many fantastical and engaging futuristic tales (e.g. about a world free of suffering)', and 'routinely make proclamations about the promise and potential of their work in ways which, I argue, often contributes to "confusion about what is possible and what is not"' (82).

Such remarks illustrate a general trend in post-empiricist history and philosophy of science whereby creative elements, such as imaginary narratives and hypothesis formation, have been reinstated as internal to scientific procedure. This tendency is manifest in challenges to the supposed distinction between the creative ferment found in the 'context of discovery' (hypothesis formation, hunches, accidents, aesthetic considerations, ...), and the systematic method of the analytically separate 'context of justification'. This was a distinction supported by Karl Popper, who proposes to 'distinguish sharply between the process of conceiving a new idea, and the methods and results of examining it logically' (8): the 'logical analysis of scientific knowledge' has no interest in the psychologistic issue of 'how it happens that a new idea occurs to a man – whether it is a musical theme, a dramatic conflict, or a scientific theory' (7). Naturally, the promulgation and circulation of science fiction narratives imagining a particular scientific extrapolation and its potential applications would therefore lie outwith the context of justification, and be at best part of the context of discovery (if not simply relegated to pop science). The discovery versus justification distinction has, as Paul Feyerabend observes, been used as a bulwark against the complexities and contingencies assiduously brought to light by historical investigations of scientific practice: '*Discovery* may be irrational and need not follow any recognized method. *Justification*, on the other hand, or – to use the Holy Word of a different school – *criticism*, starts only *after* the discoveries have been made, and it proceeds in an orderly way' (147). The distinction, argues Feyerabend, is invalid:

> Now there is, of course, a very noticeable difference between the rules of testing as 'reconstructed' by philosophers of science and the procedures which scientists use in actual research. This

difference is apparent to the most superficial examination. On the other hand, a most superficial examination also shows that a determined application of the methods of criticism and proof which are said to belong to the context of justification would wipe out science as we know it – and would never have permitted it to arise. Conversely, the fact that science exists proves that these methods were frequently overruled. They were overruled by procedures which belong to the context of discovery. (148)

In Feyerabend's methodological anarchy, the weight of historical evidence compels the conclusion that within the actual procedures of science (as opposed to dogma of 'the scientific method'), 'scientists often make moves that are forbidden by methodological rules. For example, they interpret the evidence so that it fits their fanciful ideas, eliminate difficulties by *ad hoc* procedures, push them aside, or simply refuse to take them seriously' (148).

Rather than viewing science fiction narrative within psychological discourse as merely a tactic to popularize expert knowledge, or as creative 'inspiration', it is possible to understand science fiction extrapolation within psychology as an intradisciplinary strategy of validation – regardless of whether this aim is pursued consciously or not. Corinne Squire has directly faced the issue of literary narrative within supposedly 'objective' or 'neutral' psychological discourse. She observes that '[p]sychological writing declares itself to be about knowledge, not pleasure. But although psychological papers give scientific expositions of the realities of subjectivity, they are also studded with sanctioned narrative elements and illegitimate anecdotes, which provide conventional fictional pleasure' ('Science' 193). Psychology as a discourse is rendered 'more permeable and unstable' by the intrusion of 'incomplete theories and vague, suggestive hypotheses which characterize psychological writing and which, as in science fiction, comment and speculate on scientific knowledge of realities' (193). Squire focusses particularly on science fiction extrapolation in the discipline of social psychology, albeit with some reinstatement of the discovery versus justification distinction: 'science-fictional speculations generate the new hypotheses, models and theories which sustain social psychology as a discipline. The mainstream discourse's denial of such speculations leaves processes like hypothesis formation in the realm of mystery, or reduces them to deduction' ('Crisis' 44–45).

The use of science fiction extrapolations as an avenue of narrative legitimation for psychological discourses may be illustrated by reference to Steven Pinker's 1997 popularization of cognitive psychology, *How the Mind Works*. In a remarkable passage, Pinker discusses John R. Searle's philosophical objection to certain models of artificial intelligence. Searle argues in his landmark article, 'Minds, Brains & Programs', and in a series of later refinements and modifications, that '[t]he explanation of how the brain produces intentionality cannot be that it does it by instantiating a computer program' (417). His 'Chinese Room' thought experiment is well known, and a classic philosophical paper. He imagines a scenario in which he, Searle (or any other individual who does not understand Chinese), follows a series of instructions for manipulating Chinese characters, so that 'from the point of view of somebody outside the room in which I am locked – my answers to the questions [in written Chinese] are absolutely indistinguishable from those of native Chinese speakers' (418). Searle provides 'answers by manipulating uninterpreted formal symbols', so that '[a]s far as the Chinese is concerned, I simply behave like a computer; I perform computational operations on formally specified elements' (418). But does he thereby understand Chinese? The answer is 'no': 'I have everything that artificial intelligence can put into me by way of a program, and I understand nothing' (418). He concludes, 'whatever purely formal principles you put into the computer, they will not be sufficient for understanding, since a human will be able to follow the formal principles without understanding anything' (418).

Pinker, for his part, thinks that Searle has only managed to articulate the common-sense meaning of various cognitive concepts and, particularly, the verb, 'to understand'. But a folk theory of understanding, argues Pinker, offers no obstacle to a scientific account that grasps the essential reality of understanding (95). Of course, for his conclusion to be valid, Pinker must in fact establish that the counter-intuitive account of understanding, rather than the supposedly intuitive account ascribed to Searle, articulates the essence of the phenomenon. Pinker's engagement with the arguments and counter-arguments surrounding the Chinese Room thought experiment are, however, superficial and desultory. 'The Chinese Room has kicked off a truly unbelievable amount of commentary. More than a hundred published articles have replied to it', announces Pinker (94) – a research base from which he then summarizes three responses, and discusses one more in slightly greater depth. The most original and forceful part of Pinker's vindication of his position is not his argumentative engagement – which is rather fleeting – but a rhetorical strategy of imaginative narration. Searle, for instance, is given some entirely imaginary direct discourse (one quite at odds with his manner in speech and writing): 'You can almost hear him saying, "Aw, c'mon! You mean to claim that *the guy understands Chinese*??!!! Geddadahere!"' (94). Pinker's most sustained citation against Searle is a page-long appeal via the medium of science fiction narrative: 'Perhaps the ultimate reply to Searle's Chinese Room may be found in a story by the science-fiction writer Terry Bisson, widely circulated on the Internet, which has the incredulity going the other way. It reports a conversation between the leader of an interplanetary explorer fleet and his commander in chief' (95–96). The dialogue in Bisson's story, 'They're Made out of Meat', predictably, is between two thinking machines confronted with the discovery of sentient organic life: '"Thinking meat! You're asking me to believe in thinking meat!" "Yes, thinking meat! Conscious meat! Loving meat. Dreaming meat. The meat is the whole deal! Are you beginning to get the picture or do I have to start all over?"' (Bisson).

The temptation may be simply to dismiss such story-telling as an accidental feature of Pinker's popularizing, journalistic rhetoric. Yet Pinker's text invites an investigation of to what extent investment in a psychological programme of research relies upon suasive strategies such as narrative and, specifically, science fiction extrapolation. The debate between Pinker and Searle on the Chinese Room experiment is essentially on the validity of 'any Turing machine simulation of human mental phenomena' (Searle 417). Janis Svilpis notes, and elaborates, the lengthy genealogy of proto-Turing Tests in the Golden Age of science fiction:

> [T]here should be no mystery in the Test's appearance before 1950. The kind of thinking that underlies it (what would a dialogue with a computer or alien be like?) is present in science fiction from a very early date. The robot/replicant-identification game and the first-contact game in science fiction sometimes lead to the Test, because the determination of human(-like) intelligence can be central in both. (431)

For Svilpis, this continuity between science fiction and philosophical paper 'testifies to the fruitfulness of pulp-magazine science fiction's long-continued conversation as well as to the acumen and inventiveness of its finest writers' (448–49). It also testifies, though, to the persuasive force of stock elements of the science fiction megatext that have been reified into conventional elements of a hegemonic imagined future. Turing's 'Computing Machinery and Intelligence' drives towards its conclusion on the basis of a possibility that has become somehow credible because of the sedimentation of science fiction stories in wider discourses of the future – hence Turing's harping on about intelligent machines as 'possibilities of the near future, rather than Utopian dreams' (449). Indeed, Turing even locates his argument within another far-out possibility, when he discusses modifications to the Test in light of extra-sensory perception: 'I assume that the reader is familiar with the idea of extra-sensory perception, and the meaning of the four items of it, *viz.* telepathy, clairvoyance, precognition and psycho-kinesis. These disturbing phenomena seem to deny all our usual scientific ideas. How we should like to discredit them! Unfortunately, the statistical evidence, at least for telepathy, is overwhelming' (453). Fortunately, another presumably near-future science fiction innovation, the 'telepathy-proof room' will allow the Test to run in modified form (454).

These generic and rhetorical features of Turing's 1950 paper indicate that Pinker's narrative legitimation is less eccentric than it appears. Rather than being merely a feature of popular discourse, Pinker's recourse to science fiction extrapolation elaborates the earlier narrative authorization of the Turing Test. Such textual comparisons support John Bowers's suspicion (presented with respect to cognitive psychology rather than AI) that tacit agreement on the Test's presuppositions follows from 'the seductiveness of a dramatic scenario rather than a set of actual institutional arrangements, a *narrative* and not an *institutional a priori*' (131). Further evidence for 'fragments of unconscious science fiction narrative' is provided in Squire's discussion of Sandra L. Bem's social-cognitive 'account of gender schema theory' ('Crisis' 45). Bem's theory provides a cognitive framework in which '[a] schema functions as an anticipatory structure, a readiness to search for and to assimilate incoming information in schema-relevant terms' (Bem 603). With respect to gender, 'sex typing derives in large measure from gender-schematic processing, from a generalized readiness on the part of the child to encode and to organize information [...] according to the culture's definitions of maleness and femaleness' (603). The theory is thus cognitivist since 'sex typing is mediated by the child's own cognitive processing', but also social since 'gender-schematic processing is itself derived from the sex-differentiated practices of the social community' (603). As Squire explains, Bem's argument takes a speculative turning point when it begins

> to plot parental strategies for teaching children that sex differences, but not gender differences, are important; and for giving them alternative, subversive, sexism schemata, to inoculate them against the wider gender-schematic world. Bem sees her work as preliminary, not definitive; yet, with deliberate boldness, she wonders how such practices could be adopted more generally, and pictures the gender-aschematic future which might result. And so the paper manages to be, as she later described it, both a 'feminist utopia', and an example of 'theory-building and logical inference in an empirical science'. ('Crisis' 45)

Indeed, the narrative departure into feminist utopianism is frank, for Bem concedes our present inability 'to describe concretely the particular kinds of socialization histories that enhance or diminish gender-schematic processing', but nonetheless offers 'a number of plausible strategies that are consistent with gender schema theory for raising a gender-aschematic child in the midst of a gender-schematic society' (Bem 609). These are, in essence, (1) to shield children from their 'culture's sex-linked associative network' while advancing their 'knowledge of sex's biological correlates', and (2) to provide 'alternative schemata [that] "build up one's resistance" to the lessons of the dominant culture and thereby enable one to remain gender-aschematic' (610).

Squire's description of Bem's narrative as 'unconscious' is somewhat misleading, for Bem is explicit in her science fiction extrapolation of a future society in which sexism is greatly reduced – perhaps the generic affinity is 'unconscious', but not the narrative authorization *per se*. Bem offers a practical manifesto to leverage investment in her research programme, and also suggests that large-scale societal transformation will be necessary for empirical investigation of her gender schema theory. Bem is thus candid about the extent to which her theory is embedded in a practical, political context. She makes little or no attempt to banish futurology to the margins of theory, or to deny its disciplinary significance. The same cannot be said of Randy Thornhill and Craig T. Palmer's evolutionary psychological account of a supposed 'rape module' in the human male. Their work has been subject to substantial, and withering critique from within and outside evolutionary psychology (Travis). One further, unexamined question is the extent to which they offer a narrative legitimation based on their own vision of a preferred, psychologically informed future. Towards the end of their monograph, Thornhill and Palmer offer what they present as the unarguable extrapolation of their analysis, in the form of a programme of education for both sexes about the male's innate propensity to rape. For young men, they envisage 'an evolutionarily informed educational program [...] that focuses on increasing their ability to restrain their sexual behaviour' (179). Young women get the same course, with 'some instruction in self-defense' (180), supplemented by a further sex-specific program that

> address[es] how other elements of attractiveness (including health, symmetry, and hormone markers such as waist size), and clothing and makeup that enhance them, may influence the likelihood of rape [...]. This is not to say that young women should constantly attempt to look ill and infertile; it is simply to say that they should be made aware of the costs associated with attractiveness. (181)

Moreover, women need to know that evolution 'has produced men who will be quickly aroused by signals of a female's willingness to grant sexual access', and who will 'tend to read signals of acceptance into a female's actions even when no such signals are intended' (181). The narrative legitimation is readily apparent: their vision is essentially an attenuated version of the society imagined by, for instance, Margaret Atwood's *The Handmaid's Tale*, but without the feminist, dystopian sensibility. Thornhill and Palmer's psychology promises its intended audience a rollback of the 1960s, and restores a sinister patriarchal tradition in which women invite sexual assault as one of 'the costs associated with attractiveness'. Indeed, the authors' patriarchal assumptions prevent them from even noticing the possibility of other extrapolations from their supposedly objective insights. For instance, if men really are innately predisposed to rape, why not chemically castrate them all, with special dispensation allowed only in cases of explicit mutual consent?

Bem, Thornhill and Palmer, Pinker, and Turing, invoke in their different ways science fiction extrapolations of the future as a way to legitimate their particular psychological claims. Each draws upon the cultural legitimacy of a particular vision of 'the future' as conceived in their contemporaneous context, and each gives a weight and seriousness to the literary playfulness of science fiction storytelling. Such narrative construction of the future is theorized more generally by the 'sociology of expectations', which proceeds from 'the difference between *looking into* the future and *looking at* the future' (Borup *et al.* 296). Rather than engaging in naïve futurology ('looking into' the future) scholars in science studies investigate the construction of 'the future' as a persuasive device in the here-and-now. By 'looking at' the future, science studies show how

> [n]ovel technologies and fundamental changes in scientific principle do not substantively pre-exist themselves, except and only in terms of the imaginings, expectations and visions that have shaped their potential. As such, future-oriented abstractions are among the most important objects of enquiry for scholars and analysts of innovation. Such expectations can be seen to be fundamentally 'generative', they guide activities, provide structure and legitimation, attract interest and foster investment. (285–86)

By drawing upon, and in some cases reworking, stock representations of 'the future' as imagined in the present, psychologists too can guide the development of their discipline and ensure its wider public legitimacy.

Science fiction extrapolation borrows tropes from the literary genre and transplants them into modern future-orientated discourses. But alongside such borrowings from the genre, psychology also uses science fiction in its cognitive-estranging mode – a more recognized literary function in which the genre provokes critical reflection upon supposedly common-sense ideologies. Admittedly, this properly literary deployment of science fiction may seem somewhat unlikely given the often unsophisticated use of the genre in the pedagogy of science fiction. Steven J. Kirsh, for instance, describes his pedagogic research on 'the efficacy of using a science fiction text, *Ender's Game*, as a medium for having students apply concepts and theories in a developmental psychology course' (48). Orson Scott Card's 1985 novel of futuristic child soldiers pitted against an apparently hostile alien race ('The Buggers') is treated as a series of entertaining illustrations of child development that can be scrutinized for their accuracy:

> Students analyzed *Ender's Game* based on developmental theory and research that was either presented in class or found in their textbook. For each aspect of development they identified, students were to provide at least one example from *Ender's Game* and then to explain clearly how the example depicted that aspect of development. I encouraged students to discuss both accurate and inaccurate applications/depictions of developmental concepts in the book. For instance, an inaccurate depiction of a developmental concept is the fact that Ender engages in abstract thinking at age 6, which, according to Piaget's theory of child development, is five years before he is supposed to be able to do so. (50)

Science fiction is deployed by Kirsh as a way of addressing his students' deficit in psychological knowledge, much as – more generally – scientific actors and organizations hope that entertainment media may be used to improve public understanding of science. (Although, unlike the public, Kirsh's students have the advantage of a well-stocked library, previous training, and a psychology professor, to help them identify supposed 'distortions'.) Kirsh is not unique: a similar model implicitly informs Jim Ridgway and Michele Benjamin's 1987 anthology *PsiFi: Psychological Theories and Science Fictions*. The volume, published by the British Psychological Association, anthologizes a number of science fiction short stories, with each followed by an introduction to a psychological topic pertaining to the fictional narrative. For instance, the short story, 'Burden of Proof', by Bob Shaw, prefaces what is effectively a written mini-lecture by Ridgway and Benjamin on the reliability of eyewitness testimony (Ridgway and Benjamin 30–55). (Shaw, for his part, offers a foreword to the volume in which he seems to think of science fiction as an exercise in thought experiment, describing the genre as an extension of 'the experimental method', where 'the author has unique facilities for creating analogues of fully controlled laboratory conditions. [...] he can manipulate the fictional environment in such a way as to excise every extraneous or clouding factor which might contaminate the experimental data' (viii).)

However, there are more complex and suggestive deployments of science fiction within the pedagogy of psychology, such as Hilary M. Lips's work. At first glance, Lips's approach might seem like Kirsh's, since it involves setting her students science fiction texts addressing a common topic in psychology (sex and gender, in her case, rather than developmental psychology). Yet the function of science fiction is quite different, and far more effectively theorized. Citing the Bems, Lips continues:

> We are like the fish that are too surrounded by water to understand what it means to be wet. When teaching about the psychology of sex and gender, I use science fiction to increase students' awareness of this nonconscious ideology. In recent years, a host of feminist writers of science fiction have elaborated worlds in which new possibilities for gender and/or sex are explored [...]. I use the worlds two of these writers have created to jolt my students into thinking about how much they take gender for granted and to help them imagine how things could be different. (197)

Lips introduces a far more complex theoretical context, one in which science fiction engages with the Bems' concept of gender as prereflective 'nonconscious ideology': '[W]hat happens when all [an individual's] reference groups agree, when his religion, his family, his peers, his teachers, and the mass media all disseminate the same message? The consequence is a nonconscious ideology, a set of beliefs and attitudes which he accepts implicitly but which remains outside his awareness because alternative conceptions of the world remain unimagined' (Bem and Bem 89). Non-conscious ideology both informs 'hidden prejudices about the woman's "natural" role' and 'motivate[s] a host of subtle practices that are dramatically effective at keeping her "in her place"' (89). In Lips's pedagogic deployment of science fiction, the text offers a Suvin-like cognitive estrangement of the students' 'nonconscious ideology'. Through reading Ursula Le Guin's well-known novel of sex-shifting humanoid aliens, *The Left Hand of Darkness* (1969), Lips's students 'speculate in their discussions about how "things might be different" if men could become pregnant', and 'they often come to the conclusion that "things could be different," even with our current biological arrangement' (197).

Alongside Lips's pedagogic practice, there is also testimony from feminist academics about the extent to which science fiction has informed and motivated their research on the social psychology of gender. At a relatively untheorized level, the feminist psychologist Rhoda K. Unger describes science fiction stories as having a formative intellectual influence: 'I am uncertain about whether I would have become a feminist psychologist without my father's cast-off pulp fiction, but I am certain that I would have been more apprehensive about what kinds of questions I could ask' ('Science' 116). In an echo of Suvin's statement that science fiction is 'a developed oxymoron, a realistic irreality' (viii), the feminist sociologist Ann Oakley, writing for the journal *Feminism and Psychology*, characterizes science fiction as 'a complete contradiction in terms', for it provides 'stories that are about the truth' ('Fallacies' 120). Indeed, Suvin's work seems a conscious (if implicit) reference point, for Oakley celebrates a feminist 'denaturalization' or 'estrangement from one's own culture':

> World-travelling is an essential device of science fiction because it's an act capable of breaking the links between nature and culture which tie us down – both materially and metaphorically – in *this* world. Since the 1970s there's been a flowering of science fiction written by women, and much of this has led into a whole new laboratory of experiments about sex and gender. (*Gender* 201)

Thus, argues Oakley, 'Estrangement from one's own culture (a perception of it as fiction) leads to the questioning of all stories (aka facts) about human nature' ('Fallacies' 120).

The awareness of cognitive estrangement among feminist social scientists suggests that psychological discourse itself may adopt these strategies from science fiction, even without a conscious articulation of Suvin's theoretical position. The Bems' work is again a useful source, for it contains a defamiliarizing, estranging rhetoric that confronts nonconscious ideology. Their promotion during the late 1960s of the then relatively unknown term 'sexism' consciously employs an analogy with racism. To justify this new vocabulary, they present narratives resembling brief vignettes of science fiction:

> [E]ven though our society has become sensitive to negative sex stereotypes and has begun to expunge them from the media and from children's literature, it remains blind to its gratuitous emphasis on the gender dichotomy itself. In elementary schools, for example, boys and girls line up separately or alternately; they learn songs in

which the fingers are 'ladies' and the thumbs are 'men'; they see boy and girl paper-doll silhouettes alternately placed on the days of the month in order to learn about the calendar. Children, it will be noted, are not lined up separately or alternately as blacks and whites; fingers are not 'whites' and thumbs 'blacks'; black and white dolls do not alternately mark the days of the calendar. Our society seeks to deemphasize racial distinctions but continues to exaggerate sexual distinctions. (Bem 609)

More fully developed, this could be a brief, although no doubt rather crude, narrative in which extrapolation provides a cognitive estrangement of gender within late 1960s US society and culture.

In the work of feminist social scientists such as Unger, Oakley, and the Bems, the estranging function of science fiction discourses is consciously recognized. However, the estranging function can also appear 'unconsciously' in psychological discourses. The famed obedience experiments conducted, and publicized, by Stanley Milgram (1933–1984) in the 1960s and 1970s, show unacknowledged estrangement of their contemporaneous social, cultural, and political context. Milgram's experiments provide a fantastic voyage between the everyday world of North America and the implicit dystopian spectacle of his experiments. In his original 1963 paper, 'Behavioral Study of Obedience', Milgram outlines his famous laboratory experiment for testing obedience, a procedure that 'consists of ordering a naive S[ubject] to administer increasingly more severe punishment to a victim in the context of a learning experiment' ('Behavioral' 371). The experimental subject is duped by the use of a fake shock generator, and is ordered to apply increasingly powerful shocks to the victim, who is in fact a stooge who dissimulates increasing degrees of pain and distress (372). The experiment is standardized, and pre-scripted, so that the investigators can assign a reliable 'quantitative value' to the experimental subject's behaviour 'based on the maximum intensity shock he is willing to administer before he refuses to participate further' (372). The extent of the subjects' obedience is, Milgram argues, counter-intuitive, and depressing: 'Of the 40 subjects, 26 obeyed the orders of the experimenter to the end, proceeding to punish the victim until they reached the most potent shock available on the shock generator' (376). These results show 'the sheer strength of obedient tendencies' even though many of the participants are 'acting against their own values' (376). The ease with which such destructive obedience can be evoked, Milgram infers, explains how 'millions of innocent persons were systematically slaughtered on command' in the Nazi genocide (371).

In his later, popular monograph *Obedience to Authority* (1974), Milgram gives an overall hypothesis to explain the results of the obedience experiments, which by that point he had extrapolated and developed in many different ways. They work, he speculates, by activating a neurological switch that has developed in humans because of the evolutionary advantages of group co-operation. By, as it were, flicking 'the switch that controls the transition from an autonomous to a systemic mode' (133), Milgram has in effect turned off the individual conscience in the majority of his subjects, and placed them into a different mode of operation, the so-called *'agentic state'* in which 'the person entering an authority system no longer views himself as acting out of his own purposes but rather comes to see himself as an agent for executing the wishes of another person' (133). The activated agentic state heralds the emergence of 'a new creature' that 'replaces autonomous man', and is 'unhindered by the limitations of individual morality, freed of humane inhibition, mindful only of the sanctions of authority' (188). The danger of the agentic state in modern social organization is, for Milgram, explicitly evidenced in the Shoah, and can still be seen in the contemporaneous war in Vietnam, most egregiously in the My Lai massacre (183). Indeed, the 'new creature' is especially dangerous when granted control of weapons of mass destruction, since 'evolution has not had a chance to build inhibitors against these remote forms of aggression' (157): 'There are virtually no psychological inhibitions against coastal bombardment or dropping napalm from a plane twenty thousand feet overhead. As for the man who sits in front of a button that will release Armageddon, depressing it has about the same emotional forces as calling for an elevator' (157).

Ian Nicholson has been particularly scathing of the ethics and validity of the obedience experiments, referring to '[t]he unfair, manipulative character of Milgram's experiment and the banality of its central finding' ('Torture' 750). In his historical re-analysis of the experiments, he argues that 'Milgram played on the trust of his participants, their sense of the "special" character of the psychological laboratory and their desire to look competent while playing the role of experimental participant' (749). Milgram therefore

> demonstrated little beyond the commonplace observation that people in unfamiliar environments will trust authority figures and as a consequence can be deceived, manipulated, and taken advantage of. Milgram claimed to be divining dark and hitherto unexamined reaches of human nature when what he was really doing was toying with his participants' self-worth and physical

well-being for the sake of a psychological study and his own professional advantage. (750)

Indeed, for Nicholson, the most shocking aspect of the experiments is not their (arguably) banal conclusion, but rather the blithe enthusiasm with which Milgram and his team 'knowingly and repeatedly applied "enhanced" stress techniques to innocent people', creating a 'functioning theatre of pain that reduced many able, self-possessed participants to trembling wrecks, several of whom conveyed their anguish to Milgram shortly after their participation' ('Normalization' 641). In this view of the obedience experiments, Milgram and his team were engaged in an unethical staging of scenarios that merely pretended to investigate the nature of human obedience.

The highly speculative character of Milgram's conclusions is apparent not only in the dubious validity of his experiments, but also in the careful hedging of his statements about the neurological switching to the agentic state. He confesses that it is 'totally beyond our technical skill to specify this event at the chemoneurological level', and that his evidence is restricted to the 'phenomenological expression of this shift to which we do have access' (*Obedience* 133). Milgram's neurological 'switch' is, in truth, a *novum* hidden in plain sight – a science fiction extrapolation borrowing from methodical cognition (the discipline of psychology) but embedded in a putatively non-fiction narrative rather than the pages of *Analog* magazine. By recognizing this generic overlap with science fiction, one can bring a more systematic approach to scholarship that shows how Milgram's work is an artistic commentary on his social, cultural, and historical context. The experiments' fictional shocks were intended to metaphorically shock the post-war US populace out of its moral complacency. Kathryn Millard, for instance, describes Milgram's widely screened 1965 documentary film *Obedience* 'as a filmed morality play transposed to a social psychology laboratory', in which Milgram 'imposed a predetermined argument onto footage that simply did not deliver the desired results' – subjects in the filmed experimental variant in fact 'did not display high levels of obedience, and that which they did display was far from blind' (452). Milgram was more than just an improvisational dramatist and neo-realist film-maker; he also aspired (albeit unsuccessfully) to write fiction. Nicholson records how, '[a]fter the obedience experiment was completed, Milgram contacted a literary agent to facilitate his artistic talents. "For my own amusement I have always written epigrams and anecdotes" he remarked. "Now I would like to write fiction for an audience. It is a natural outgrowth of my temperament"' ('Torture' 755).

Milgram's aim in his science fiction theatre of cruelty was to confound the public's belief, as he has it in *Obedience to Authority*, that '[o]rdinary people [...] do not administer painful shocks to a protesting individual simply because they are ordered to do so. Only Nazis and sadists perform this way' (169). It was this application to the domestic political sphere, rather than the purported explanation of Nazi genocide, that captivated the US media: 'His empirical findings were embedded in a discourse of national decline that centred on the idea that American culture was losing its ability to produce autonomous, strong-willed individuals' (Nicholson 'Shocking' 246). Among the pre-existing discourses that helped Milgram's findings resonate in public consciousness, was post-war science fiction, which

> further popularized the idea of a malevolent, conformist presence beneath the placid, benign exterior of middle America. In these films and shows, fundamental American values and beliefs are torn away – but not by outside forces or aliens. The real threat is from those close to you – ordinary Americans who willingly give up their individuality. This 'enemy within' theme is clearly evident in two of the best-known works of science fiction from the era: the iconic film *Invasion of the Body Snatchers* (1956) and the television series *Twilight Zone* (1959–1964). (258)

Milgram's body of work, and particularly his mass-market output, such as the documentary *Obedience*, and his full-length book, *Obedience to Authority*, can thus productively be interpreted as science fiction, despite the probable intentions of the author, and the likely generic presumption of its readership, that this corpus represented sober psychological scholarship. By bracketing or neglecting the validity of Milgram's social psychology, one can instead understand Milgram's 'new creature' as a speculative *novum*. His texts and films ask: *what if* there were a technology that could heighten the unreflective obedience of 'the "organization man"' (Nicholson 'Shocking' 247)? If there were such a technology, it would manipulate subjects in the way imagined by Milgram's theatrical pseudo-experiments. By confronting the theatrical, filmic, and textual spectacle of the obedience experiments, Milgram's audience were invited to view their contemporaneous reality with fresh eyes:

> The experiments' popularity and standing in American politics and jurisprudence is no less remarkable. In the early 1970s Milgram's work was used to critique aspects of the Vietnam War, and in the aftermath of Watergate the experiments were used to explain the

conduct of President Nixon's staff. During the famous 1974 trial of Patty Hearst, Milgram's research was cited to explain how the kidnapped heiress could have come to obey the instructions of the Symbionese Liberation Army. (239)

Whatever the merits of Milgram's work as social psychology, it was undoubtedly successful in defamiliarizing the taken-for-granted fabric of organizational conformity in US life, thereby providing an unself-conscious 'cognitive estrangement' for its audience.

Conclusion

The preceding analysis of science fiction discourses within the discipline of psychology is necessarily tentative and far more provisional than this monograph's investigation of psychology within science fiction. Despite the boundary work that might aim to segregate science fiction from scientific practice, there is clearly deployment of science fiction narrative within the discipline of psychology itself. This may be relatively unself-conscious – a persuasive tactic that supposedly belongs to the realms of popularization. But it may also be consciously pursued within a larger sense of the contingencies and cultural underpinnings of psychological research. Such science fiction narration may have a variety of purposes. Admittedly, the pedagogic use, like the popularizing deployment, may be somewhat simplistic – a matter of sugar-coating pre-packaged expert knowledge. But a more sophisticated deployment of psychology may – wittingly or unwittingly – mobilize narratives of the future that borrow science fiction tropes in order to legitimate a particular programme of psychological research. Psychology, like the other sciences, has its own relationship to the technoscientific imaginary within contemporary society and culture, and stakes its claims within and against certain hegemonic narratives of the future. Perhaps more surprisingly, psychology can also play (consciously or otherwise) the literary game of cognitive estrangement. This science fiction aesthetic, which came to particular self-consciousness in the literature and criticism of the countercultural New Wave, clearly informs the discursive strategies of certain psychologists from the 1960s onwards. Wittingly, or unwittingly, psychology allows the telling and performance of narratives based on supposedly real, or imminent, psychological technologies – stories that, like those of literary science fiction, take the reader to an estranged, critically distanced, version of their own reality.

Works Cited

Abbott, Carl. *Frontiers Past and Future: Science Fiction and the American West.* Lawrence, KS: UP of Kansas, 2006.

Adler, Alfred. *The Neurotic Constitution: Outlines of a Comparative Individualistic Psychology and Psychotherapy.* Trans. Glueck, Bernard and John E. Lind. The International Library of Psychology. London: Kegan Paul, Trench, Trubner, 1921.

Allport, Gordon W. *Becoming: Basic Considerations for a Psychology of Personality.* New Haven, CT: Yale UP, 1955.

Appiah, Kwame Anthony. *The Ethics of Identity.* Princeton, NJ: Princeton UP, 2005.

Aquinas. *Basic Writings of Saint Thomas Aquinas.* Vol. 2. 2 vols. New York: Random House, 1945.

Asimov, Isaac. *I, Robot.* 1967. London: HarperCollins, 2013.

Atwood, Margaret. *The Handmaid's Tale.* 1985. London: Vintage, 1996.

Badmington, Neil. 'Pod Almighty!; or, Humanism, Posthumanism, and the Strange Case of *Invasion of the Body Snatchers.*' *Textual Practice* 15.1 (2001): 5–22.

Ballard, J.G. 'Which Way to Inner Space?' *A User's Guide to the Millennium: Essays and Reviews.* 1962. London: HarperCollins, 1996. 195–98.

Banks, Iain. *Walking on Glass.* 1985. London: Abacus, 1990.

Bartholomew, Robert E., and Jeffrey S. Victor. 'A Social-Psychological Theory of Collective Anxiety Attacks: The "Mad Gasser" Reexamined.' *Sociological Quarterly* 45.2 (2004): 229–48.

Bartlett, Frederic C. *Remembering: A Study in Experimental and Social Psychology.* 1932. Cambridge: Cambridge UP, 1995.

Bazin, Nancy Topping. 'Androgyny or Catastrophe: The Vision of Doris Lessing's Later Novels.' *Frontiers: A Journal of Women Studies* 5.3 (1980): 10–15.

de Beauvoir, Simone. *The Ethics of Ambiguity.* 1947. Trans. Frechtman, Bernard. New York: Open Road Integrated Media, 2018.

Bem, Sandra L. 'Gender Schema Theory and Its Implications for Child Development: Raising Gender-Aschematic Children in a Gender-Schematic Society.' *Signs* 8.4 (1983): 598–616.

Bem, Sandra L., and Daryl J. Bem. 'Case Study of a Nonconscious Ideology: Training the Woman to Know Her Place.' *Beliefs, Attitudes, and Human Affairs*. By Daryl J. Bem. Basic Concepts in Psychology. Brooks/Cole Publishing Company: Belmont, CA, 1970. 89–99.

Berlin, Isaiah. 'The Decline of Utopian Ideas in the West.' *The Crooked Timber of Humanity: Chapters in the History of Ideas*. 1978. Ed. Hardy, Henry. London: John Murray, 1990. 20–48.

Berman, Jeffrey. *The Talking Cure: Literary Representations of Psychoanalysis*. New York: New York UP, 1985.

Berryman, Charles. 'Vonnegut and Evolution: *Galápagos*.' *Critical Essays on Kurt Vonnegut*. Ed. Merrill, Robert. Boston, MA: G.K. Hall, 1990. 188–99.

Bester, Alfred. *The Demolished Man*. 1953. SF Masterworks. London: Gollancz, 1999.

———. 'Oddy and Id.' *Virtual Unrealities: The Short Fiction of Alfred Bester*. 1950. New York: Vintage, 1997. 22–37.

Birke, Lynda. *Feminism, Animals and Science: The Naming of the Shrew*. Buckingham, UK: Open University, 1994.

Bisson, Terry. 'They're Made out of Meat.' 2016. Web. 1 March 2019. <http://www.terrybisson.com/page6/page6.html>.

Bloch, Ernst. *The Principle of Hope*. 1959. Trans. Plaice, Neville, Stephen Plaice and Paul Knight. Vol. 1. 3 vols. Oxford: Blackwell, 1986.

———. *The Principle of Hope*. 1959. Trans. Plaice, Neville, Stephen Plaice, and Paul Knight. Vol. 2. 3 vols. Oxford: Blackwell, 1986.

Blum, D. Steven. *Walter Lippmann: Cosmopolitanism in the Century of Total War*. Ithaca, NY: Cornell UP, 1984.

Bolling, Douglass. 'Structure and Theme in *Briefing for a Descent into Hell*.' *Contemporary Literature* 14.4 (1973): 550–64.

Booker, M. Keith. 'Woman on the Edge of a Genre: The Feminist Dystopias of Marge Piercy.' *Science Fiction Studies* 21.3 (1994): 357–50.

Borup, Mads, et al. 'The Sociology of Expectations in Science and Technology.' *Technology Analysis & Strategic Management* 18.3–4 (2006): 285–98.

Bottom, William P., and Dejun Tony Kong. '"The Casual Cruelty of Our Prejudices": On Walter Lippmann's Theory of Stereotype and Its "Obliteration" in Psychology and Social Science.' *Journal of the History of the Behavioral Sciences* 48.4 (2012): 363–94.

Bowers, John. 'All Hail the Great Abstraction: Star Wars and the Politics of Cognitive Psychology.' *Deconstructing Social Psychology*. Eds. Parker, Ian and John Shotter. London: Routledge, 1990. 127–40.

Bowlby, John. *Attachment: Attachment and Loss*. The International Psycho-Analytical Library. Vol. 1. 3 vols. London: Hogarth and The Institute for Psycho-Analysis, 1969.

———. 'Foreword.' *The Origins of Love and Hate*. By Ian D. Suttie. London: Free Association, 1988. xv–xviii.

———. *A Secure Base: Clinical Applications of Attachment Theory*. London: Routledge, 1988.

Boyer, Pascal. 'Religion: Bound to Believe?' *Nature* 455.7216 (2008): 1038–39.

Brecht, Bertholt. 'Short Description of a New Technique of Acting That Produces a *Verfremdung* Effect.' Trans. Willett, John and Marc Silberman. *Brecht on Theatre*. Eds. Silberman, Marc, Steve Giles, and Tom Kuhn. 3rd ed. London: Bloomsbury, 1978. 184–95.
Breland, Keller, and Marian Breland. 'A Field of Applied Animal Psychology.' *American Psychologist* 6.6 (1951): 202–04.
———. 'The Misbehavior of Organisms.' *American Psychologist* 16.11 (1961): 681–84.
Broderick, Damien. *Psience Fiction: The Paranormal in Science Fiction Literature*. Jefferson, NC: McFarland, 2018.
———. *Reading by Starlight: Postmodern Science Fiction*. London: Routledge, 1995.
Brosco, Jeffrey P., and Diane B. Paul. 'The Political History of PKU: Reflections on 50 Years of Newborn Screening.' *Pediatrics* 132.6 (2013): 987–89.
Brown, Roger, and James Kulik. 'Flashbulb Memories.' *Cognition* 5.1 (1977): 73–99.
Buller, David J. *Adapting Minds: Evolutionary Psychology and the Persistent Quest for Human Nature*. Cambridge, MA: MIT, 2006.
Bultmann, Rudolf. 'New Testament and Mythology: The Problem of Demythologizing the New Testament Proclamation.' Trans. Ogden, Schubert M. *New Testament and Mythology and Other Basic Writings*. Ed. Ogden, Schubert M. London: SCM, 1984. 1–43.
Burgess, Anthony. *1985*. London: Hutchinson, 1978.
———. *A Clockwork Orange*. 1962. Penguin Classics. London: Penguin, 2000.
Burn, Stephen J. 'Neuroscience and Modern Fiction.' *Modern Fiction Studies* 61.2 (2015): 209–25.
Burnham, John C. 'The "New Freud Studies": A Historiographical Shift.' *The Journal of the Historical Society* 6 (2006): 213–33.
Buss, David M. 'Sex Differences in Human Mate Preferences: Evolutionary Hypotheses Tested in 37 Cultures.' *Behavioral and Brain Sciences* 12.1 (1989): 1–49.
Butler, Andrew M. 'Psychoanalysis.' *The Routledge Companion to Science Fiction*. Eds. Bould, Mark, et al. Abingdon: Routledge, 2009. 288–97.
Butler, Octavia E. *Parable of the Sower*. 1993. London: Women's Press, 1995.
Callenbach, Ernest. *Ecotopia: A Novel About Ecology, People and Politics in 1999*. 1975. London: Pluto, 1978.
Camus, Albert. *The Myth of Sisyphus*. 1942. Trans. O'Brien, Justin. Penguin Books Great Ideas. London: Penguin, 2005.
Canavan, Gerry. *Octavia E. Butler*. Modern Masters of Science Fiction. Urbana, IL: U of Illinois P, 2016.
Carroll, Noel. *The Philosophy of Horror: Or Paradoxes of the Heart*. London: Routledge, 1990.
Chesler, Phyllis. *Women and Madness*. 1972. London: Allen Lane, 1974.
Chiang, Ted. 'Story Notes.' *Stories of Your Life and Others*. London: Pan Macmillan, 2015. 329–38.
———. 'Story of Your Life.' *Stories of Your Life and Others*. 1998. London: Pan Macmillan, 2015. 109–72.

Chomsky, Noam. 'A Review of B.F. Skinner's *Verbal Behavior.*' *The Structure of Language: Readings in the Philosophy of Language.* 1959. Eds. Fodor, Jerry A. and Jerrold J. Katz. Englewood Cliffs, NJ: Prentice-Hall, 1964. 547–78.
Christopher, John. *The Death of Grass.* 1956. Penguin Classics. London: Penguin, 2009.
Cleary, Maureen Anne. 'Phenylketonuria.' *Paediatrics and Child Health* 21.2 (2011): 61–64.
Collini, Stefan. *Absent Minds: Intellectuals in Britain.* Oxford: Oxford UP, 2006.
Condon, Richard. *The Manchurian Candidate.* 1959. London: Orion, 2013.
Conley, Tim, and Stephen Cain. 'The Embedding.' *Encyclopedia of Fictional and Fantastic Languages.* Westport, CT: Greenwood, 2006. 56–58.
Cooper, Edmund. *Who Needs Men?* London: Hodder and Stoughton, 1972.
Cordle, Daniel. 'Changing of the Old Guard: Time Travel and Literary Technique in the Work of Kurt Vonnegut.' *The Yearbook of English Studies* 30 (2000): 166–76.
Crigger, Nancy J. 'The Trouble with Caring: A Review of Eight Arguments against an Ethic of Care.' *Journal of Professional Nursing* 13.4 (1997): 217–21.
Crowther-Heyck, Hunter. 'George A. Miller, Language, and the Computer Metaphor of Mind.' *History of Psychology* 2.1 (1999): 37–64.
Csicsery-Ronay, Istvan. 'Cyberpunk and Neuromanticism.' *Mississippi Review* 16.2/3 (1988): 266–78.
———. 'Science Fiction/Criticism.' *A Companion to Science Fiction.* Ed. Seed, David. Blackwell Companions to Literature and Culture. Oxford: Blackwell, 2005. 43–59.
———. *The Seven Beauties of Science Fiction.* 2008. Middletown, CT: Wesleyan UP, 2011.
De Groot, Jerome. *The Historical Novel.* The New Critical Idiom. Abingdon: Routledge, 2010.
Deighton, Len. *The Ipcress File.* London: Hodder & Stoughton, 1962.
Delany, Samuel R. *Babel-17.* 1966. SF Masterworks. London: Gollancz, 2010.
Dick, Philip K. 'We Can Remember It for You Wholesale.' *We Can Remember It for You Wholesale.* 1966. Vol. 5. The Collected Short Stories of Philip K. Dick. London: Orion, 2000. 157–74.
Dilthey, W. 'The Construction of the Historical World in the Human Studies.' Trans. Rickman, H.P. *W. Dilthey: Selected Writings.* Ed. Rickman, H.P. Cambridge: Cambridge UP, 1976. 168–245.
Donovan, Josephine. 'Attention to Suffering: Sympathy as a Basis for Ethical Treatment of Animals.' *The Feminist Care Tradition in Animal Ethics: A Reader.* Eds. Donovan, Josephine and Carol J. Adams. New York: Columbia UP, 2007. 174–97.
———. 'Caring to Dialogue: Feminism and the Treatment of Animals.' *The Feminist Care Tradition in Animal Ethics: A Reader.* Eds. Donovan, Josephine and Carol J. Adams. New York: Columbia UP, 2007. 360–69.
Drummond, Henry. *The Lowell Lectures on the Ascent of Man.* London: Hodder and Stoughton, 1894.

Dunn, Thomas P. 'Theme and Narrative Structure in Ursula K. Le Guin's *The Dispossessed* and Frederik Pohl's *Gateway*.' *Reflections on the Fantastic: Selected Essays from the Fourth International Conference on the Fantastic in the Arts*. Ed. Collings, Michael R. Contributions to the Study of Science Fiction and Fantasy. Westport, CT: Greenwood, 1986. 87–95.

DuPlessis, Rachel Blau. 'The Feminist Apologues of Lessing, Piercy, and Russ.' *Frontiers: A Journal of Women Studies* 4.1 (1979): 1–8.

Ellenberger, Henri F. *The Discovery of the Unconscious: The History and Evolution of Dynamic Psychiatry*. New York: Basic Books, 1970.

Elms, Alan C. 'Skinner's Dark Year and *Walden Two*.' *American Psychologist* 36.5 (1981): 470–79.

Eyer, Diane E. *Mother–Infant Bonding: A Scientific Fiction*. New Haven, CT: Yale UP, 1992.

Fancourt, Donna. 'Accessing Utopia through Altered States of Consciousness: Three Feminist Utopian Novels.' *Utopian Studies* 13.1 (2002): 94–113.

Feeney, Judith, and Patricia Noller. *Adult Attachment*. Sage Series on Close Relationships. Thousand Oaks, CA: Sage, 1996.

Ferguson, Oliver W. 'History and Story: Leon Trout's Double Narrative in *Galápagos*.' *Critique* 40.3 (1999): 230–38.

Feyerabend, Paul. *Against Method*. 3rd ed. London: Verso, 1993.

Fine, Cordelia. *Delusions of Gender: The Real Science Behind Sex Differences*. London: Icon, 2010.

Fink, Bruce. *A Clinical Introduction to Lacanian Psychoanalysis: Theory and Technique*. Cambridge, MA: Harvard UP, 1997.

Finney, Jack. *The Body Snatchers*. 1955. SF Masterworks. London: Gollancz, 2010.

Fishburn, Katherine. 'Doris Lessing's *Briefing for a Descent into Hell*: Science Fiction or Psycho-Drama?' *Science Fiction Studies* 15.1 (1988): 48–60.

Frankl, Viktor E. *Man's Search for Meaning: An Introduction to Logotherapy*. 1946. Trans. Lasch, Ilse. Rev. and enlarged ed. London: Hodder & Stoughton, 1964.

Freedman, Carl. *Critical Theory and Science Fiction*. Hanover, NH: Wesleyan UP, 2000.

———. 'Remembering the Future: Science and Positivism from Isaac Asimov to Gregory Benford.' *Extrapolation* 39.2 (1998): 128–38.

Freese, Peter. 'Surviving the End: Apocalypse, Evolution, and Entropy in Bernard Malamud, Kurt Vonnegut, and Thomas Pynchon.' *Critique* 36.3 (1995): 163–76.

Freud, Sigmund. 'Civilization and Its Discontents.' Trans. Strachey, James. *The Future of an Illusion, Civilization and Its Discontents, and Other Works*. 1930. Vol. 21. The Standard Edition of the Complete Psychological Works of Sigmund Freud. London: Hogarth and the Institute of Psycho-Analysis, 1961. 57–145.

———. 'The Dynamics of Transference.' Trans. Strachey, James. *The Case of Schreber, Papers on Technique, and Other Works*. 1912. Vol. 12. The Standard Edition of the Complete Psychological Works of Sigmund Freud. London: Hogarth and the Institute of Psycho-Analysis, 1958. 97–108.

―――. 'The Future of an Illusion.' Trans. Strachey, James. *The Future of an Illusion, Civilization and Its Discontents, and Other Works*. 1927. Vol. 21. The Standard Edition of the Complete Psychological Works of Sigmund Freud. London: Hogarth and the Institute of Psycho-analysis, 1961. 1–56.

―――. 'Instincts and Their Vicissitudes.' Trans. Strachey, James. *On the History of the Psycho-Analytic Movement, Papers on Metapsychology, and Other Works*. 1915. Vol. 14. The Standard Edition of the Complete Psychological Works of Sigmund Freud. London: Hogarth and the Institute of Psycho-Analysis, 1957. 109–40.

Fromm, Erich. *The Crisis of Psychoanalysis*. London: Jonathan Cape, 1971.

―――. *The Fear of Freedom*. 1942. London: Routledge & Kegan Paul, 2001.

―――. 'The Social Philosophy of "Will Therapy."' *Psychiatry* 2.2 (1939): 229–37.

Gannon, Charles E. *Rumors of War and Infernal Machines: Technomilitary Agenda-Setting in American and British Speculative Fiction*. Liverpool: Liverpool UP, 2003.

Gardiner, Judith Kegan. 'Empathic Ways of Reading: Narcissism, Cultural Politics, and Russ's *Female Man*.' *Feminist Studies* 20.1 (1994): 87–111.

―――. 'Evil, Apocalypse, and Feminist Fiction.' *Frontiers: A Journal of Women Studies* 7.2 (1983): 74–80.

Gellner, Ernest. *The Psychoanalytic Movement: Or the Coming of Unreason*. Paladin Movements and Ideas. London: Paladin, 1985.

Gergen, Kenneth J. 'Metaphor and Monophy in the Twentieth-Century Psychology of Emotions.' *Historical Dimensions of Psychological Discourse*. Eds. Graumann, Carl F. and Kenneth J. Gergen. Cambridge: Cambridge UP, 1996. 60–82.

―――. 'The Social Constructionist Movement in Modern Psychology.' *American Psychologist* 40.3 (1985): 266–75.

―――. 'Social Psychology as History.' *Journal of Personality and Social Psychology* 26.2 (1973): 309–20.

Gibson, William. *Neuromancer*. 1984. London: HarperCollins, 1995.

Gieryn, Thomas F. *Cultural Boundaries of Science: Credibility on the Line*. Chicago, IL: U Chicago P, 1999.

Gilligan, Carol. *In a Different Voice: Psychological Theory and Women's Development*. Cambridge, MA: Harvard UP, 1982.

Glassy, Mark C. *The Biology of Science Fiction Cinema*. Jefferson, NC: McFarland, 2001.

Gomel, Elana. *Science Fiction, Alien Encounters, and the Ethics of Posthumanism: Beyond the Golden Rule*. Basingstoke: Palgrave Macmillan, 2014.

Goodall, Jane, and Phillip Berman. *Reason for Hope: An Extraordinary Life*. London: HarperCollins, 2000.

Goodwin, C. James. *A History of Modern Psychology*. 4th ed. Hoboken, NJ: Wiley, 2012.

Gould, Stephen Jay. 'More Things in Heaven and Earth.' *Alas, Poor Darwin: Arguments against Evolutionary Psychology*. Eds. Rose, Hilary and Steven Rose. London: Vintage, 2001. 85–105.

Grant, Barry Keith. *Invasion of the Body Snatchers*. 2010. BFI Film Classics. London: Bloomsbury & British Film Institute, 2018.

Gross, Alan G. 'The Roles of Rhetoric in the Public Understanding of Science.' *Public Understanding of Science* 3.1 (1994): 3-23.

Hague, Euan, and David Stenhouse. 'A Very Interesting Place: Representing Scotland in American Romance Novels.' *The Edinburgh Companion to Contemporary Scottish Literature*. Ed. Schoene, Berthold. Edinburgh: Edinburgh UP, 2007. 354-61.

Haldeman, Douglas C. 'The Practice and Ethics of Sexual Orientation Conversion Therapy.' *Journal of Consulting and Clinical Psychology* 62.2 (1994): 221-27.

Hamilton, Richard. 'The Darwinian Cage: Evolutionary Psychology as Moral Science.' *Theory, Culture & Society* 25.2 (2008): 105-25.

Haraway, Donna. 'A Manifesto for Cyborgs: Science, Technology and Socialist Feminism in the 1980s.' *Norton Anthology of Theory and Criticism*. Ed. Leitch, Vincent B. London: Norton, 2001. 2269-99.

Hardesty, William H. 'Semiotics, Space Opera and *Babel-17*.' *Mosaic* 13.3 (1980): 63-69.

Hardin, Nancy Shields. 'Doris Lessing and the Sufi Way.' *Contemporary Literature* 14.4 (1973): 565-81.

Harlow, Harry F. 'Mice, Monkeys, Men, and Motives.' *Psychological Review* 60.1 (1953): 23-32.

Harris, Ben. 'Letting Go of Little Albert: Disciplinary Memory, History, and the Uses of Myth.' *Journal of the History of the Behavioral Sciences* 47.1 (2011): 1-17.

Hawkins, Mike. *Social Darwinism in European and American Thought, 1860-1945: Nature as Model and Nature as Threat*. Cambridge: Cambridge UP, 1997.

Hayles, N. Katherine. *How We Became Posthuman: Virtual Bodies in Cybernetics, Literature, and Informatics*. Chicago, IL: U Chicago P, 1999.

Heelas, Paul. *The New Age Movement: The Celebration of the Self and the Sacralization of Modernity*. Oxford: Blackwell, 1996.

Heidegger, Martin. *Being and Time*. 1927. Trans. Macquarrie, John and Edward Robinson. Oxford: Blackwell, 1962.

Heinlein, Robert A. *The Moon Is a Harsh Mistress*. SF Masterworks. London: Gollancz, 2001.

Henderson, Ian. *Myth in the New Testament*. Studies in Biblical Theology. London: SCM, 1952.

Herbert, Frank. *The Dragon in the Sea*. 1956. London: Gollancz, 1984.

Herbrechter, Stefan. *Posthumanism: A Critical Analysis*. 2009. London: Bloomsbury, 2013.

Hilgartner, Stephen. 'The Dominant View of Popularization: Conceptual Problems, Political Uses.' *Social Studies of Science* 20.3 (1990): 519-39.

Hird, Myra J. *Sex, Gender, and Science*. Houndmills, Basingstoke: Palgrave Macmillan, 2004.

Hirshbein, Laura. 'L. Ron Hubbard's Science Fiction Quest against Psychiatry.' *Medical Humanities* 42.4 (2016): e10-e14.

Hite, Molly. 'Doris Lessing's *The Golden Notebook* and *The Four-Gated City*: Ideology, Coherence, and Possibility.' *Twentieth Century Literature* 34.1 (1988): 16-29.

Hodder, Alan D. *Thoreau's Ecstatic Witness*. New Haven, CT: Yale UP, 2001.
Hunt, Caroline. 'Young Adult Literature Evades the Theorists.' *Children's Literature Association Quarterly* 21.1 (1996): 4–11.
Huxley, Aldous. *Brave New World*. 1932. London: Vintage, 2004.
———. *Heaven and Hell*. London: Chatto & Windus, 1956.
Jameson, Fredric. *Archaeologies of the Future: The Desire Called Utopia and Other Science Fictions*. London: Verso, 2005.
———. *The Political Unconscious: Narrative as a Socially Symbolic Act*. London: Methuen, 1981.
Jaspers, Karl. *General Psychopathology*. 1913. Trans. Hoenig, J. and Marian W. Hamilton. Manchester: Manchester UP, 1963.
Johnson, Glen M. '"We'd Fight ... We Had To". *The Body Snatchers* as Novel and Film.' *The Journal of Popular Culture* 13.1 (1979): 5–16.
Jung, C.G. 'The Concept of the Collective Unconscious.' Trans. Hull, R.F.C. *The Archetypes and the Collective Unconscious*. 1936/37. Eds. Read, Herbert, Michael Fordham, and Gerhard Adler. Vol. 9.1. The Collected Works of C.G. Jung. London: Routledge & Kegan Paul, 1959. 42–53.
———. 'Flying Saucers: A Modern Myth of Things Seen in the Skies.' Trans. Hull, R.F.C. *Civilization in Transition*. 1958. Eds. Read, Herbert, Michael Fordham, and Gerhard Adler. Vol. 10. The Collected Works of C.G. Jung. London: Routledge & Kegan Paul, 1964. 307–433.
———. *Psychological Types*. Trans. Baynes, H.G. and R.F.C. Hull. Eds. Read, Herbert, *et al*. Vol. 6. The Collected Works of C.G. Jung. London: Routledge & Kegan Paul, 1971.
———. 'Psychology and Religion.' Trans. Hull, R.F.C. *Psychology and Religion: West and East*. 1937. Eds. Read, Herbert, Michael Fordham, and Gerhard Adler. Vol. 11. The Collected Works of C.G. Jung. London: Routledge & Kegan Paul, 1958. 3–106.
———. 'Psychotherapy Today.' Trans. Hull, R.F.C. *The Practice of Psychotherapy: Essays on the Psychology of the Transference and Other Subjects*. 1946. Eds. Read, Herbert, Michael Fordham, and Gerhard Adler. Vol. 16. The Collected Works of C.G. Jung. London: Routledge & Kegan Paul, 1954. 94–110.
———. 'The Undiscovered Self (Present and Future).' Trans. Hull, R.F.C. *Civilization in Transition*. 1957. Eds. Read, Herbert, Michael Fordham, and Gerhard Adler. Vol. 10. The Collected Works of C.G. Jung. London: Routledge & Kegan Paul, 1964. 245–306.
Kant, Immanuel. *Critique of Pure Reason*. Trans. Kemp Smith, Norman. London: MacMillan, 1929.
Kaplan, Bert. 'Introduction.' *The Inner World of Mental Illness: A Series of First-Person Accounts of What It Was Like*. Ed. Kaplan, Bert. New York: Harper and Row, 1964. vii–xii.
Karl, Frederick R. 'Doris Lessing in the Sixties: The New Anatomy of Melancholy.' *Contemporary Literature* 13.1 (1972): 15–33.
Keyes, Daniel. *Flowers for Algernon*. 1966. London: Gollancz, 2011.
Kirschenbaum, Howard. 'Carl Rogers's Life and Work: An Assessment on the 100th Anniversary of His Birth.' *Journal of Counseling & Development* 82.1 (2004): 116–24.

Kirsh, Steven J. '*Ender's Game*: Using Science Fiction to Teach Child Development.' *Journal on Excellence in College Teaching* 9.2 (1998): 47–53.

Kitsi-Mitakou, Katerina. '"None of Woman Born": Colonizing the Womb from Frankenstein's Mother to Naomi Mitchison's Clone Mums.' *Biotechnological and Medical Themes in Science Fiction*. Ed. Pastourmatzi, Domna. Thessaloniki: University Studio Press, 2002. 208–21.

Kitzinger, Jenny. 'Questioning the Sci-Fi Alibi: A Critique of How "Science Fiction Fears" Are Used to Explain Away Public Concerns About Risk.' *Journal of Risk Research* 13.1 (2010): 73–86.

Kuhn, Thomas S. *The Structure of Scientific Revolutions*. 1962. 4th ed. Chicago, IL: U of Chicago P, 2012.

Laing, R.D. *The Divided Self: An Existential Study in Sanity and Madness*. 1960. Harmondsworth: Pelican, 1965.

———. *The Politics of Experience and the Bird of Paradise*. London: Penguin, 1967.

Laing, R.D., and Aaron Esterson. *Sanity, Madness and the Family: Families of Schizophrenics*. 1964. London: Pelican, 1970.

van Langenhove, Fernand. *The Growth of a Legend: A Study Based Upon the German Accounts of Francs-Tireurs and 'Atrocities' in Belgium*. London: G.P. Putnam's, 1916.

Latham, Rob. 'Sextrapolation in New Wave Science Fiction.' *Science Fiction Studies* 33.2 (2006): 251–74.

Le Guin, Ursula K. 'The Child and the Shadow.' *The Language of the Night: Essays on Fantasy and Science Fiction*. 1975. Ed. Wood, Susan. London: Women's Press, 1989. 49–60.

———. *The Lathe of Heaven*. 1971. SF Masterworks. London: Gollancz, 2001.

———. 'Myth and Archetype in Science Fiction.' *The Language of the Night: Essays on Fantasy and Science Fiction*. 1976. Ed. Wood, Susan. London: Women's Press, 1989. 61–69.

———. 'On Norman Spinrad's *The Iron Dream*.' Rev. of *The Iron Dream*, Norman Spinrad. *Science Fiction Studies* 1.1 (1973): 41–44.

———. 'Vaster Than Empires and More Slow.' *The Wind's Twelve Quarters*. 1971. London: Gollancz, 1976. 181–217.

———. *The Word for World Is Forest*. 1972. SF Masterworks. London: Gollancz, 2015.

Leahey, Thomas Hardy, and Grace Evans Leahey. *Psychology's Occult Doubles: Psychology and the Problem of Pseudoscience*. Chicago, IL: Nelson–Hall, 1983.

Lessing, Doris. *The Four-Gated City*. 1969. London: Paladin, 1990.

———. 'The Small Personal Voice.' *A Small Personal Voice: Essays, Reviews, Interviews*. 1957. Ed. Schlueter, Paul. New York: Alfred A. Knopf, 1974. 3–21.

Levitas, Ruth. *Utopia as Method: The Imaginary Reconstitution of Society*. Basingstoke: Palgrave Macmillan, 2013.

Lindner, Robert. *The Fifty-Minute Hour: A Collection of True Psychoanalytic Tales*. 1954. New York: Other, 1999.

———. 'The Jet-Propelled Couch: Part I: The Man Who Traveled through Space.' *Harper's Magazine* 1 December 1954: 49–57.

———. 'The Jet-Propelled Couch: Part II: Return to Earth.' *Harper's Magazine* 1 January 1955: 76–84.

Lippmann, Walter. *Public Opinion*. 1922. New York: MacMillan, 1929.

Lips, Hilary M. 'Using Science Fiction to Teach the Psychology of Sex and Gender.' *Teaching of Psychology* 17.3 (1990): 197–98.

Lloyd, Vincent. 'Post-Racial, Post-Apocalyptic Love: Octavia Butler as Political Theologian.' *Political Theology* 17.5 (2016): 449–64.

López-Muñoz, Francisco, et al. 'History of the Discovery and Clinical Introduction of Chlorpromazine.' *Annals of Clinical Psychiatry* 17.3 (2005): 113–35.

Lovecraft, H.P. 'The Colour out of Space.' *The Call of Cthulhu and Other Weird Stories*. 1927. Ed. Joshi, S.T. London: Penguin, 1999. 170–99.

Lowentrout, Peter M. '*Psi*fi: The Domestication of *Psi* in Science Fiction.' *Extrapolation* 30.4 (1989): 388–400.

Luckhurst, Roger. *Science Fiction*. Cultural History of Literature. Cambridge: Polity, 2005.

Lukács, Georg. *The Historical Novel*. 1937. Trans. Mitchell, Hannah and Stanley Mitchell. London: Merlin, 1962.

Lutz, Catherine. 'Cultural Politics by Other Means: Gender and Politics in Some American Psychologies of Emotions.' *Historical Dimensions of Psychological Discourse*. Eds. Graumann, Carl F. and Kenneth J. Gergen. Cambridge: Cambridge UP, 1996. 125–44.

McCormack, Michael Brandon. '"Your God Is a Racist, Sexist, Homophobic, and a Misogynist...Our God Is Change": Ishmael Reed, Octavia Butler and Afrofuturist Critiques of (Black) American Religion.' *Black Theology* 14.1 (2016): 6–27.

McHugh, Vincent. *I Am Thinking of My Darling*. 1943. New York: Yarrow, 1991.

Maciunas, Billie. 'Feminist Epistemology in Piercy's *Woman on the Edge of Time*.' *Women's Studies: An Interdisciplinary Journal* 20.3–4 (1992): 249–58.

Mackenzie, Brian D. *Behaviourism and the Limits of Scientific Method*. International Library of Philosophy and Scientific Method. London: Routledge & Kegan Paul, 1977.

Malinowski, Bronislaw. *Sex and Repression in Savage Society*. 1927. London: Routledge & Kegan Paul, 1960.

———. *The Sexual Life of Savages in North-Western Melanesia*. 3rd ed. London: Routledge, 1932.

Malmgren, Carl. 'The Languages of Science Fiction: Samuel Delany's *Babel-17*.' *Extrapolation* 34.1 (1993): 5–17.

Malzberg, Barry N. *Herovit's World*. New York: Random House, 1973.

———. *The Remaking of Sigmund Freud*. New York: Ballantine, 1985.

Mangione, Jerre Gerlando. *The Dream and the Deal: The Federal Writers' Project, 1935–1943*. Syracuse, NY: Syracuse UP, 1996.

Maslow, Abraham H. *Religions, Values, and Peak-Experiences*. 1964. London: Penguin, 1976.

———. *Toward a Psychology of Being*. 1962. 2nd ed. New York: Van Nostrand, 1968.

May, Rollo. 'The Origins and Significance of the Existential Movement in Psychology.' *Existence: A New Dimension in Psychiatry and Psychology.* Eds. May, Rollo, Ernest Angel, and Henri F. Ellenberger. New York: Basic Books, 1958. 3–36.
Mayhew, Ben. 'Between Love and Aggression: The Politics of John Bowlby.' *History of the Human Sciences* 19.4 (2006): 19–35.
Mercer, Philip. *Sympathy and Ethics: A Study of the Relationship between Sympathy and Morality with Special Reference to Hume's Treatise.* Oxford: Clarendon, 1972.
Midgley, Mary. *The Ethical Primate: Humans, Freedom and Morality.* London: Routledge, 1994.
——. *Evolution as a Religion: Strange Hopes and Stranger Fears.* 1985. Revised ed. London: Routledge, 2002.
Miéville, China. 'Cognition as Ideology: A Dialectic of SF Theory.' *Red Planets: Marxism and Science Fiction.* Eds. Bould, Mark and China Miéville. London: Pluto, 2009. 231–48.
——. 'Editorial Introduction.' *Historical Materialism* 10.4 (2002): 39–49.
Milgram, Stanley. 'Behavioral Study of Obedience.' *The Journal of Abnormal and Social Psychology* 67.4 (1963): 371–78.
——. *Obedience to Authority: An Experimental View.* London: Tavistock, 1974.
Millard, Kathryn. 'Revisioning Obedience: Exploring the Role of Milgram's Skills as a Filmmaker in Bringing His Shocking Narrative to Life.' *Journal of Social Issues* 70.3 (2014): 439–55.
Miller, Gavin. 'Animals, Empathy, and Care in Naomi Mitchison's *Memoirs of a Spacewoman*.' *Science Fiction Studies* 35.2 (2008): 251–65.
——. 'The Apathetic Fallacy.' *Philosophy and Literature* 34.1 (2010): 48–64.
——. 'Literary Narrative as Soteriology in the Work of Kurt Vonnegut and Alasdair Gray.' *Journal of Narrative Theory* 31.3 (2001): 299–323.
——. 'Political Repression and Sexual Freedom in *Brave New World* and *1984*.' *Huxley's Brave New World: Essays.* Eds. Izzo, David Garrett and Kim Kirkpatrick. Jefferson, NC: McFarland, 2008. 17–25.
——. 'A Wall of Ideas: The "Taboo on Tenderness" in Theory and Culture.' *New Literary History* 38.4 (2007): 667–81.
Miller, George A. 'The Magical Number Seven, Plus or Minus Two: Some Limits on Our Capacity for Processing Information.' *Psychological Review* 63.2 (1956): 81–97.
Miller, George A., and Noam Chomsky. 'Finitary Models of Language Users.' *Handbook of Mathematical Psychology.* Vol. 2. New York: Wiley, 1963. 419–91.
Milner, Andrew. *Locating Science Fiction.* Liverpool Science Fiction Texts and Studies. Liverpool: Liverpool UP, 2012.
Misiak, Henryk, and Virginia Staudt Sexton. *Phenomenological, Existential, and Humanistic Psychologies: A Historical Survey.* New York: Grune & Stratton, 1973.
Mitchison, Naomi. *All Change Here: Girlhood and Marriage.* London: Bodley Head, 1975.
——. 'Comfort.' *A Girl Must Live: Stories and Poems.* Glasgow: Richard Drew, 1990. 135–36.

———. 'Conversation with an Improbable Future.' *A Girl Must Live: Stories and Poems*. Glasgow: Richard Drew, 1990. 221–31.
———. *The Corn King and the Spring Queen*. 1931. London: Virago, 1983.
———. *Memoirs of a Spacewoman*. 1962. London: Women's Press, 1985.
———. *Small Talk ... : Memories of an Edwardian Childhood*. London: Bodley Head, 1973.
———. *Solution Three*. 1975. New York: Feminist Press at City U of New York, 1995.
Moon, Elizabeth. *Speed of Dark*. London: Orbit, 2002.
Morawski, J.G. 'Assessing Psychology's Moral Heritage through Our Neglected Utopias.' *American Psychologist* 37.10 (1982): 1082–95.
Morris, David. 'Octavia Butler's (R)evolutionary Movement for the Twenty-First Century.' *Utopian Studies* 26.2 (2015): 270–88.
Morse, Donald E. 'Thinking Intelligently About Science and Art: Kurt Vonnegut's *Galápagos* and *Bluebeard*.' *Extrapolation* 38.4 (1997): 292–303.
Moylan, Tom. *Demand the Impossible: Science Fiction and the Utopian Imagination*. London: Methuen, 1986.
———. *Scraps of the Untainted Sky: Science Fiction, Utopia, Dystopia*. Cultural Studies Series. Boulder, CO: Westview, 2000.
Neisser, Ulric. *Cognitive Psychology*. The Century Psychology Series. New York: Appleton-Century-Crofts, 1967.
Newman, Leonard S. 'Was Walter Lippmann Interested in Stereotyping?: *Public Opinion* and Cognitive Social Psychology.' *History of Psychology* 12.1 (2009): 7–18.
Nicholson, Ian. 'The Normalization of Torment: Producing and Managing Anguish in Milgram's "Obedience" Laboratory.' *Theory & Psychology* 25.5 (2015): 639–56.
———. '"Shocking" Masculinity: Stanley Milgram, "Obedience to Authority", and the "Crisis of Manhood" in Cold War America.' *Isis* 102.2 (2011): 238–68.
———. '"Torture at Yale": Experimental Subjects, Laboratory Torment and the "Rehabilitation" of Milgram's "Obedience to Authority."' *Theory & Psychology* 21.6 (2011): 737–61.
O'Neill, Joseph. *Land under England*. 1935. SF Masterworks. London: Gollancz, 2018.
Oakley, Ann. *Gender on Planet Earth*. Cambridge: Polity, 2002.
———. 'Fallacies of Fact and Fiction.' *Feminism & Psychology* 19.1 (2009): 118–22.
Orwell, George. *Nineteen Eighty-Four*. 1949. Harmondsworth, Middlesex: Penguin, 1954.
Paul, Terri. '"Sixty Billion Gigabits": Liberation through Machines in Frederik Pohl's *Gateway* and *Beyond the Blue Event Horizon*.' *The Mechanical God: Machines in Science Fiction*. Eds. Dunn, Thomas P. and Richard D. Erlich. Contributions to the Study of Science Fiction and Fantasy. Westport, CT: Greenwood, 1982. 53–62.
Pavlov, I.P. *Conditioned Reflexes: An Investigation of the Physiological Activity of the Cerebral Cortex*. 1924. Trans. Anrep, G.V. Oxford: Oxford UP, 1927.

Phillips, Jerry. 'The Intuition of the Future: Utopia and Catastrophe in Octavia Butler's *Parable of the Sower.' Novel: A Forum on Fiction* 35.2–3 (2002): 299–311.
Pickren, Wade E., and Alexandra Rutherford. *A History of Modern Psychology in Context*. Hoboken, NJ: Wiley, 2010.
Piercy, Marge. *Sleeping with Cats: A Memoir*. London: Middlemarsh, 2002.
———. *Woman on the Edge of Time*. 1976. London: Women's Press, 1979.
Pinker, Steven. *How the Mind Works*. 1997. London: Penguin, 1999.
Pohl, Frederik. *Gateway*. London: Gollancz, 1977.
———. *Heechee Rendezvous*. London: Gollancz, 1984.
Popper, Karl. *The Logic of Scientific Discovery*. 1935. London: Routledge, 2002.
Poulin, Carmen. 'It Made Us Think Differently: Unger's "Toward a Redefinition of Sex and Gender."' *Feminism & Psychology* 17.4 (2007): 435–41.
Pytell, Timothy. 'The Missing Pieces of the Puzzle: A Reflection on the Odd Career of Viktor Frankl.' *Journal of Contemporary History* 35.2 (2000): 281–306.
Rabinovitz, Rubin. 'Mechanism vs. Organism: Anthony Burgess' *A Clockwork Orange.' Modern Fiction Studies* 24.4 (1978/1979): 538–41.
Radcliffe-Brown, A.R. *Structure and Function in Primitive Society*. London: Cohen & West, 1952.
Reiss, Timothy J. 'How Can "New" Meaning Be Thought?: Fictions of Science, Science Fictions.' *Canadian Review of Comparative Literature* 12.1 (1985): 88–126.
Richards, Graham. *Putting Psychology in Its Place: An Introduction from a Critical Historical Perspective*. London: Routledge, 1996.
Ricoeur, Paul. *Freud and Philosophy: An Essay on Interpretation*. 1965. Trans. Savage, Denis. New Haven, CT: Yale UP, 1970.
Ridgway, Jim, and Michele Benjamin. *Psifi: Psychological Theories and Science Fictions*. Leicester: British Psychological Society, 1987.
Rilling, Mark. 'The Mystery of the Vanished Citations: James Mcconnell's Forgotten 1960s Quest for Planarian Learning, a Biochemical Engram, and Celebrity.' *American Psychologist* 51.6 (1996): 589–98.
Roazen, Paul. *The Historiography of Psychoanalysis*. New Brunswick, NJ: Transaction Publishers, 2001.
Roberts, Adam. *The History of Science Fiction*. Palgrave Histories of Literature. Basingstoke: Palgrave Macmillan, 2006.
Robinson, Kim Stanley. 'Notes for an Essay on Cecelia Holland.' *Foundation: The Review of Science Fiction* 40 (1987): 54–61.
'Rocky Mountain Spotted Fever (RMSF) | CDC.' Web. 1 March 2019. <https://www.cdc.gov/rmsf/index.html>.
Roemer, Kenneth M. 'Mixing Behaviorism and Utopia: The Transformations of *Walden Two.' No Place Else: Explorations in Utopian and Dystopian Fiction*. Eds. Rabkin, Eric S., Martin H. Greenberg, and Joseph D. Olander. Carbondale and Edwardsville, IL: Southern Illinois UP, 1983. 125–46.
Rose, Nikolas. *Governing the Soul: The Shaping of the Private Self*. London: Routledge, 1990.

———. *Inventing Our Selves: Psychology, Power and Personhood*. Cambridge: Cambridge UP, 1996.

Rose, Nikolas, and Joelle M. Abi-Rached. *Neuro: The New Brain Sciences and the Management of the Mind*. Princeton, NJ: Princeton UP, 2013.

Rose, Steven, R.C. Lewontin, and Leon J. Kamin. *Not in Our Genes: Biology, Ideology and Human Nature*. Harmondsworth: Penguin, 1984.

Ross, Andrew. *Strange Weather: Culture, Science, and Technology in the Age of Limits*. London: Verso, 1991.

Rotberg, Robert I. 'The Failure and Collapse of Nation-States: Breakdown, Prevention, and Repair.' *When States Fail: Causes and Consequences*. Ed. Rotbert, Robert I. Princeton, NJ: Princeton UP, 2004. 1–49.

Ruddick, Sara. 'Maternal Thinking.' *Feminist Studies* 6.2 (1980): 342–67.

Russ, Joanna. '*Amor Vincit Foeminam*: The Battle of the Sexes in Science Fiction ' *To Write Like a Woman: Essays in Feminism and Science Fiction*. 1980. Bloomington and Indianapolis, IN: Indiana UP, 1995. 41–59.

———. *The Female Man*. 1975. SF Masterworks. London: Gollancz, 2010.

———. 'On the Fascination of Horror Stories, Including Lovecraft's.' *To Write Like a Woman: Essays in Feminism and Science Fiction*. 1980. Bloomington and Indianapolis, IN: Indiana UP, 1995. 60–64.

———. 'Towards an Aesthetic of Science Fiction.' *To Write Like a Woman: Essays in Feminism and Science Fiction*. 1975. Bloomington and Indianapolis, IN: Indiana UP, 1995. 3–14.

———. 'What Can a Heroine Do? Or Why Women Can't Write.' *To Write Like a Woman: Essays in Feminism and Science Fiction*. 1972. Bloomington and Indianapolis, IN: Indiana UP, 1995. 79–93.

Sargent, Lyman Tower. 'The Three Faces of Utopianism Revisited.' *Utopian Studies* 5.1 (1994): 1–37.

Sartre, Jean-Paul. *Being and Nothingness: An Essay on Phenomenological Ontology*. 1943. Trans. Barnes, Hazel E. London: Routledge, 1969.

———. *Nausea*. 1938. Trans. Baldick, Robert. London: Penguin, 1965.

Saxton, Josephine. 'The Backlash: The Further Travails of Jane Saint.' *The Consciousness Machine, Jane Saint and the Backlash: The Further Travails of Jane Saint*. London: Women's Press, 1989. 41–167.

———. 'Introduction.' *The Consciousness Machine, Jane Saint and the Backlash: The Further Travails of Jane Saint*. London: Women's Press, 1989. 1–6.

Searle, John R. 'Minds, Brains and Programs.' *The Behavioral and Brain Sciences* 3 (1980): 417–57.

Seed, David. *Brainwashing: The Fictions of Mind Control: A Study of Novels and Films since World War II*. Kent, OH: Kent State UP, 2004.

Shamdasani, Sonu. *Jung and the Making of Modern Psychology: The Dream of a Science*. Cambridge: Cambridge UP, 2003.

Shands, Kerstin W. *The Repair of the World: The Novels of Marge Piercy*. Contributions in Women's Studies. Westport, CT: Greenwood, 1994.

Shaw, Bob. 'Foreword.' *Psifi: Psychological Theories and Science Fictions*. By Ridgway, Jim and Michele Benjamin. Leicester: British Psychological Society, 1987. vii–ix.

Shaw, Sarah. 'Monstrous Sex: The Erotic in Naomi Mitchison's Science Fiction.' *Michigan Feminist Studies* 16 (2002): 141–68.
Sheckley, Robert. 'Bad Medicine.' *The Robert Sheckley Omnibus*. Ed. Conquest, Robert. Harmondsworth: Penguin, 1975. 207–26.
Shelton, Robert 'The Social Text as Body: Images of Health and Disease in Three Recent Feminist Utopias.' *Literature and Medicine* 12.2 (1993): 161–77.
Shepard, Glenn H., and Douglas W. Yu. 'Is Beauty in the Eye of the Beholder?' *Nature* 396.6709 (1998): 321–22.
Shklovsky, Viktor. 'The Resurrrection of the Word.' Trans. Sherwood, Richard. *Russian Formalism: A Collection of Articles and Texts in Translation*. 1914. Eds. Bann, Stephen and John E. Bowlt. 20th Century Studies. Edinburgh: Scottish Academic Press, 1973. 41–47.
Silverberg, Robert. *Dying Inside*. 1972. SF Masterworks. London: Gollancz, 2005.
Singh, Devendra. 'Body Shape and Women's Attractiveness: The Critical Role of Waist-to-Hip Ratio.' *Human Nature* 4.3 (1993): 297–321.
Skinner, B.F. *About Behaviourism*. London: Jonathan Cape, 1974.
———. *The Behavior of Organisms: An Experimental Analysis*. Century Psychology Series. New York: Appleton-Century-Crofts, 1938.
———. *Beyond Freedom and Dignity*. 1971. London: Jonathan Cape, 1972.
———. *Science and Human Behavior*. New York: Free Press, 1953.
———. '"Superstition" in the Pigeon.' *Journal of Experimental Psychology* 38.2 (1948): 168–72.
———. *Walden Two*. 1948. Indianapolis, IN: Hackett, 1976.
Sleator, William. *House of Stairs*. 1974. New York: Penguin, 2004.
Smith, Philip E. 'The Evolution of Politics and the Politics of Evolution: Social Darwinism in Heinlein's Fiction.' *Robert A. Heinlein*. Eds. Olander, Joseph D. and Martin Harry Greenberg. Writers of the 21st Century. New York: Taplinger, 1978. 137–71.
Smith, Roger. *Being Human: Historical Knowledge and the Creation of Human Nature*. Manchester: Manchester UP, 2007.
———. 'Does Reflexivity Separate the Human Sciences from the Natural Sciences?' *History of the Human Sciences* 18.4 (2005): 1–25.
———. 'Does the History of Psychology Have a Subject?' *History of the Human Sciences* 1.2 (1988): 147–77.
Somay, Bülent. 'Towards an Open-Ended Utopia.' *Science Fiction Studies* 11.1 (1984): 25–38.
Sommer, Andreas. 'Psychical Research and the Origins of American Psychology: Hugo Münsterberg, William James and Eusapia Palladino.' *History of the Human Sciences* 25.2 (2012): 23–44.
Spilka, Mark. 'Lawrence's Quarrel with Tenderness.' *Critical Quarterly* 9.4 (1967): 363–77.
Spinrad, Norman. *The Iron Dream*. 1972. St Albans: Panther, 1974.
Squier, Susan M. 'Afterword: Naomi Mitchison: The Feminist Art of Making Things Difficult.' *Solution Three*. By Naomi Mitchison. New York: Feminist Press at the City U of New York, 1995. 161–83.

Squire, Corinne. 'Crisis What Crisis?: Discourses and Narratives of the "Social" in Social Psychology.' *Deconstructing Social Psychology*. Eds. Parker, Ian and John Shotter. London and New York: Routledge, 1990. 33–46.

———. 'Science Fictions.' *Feminism & Psychology* 1.2 (1991): 181–99.

Stableford, Brian. 'Slaves of the Death Spiders: Colin Wilson and Existentialist Science Fiction.' *Foundation: The International Review of Science Fiction*. 38 (1986/1987): 63–67.

Steiner, Peter. *Russian Formalism: A Metapoetics*. Ithaca, NY: Cornell UP, 1984.

Stern, Daniel N. *The Interpersonal World of the Infant: A View from Psychoanalysis and Developmental Psychology*. 1985. London: Karnac, 1998.

Stinson, John J. 'Better to Be Hot or Cold: *1985* and the Dynamic of the Manichean Duoverse.' *Modern Fiction Studies* 27.3 (1981): 505–16.

Sturgeon, Theodore. 'And Now the News ... .' *A Touch of Sturgeon: Stories by Theodore Sturgeon*. 1956. London: Simon & Schuster, 1987. 183–200.

Suttie, Ian D. *The Origins of Love and Hate*. London: Kegan Paul, 1935.

Suvin, Darko. *Metamorphoses of Science Fiction: On the Poetics and History of a Literary Genre*. New Haven, CT: Yale UP, 1979.

Svilpis, Janis. 'The Science-Fiction Prehistory of the Turing Test.' *Science Fiction Studies* 35.3 (2008): 430–49.

Tacitus. 'Agricola.' Trans. Birley, Anthony R. *Agricola and Germany*. Oxford World's Classics. Oxford: Oxford UP, 1999. 1–34.

Thoreau, Henry David. *Walden; or, Life in the Woods*. Boston, MA: Ticknor and Fields, 1854.

Thorndike, Edward L. *Animal Intelligence: Experimental Studies*. New York: Macmillan, 1911.

Thornhill, Randy, and Craig T. Palmer. *A Natural History of Rape: Biological Bases of Sexual Coercion*. Cambridge, MA: MIT Press, 2000.

Tirohl, Blu. '"We Are the Dead ... You Are the Dead". An Examination of Sexuality as a Weapon of Revolt in Orwell's *Nineteen Eighty-Four*.' *Journal of Gender Studies* 9.1 (2000): 55–61.

Tooby, John, and Leda Cosmides. 'The Psychological Foundations of Culture.' *The Adapted Mind: Evolutionary Psychology and the Generation of Culture*. Eds. Barkow, Jerome H., Leda Cosmides, and John Tooby. Oxford: Oxford University, 1992. 19–136.

Tóth, János I., and Katalin Csala-Gáti. 'The Socio-Biological and Human-Ecological Notions in *The Time Machine*.' *The Wellsian: Selected Essays on H.G. Wells*. Ed. Partington, John S. Oss, Netherlands: Equilibris, 2003. 19–30.

Travis, Cheryl Brown, ed. *Evolution, Gender, and Rape*. Cambridge, MA: MIT Press, 2003.

Turing, A.M. 'Computing Machinery and Intelligence.' *Mind* 59.236 (1950): 433–60.

Unger, Rhoda K. 'Science Fictive Visions: A Feminist Psychologist's View.' *Feminism & Psychology* 19.1 (2009): 113–17.

———. 'Toward a Redefinition of Sex and Gender.' *American Psychologist* 34.11 (1979): 1085–94.

Väliverronen, Esa. 'Biodiversity and the Power of Metaphor in Environmental Discourse.' *Science Studies* 11.1 (1998): 19–34.
Vickers, A. Leah, and Philip Kitcher. 'Pop Sociobiology Reborn: The Evolutionary Psychology of Sex and Violence.' *Evolution, Gender, and Rape*. Ed. Travis, Cheryl Brown. Cambridge, MA and London: MIT P, 2003. 139–68.
Vint, Sherryl. 'Afterword: The World Gibson Made.' *Beyond Cyberpunk: New Critical Perspectives*. Eds. Murphy, Graham J. and Sherryl Vint. Routledge Studies in Contemporary Literature. London: Routledge, 2010. 228–33.
———. *Bodies of Tomorrow: Technology, Subjectivity, Science Fiction*. Toronto: U of Toronto P, 2007.
———. *Science Fiction: A Guide for the Perplexed*. Guides for the Perplexed. London: Bloomsbury, 2014.
Vlastos, Marion. 'Doris Lessing and R.D. Laing: Psychopolitics and Prophecy.' *PMLA* 91.2 (1976): 245–58.
Vonnegut, Kurt. *Galápagos*. 1985. London: Paladin, 1990.
Waage, Fred. 'Traumatic Conformity: Robert Lindner's Narratives of Rebellion.' *Journal of American Culture* 22.2 (1999): 25–32.
Wagemans, Johan, et al. 'A Century of Gestalt Psychology in Visual Perception: I. Perceptual Grouping and Figure–Ground Organization.' *Psychological Bulletin* 138.6 (2012): 1172–217.
Watrin, João Paulo, and Rosângela Darwich. 'On Behaviorism in the Cognitive Revolution: Myth and Reactions.' *Review of General Psychology* 16.3 (2012): 269–82.
Watson, Ian. *The Embedding*. 1973. London: Gollancz, 2000.
———. 'Towards an Alien Linguistics.' *The Book of Ian Watson*. Willimantic, CT: Mark V. Ziesing, 1985. 43–61.
Watson, John B. 'Psychology as the Behaviorist Views It.' *Psychological Review* 20.2 (1913): 158–77.
———. 'Should a Child Have More Than One Mother?' *Liberty Magazine* 29 June 1929: 31–35.
Watson, John B., and Rosalie Rayner. 'Conditioned Emotional Reactions.' *Journal of Experimental Psychology* 3.1 (1920): 1–14.
Weikart, Richard. 'The Role of Darwinism in Nazi Racial Thought.' *German Studies Review* 36.3 (2013): 537–56.
Weizenbaum, Joseph. *Computer Power and Human Reason: From Judgment to Calculation*. San Francisco: W.H. Freeman, 1976.
Wells, H.G. *The Croquet Player: A Story*. London: Chatto & Windus, 1936.
———. *The Island of Doctor Moreau*. 1896. Penguin Classics. London: Penguin, 2005.
———. *A Modern Utopia*. 1905. Penguin Classics. London: Penguin, 2005.
———. *The Time Machine*. 1895. Penguin Classics. London: Penguin, 2005.
———. *The War of the Worlds*. 1898. Penguin Classics. London: Penguin, 2005.
Wheeler, Pat. '"That Is Not Me. I Am Not That": Anger and the Will to Action in Joanna Russ's Fiction.' *On Joanna Russ*. Ed. Mendlesohn, Farah. Middletown, CT: Wesleyan UP, 2009. 99–113.

Whitley, Richard. 'Knowledge Producers and Knowledge Acquirers: Popularisation as a Relation between Scientific Fields and Their Publics.' *Expository Science: Forms and Functions of Popularisation*. Eds. Shinn, Terry and Richard Whitley. Sociology of the Sciences. Dordrecht: Reidel, 1985. 3–28.
Whorf, Benjamin Lee. 'Science and Linguistics.' *Language, Thought, and Reality: Selected Writings of Benjamin Lee Whorf*. 1940. Ed. Carroll, John B. Cambridge, MA: MIT P, 1956. 207–19.
Wiener, Norbert. *Cybernetics: Or Control and Communication in the Animal and the Machine*. 2nd ed. Cambridge, MA: MIT, 1961.
Wilson, Colin. *The Mind Parasites*. 1967. St Albans: Panther, 1969.
———. *New Pathways in Psychology: Maslow and the Post-Freudian Revolution*. London: Gollancz, 1972.
———. *Science Fiction as Existentialism*. Bran's Head Library of Science Fiction Criticism. Eds. Young, Grahame Barrasford and Richard S. Kirby. Hayes: Bran's Head, 1978.
———. *The Space Vampires*. London: Hart-Davis, MacGibbon, 1976.
Wilson, Edward O. *Sociobiology: The New Synthesis*. Cambridge, MA: Harvard UP, 1975.
Wimsatt, W.K., and M.C. Beardsley. 'The Intentional Fallacy.' *The Sewanee Review* 54.3 (1946): 468–88.
Yaszek, Lisa, and Jason W. Ellis. 'Science Fiction.' *The Cambridge Companion to Literature and the Posthuman*. Eds. Clarke, Bruce and Manuela Rossini. Cambridge Companions to Literature. Cambridge: Cambridge UP, 2016. 71–83.
Žižek, Slavoj. *Welcome to the Desert of Real!: Five Essays on September 11 and Related Dates*. London: Verso, 2002.

Index

Abi-Rached, Joelle M. 13–15
Allport, Gordon W. 169–71
attachment theory 67–68, 71–72, 78–79, 161

Banks, Iain M.
   Player of Games 101
   Walking on Glass 34
Bartholomew, Robert E. 217–18
Bartlett, Fredric 202, 227
de Beauvoir, Simone 198–99
behaviourist psychology
   dystopian extrapolation 141–49
   reflexivity 137–49
   salvational narratives in 137–38
   summary 128–32
   technocracy 133, 138–39
   utopian extrapolation 133–41
Bem, Daryl 252–54
Bem, Sandra L. 40, 248–49, 252–54
Benjamin, Michele 251–52
Berlin, Isaiah 164–65
Bester, Alfred
   The Demolished Man 111–12
   'Oddy and Id' ['The Devil's Invention'] 89
Bisson, Terry
   'They're Made out of Meat' 247
Bloch, Ernst 125
Blum, Steven D. 219–20
Borup, Mads 250
Bottom, William P. 212–13

Bowlby, John 67–68, 71–72, 78
   see also attachment theory
Breland, Keller and Marian 131–32
Brosco, Jeffrey P. 113–14
Buller, David J. 48–49, 64
Bultmann, Rudolf 184
Burgess, Anthony
   1985 143
   A Clockwork Orange 142–43
Butler, Octavia
   Parable of the Sower 54–60
   Parable of the Talents 54–55

Cain, Stephen 228
Callenbach, Ernest
   Ecotopia 101–02
Canavan, Gerry 54–55, 57, 60
Chesler, Phyllis 195
Chiang, Ted
   'Story of Your Life' 228–30
Chomsky, Noam 132, 140, 204–05, 222–23, 225–26, 228
Christopher, John
   The Death of Grass 88–89, 162
cognition effect 5–7
cognitive estrangement 4–6, 27–30, 36–37, 40, 72–79, 85, 113–14, 154, 159–60, 163–64, 184–87, 193–94, 197–98, 219–20, 239–40, 252–58
cognitive psychology
   cognitive linguistics 220–33

memory 226–31
Sapir-Whorf hypothesis 222–23
stereotypes 211–20
summary 201–05
Collini, Stefan 179
Conley, Tim 228
Cooper, Edmund
Gender Genocide [*Who Needs Men?*] 155–57
Cosmides, Leda 47–48
Csala-Gáti, Katalin 50
Csicsery-Ronay, Istvan 4–6, 14, 23, 24, 28, 240
cybernetics 68
cyberpunk 14, 205, 220–21

Delany, Samuel
Babel-17 222–24, 227
Dick, Philip K.
'We Can Remember it for you Wholesale' 227–28
didacticism 21–23, 39–40, 50–54, 134–35, 153–54, 179–89, 212–20, 236, 242–44, 251–52
Dilthey, Wilhelm 194–95
Donovan, Josephine 69
Drummond, Henry 74–75
DuPlessis, Rachel 198
dystopianism 26–27, 90–101, 141–49, 152–64, 195, 254–58

Ellenberger, Henri F. 84
Ellis, Jason W. 205, 220
empathy 54, 58–60, 68–79, 172–73, 193–97, 206–08, 231
evolutionary psychology 38
  Atavistic Misfit Hypothesis 64–67
  EEA (Environment of Evolutionary Adaptedness) 49, 64–67
  EP (Evolutionary Psychology, formal programme of) 47–49, 60–61, 64–67
  hermeneutics of suspicion 48–49

narrative of Fall 65–67
reflexivity 60–67
rejection of social science 47–48, 67
summary 45–49
topos of renewed selection 50–60
utopian extrapolation 67–79
see also attachment theory; Social Darwinism; sociobiology
existential-humanistic psychology 114–16, 148–49
  human apotheosis 19, 179–89
  psychiatric critique by 190–99
  summary 168–73
  utopian extrapolation 173–78

Feyerabend, Paul 244–45
Finney, Jack
  The Body Snatchers 206–20
Fishburn, Katherine 192–93
Frankl, Victor 169–70
Freedman, Carl 4–6, 19–20
Freud, Sigmund 82–84, 90, 98–101
  see also psychoanalytic psychology
Fromm, Erich 99–100, 168–69
futurology 21–23, 24, 40, 50–57, 175–76, 182–84, 188–89, 240–41, 244–50

Gardiner, Judith Kegan 152–53, 197
Gellner, Ernest 94
Gennep, Arnold von 214–15
Gergen, Kenneth J. 9, 149–51, 242
Gomel, Elena 206
Goodwin, C. James 202–03
Gould, Stephen Jay 49, 64
Gross, Alan G. 243

Hamilton, Richard 49, 64, 67, 80
Hawkins, Mike 45–47, 52, 74
Heelas, Paul 189

INDEX

Heinlein, Robert A. 22, 33
  The Moon is a Harsh Mistress 52–53
Herbert, Frank
  The Dragon in the Sea 104–05
Herbrechter, Stefan 205, 207
Hilgartner, Stephen 23, 40, 242–43
Hird, Myra J. 79
Huxley, Aldous
  Brave New World 90–98, 141
  Heaven and Hell 182–83

Jameson, Fredric 101–02, 125, 144
Jaspers, Karl 172
Johnson, Glen M. 206–10, 218
Jung, C.G. 102–10

Kaplan, Bert 193
Keyes, Daniel
  Flowers for Algernon 112–19
Kirsh, Steven J. 40, 251
Kitzinger, Jenny 40, 243–44
Kong, Tony 212–13
Kuhn, Thomas 35

Laing, R.D. 153, 172–73, 192–96
Latham, Rob 152
Le Guin, Ursula 33, 252
  The Lathe of Heaven 143–46
  views on Jung 102–04
  The Word for World is Forest 105–10
Lessing, Doris 192–93
  The Four-Gated City 186–88
Levitas, Ruth 24–26
Lindner, Robert
  'The Jet-Propelled Couch' 30–33
Lippman, Walter 212–19
Lips, Hilary M. 252

McHugh, Vincent
  I Am Thinking of My Darling 173–78, 192
MacKenzie, Brian D. 128, 132
Mad Gasser of Mattoon 217–18

Malinowski, Bronislaw 92
Malzberg, Barry
  Herovit's World 34
  Remaking of Sigmund Freud 98–101
Maslow, Abraham 170–72, 181–82
May, Rollo 168
Mercer, Philip 59
metafiction 30–34, 102–10, 140–41, 178, 187–88, 219–20
Miéville, China 6
Milgram, Stanley 40, 242, 254–58
Millard, Kathryn 256
Miller, George A. 204–05, 226
Milner, Andrew 7–8, 238–39
Mitchison, Naomi
  'Comfort' 70–71
  'Conversation with an Improbable Future' 69, 71
  The Corn King and the Spring Queen 70
  Memoirs of a Spacewoman 67–79, 193–94
  Solution Three 158–64
Morawski, J.G. 133
Moylan, Tom 25–27, 55, 147

Neisser, Ulrich 203–04
neuroscience 13–15, 17–18, 190–92, 195–99
Newman, Leonard S. 212
Nicholson, Ian 40, 242, 255–58

Oakley, Ann 40, 253
Orwell, George
  1984 90–98

Palmer, Craig T. 38, 249–50
Paul, Diane B. 113–14
Paul, Terri 121
Pavlov, Ivan 128–29, 149
Pickren, Wade 12, 36, 202, 204
Piercy, Marge
  Woman on the Edge of Time 195–99
Pinker, Steven 48, 64–65, 245–47

PKU [phenylketonuria] 112–14
Pohl, Frederik
  Gateway 119–24, 220
  Heechee Rendezvous 124
Popper, Karl 244
prophecy *see* futurology
psychoanalytic psychology 148–49
  adaptation to cultural context 126
  analytic relationship 111–24
  anti-utopianism 99–101, 125
  collective unconscious 101–10, 111
  diagnosis of science fiction 30–34
  functionalism 94–95
  ideological function critiqued 119–24
  Jungian views on tradition 106–07
  libidinal economics 90–101
  Nietzschean antecedents 84–89
  play theorized 101–02
  reflexivity 36–37, 98–101, 112–24
  summary 82–84
  tenderness theorized 70–71, 97–98
psychology
  definition 11–20
  fictional psychologies 19–20
  functions in science fiction 20–39, 236–37
  see also cognitive estrangement; didacticism; dystopianism; futurology; metafiction; reflexivity; utopianism
  history of psychology 8–9, 11–15, 237–38
  narrative legitimation 245–50
  non-paradigmatic science 35–36
  parapsychology 18–19
  popularization 242–44
    see also didacticism
  post-empiricist history and philosophy of 244–45, 250
  psychologization 9, 13
  science fiction discourse in 39–40, 242–58
  selection for literary analysis 15–20
  see also attachment theory; behaviourist psychology; cognitive psychology; evolutionary psychology; existential-humanistic psychology; neuroscience; psychoanalytic psychology; reflexivity; social constructionist psychology; sociobiology

Radcliffe-Browne, A.R. 94
reflexivity 35–39, 60–67, 77–79, 112–24, 136–41, 141–49, 149–50, 154, 190–99, 224, 232–33
Richards, Graham 12, 38–39
Ridgway, Jim 251–52
Robinson, Kim Stanley 240
Roemer, Kenneth M. 134, 136
Rose, Nikolas 13–15
Rose, Steven 60
Russ, Joanna 21, 41, 155–58
  The Female Man 152–55
Rutherford, Alexandra 12, 36, 202, 204

Sargent, William 25–26
Sartre, Jean-Paul 115–16, 170–71, 183
Saxton, Josephine
  Jane Saint and the Backlash 110–11
science fiction
  definition 2–8
  historical novel and 239–40
  literary type 239–41
  and psychologization 238–41

in psychology 39–40,
  242–58
psychology's function in 20–39,
  236–37
selection for analysis 9–11
see also cognitive estrangement;
  didacticism; dystopianism;
  futurology; metafiction;
  reflexivity; utopianism
Searle, John R. 246–47
Seed, David 95, 133, 141
Shamdasani, Sonu 36, 106–07
Shaw, Bob 251–52
Shaw, Sarah 70–71
Sheckley, Robert
  'Bad Medicine' 36–37
Silverberg, Robert
  Dying Inside 189
Skinner, B.F. 128, 131–32,
  146–49
  Walden Two 22, 24–25, 133–41
Sleator, William
  House of Stairs 146–49
Smith, Roger 12–13, 35–36
social constructionist psychology
  cultural diversity and 160–64
  dystopian extrapolation from
    155–64
  feminism 152–64
  summary 149–52
Social Darwinism 45–47, 50–54
sociobiology 60–67
Somay, Bülent 197–98
Spilka, Mark 71
Spinrad, Norman
  The Iron Dream 33
Squire, Corinne 40, 245,
  248–49
Stableford, Brian 188
Sturgeon, Theodore
  'And Now the News' 190–92
Suttie, Ian D. 71, 96–98
Suvin, Darko 2–8, 23, 27–30, 220,
  253
  see also cognitive estrangement
Svilpis, Janet 247

Thoreau, Henry David 133–35
Thorndike, Edward 128,
  130–31
Thornhill, Randy 38, 249–50
Tooby, John 47–48
Tóth, János I. 50
Turing, Alan 247–48

Unger, Rhoda K. 151–52,
  253
utopianism 24–27, 40, 51–52,
  58–60, 61–67, 67–79, 100–01,
  101–02, 125–26, 133–41, 155,
  164–65, 173–78, 188, 195–99,
  248–49
  see also dystopianism

Väliverronen, Esa 164
Victor, Jeffrey S. 217–18
Vint, Sherryl 14, 19, 220–21
Vonnegut, Kurt
  Galápagos 61–67
  Slaughterhouse-Five 229–30

Watson, Ian
  The Embedding 221–33
  'Towards an Alien Linguistics'
    222–23
Watson, John B. 128–30, 133
Weikart, Richard 46–47, 53
Weizenbaum, Joseph 121
Wells, H.G.
  The Croquet Player 86–87
  The Island of Doctor Moreau
    85–86
  A Modern Utopia 51–52
  The Time Machine 50–51
Whitley, Richard 243–44
Whorf, Benjamin Lee 222–23
Wilson, Colin 187–88
  The Mind Parasites 179–85
  Science Fiction as Existentialism
    184
  The Space Vampires 185

Yaszek, Lisa 205, 220

9 781789 620603

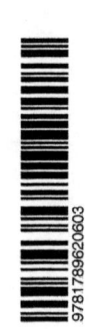